NATIONAL ECONOMIC POLICIES

NATIONAL ECONOMIC POLICIES

DOMINICK SALVATORE
EDITOR

HANDBOOK OF COMPARATIVE ECONOMIC POLICIES
VOLUME 1

GREENWOOD PRESS
New York • Westport, Connecticut • London

Library of Congress Cataloging-in-Publication Data

National economic policies / Dominick Salvatore, editor.
     p.   cm.—(Handbook of comparative economic policies, ISSN 1054–7681 ; v. 1)
    Includes bibliographical references and index.
    ISBN 0–313–26591–7 (alk. paper)
    1. Economic policy. 2. Comparative economics.   I. Salvatore,
Dominick.   II. Series.
    HD87.N38 1991
    338.9—dc20   91–178

British Library Cataloguing in Publication Data is available.

Library of Congress Catalog Card Number: 91–178
ISBN: 0–313–26591–7
ISSN: 1054–7681

First published in 1991

Greenwood Press, 88 Post Road West, Westport, CT 06881
An imprint of Greenwood Publishing Group, Inc.

Printed in the United States of America

The paper used in this book complies with the
Permanent Paper Standard issued by the National
Information Standards Organization (Z39.48–1984).

10 9 8 7 6 5 4 3 2 1

CONTENTS

ILLUSTRATIONS

PREFACE

The present volume is the first in a series of comparative economics handbooks. It presents an overview of national economic policies in the world's most important countries or groupings of countries. Future volumes will deal with more specific aspects of economic policies such as trade, monetary, fiscal, economic development, and environmental policies.

With increased economic competition among industrial countries, the need for rapid economic development in less developed countries, and the collapse of the centrally planned regimes in Eastern Europe, economic policies have moved to the forefront relative to political, defense, and other policies followed by most nations of the world (although, of course, all policies are interrelated). Few, however, would dispute that a well-managed economic system with high rates of growth and development, full employment, and little or no inflation, as well as a concern for the environment, are not among the top priorities of national governments throughout the world today.

Nations use fiscal, monetary, industrial, trade, and regulatory policies to achieve their economic goals. The purpose of this volume is to examine and compare the policies followed by different types of countries and examine their effects. There is today a great need to conduct this type of comparative study. Industrial, developing, and Eastern European countries can all learn a great deal from such a comparative study.

This volume contains a chapter on each of the largest countries in the world (the United States, Japan, India, the Soviet Union, and China) as well as a chapter on each of several homogeneous groupings of countries (the European Economic Community, the newly industrializing countries [NICs], and the countries of Latin America, Africa, and Eastern Europe). Of course, no two countries are identical, but similarities among countries in a specific group are greater than differences; to that extent, it is useful to deal with them together. By comparing the policy used, the policy instruments utilized, and the outcomes of the policies adopted by different countries or groups of fairly homogeneous countries, the hope is that all countries can learn something useful. Although numerous studies have been published on how individual countries conduct economic policies, few if any comparative studies, such as the present one, have been issued.

This handbook can be of great use to students of comparative economic systems in general and to economists, policymakers, and the general informed public as a source of reference and comparison. The references at the end of each chapter and the selected bibliography at the end of the volume indicate the most important sources of additional information and detail on the economic policies of the most important countries in the world.

PART I

INTRODUCTION

1

NATIONAL ECONOMIC POLICIES: AN OVERVIEW

Dominick Salvatore

INTRODUCTION

Most nations of the world, developed as well as developing, market economies as well as those that are now shifting from a centrally planned system to a market economy, share a number of important common objectives: full employment of domestic resources (especially labor), an "acceptably" low rate of inflation, a "reasonable" rate of growth, an "equitable" distribution of income, and, more recently, control over environmental pollution. The tools generally available to achieve these goals are fiscal and monetary policies, industrial policies, trade and exchange rate policies, and regulation. Different types of countries choose a different mix of these policies and utilize somewhat different means to carry them out.

This volume seeks to identify and compare the policies followed by different types of countries, the instruments that the various countries use to achieve their goals, and the results obtained. Admittedly, this is an ambitious task. There is, however, a great need to conduct this type of comparative study of national economic policies. The optimal policies in one country or group of countries are not necessarily, or even usually, the best policies for other countries operating under a different institutional setting. Thus, comparative studies become essential.

Much can be learned from such comparative studies of national economic policies. Major industrial countries can better evaluate their own policies by comparing them to similar policies conducted by other industrial countries. They can also acquire a deeper understanding of why some countries adopt specific policies and the reason why they utilize particular policy instruments rather than others. Developing countries can learn from the experience of industrial countries and possibly avoid repeating the same mistakes that the industrial countries made during their course of economic development. Particular developing countries can also learn from the experience of other developing countries. Finally, the countries of Eastern Europe, the Soviet Union, and China can learn from the experience of developed and developing countries in identifying the institutions that are essential for the structural adjustment they are now undertaking in their road to a market economy, in choosing the most appropriate instruments available, and in learning how to conduct national economic policies.

Space limitations do not permit us to deal with all countries. Indeed, it may not even be necessary to cover the world lest we get lost in a sea of details. In this volume, we include a chapter on each of the largest countries (the United States, Japan, India, the Soviet Union, and China) as well as a chapter on each of several homogeneous groupings of countries—the European Economic Community (EEC), the newly industrializing countries (NICs), and the countries of Latin America, Africa, and Eastern Europe. Of course, no two countries are identical, but similarities among the various countries in a specific group are greater than the differences, and, to that extent, it is useful to deal with them together. By comparing the policy used, the policy instruments utilized, and the outcomes of the policies adopted by different countries or groups of fairly homogeneous countries, we hope that all countries can learn something useful. While there are numerous studies on how individual countries conduct economic policies, few if any comparative studies, such as the present one, have been published.

Of course, national economic policies in most countries have undergone significant changes during the past decade. While the various chapters of this volume take a historical approach, much of the focus is necessarily on the economic policies of the 1980s since it is these policies that are most useful to determine optimal policies for the future. The most important policy changes occurred in the field of *fiscal policies* and were stimulated by the huge and persistent budget deficits that arose in many countries during the past decade. These deficits exacerbated low and declining national savings rates and reduced economic efficiency and growth. The *monetary policy* objectives of most countries were price stability, support for economic growth, and equilibrium in the balance of payments. *Industrial policies* were regarded as crucial for economic development in the Third Word. *Trade and exchange rate policies* led to a more open world trading and financial system, but the large U.S. trade deficits have encouraged new forms of protectionism as well as attempts at international economic policy coordination. *Environmental policies* have also become very important as nations became increasingly concerned with the impact of pollution and other "social evils" on their economies. Petroleum shocks, worldwide inflation, recurrent recessions, and lagging economic development in the Third World, however, have all tended to dampen greater environmental efforts. In recent years, the world has also witnessed the birth of economic policy in the European Community as well as radical economic reforms in socialist or former socialist countries.

ECONOMIC POLICIES IN THE UNITED STATES

During the 1980s the policy emphasis changed in the United States from an overriding concern for unemployment and the environment to reducing government involvement in the economy, reducing the rate of inflation, as well as stimulating economic growth by relying on individual initiative and free markets. This new strategy was, for the most part, successful. Inflation was brought under control and the United States experienced an unprecedented long period of growth. Nevertheless, the 1980s were marked by huge budget and trade deficits, stagnant wages, and rising inequality.

For the next decade, the key policy issues are how to revive the national savings rate, reduce the "twin" budget and current account deficits, reduce inflation, and deal constructively with income inequality and preservation of the environment.

- The large budget deficit exacerbates the low national savings rate in the United States and undermines the renewed emphasis on economic efficiency and growth. Reducing the budget deficit is also a promising means of reducing the large U.S. current account deficit.

- In the area of tax policy, the United States continues to grapple with the problem of achieving a more rational tax system, particularly with respect to taxing capital gains and the income from various forms of capital without adding to inequality.

- In response to the problem of inequality and poverty, policy initiatives to assist lower income workers may emphasize the need for employers to furnish more benefits to their employees.

- In the regulatory area, there is a new appreciation that laissez faire can lead to a dirty environment and to costly bailouts in the case of deposit insurance for the thrift industry. The future thrust of policy in the environmental area will likely be to develop improved tools of government regulation to control environmental degradation while preserving a high degree of market flexibility.

ECONOMIC POLICIES IN THE EUROPEAN ECONOMIC COMMUNITY

Since its formation the EC has not had a single economic policy. Monetary policy was run by the twelve separate Central banks of member states and budgetary and fiscal policies resulted from negotiation between national governments and national parliaments with no concern about Community interests. Structural policies were directed at domestic goals and interests.

This policy incongruence and the resulting policy confusion are likely to end soon, as the European Community strives to establish a truly unified internal market by 1992, an economic and monetary union soon after, and eventually, a political union. Indeed, the 1990s will witness the birth of European Community economic policy, with a single currency and a single monetary authority, supported by coordinated budgetary and fiscal policy, and with microeconomic management agreed on at the Community level.

ECONOMIC POLICIES IN JAPAN

During the first five years after the war, efforts were undertaken to rebuild Japan's agricultural and industrial sectors and reduce inflation. Over the next fifteen years, Japanese economic growth overshadowed the business cycles, generated periodic constraints in foreign exchange, and propelled Japan to the ranks of the leading industrial nations of the world.

During the postwar period, Japan's main fiscal objectives were to achieve control of an excessive aggregate demand, promote productive investment, low-cost financing for strategic sectors of the economy, and a relatively small budget as a percentage of GNP. At the same time, Japan's fiscal policy attempted to assist, through government subsidies, the low productivity sectors of the economy, such as agriculture and small-scale firms, and to adjust income distortions caused by the imbalance of its rapid growth.

Monetary policy objectives are generally stated to be price stability, support of economic growth, and equilibrium in the balance of payments. Until the end of the 1960s there were no tradeoffs between these objectives in Japan. In the period of rapid growth, the Central Bank and the government followed a stop-and-go policy; whenever there was a deficit in the balance of payments, monetary policy was tightened and whenever there was a surplus, the policy was relaxed. By the end of the 1960s, however, monetary inflation and the balance-of-payments surplus began to coexist, creating a need to choose between the goals. Other instruments like the discount rate, open market operations, and changes in the reserve requirement played a greater role.

In the early decades after World War II, Japan became accustomed to protecting infant industries and nursing them to bring them to international competitive standards. In the 1970s and 1980s, as its exports systematically undermined Western industries, Japan's practices became known as ''adversarial trade'' and were distinguished from ''competitive trade'' whereby a country also imports manufactures of the same kind as it exports (i.e., intra-industry trade). Since the early 1970s, as a result of international friction, many formal barriers to trade in Japan have been gradually removed. Today the Japanese genuinely believe that they have lower tariffs than most nations and that the tariffs they do have are among the world's lowest.

Japanese authorities have actively intervened in the foreign exchange market in response to exchange-rate movements since World War II. Even under the regime of flexible exchange rates, however, Japan was unable to leave exchange-rate determination completely to market forces because the exchange rate was used as another parameter to be controlled in managing the domestic economy. The main policy measures taken in response to exchange-rate movements have been discount rate adjustments, capital controls, and market intervention.

ECONOMIC POLICIES IN OTHER MAJOR OECD COUNTRIES

The countries analyzed in this section, namely, Austria, Australia, Canada, and Sweden, are small, open, and, with one exception, highly industrialized. Therefore, they are closely integrated into the world economy without being able to exert influence on global trends.

Austria has had a long history of giving top priority to full employment, the tradeoff being a rising fiscal deficit and increasing restrictions on market forces. As a consequence, unemployment could be kept well below the Organization of Economic Cooperation and Development (OECD) average while public indebtedness rose sharply and now accounts for some 50 percent of gross domestic product (GDP). Only in the 1980s was fiscal consolidation assigned top priority alongside price stability. The prime task of the Austrian National Bank is to pursue a monetary policy conducive to price stability. The Bank has also pioneered an exchange-rate approach which it terms the hard currency policy. In practice, this policy means the de facto peg of the schilling to the Deutsche mark. Austria's possible future membership in the EC would end its autonomous trade policy.

The objective of full employment has always been given very high priority in Swedish economic policy, independently of the parties in power. As a consequence, labor market performance and policy in Sweden have been distinctly different from those in other OECD countries. Contrary to what happened in most other OECD countries, the emphasis placed on full employment in Sweden resulted in unemployment rates that did not rise significantly after the two oil price shocks of the 1970s. Low wage differentials are another characteristic feature of the Swedish economy, based on the concept of social justice. Therefore, in an international comparison, both intersectoral and interprofessional wage dispersion, is very low. In addition, Sweden has long closed itself off to foreign financial influence. A plethora of restrictions have been used to impede the inward movement of foreign investment and foreign ownership of Swedish industry and services.

The basic aim of Canada's economic policy during the second half of the 1980s was set out in the government's Agenda for Economic Renewal in November 1984. In order to create conditions for sustained economic growth, a mixture of microeconomic reforms and macroeconomic stabilization policies was put together. The main ingredient was deregulation of the economy (especially of the energy, transportation, and foreign investment areas), tax reform, budget deficit consolidation, and stimulation of private sector growth.

The basic goal of Australian economic policy is to sustain economic growth, ensure equitable income distribution, and strive for internal and external equilibrium. There is a strong belief in comparative wage justice. In the postwar period, the Australian economy faced significant government intervention. The creation of a large and diverse manufacturing base was highly important to successive governments. This strategy was pursued through an import substitution policy, supported first by import licensing and then by various tariffs. Since the early 1980s governments have reduced their reliance on protection and have moved away somewhat from the use of tariffs for the protection that remains. Immigration policy has also been traditionally used as a tool for economic development.

ECONOMIC POLICIES IN NEWLY INDUSTRIALIZING COUNTRIES

The performance of the four newly industrialized countries, namely, Hong Kong, Singapore, Taiwan, and Korea, has been remarkable in recent years. During the 1986–89 period the economies of these nations grew at an annual rate of almost 10 percent, prices were stable, and the balance-of-payment surplus continued to rise.

There is general agreement that the economic success of these countries depends heavily on prudent economic policies.

- The fiscal policies of the Asian NICs have traditionally been quite conservative, with budgets normally showing a slight surplus, especially in the 1980s. They have had well-organized tax systems from an early stage of development, and the principle of a small government has prevailed in determining the size of the budget. Total government spending has been constrained not to increase at a higher rate than the expected nominal gross national product (GNP) growth rate.

- The environment under which the monetary policy is implemented is substantially different among Asian NICs. Hong Kong has no central bank, whereas in Singapore, through its monetary authority, the government actually performs the role of the central bank. Both Taiwan and Korea have legitimate central banks, that is, the Bank of Taiwan and the Bank of Korea.

  In terms of financial market development, Hong Kong and Singapore are far ahead of Korea and Taiwan. Hong Kong and Singapore have liberalized and quite sophisticated financial systems, while financial development has been relatively slow in the other two countries, owing to governmental control and intervention. Notwithstanding the differences in their financial systems, the four countries have one common feature: they have successfully controlled the money supply and thereby contained inflation.

- One common characteristic shared by the NICs is a high degree of openness. As they have depended on trade for economic growth, the trade/GNP ratio is extremely high. In Singapore the ratio in 1988 was over 300 percent; even in Korea, which had the lowest among the four, it was 65 percent. By pursuing an export-oriented development strategy, these economies have achieved rapid growth of exports and income.

ECONOMIC POLICIES IN LATIN AMERICA

The 1980s saw major changes in national economic policies throughout Latin America. Although each country followed a somewhat different set of policies, four common elements were evident. First, the role of the public sector in production and distribution was reevaluated and aimed at increasing the role of the private sector in these activities. Second, there was an increasing awareness of the need to reduce budget deficits in order to reduce inflation and current account deficits. Third, Latin America recognized the need to reduce the anti-export bias in trade policies. Fourth, the area acknowledged the need to introduce structural reforms in the labor market, financial markets, and domestic trade.

These reforms were started in Mexico in 1983, in Uruguay and Chile in 1984, in Costa Rica in 1985, and in Venezuela in 1989. Brazil and Argentina are still struggling to control inflation, while Peru and Nicaragua have postponed structural adjustment. The most difficult reforms to implement have been those relating to the public sector and the labor and domestic markets. Reforms of the public sector have faced the strong opposition of rent seekers, such as suppliers of the public sector and trade unions, especially in Argentina and Brazil. Major progress has been achieved in controlling inflation in Bolivia, Costa Rica, Chile, and Mexico, and in opening the economy in Mexico, Costa Rica, Bolivia, and Venezuela. The inability to finance current account deficits and the debt overhang accumulated during the easy spending years of the late 1970s have severely limited growth in most of Latin America since the early 1980s.

ECONOMIC POLICIES IN INDIA

A framework of Indian economic policies evolved out of the medley of different political beliefs and, as such, lacked clarity both with regard to their goals and how they should be accomplished. Since the 1950s the basis for the economic policy and the type of instruments used were influenced by a strong perception that the Indian system was characterized by pervasive market failures and that these required frequent and decisive government intervention to be overcome.

The Congress party, which was in power throughout most of the postindependence period, pushed for a mixed economy with public and private sectors comingling in such a way as to assure rapid economic development and a rising standard of living, while promoting an equitable distribution of income. This type of mixed economy, however, involved a grab bag of policy measures that gravitated neither toward a market economy nor toward a total command economy. The resulting fuzziness in economic policy formulation and implementation served the purpose well for a while, with a virtual national consensus on major economic issues. However, as the economy progressed and some initial good results were achieved, the policy framework did not change as was required by emerging changing conditions in the economy. This resulted in large vested interests, which impaired economic efficiency and significant waste of resources.

In order to resolve the riddles of economic power management in India, it is necessary to probe into the political economy of Indian economic development, the anatomy of a rent-seeking society (which spawns inefficient policies), and the political process (which strongly makes for interventionist policies).

ECONOMIC POLICIES IN AFRICA

African countries share not only the usual characteristics of underdevelopment, but also the cherished objectives of rapid development and transformation, the desire to improve the standards of living of the people, and the quest for economic independence as a guarantee to political sovereignty. They present different approaches to national economic management, ranging from strong public sector dominance in economic activities at one extreme, a mixed economy (with the government exercising substantial control over the operations of the private sector) in the middle, to a more liberal free enterprise economy.

Thirty years after independence, the economies of Egypt, Kenya, and Nigeria (the three countries on which the African chapter focuses) generally face excessive dependence on external trade and on a limited range of commodities for export earnings. Neither the development strategies and economic policies adopted during the 1960s and 1970s nor the policies incorporated in the reform and adjustment programs of the 1980s produced the desired effects on African economic development in terms of its long-term development objectives.

Given Africa's long-term objectives to establish a self-sustaining process of economic growth and development, and a human-centered development, it needs to reorient some of its economic policies.

1. In the area of fiscal policy, the restraint on public spending has to be applied selectively, if adverse effects on long-term development are to be averted.

2. In the area of monetary policy, there is a need to use selective interest rates in such a way that interest rates on loans for speculative activities will be greater than the rates on loans for productive activities.

3. Finally, given their economic conditions, African countries recognize that trade liberalization is not generally in their best interest. Import liberalization leads to greater external dependence, jeopardizes national priorities such as food self-sufficiency, and threatens the survival of infant industries. Hence, future trade policy should be in the direction of using a combination of tariff and tax measures to change the consumption pattern, protect local industries, and encourage domestic sourcing of industrial raw materials.

ECONOMIC POLICIES IN THE USSR

Since Mikhail Gorbachev became the General Secretary of the Communist party of the Soviet Union in March 1985, the Soviet Union has undergone spectacular change in the economic sphere and even greater political transformation. This transformation began in early 1986, and its pace accelerated in mid-1987. Both macro- and micro-economic policies have been and are being used to transform the economy of the Soviet Union. The road to *perestroika* has been both bold and difficult.

The major aim of perestroika has been to transform the economy of the Soviet

Union from a centrally planned system to a market system. This transformation has been much more difficult than originally envisioned. The root of the problem and the intensity of the cure required to overcome problems were repeatedly underestimated. It is important, however, to closely examine the transitional phase of the reform and the direction in which it may be heading so that we can clearly assess the serious problems facing the Soviet economy.

Future policies should be constructed around three major themes:

1. Gaining control over monetary and fiscal affairs in a decentralizing environment
2. Addressing the issues of reform during the transition phase
3. Formulating proper macroeconomic policies, which continues to be a critical task. In this connection, questions arise as to the role of monetary and fiscal policies in a society that professes to be socialist and the degree to which they need to be complemented with incomes and price policies to safeguard social priorities without exacerbating inflationary pressures

ECONOMIC POLICIES IN EASTERN EUROPE: POLAND

Launched in the period of dramatic social struggle, the Polish economy reform quickly lost its momentum and got stuck in endless bureaucratic debates and procedures, without producing any significant results in terms of increased efficiency and competitiveness, accelerated growth, or structural change.

Attempts to introduce a market-oriented system as envisaged in the reform blueprint prepared in 1981 were effectively blocked by short-term economic policy measures aimed at maintaining political control over the economy. Furthermore, the reform project itself was based on an erroneous assumption about the practical feasibility of combining central planning and predominantly state ownership with arbitrarily selected elements of market mechanism into a sort of hybrid system called market socialism. Finally, the imposition of martial law in December 1981 under pressure from the Soviet Union and other conservative regimes in Eastern Europe created the least favorable environment for any kind of systemic change at variance with traditional socialist principles.

In order to revitalize the Polish economy, effective measures should be adopted as follows:

- While still adhering to the principle of positive interest rates in real interest rates, the government should be more active in applying preferential credit conditions in selected sectors, mainly agriculture, exports, and private sector activities.
- Far more investments need to be made to improve infrastructures.
- The prohibitive wage restraint system should be replaced by a flat tax rate on all wages. This move should be combined with introducing serious limitations on the powers of Workers' Councils in order to protect state-owned companies from spending an excessive proportion of revenues on wages and salaries.

• The basic exchange rate of the domestic economy with respect to the U.S. dollar for dollar should be changed to serve as an important stabilization "anchor." However, a wide range of export promotion schemes should be introduced to supplement custom tariff suspension in order to make trade policy more export-oriented and less protective for import substitution.

ECONOMIC POLICIES IN CHINA

During 1978–88 the world witnessed many dramatic changes in the economy of China. In such a centrally planned economy, the management of the macroeconomic system and the policies adopted have played a key role in the reform. This significantly increased the financial power of the local governments and state-owned enterprises. The transfer of profits of state-owned enterprises to the state was replaced by taxation, and financial allocations to state-owned enterprises were replaced by taxation. Financial allocation to the state-owned enterprises was replaced by bank credits.

Through financial reforms during the past ten years, China has acquired a primary modern financial system, which includes a central bank, an interest rate mechanism, a variety of credit systems, and an initial link with international markets. China must now learn how to stabilize the value of its currency or money supply, tighten the monetary policy to constrain the rapid expansion of social demand, and learn how to resolve the conflict between the central bank and the government.

Based on an evaluation of China's industrial management system and its historical changes, we predict that future policies will emphasize industrial development, the coordination of industrial and agricultural development policies, the encouragment of a rational structure within the industrial sector, and the stimulation of technological progress and innovation.

PART II

NATIONAL ECONOMIC POLICIES
IN INDUSTRIAL COUNTRIES

2

NATIONAL ECONOMIC POLICIES IN THE UNITED STATES: A REVIEW OF THE 1980s AND THE OUTLOOK FOR THE 1990s

George Iden

INTRODUCTION

The United States began the 1980s with a new administration and a new focus for national economic policy. Instead of lower unemployment and the environment, the new policy emphasis of the Reagan administration was less government involvement, lower taxes, and lower inflation. The overriding objective was more rapid economic growth through a strategy of reliance on individual initiative and free markets. The new strategy was partially successful in that the decade was marked by considerable progress in controlling inflation and in achieving an economic expansion of record length, which brought unemployment to its lowest level in more than fifteen years. But there was no supply-side miracle or gain in reducing inflation without significantly higher unemployment during the first half of the decade. In addition, the record of the 1980s was marred by large fiscal and trade deficits, stagnant real wages, rising inequality, and retreat and debacle in government regulation. In brief, gains were made in some important areas, but other areas, critical for the quality of life and future living standards, were neglected.

As we look to the 1990s, the key policy issues are how to revive the national saving rate, reduce the "twin" budget and current account deficits, reduce inflation, and deal constructively with income inequality and preservation of the environment. In the fiscal/tax and monetary policy areas, much unfinished business remains. In addition, after a decade of neglect, new initiatives are again being considered to deal with rising income inequality and a poverty rate that has stagnated at a considerably higher level than prevailed a decade ago. Public concern about the environment is also being revived. It is becoming increasingly clear that the public cares about the environment, and policymakers are beginning to respond. But they are seeking ways to control pollution with greater use of market approaches—to preserve efficiency and the environment.

Today the quality and tone of debate on economic policy are better and more promising than they were during much of the 1980s. We now have greater appreciation of the advantages of markets, of price stability, and of low, uniform tax rates than before the Reagan administration took office. At the same time, the tone of policy discussions has become more realistic and less strident. There is a also renewed recognition that government involvement is not necessarily bad. The claims represented by the various points of view have become less inflated, though strong disagreements and controversies remain. Few politicians or economists continue to argue that inflation can be substantially lowered without significant, though temporary, costs of higher unemployment, or that lowering taxes stimulates work and saving enough to prevent the budget deficit from rising. But heated debate continues on such issues as the extent to which federal deficits raise interest rates, lower national saving, and contribute to current large trade deficits; the magnitude of the costs from further reducing inflation; and the feasibility of maintaining or even lowering unemployment further without an acceleration in inflation. Economists and policymakers are again debating policy issues and options for reducing inequality without seriously undermining economic incentives. Nonetheless, major differences of opinion exist about the causes of poverty and appropriate policy responses.

This chapter gives a broad overview of U.S. economic policy. Its focus is on long-run trends and major issues, not on the most recent developments and proposals. The discussion of policy developments emphasizes the period of the Reagan administration from 1981 to 1988 and makes only passing reference to the current Bush administration. The chapter briefly describes the current policy context and summarizes recent economic trends, respectively; discusses recent developments and current issues in the area of macroeconomic policy—fiscal policy, monetary policy, and international trade and finance; and focuses on microeconomic policy, specifically government regulation and industrial or growth policy.

POLICY CONTEXT

The current focus in U.S. national economic policymaking is on raising the national saving rate—particularly by reducing the federal budget deficit—on reducing the trade deficit, on further reducing inflation, and on achieving the right mix of government involvement and free markets in the areas of government regulation, industry policies, and antipoverty efforts. To gain a perspective on these issues, it is useful to review recent policy debates in and economic trends.

Overview of Reaganomics

The Reagan administration established the framework for economic policy and for the economic policy debate during the 1980s early in its tenure.[1] In early

1981 the new administration issued a report that laid out four basic objectives of its economic policy:

1. A budget plan to cut the rate of growth in federal spending and to shift budget priorities away from domestic programs and toward defense
2. A series of proposals to reduce personal income tax rates by approximately 10 percent a year over three years and to provide tax incentives for business investment by accelerating depreciation on capital investments
3. A far-reaching program of regulatory relief
4. In cooperation with the Federal Reserve Board, a new commitment to a monetary policy that would reduce inflation and restore a stable currency and healthy financial markets

For the most part, the Reagan administration initially got much of what it wanted in its economic program. Personal and business taxes were cut dramatically by the Tax Reduction and Economic Growth Act of 1981; and marginal tax rates were cut further and the tax base broadened by the Tax Reform Act of 1986. Growth in government spending was slowed and domestic programs were cut substantially, though not by as much as the administration wanted. Government regulations were loosened through lax enforcement, and, in a number of instances, the resources for enforcement were cut substantially. Finally, although monetary policy in the United States is conducted by a relatively independent Federal Reserve, the administration reaped much of the credit for bringing inflation under control because it supported the policies of the Federal Reserve, or at least acquiesced to them. At any rate, the policy of monetary stringency that was begun in October 1979 was continued until inflation was dramatically reduced.

As the economic record makes clear, however, these initiatives accomplished less than many of their proponents, both inside and outside the administration, claimed. Taxes were cut, but revenues declined compared with prior law. Some enthusiastic proponents of supply-side economics had argued that the tax cuts might actually increase revenues, and they offered a Laffer curve as an explanation.[2] Those who subscribed to this view explained that beyond some point taxes could be so high that further increases would eventually result in less revenue rather than more. Thus, cutting tax rates, they argued, would raise revenue, or at least not reduce it. While that theory is difficult to dispute as an abstract proposition, the crucial question is whether taxes in the United States were at that point on the curve. At the time most economists argued that tax rates in the United States were not that high, and subsequent developments indicate that they were right.

It is not unusual for an administration to claim more for its economic policy proposals than it delivers in retrospect. What is unusual for the United States, however, is for the proponents to make such extravagant claims for their "supply-side" proposals, with so little to back them up in terms of economic analysis.

Moreover, policymakers generally want to claim more for policies than their economic advisers claim. But in the early years of the Reagan administration, the claims of the economic advisers seemed as extravagant as those of the politicians. This situation slowly changed as the decade wore on and as more middle-of-the-road economists were appointed to positions of responsibility.

Similarly, with respect to monetary policy, some proponents of tight money argued that, because of rational expectations, tighter monetary policy could dramatically reduce inflation without resulting in significantly higher unemployment. A key aspect of this argument was that the policy change had to be announced in advance and have credibility. That also proved not to be the case. Tight monetary policy did substantially reduce inflation, but at a cost of one of the deepest recessions in the post–World War II period. The unemployment rate rose from approximately 7 percent in 1980 to a high of almost 11 percent in late 1982.

In the international area, the Reagan administration generally emphasized free market solutions and a policy of laissez faire, although there were exceptions in the area of protectionism. The dollar rose strongly in foreign exchange markets during the first half of the 1980s, putting great competitive pressures on trade-dependent sectors of the U.S. economy. Throughout most of this rise, the administration argued that the value of the dollar was not a policy concern, because exchange markets determined this anyway. It was argued that the dollar's strength was due to a great improved climate for business and investment in the United States and to the United States being a safe haven for investors. Of course, the conventional view of economists was that the very large fiscal stimulus associated with the tax cuts and increased defense spending played a major role in the appreciation of the dollar.

In dealing with developing countries, the Reagan administration also emphasized greater reliance on free market solutions and less reliance on foreign aid. This philosophy collided with reality in at least one major area—the debt problems of Third World countries. It became increasingly clear that the Third World's debt problems were threatening its economic future and political stability. During most of the 1980s, however, the U.S. administration and the Federal Reserve refused to consider plans involving debt reduction. A major theme was that Third World nations in difficulty should tighten their belts, emphasize market solutions, and grow their way out of their staggering debt burdens.[3]

Not surprisingly, economists hold very different opinions about the economic effects of Reaganomics and about the overall success of the program. At one extreme are the extreme supply-siders, who believe that the decreases in marginal tax rates have dramatically increased incentives, effort, and capital investment. In the middle is a group that believes that the cuts in marginal rates and increases in investment incentives had modest effects and would gradually spur long-run economic growth. At the other extreme, some economists believe that the supply-side effects of the Reagan program were quite modest and that budget deficits undid much of the positive effects of other features of the program on economic growth. For instance, most measures of the saving rate decreased during the 1980s—not increased.

Probably the most severe criticism has been leveled at the large budget deficits during the Reagan years, as well as the implications for income distribution stemming from the budget outlay reductions and tax policies.[4] In particular, the budget deficits may have undone much of the positive effects on long-run economic growth resulting from the supply-side tax changes and the loosening of environmental regulations. The reductions in budget outlays were focused on social programs; therefore, they had the most severe effects on lower income individuals. On the tax side, wealthy individuals obviously benefited most from the reductions in marginal tax rates and the shift in emphasis from individual and corporate income taxes to social security or payroll taxes.

There is widespread agreement that the Reagan economic program changed the terms of debate on macroeconomic policies and shifted priorities. Since the passage of the Employment Act of 1946, reducing unemployment had been a primary objective of macroeconomic policy. However, in the 1980s under President Reagan's leadership, controlling inflation and economic growth received more emphasis, relative to the employment goal. Incomes policy was once a standard approach to fighting inflation, but it is not even discussed any more. Currently, there are no federal jobs programs to assist the poor. When the next recession does come, there is apt to be much less emphasis on standard anti-recession measures, such as extended unemployment insurance benefits, jobs programs, and income tax reductions. In general, the focus of attention has been shifted from economic stabilization and equity or fairness, to economic efficiency and growth. Nevertheless, the budget deficit and low private saving rate tended to undermine the Reagan administration's stated objective of achieving more rapid economic growth.

What kind of hard evidence is there on the success or failure of the Reagan program? Many analysts would argue that the supply-side tax cuts are the most likely feature of the Reagan program to have positive long-run effects on economic growth. There are two types of evidence: empirical studies of the effects of changes in marginal tax rates on saving and labor supply, and analyses of actual data following the implementation of the program.

With respect to knowledge about supply response, there is more agreement about labor supply than about the response of saving. Evidence suggests that there is a significant and positive labor response from a reduction in marginal tax rates, if incomes are held constant. But personal incomes were not held constant in either of the two major tax laws of the 1980s—both contained cuts in average tax rates for individuals. The literature on the elasticity of saving is inconclusive (Tanzi, 1987).

According to Feldstein (1986b) and Feldstein and Elmendorf (1989), whose work was based on an analysis of data after the policy changes, business investment was especially strong during the first two years of the economic recovery. However, there was no evidence that the size of the labor force had been affected by the tax cuts or that private saving had been positively affected. Feldstein (1989) argued that the recovery was driven primarily by monetary policy, but that fiscal policy had made a contribution in appreciating the dollar, which in turn had exerted downward pressure on inflation.

Some economists argue that other dimensions of labor supply, besides labor force participation rates, have been affected. For instance, it is possible that effort and mobility could have increased or that some groups of professionals now work harder as a result of the declines in marginal tax rates. In addition, some underground economic activity could have been shifted above ground in response to lower marginal tax rates. The principal evidence cited for large supply-side effects comes from data on the personal income tax, which show that despite lower top tax rates the high income groups paid a larger share of taxes than before rates were reduced. But that result seems to be attributable to increases in the inequality of income rather than to any supply-side stimulus per se (see Congressional Budget Office, 1987a). In addition, there seems to be little supporting evidence for large supply-side effects, such as a sudden rise in productivity or an acceleration in economic growth.

In sum, the supply-side economic policies of the Reagan period draw mixed reviews. Based on public finance literature, reductions in marginal tax rates while holding average taxes constant should increase the supply of labor. However, there seems to be little evidence that labor force participation rates have been affected by the tax measures of the 1980s. Some economists argue that other dimensions of labor supply have been affected, but the only support seems to be tax collections from high income groups which can be interpreted simply as an increase in inequality. In addition, while there is some evidence that business fixed investment responds to tax incentives such as those contained in the 1981 tax legislation, economists and policymakers are no longer as enthusiastic about such measures because they are distortionary. Finally, the budget deficits threaten to offset whatever benefits to economic growth there may have been from the supply-side measures.

Overview of the Bush Administration's Economic Policies and Current Issues

The Bush administration, which came to office in early 1989, continued the broad economic policies of the Reagan administration, with its emphasis on no tax increases, lower government spending, free markets, and minimal government regulation. No major new initiatives have been put forth by the Bush administration, and none seems imminent at the time of this writing. In the campaign, Bush stated emphatically that he would oppose any new taxes, or in his words, "Read my lips. No new taxes." Paradoxically, one of the ways that the Bush administration proposed to reduce the deficit was to cut the tax rate on capital gains. It argued that increased trading of assets would more than make up for the lower tax rate on capital gains and that cutting the tax would be a net revenue raiser.

In general, the stance of the Bush administration on the role of government has been less doctrinaire and more flexible than the Reagan administration. The new president at least verbally stressed the need to solve drug, education, and environmental problems, although he has proposed little in the way of additional federal budget resources.[5] The administration also moved swiftly to begin cleaning up the financial problems of the thrift industry, which had been created in part by lax regulatory policies earlier in the 1980s.

With regard to current economic policy issues, attention is being focused on the low U.S. saving rate and ways to address it, to the trade deficit, and to problems of the nation's low income population. The national saving rate has fallen to extremely low levels, relative to historical levels in the United States or relative to other countries. In turn, the low rate is associated not only with large government deficits, but also with a decline in the private saving rate. A low national savings rate, in turn, is the major cause of the inflow of foreign capital and the trade deficit, which encourages protectionism. In the area of fiscal policy, the dominant issue is how to deal with the budget deficit and which alternative is worse for economic growth: letting deficits run or raising taxes. In addition, tax reform is only partially complete, and much remains to be done to broaden the income tax base, rationalize the tax treatment of different types of income, and, at the same time, encourage more private saving. Dealing with the budget deficit and raising the national saving rate would go a long way in addressing the trade deficit problem, but many analysts believe that the United States also faces mounting long-run competitiveness problems. Since a hallmark of U.S. policy has been the encouragement of the free market system, there is considerable uncertainty about the best way to meet the challenge of foreign competition, particularly when some of the most successful competitors appear to practice more focused industry policy.

THE ECONOMIC ENVIRONMENT

During the 1980s the economy's performance improved in some areas but not in others. Probably the most notable improvement is that the economy now seems less inflation prone than during the 1970s. Inflation came down and stabilized, despite sustained economic growth that brought the unemployment rate to a fifteen-year low. In 1988–89 the economy operated at essentially its NAIRU (nonaccelerating inflation of unemployment)—the lowest unemployment rate compatible with stable inflation. In addition, productivity growth partially rebounded from the dismal performance of the 1970s. On the other hand, both the national saving rate and net exports fell markedly during the 1980s, which do not bode well for future growth in living standards. One of the main reasons for the lower national saving rate has been the large federal deficits. The federal debt rose from approximately 26 percent of GNP in 1981 to 43 percent in 1989, leaving a legacy of much higher debt service cost and possibly higher interest rates, among other effects. In addition, inequality rose during the decade, and there was no progress in reducing poverty.

Inflation and Unemployment

Recent trends in inflation and unemployment are summarized in Figure 2.1. As the 1980s began, inflation was relatively high. The Consumer Price Index (CPI) increased at an annual rate of 12.5 percent in 1980, but by 1982 it had slowed to a 3.8 percent rate. There were two main reasons for this marked decline. First, energy prices rose sharply in 1979 and 1980 and then declined in the early 1980s. The oil price shock caused a temporary boost in overall measures of inflation, which was then followed by a downward shock. Core inflation, or the CPI adjusted for food, energy, and used cars, was not nearly as volatile as the overall index (see the top panel in Figure 2.1).

A second factor behind the rapid improvement in inflation was the tight monetary policy pursued by the Federal Reserve and supported by the Reagan administration. Tight monetary policy reduced the growth in aggregate nominal spending, but it also caused an actual decline in real spending. Thus, the United States experienced two recessions in the early 1980s, which were nearly back to back. The unemployment rate reached a high of 10.8 percent in November 1982—the highest rate since the Great Depression of the 1930s. Although the unemployment rate began a slow decline in 1983, it remained relatively high for several years. By the end of the decade, however, the unemployment rate had gradually fallen to slightly above 5 percent—the lowest level since the early 1970s (see the lower panel in Figure 2.1).

The broad nature of the relationship between inflation and unemployment in the United States continues to be a subject of debate among economists—as elsewhere. The conventional view focuses on the hypothesis that there is an identifiable NAIRU. The basic idea that underlies NAIRU is that there is some relatively stable level of unemployment below which inflation will increase and above which inflation will decrease.[6]

The fact that inflation and unemployment at times increased together during the 1970s caused many economists and policymakers to challenge this view. It seemed to them that the theory did not hold. However, the challenges seemed to be aimed at an early naive version of the Phillips curve, in which inflation was depicted as a stable inverse relationship between inflation and unemployment. This naive version implied that lower unemployment could be permanently "bought" by accepting a somewhat higher level of inflation. The later augmented theory, however, postulated a relationship between changes in the current inflation rate, the past inflation rate, and the difference between the actual level of unemployment and the estimated level of NAIRU. There is considerable empirical evidence to suggest that this latter explanation has held up rather well in the United States, in contrast to countries of Western Europe which experienced

Figure 2.1
U.S. Inflation and Unemployment

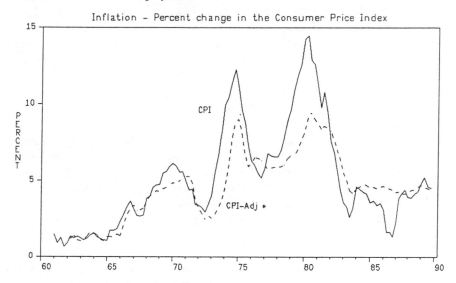

Inflation - Percent change in the Consumer Price Index

Source: U.S. Bureau of Labor Statistics.

Note: CPI-Adj is CPI less food, fuel, and used cars.

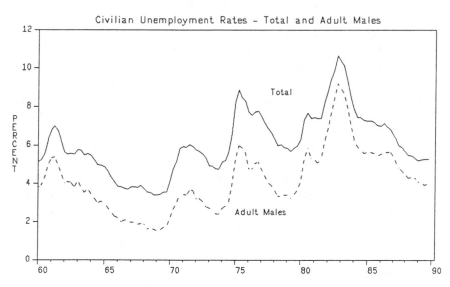

Civilian Unemployment Rates - Total and Adult Males

Source: U.S. Bureau of Labor Statistics.

Note: Adult males ages 25 to 54.

persistently high unemployment rates during much of the 1980s (see Schultze, 1987 and Blinder, 1987).

At any rate, the lowest noninflationary rate of unemployment in the United States has not been a constant during the last two decades. During the 1970s several factors tended to raise the level of NAIRU. First, divergences between workers' notions of fair wage increases and feasible wage increases can produce inflationary biases in the economy for considerable periods of time. During the 1973–81 period productivity growth slowed to less than 1 percent per year. But workers continued to act on the assumption that they could expect an inflation adjustment plus a productivity adjustment of 2 or 3 percent per year (see Schultze, 1987). For the economy as a whole, this obviously was not feasible, and one result was that profit margins were squeezed. Second, the demographic composition of the labor force changed toward a greater proportion of groups with relatively high rates of unemployment, such as teenagers and adult women. Third, there were inflationary shocks in the form of sharply higher oil prices and a fall in the foreign exchange value of the dollar.

During the 1980s several factors worked in the opposite direction to reduce the noninflationary level of unemployment. One is that the economy experienced two recessions during the early 1980s, which produced a sustained period of relatively high unemployment rates and shocked workers into accepting more modest wage increases. Second, the dollar increased rapidly during the first half of the decade, which increased competitive pressures in product and labor markets. Third, deregulation in such markets as the airlines, trucking, and telephone communication—a process that began in the late 1970s under the Carter administration—also increased competitive pressures in labor markets. Fourth, demographic factors began shifting in a direction that favored lower unemployment rates. The proportion of youth labor declined. In addition, the unemployment rate for women moved closer to the unemployment rate for men, reflecting lower frictional unemployment for women. Finally, after a series of inflationary shocks in the 1970s, there were some deflationary shocks during the 1980s as the price of oil, and to a lesser extent the price of food and raw materials, declined substantially.

As a result of these developments, estimates of NAIRU for the United States increased from around 4 percent in the 1950s and 1960s to around 6 to 7 percent in the 1970s, before falling to the 5 to 6 percent range by the end of the 1980s. The Congressional Budget Office assumes that currently NAIRU is approximately 5.5 percent. Based on its statements about the economy, the Federal Reserve seems to hold a similar view about the level of NAIRU. However, the administration seems to have made a somewhat more optimistic assessment of NAIRU. Its economic assumptions for the budget show the unemployment rate falling to approximately 5 percent in 1994 and, at the same time, inflation declining. On the other hand, based on his analysis of inflation, Gordon (1988) concludes that the natural rate of unemployment has not fallen below 6 percent.[7]

Table 2.1
U.S. Unemployment Rates by Census Regions and Divisions, 1988, All Races and Black (percent unemployment)

	All Races		Black	
	Total	16-19 Years	Total	16-19 Years
Northeast	4.0	11.1	8.1	24.7
New England	3.1	8.6	5.5	n.a.
Middle Atlantic	4.4	12.2	8.4	26.0
Midwest	5.8	14.5	16.1	38.8
East North Central	6.3	14.6	16.7	40.2
West North Central	4.7	14.3	13.5	n.a.
South	6.1	17.9	11.5	31.4
South Atlantic	4.8	14.8	9.0	26.0
East South Central	7.1	18.8	14.3	41.1
West South Central	7.8	22.0	15.7	40.3
West	5.6	15.9	11.0	36.5
Mountain	6.2	16.8	11.3	n.a.
Pacific	5.4	15.5	10.9	37.7
United States	5.5	15.3	11.7	32.4

Source: U.S. Bureau of Labor Statistics, *Geographic Profile of Employment and Unemployment*, Bulletin 2327 (Washington, D.C.: U.S. Government Printing Office, May 1989), Table 1.
Note: n.a. = not available.

Marked disparities in unemployment rates by race and region characterized much of the 1980s, although these disparities diminished as labor markets tightened toward the end of the decade. The recession of 1982 hit the Midwest especially hard because it exacerbated longer run competitive problems of some of the traditional capital and durable goods industries. Next, the sharp rise in the dollar compounded the difficulties of traditional factory-dominated areas. At the same time, conditions were much more prosperous in the Northeast with its specialization in service and defense industries. Layoffs in petroleum-related industries raised unemployment in the South Central and Mountain regions (Table 2.1).

As indicated in Table 2.1, in 1988 unemployment rates among black workers were roughly double the rates for all races. In particular, unemployment rates among black teenagers were disastrously high in all regions, especially in the industrial Midwest.

Table 2.2
U.S. Real GNP, Productivity and Employment: 1980s Compared to 1960s and 1970s (annual percent change, compounded)

	1960-1970	1970-1980	1980-1989
Real GNP	3.8	2.8	2.7
Productivity[a]	2.4	1.1	1.4
Employment[b]	1.8	2.4	1.7

Sources: U.S. Bureau of Labor Statistics; U.S. Bureau of Economic Analysis.

[a] Output per hour in the nonfarm business sector.

[b] Total civilian employment.

Longer Run Economic Performance—Output, Productivity, Employment, and Wages

Measures of longer term U.S. economic performance are summarized in Table 2.2, which compares economic series for the 1980–89 period with those of the earlier two decades. In brief, the growth rate in real GNP was similar in the 1980s and the 1970s but roughly a percentage point lower than in the 1960s. When we compare the 1980s with the 1970s, however, we see that the growth in output was achieved with somewhat faster growth in productivity and somewhat slower growth in employment. Nevertheless, the U.S. performance in creating jobs during the 1980s has been impressive compared with that of other industrial countries. Civilian employment grew by more than 18 million from 1980 to 1989, or at a compound rate of about 1.7 percent annually.

The decline in long-run productivity growth became one of the dominant issues of the late 1970s and early 1980s. The key role of productivity growth in raising standards of living is widely appreciated, and the decline in productivity growth during the 1970s produced a quest for ways to reverse the decline. Productivity growth declined markedly after the "golden years" following World War II until the mid–1960s. From 1973 to 1979 productivity grew at scarcely a perceptible rate—about one-half percent per year. During the 1980s productivity growth revived somewhat, but it remained substantially below the pace of the postwar period to the early 1970s period (see Table 2.2).

There is little agreement about the quantitative importance of factors that have influenced productivity growth. Economists continue to debate the causes of the productivity slowdown in the United States—since the productivity slowdown was a worldwide phenomenon. A substantial part of the productivity slowdown—perhaps half—remains unexplained by conventional growth-accounting analysis. Part of the slowdown may be an artifact of measurement, since productivity is especially difficult to measure in the service-producing sectors of the economy. In addition, there is considerable agreement about some of the causes, though not about their relative weights.[8] A common list of relatively specific factors includes the following:

- Oil price shocks, both in 1974 and again in 1979–80
- Demographic changes, notably increases in the relative size of the youth cohorts in the labor force and increases in the proportion of women in the labor force relative to men
- Increases in government "social" regulation, that is, measures to protect the environment and to promote occupational health and safety
- Slower growth in the capital–labor ratio, particularly when adjusted for capital investment required by government regulations
- Declines in research and development investments relative to GNP
- Completion of the shift in employment from the low-productivity agricultural sector to the higher productivity nonagricultural sector

Some economists and policymakers, however, emphasize broader determinants of productivity growth pertaining to the economic environment—influences that are even more difficult to measure than those from the above list. This group emphasizes impediments associated with government, such as increases in marginal tax rates, inflation, and government regulations. In addition, some analysts argue that measures aimed at reducing poverty had undermined economic incentives enough to be a factor in the productivity slowdown; but it is difficult to see how these measures could have had that great an effect. At any rate, the recommendations of the Reagan administration were designed to address these broad, government-related factors.[9]

There are fundamental differences in views about the importance of government and inflation as explanations of the productivity slowdown. Most economists would concur that these government influences matter for productivity performance, but there is much less agreement on their quantitative importance. For instance, inflation tends to distort decisions and to cause some resources to be misallocated, but there is little quantitative evidence on the importance of this factor in slowing productivity growth. Thus, the views of economists and policymakers on this issue tend to be determined on an ideological rather than on an empirical basis.

As alluded to above, the 1980s witnessed some modest recovery of productivity growth. To some extent, this recovery was due to a reversal of a number of factors that contributed to the slowdown in the 1970s. Energy prices not only stopped rising but also declined substantially. The bulge in the teenage labor force turned into a bust, as the number of teenagers in the labor force began declining in absolute terms and as a percentage of the labor force. Private research and development recovered. For those who emphasized more general causes, inflation declined, and government regulations were loosened. Still, a key question is how much more productivity growth will recover, particularly since the causes of the productivity slowdown are so poorly understood. The answer affects, among other things, the outlook for the budget deficit and the future standard of living in general.

Whatever the causes of the productivity slowdown, the implications for real wage growth have been profound. From the end of World War II until approximately 1973, real wages in the United States increased strongly and steadily. However, with the break in productivity growth, in about 1973, real wage growth slowed dramatically—and by some measures came to a virtual halt.

In addition to the slowdown in aggregate wage growth, profound changes have taken place in the distribution of wages. Conventional measures of real wages for production and nonsupervisory workers show essentially no growth since the early 1970s. That trend has not been altered despite some recovery in productivity growth during the 1980s. By contrast, broader measures that include higher paid managerial and professional workers have shown more growth. In addition, measures of compensation that include fringe benefits show more growth than more narrow measures of wages and salaries. Fringe benefits, such as employer-provided medical insurance, and payroll taxes to support social insurance programs have accounted for an increased share of overall compensation.

Although the rapid growth of U.S. employment has excited envy in countries where employment has stagnated, it has been the subject of controversy in the United States. Here the debate has centered on the quality of jobs, with some analysts such as Harrison et al. (1986) arguing that employment growth has been highly concentrated in low-paying service sectors. Other economists, such as Kosters and Ross (1988), argue that the proportion of low-paying jobs has not grown, although aggregate real wage growth has slowed along with productivity growth. In their view, the policy implications, if any, pertain to measures that could stimulate overall productivity growth. Still, the debate continues: whether low-wage, predominately service jobs, are growing disproportionately and, if so, whether there are specific policy implications.

Savings, Interest Rates, and the Composition of Output

Several characteristics of the economy stand out as being different during the 1980s.[10] As will be discussed in detail, the federal budget deficit as a share of GNP was unusually large during this decade. The higher deficits, unless offset by a higher private saving rate, imply a lower rate of saving for the economy as a whole. In addition, there was a substantial decline in the private saving rate during the 1980s. As a result of the decline in the private saving rate and the government deficits, the net national savings rate fell precipitously in the 1980s

Figure 2.2
U.S. Net Saving, Net Domestic Investment, and Net Foreign Investment as
Percentages of Net National Product

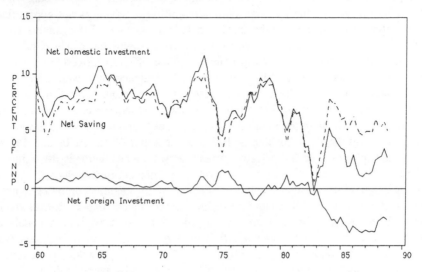

Source: U.S. Bureau of Economic Analysis.

(see Figure 2.2). Moreover, the U.S. savings rate is one of the lowest of any industrial country.

At the same time, the scarcity of domestic savings has been made up by an extraordinary increase in net foreign investment in the United States and the associated deficit in the U.S. current account. Net domestic investment as a share of net national product was also somewhat lower during the 1980s. Consistent with the lower saving rate and only moderately lower rate of net investment, the real interest rate was unusually high during the last decade—although it has declined in recent years.

According to some economists (see Council of Economic Advisers, 1989), the performance of investment should be measured gross of depreciation rather than net of depreciation. Since depreciation has grown especially rapidly, the performance of gross investment has not been unusually weak during the current decade. The proponents of this view argue that gross investment is important because it embodies new technology and because economic depreciation is difficult to measure accurately. On the other hand, net investment represents the net addition to the capital stock, and, according to most models of economic growth, the capital stock plays an especially important role in determining output and, therefore, living standards.

An issue that has come to dominate much policy debate concerns the causes of the decline in the national saving rate and the appropriate policy response, if any. The decline in the private saving rate has occurred despite the increase in the budget deficit. According to the Ricardian Equivalence view, the private sector can be expected to offset the government deficit by saving more. Instead, the private saving rate has fallen. Proponents of the Ricardian Equivalence view, however, argue that the national income definition of saving is not appropriate for analyzing saving behavior because it excludes capital gains. If we take account of capital gains, they argue, the decline in the private saving rate can be explained. Even so, it is difficult to see how private saving has offset the government deficit, which would need to occur if the Ricardian Equivalence view were correct.

Several explanations have been offered for the marked decline in the U.S. private saving rate during the 1980s. One factor is the increase in household wealth associated with the boom in the U.S. stock market during the 1980s, the large gains in the value of houses during the last half of the 1970s and 1980s, and the tripling of the federal government debt. Another factor is the aging of the population. According to the life cycle or permanent income hypothesis, an aging population consumes a larger fraction of its income compared with a younger population. Moreover, according to one recent paper, the relatively large increases in interest income during the 1980s went disproportionately to older households which spent a relatively large share of their incomes (see Sheshinski and Tanzi, 1989). Another explanation is the growth of government social insurance programs that assume many private risks which in the past have been an important motivation for private saving. However, the timing of this factor does not seem to correspond with the decline in the saving rate. Still, some economists point out that a slowing in income growth implies that a lower saving rate is needed to keep the ratio of income-to-wealth constant. According to the latter view, a lower saving rate is no problem.[11]

Finally, some analysts argue that the conventional measure of saving is much too narrow and somewhat misleading. They favor broader measures of saving that include research and development and investments in human capital. According to these broader measures, the U.S. saving rate is not relatively low by international standards; and if there has been a decline in the relevant saving rate it has been quite modest.[12] However, it is particularly difficult to distinguish human capital investments from consumption, and to estimate depreciation rates for R&D and human capital. Moreover, for the United States, military R&D is relatively important, but it may not contribute much to productivity growth.

Trends in Income Inequality and Poverty

During the 1980s the distribution of income became more unequally distributed and seemingly less responsive to overall economic growth. One of the popular phrases that was spoken by President Kennedy and often repeated until after the early 1980s was "A rising tide lifts all boats." This means that economic growth also improves the lot of the poor because employment opportunities and real wages increase for all major groups of workers; and more tax receipts make possible larger human resource investments and more generous welfare pay-

Table 2.3
Trends in Income Distribution in the United States, 1950–88 (personal income of families)

| | Income Shares | | | Ratio | Gini |
	Lowest Fifth	Second Fifth	Highest Fifth	Top 5 Percent	Highest to Lowest	Coefficient[a]
1950	4.5	12.0	42.7	17.3	9.5	.379
1960	4.8	12.2	41.3	15.9	8.6	.364
1970	5.4	12.2	40.9	15.6	7.6	.354
1980	5.1	11.6	41.6	15.3	8.2	.365
1981	5.0	11.3	41.9	15.4	8.4	.370
1982	4.7	11.2	42.7	16.0	9.1	.381
1983	4.7	11.1	42.8	15.9	9.1	.382
1984	4.7	11.0	42.9	16.0	9.1	.383
1985	4.6	10.9	43.5	16.7	9.5	.389
1986	4.6	10.8	43.7	17.0	9.5	.392
1987	4.6	10.8	43.7	16.9	9.5	.392
1988[b]	4.6	10.7	44.0	17.2	9.6	.395

Sources: U.S. Bureau of the Census, Current Population Reports, Series P-60, No. 162, *Money Income of Households, Families, and Persons in the United States: 1987* (Washington, D.C.: U.S. Government Printing Office 1989), Table 12; and Series P-60, No. 166, *Money Income and Poverty Status in the United States: 1988*, op. cit., Table 5.

[a] The "Gini coefficient is a measure of income inequity ranging from 0 to 1. A measure of 1 indicates perfect inequality; a measure of 0 indicates perfect equality.

[b] Based on advance data from the March 1989 *Current Population Survey.*

ments. That prescription seemed to fit the U.S. economy until the 1980s. Poverty and inequality tended to rise in recessions, but after the recession rapid improvement in living standards would ensue. In the 1980s, however, economic progress after the recession of 1982 was unusually slow or nonexistent for people at the lower half of the income scale.

The new forms of inequality have several dimensions. One is rising inequality in the distribution of personal income by families (see Table 2.3). Part of this trend is due to a change in the composition of families, namely, a trend toward smaller families and toward single-parent families. A recent study by the Congressional Budget Office (1986b), however, found that, even after adjusting for family size, inequality increased between the early 1970s and the mid-1980s. Another dimension is that the wages of production and nonsupervisory workers have been essentially stagnant for more than fifteen years, while broader measures that include managers and supervisors have indicated slow but still substantial growth. Looked at another way, the earnings of college graduates have risen sharply relative to the earnings of persons with less education. Still another dimension is that the earnings of young workers have fallen absolutely and relative to the earnings of workers of middle age and older. Finally, the earnings of young college graduates have grown rapidly relative to the earnings of young workers with only a high school diploma or less.

Economists give several types of explanations for the increases in inequality in the United States during the 1980s. According to one recent study, income disparities have grown because of the increased labor force participation of women with high earnings who are married to men who also have high earnings (see Danziger et al., 1989). Other explanations involve greater international competition that may have severely limited wage increases among relatively less skilled workers in goods-producing industries. In addition, minimum wage policy departed from the past in that the real minimum was permitted to erode significantly during the 1980s. By placing a floor under wages, minimum wage policy may have reduced wage differentials in earlier years. Another explanation stresses changes in relative supplies of labor, particularly the large increase in young adult workers resulting from the postwar baby boom. A large influx of relatively unskilled immigrants—including illegal immigrants—may have added to the pressure on wages of low-skilled workers. Still another possible explanation is that there may have been a change in the nature of technological change that has resulted in major changes in relative wages (see Bound and Johnson, 1989).

During the 1980s the United States made essentially no progress in reducing poverty.[13] The index of poverty increased sharply during the period of high unemployment produced by the severe 1982 recession. Roughly 11 percent of the U.S. population was poor in 1974, 12 percent in 1979, and 15 percent in 1983. Since then, the proportion of persons in poverty has declined very slowly, and in 1988, it was still about 13 percent.

Some of the implications of the high poverty rate in the United States are a relatively high rate of infant mortality compared with that of other nations, a lack of medical insurance for millions of workers, and an unknown—but probably large—number of homeless people.

MACROECONOMIC POLICIES

The 1980s was an eventful decade for macroeconomic policies. In fiscal policy, there were major shifts toward lowering marginal tax rates and broadening the tax base, but the dominant issue was and continues to be the relatively large budget deficits. Although the policy debate should have focused on reducing the deficit and stimulating the private saving rate, much energy was expended on the capital gains issue during 1989, and it promises to be high on the economic policy agenda again in the early 1990s. Monetary policy has had major successes in controlling inflation and in nurturing a steady economic expansion that has now completed its seventh year. While the economy has essentially reached full employment, the Federal Reserve hopes to bring down the inflation rate which seems to be stuck at about 4 percent per year. In the international area, the United States has made some progress in reducing its massive current account deficit, but it still has a long way to go.

Fiscal Policy

With respect to fiscal policy, three major developments occurred during the 1980s. First, the tax base was substantially broadened and marginal tax rates were dramatically reduced; second, the long-term rise in federal government spending as a share of GNP was brought to a halt by the middle of the decade and has since declined moderately; and, third, federal budget deficits have been large by historical precedent in the United States, though not compared to those in several other countries.

Much of the current debate focuses on the economic effects of large federal budget deficits, specifically on whether their detrimental effects exceed the costs of higher taxes that might be required to reduce them substantially and, if the deficits are to be reduced, the appropriate mix and timing of the required spending cuts and tax increases. A related issue involves the funding of the social security system and the treatment of the social security trust funds in the federal budget. The latter apparent accounting issue masks deeper issues involving the appropriate target for the federal deficit and the share of the burden of financing government spending and social security in particular.

Two broad factors contributed to these major changes in fiscal policy during the 1980s. First, there was a political reassessment of the size of government and of the effects of taxes and transfers. This reassessment was fueled by a feeling of discontent over the inability of traditional stabilization policies to deal with the stagflation of the late 1970s. In addition, economic research began to build a compelling case that the tax and transfer system, as well as a "command and control" type of social regulation, was exacting a high price on economic efficiency.[14]

Trends in Federal Spending, Taxes, and Budget Deficits. Both federal government spending and taxes as shares of gross national product (GNP) were on upward trends during most of the post–World War II period—with spending rising more rapidly than tax receipts (see Figure 2.3). However, the fiscal experience of the 1980s was qualitatively different. The tax share declined rather sharply in the early 1980s, reflecting the three-year phase-in of tax cuts under the Tax Reduction and Economic Growth Act of 1981. However, federal spending as a share of GNP continued rising until the mid-1980s, after which it slowly declined. Defense spending and interest on the public debt increased as shares of total government spending, while spending on nondefense discretionary programs, such as job training and grants to state and local governments, fell significantly.

Federal deficits were extraordinarily large during the 1980s. After reaching a peak of nearly 6 percent of GNP in 1983, the federal deficit began declining slowly after 1986 and, by 1988, had reached about 3 percent of GNP.

The pattern of federal deficits and federal debt during the 1980s was something new in U.S. fiscal experience. Before then, deficits were relatively small except during periods of recession and wartime. By contrast, the federal deficit remained

Figure 2.3

U.S. Federal Budget Outlays, Receipts, and Deficits as Percentages of Gross National Product

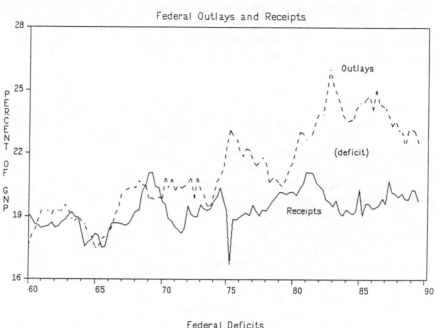

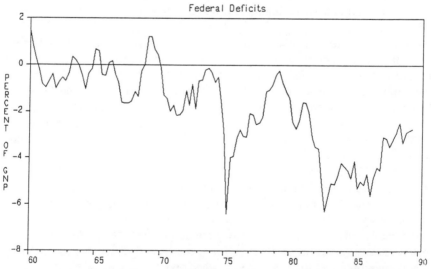

Sources: Office of Management and Budget; and U.S. Bureau of Economic Analysis.

Note: National Income and Product Accounts budget data.

at relatively high levels throughout the long recovery-expansion following the deep U.S. recession of 1981–82. As a consequence, the federal debt held by the public rose from approximately 27 percent of gross national product at the beginning of the decade to about 43 percent near its close in 1989; in current dollars, the federal debt roughly tripled during the 1980s.

A major reason why U.S. deficits are of such concern is that they are large relative to the rate of private saving. Federal deficits relative to GNP averaged more than two-thirds of the private saving rate during the 1980s. While some industrial countries, such as Italy, sometimes ran fiscal deficits relative to GNP that equaled or exceeded those of the United States during the 1980s, in most cases, such countries had comparatively high rates of private saving. In other words, some countries have been able to finance large government deficits with relative ease because they have also had relatively high rates of saving in the private sector. However, the U.S. private saving rate is among the lowest of the industrial countries of the world.

Extremely important changes were made in the U.S. tax structure during the 1980s. In general, marginal and average tax rates were reduced under the income tax, and the income tax base was broadened. In addition, the composition of tax revenues shifted toward greater reliance on social security, or payroll taxes. There were three major pieces of tax legislation: the Tax Reduction and Economic Growth Act of 1981, which partially indexed income tax rates for inflation and reduced tax rates; the Social Security Act of 1983, which provided for higher payroll taxes, phased in over a number of years; and the Tax Reform Act of 1986, which reduced marginal tax rates and broadened the tax base.

Through a series of major legislative initiatives, the top marginal tax rates under the personal income tax were reduced from 70 percent on property income at the beginning of the decade to 28 percent at the end of the decade. (Over part of the income range the marginal tax rate is 33 percent, but then it declines to 28 percent at the top of the income range.) In addition, the number of tax brackets was reduced to only two. The strategy of reducing marginal rates involved broadening the income tax base, and the tax legislation of 1986 substantially broadened the tax base by eliminating the differentially lower tax on capital gains and eliminating or limiting many deductions such as interest on consumer loans.[15]

In the tax legislation of 1981, the personal income tax brackets were indexed for inflation—which dramatically changed the way fiscal policy had been conducted. In the past, inflation along with real income growth pushed more taxpayers into higher brackets, and taxes were then periodically reduced, usually with the aim of stimulating the economy. Now, there is no such automatic tendency for budget deficits to close, or for the budget to be in a position for economic stimulus in the event of a recession.

Economists generally give high marks to the changes in the tax structure during the 1980s, although they differ substantially on just how important the supply-side benefits have been. Two aspects in particular are frequently cited as beneficial. First, the reduction in marginal tax rates should stimulate labor supply. Second, more equal tax rates on capital income should improve the efficiency with which capital is employed (see Gravelle, 1989).

Not all economists applaud the tax changes of 1986, because they believe that the investment tax credit, rapid depreciation, and individual retirement accounts—all repealed by the Tax Reform Act—were highly beneficial for economic growth (see Boskin, 1987). In some respects, the main thrust of the Tax Reform Act of 1986 ran counter to that of the Tax Reduction and Economic Growth Act of 1981, because that legislation sought to stimulate saving and investment. In any event, the broad changes in the U.S. tax structure seem to have been part of a broad international trend among industrial countries—to reduce marginal tax rates and to broaden the tax base.[16]

Economic Effects of Government Deficits.   Budget deficits that are not caused by recessions are generally a cause for concern because they can lead to faster money growth and inflation and to the crowding out of wealth and capital formation. There is some debate over whether the Federal Reserve may have partially monetized budget deficits in the post–World War II period: Generally, however, this is not believed to have been the case in the 1980s (see Barth et al., 1982 and Miller and Velz, 1989). However, based on circumstantial evidence, a case can be made that the large federal budget deficits during the 1980s were a significant factor behind the large U.S. trade deficits and the unusually low net national saving rate. But plausibility does not establish causation, and a debate has been raging over the economic effects of budget deficits.

The policy debate on federal budget deficits has been characterized by widespread disagreement about their economic effects—a disagreement that has been fed by contradictory writing on the part of economists. According to the conventional view, federal deficits raise interest rates, lower national saving, and reduce investment and net exports. However, according to a competing view, known as the Ricardian Equivalence proposition, private agents raise their own saving in order to offset the public deficits. In the latter case, government deficits would have none of the adverse effects on interest rates, saving, and the composition of output that are associated with the conventional view.

Under the conventional view, an increase in federal budget deficits raises interest rates because it adds to the demand for credit and raises the amount of government bonds relative to other forms of wealth. The interest rate rises to allocate available credit between public and private uses, and, in terms of "portfolio" models, an increase in the amount of government bonds can be absorbed only if there is an increase in the return on such bonds—namely, a rise in interest rates.

Within the conventional viewpoint, there is a broad range of views about the size and importance of the economic effects of government deficits. For one thing, with an international capital market, an increase in interest rates may be muted because of international capital flows. In the case of a large country, such as the United States, the world interest rate may be affected, but in the case of a small country there may be little or no effect on interest rates (see Tanzi, 1985). In any case, even if deficits have no perceptible effect on interest rates, they still undermine longer run growth in the standard of living because of the accumulation of dollar-denominated assets owned by foreigners. Whether the inflow of foreign capital is invested productively is important for future living standards, but it is not crucial to the conclusion that budget deficits reduce the growth of living standards.

The opposing or Ricardian Equivalence view, as developed by Robert Barro (1974) among others, concludes that under certain assumptions government deficits do not affect national saving, interest rates, or trade deficits. Among the critical assumptions are that economic agents include the economic welfare of future generations in their utility functions, that capital markets function perfectly, and that private agents can borrow or lend at the same rate of interest as the government. Rational economic agents will then conclude that the financing of a given level of government spending is immaterial and that government bonds do not add to wealth because they are matched by future debt service obligations.[17]

This debate over the seriousness of the economic consequences of government deficits has raged among academic economists, but it has also been echoed at the highest policy levels. At times, the sides have been drawn between the administration on the one hand and the Congress on the other hand. At other times, the debate seems to have been equally intense within the administration— for example, between Martin Feldstein as chairman of the Council of Economic Advisers, who represented the conventional view, and Donald Regan as secretary of the Treasury and chief economic spokesman for the administration, who represented the opposing view that deficits had minimal adverse economic effects, at least compared to tax increases. The debate culminated in early 1984 when Secretary Regan dumped the Economic Report of the Council of Economic Advisers into the waste basket; it may have been a factor in Feldstein's resignation which occurred within a few months.

The U.S. Treasury, under Secretary Regan, took the position that there was no evidence to support the claim that budget deficits raise interest rates. Treasury officials cited the contradictory findings reported in the empirical economic literature. In addition, the Treasury undertook its own empirical study and concluded that it did not find a statistically significant relationship between higher deficits and higher interest rates. Administration officials, including the Council of Economic Advisers after Feldstein, took the position that the high real interest rates during the 1980s were largely due to other factors such as an improved investment climate in the United States and the investment tax incentives contained in the 1981 tax legislation.

Reports by the Congressional Budget Office (1989b and 1985a), however, warned that sustained budget deficits do have detrimental economic effects. In particular, it argued that deficits reduce national saving and investment, including net U.S. investment abroad. The lack of consensus on whether deficits raised interest rates was attributed, among other factors, to the limited U.S. experience with peacetime deficits that were not associated with economic recessions.

Another argument challenging the seriousness of federal budget deficits pertains to measurement, and was advanced by officials of the U.S. Treasury Department (see Darby, 1987) and by Eisner (1986), among others. According to this view, the federal deficit is not large after certain adjustments are made, including an inflation adjustment, an adjustment for capital investment by government, an adjustment for the business cycle, and, finally, including the budgetary surpluses of state and local governments. The Treasury document emphasized that substantial federal debt was accumulated during the period of tight monetary policy during the early 1980s and that, consequently, debt service was considerably higher from then on. The implication is that fiscal policy was not to blame for a substantial part of the ensuing budget deficits.

In the current situation, the most important issue pertains to an inflation adjustment. Inflation reduces the real value of the public debt. In addition, interest rates tend to reflect expected inflation, and, therefore, the interest cost of servicing the public debt is higher because of this inflation premium. If wealth holders are not subject to money illusion, they will save the inflation premium contained in their interest income. Thus, an increase in nominal interest income that merely reflects higher inflation should not affect consumption and saving. Since the privately held federal debt is now about $2 trillion and inflation is running between 4 and 5 percent, an inflation adjustment for the federal deficit would result in a subtraction of $80 to $100 billion, which amounts to roughly half to two-thirds of the nominal deficit. In other words, after the inflation adjustment, the federal deficit would be as little as $50 billion, or approximately 1 percent of GNP. If the federal government does any net investment at all, then one can argue that the "true" deficit is even less than that. Moreover, since state and local governments have been running surpluses during the 1980s, the total government deficit has been still smaller.

These measurement arguments pose two problems. One is that the inflation adjustment—to the extent that wealth holders are informed and rational—and the inclusion of state and local government surpluses merely shift a given amount of national saving from the private sector to the public sector. In other words, private sector saving is reduced as much as public sector saving is increased by this adjustment. Moreover, a substantial part of the surpluses of state and local governments is associated with the accumulation of savings for the pension funds of government employees, which substitutes for private savings. The second problem, which pertains to the adjustment for public sector net investment, is that this net investment, scaled for economic growth, is no larger—and probably smaller—than it was in earlier decades.

The basic problem produced by federal deficits so far is that they have reduced national saving, which is currently extremely low. Federal deficits absorbed a larger share of net national saving during the 1980s than in any earlier decade in the post–World War II period. But the decline in saving has not been limited to the public sector. The private saving rate also declined markedly during the 1980s. Net investment was somewhat lower during the 1980s, but not as much lower as the saving rate. Thus, the shortfall in domestic saving has been made up by a large decline in U.S. net foreign investment.

In view of the importance of the issue of whether federal deficits raise interest rates and crowd out domestic investment, it is not surprising that many empirical studies in recent years have tried to test statistically for a relationship between federal budget deficits and interest rates. Despite the intense research effort, there is no consensus on whether budget deficits raise interest rates.

Some patterns in the results of the research on budget deficits and interest rates are beginning to emerge, however. The evidence appears to be stronger that deficits affect long-term interest rates than that deficits affect short-term interest rates. In addition, studies that use cyclically adjusted measures of the deficit are more apt to find that deficits raise interest rates than studies that make use of unadjusted deficit measures. Moreover, expected future deficits, or unanticipated current deficits, seem more potent for interest rates than the simple current deficit. Some studies have found that increases in federal debt, rather than deficits per se, raise interest rates. Finally, it should be emphasized that most of the controversy pertains to deficits produced by lower taxes rather than by increases in government purchases. Several studies found that increases in government purchases tended to raise interest rates, while the evidence on changes in deficits per se was more ambiguous.[18]

Another argument that has been made against trying to close the federal budget deficits through tax increases is that raising taxes would not close the deficit because policymakers would simply raise spending. There is some research to support both sides of this question, but the most sophisticated analysis has come to the conclusion that there is no quantitative evidence to support the proposition that an increase in taxes leads to an increase in spending with no effect on the deficit.[19]

Still another argument against raising taxes to close the deficit, which is related to the Laffer curve, is that raising taxes would not close the deficit because the added tax burden would result in no more taxes being collected. Conservative economists have raised this argument for many years, but the evidence to support it is notably absent.

Other Current Fiscal Policy Issues. As the 1990s begin, a paramount issue in U.S. fiscal policy is how to deal with the federal budget deficit, which has come down from peak levels in the mid-1980s but still looms relatively large. According to recent estimates by the Congressional Budget Office (1990), the budget deficit based on current policy will be about 2.5 percent of GNP in fiscal year 1990 and will decline slowly to about 1.5 percent of GNP by 1995.

There are at least three major questions connected to the deficit issue: how large are the policy changes needed, what mix of spending cuts and tax increases is appropriate, and how does the harm produced by the deficit compare with the harm that might result from raising taxes? The administration favors a strategy of spending cuts, with no tax increases. On the other hand, the Congress favors a combined strategy of lower spending and higher taxes. The end result has been a budgetary stalemate of major proportions, although the recent thaw in the cold war in Europe offers some new signs of hope. Like all administrations, the current one tends to be optimistic in its future economic projections—often termed "rosy scenario." With a rosy projection, there is less need to undertake painful spending cuts and tax increases.

As a disciplinary device for itself, Congress passed and the president signed into law the Gramm–Rudman–Hollings Deficit Reduction Act of 1985 (GRH), which provides for automatic spending cuts when its deficit reduction targets are not met. The spending cuts are across-the-board for programs that are not specifically excluded, such as social security and certain programs for the poor. As amended, GRH calls for lowering the deficit to $100 billion in fiscal year 1990, $64 billion in 1991, $28 billion in 1992, and 0 in 1993.[20]

By passing the Deficit Reduction Act, Congress put itself in a bind on the controversy with the administration over the appropriate mix of spending cuts and tax increases for reducing budget deficits. The administration favors deficit cutting by cutting spending, entirely, whereas the Congress favors a combination of spending cuts and tax increases. Since the GRH is stipulated entirely in terms of spending cuts, Congress finds itself in a quandary. If Congress insists on a balanced tax and spending approach, the administration can simply refuse to go along, in which case GRH takes effect.

Another critical issue that relates to the size of the deficit problem is the outlook for the economy, particularly for economic growth and interest rates. The administration typically adopts more optimistic assumptions about future economic growth, inflation, and interest rates than the Congressional Budget Office (CBO). For instance, in early 1989 the Reagan administration's budget projections showed the federal deficit disappearing by 1993. By contrast, the CBO's projections with the administration's policies showed the deficit at approximately $80 billion in 1993. The bulk of the difference in these budget projections can be traced to different views about the outlook for productivity growth, inflation, interest rates and, to a lesser extent, to differing views about how low unemployment can go without causing inflation to increase—NAIRU. The interest rate projections differ primarily because of differing assumptions about inflation, but also because of differing views about the effects of reducing the budget deficits on interest rates. The Bush administration—in contrast to most of the earlier spokespersons for the Reagan administration—argued that reducing the whole range of future deficits with the end result of a balanced budget would reduce interest rates by as much as two percentage points. Such a reduction in interest rates would have a major effect on the deficit; according to CBO's "rule of thumb" estimates, a reduction of one percentage point would lower the deficit by almost $30 billion by the sixth year.

Another current issue that is generating much heated debate concerns the taxation of capital gains, although this issue can be approached as part of a broader set of issues involving the tax treatment of various forms of capital income. Under the base-broadening compromise tax legislation of 1986, the distinction between capital gains and regular income was eliminated as part of the agreement to lower marginal tax rates on high-income individuals. Indeed, the highest marginal tax rate was brought down to a lower level than almost anyone expected. But the elimination of the distinction between capital gains and other income meant a substantial increase in the rate on capital gains. In addition, while income tax brackets were indexed for inflation, capital gains were not, and neither was depreciation on depreciable assets. In the case of capital gains, the absence of indexing meant that the tax on real gains could run much higher than the top 28 percent on regular income.

At the current time, there is considerable support in the United States for reducing the tax on capital gains. Some individuals believe that capital gains should not be subject to the income tax, in part to prevent capital from migrating to countries that have lower taxes on capital gains.[21]

A reduction in the capital gains tax was a major theme of candidate Bush and has become a major objective of the Bush administration. It has strongly supported a reduction in the capital gains tax as a measure that would stimulate economic growth in the long run and raise revenue in the short run. According to its proponents, a lower rate on capital gains would encourage national saving and investment.

In early 1989 the Bush administration made its proposal on capital gains. The proposal had three elements: special tax treatment, qualified assets, and a holding period requirement. Under the special tax treatment, individuals would face a maximum tax rate on capital gains on qualified assets of 15 percent. Qualified assets would include most property except depreciable property, collectibles, livestock, and assets used in a trade or business.

The administration argued that its proposal would lead to an increase in tax receipts of nearly $5 billion in 1990 and in 1991, but then a gradual decrease to about $2 billion in 1993. However, Congress' Joint Committee on Taxation estimated a gain of about $3 billion in 1990, followed by substantial losses.

Opponents of lowering the capital gains tax have argued that a lower tax on capital gains would chiefly benefit the rich and would loosen substantial revenue, except perhaps in the very short run.[22] Even if a lower capital gains tax stimulated innovation and risk taking, this would represent a small proportion of overall capital gains. If there is a desire to encourage entrepreneurial capital, critics charge that other less costly methods are available.

The fairness issue was also important in the debate over capital gains. The Democratic leadership in Congress stressed that special treatment for capital gains would benefit primarily the rich and that such a change in the tax code would violate the spirit of the 1986 agreement to dramatically lower the top marginal tax rates. Moreover, the tax reform package was designed to be neutral with respect to the tax burden among income groups; reducing the tax rate on capital gains afterward would undo the implicit agreement. As an alternative to a lower capital gains tax, the Democrats in 1989 offered proposals designed to reward savings by the middle class, such as individual retirement accounts, or savings plans that could be tapped for other purposes besides retirement, such as to purchase a home or to finance college education. The Republicans countered that many taxpayers affected by capital gains were not especially rich, but rather were cashing in on long-held assets that in many cases represented their lifetime savings.

The most important issue is not the revenue implications but the principles that should guide the taxation of capital gains and the income from capital in its various forms. For instance, rather than a lower rate for all capital gains, many economists would favor the indexing of capital gains for changes in the price level. That, at least, would more accurately measure capital gains.

The Tax Reform Act of 1986 left many of the distortions in the tax system unchanged. For instance, the ownership of a home is still accorded major tax advantages. Capital gains on homes are not taxed as long as the proceeds are reinvested in a home of equal or greater value. In addition, an exemption of $125,000 in capital gains is provided when the taxpayer reaches age fifty-five. Mortgage interest and real estate taxes are deductible from regular income, and the income in kind from owner-occupied homes is not taxed. Moreover, in some respects the Tax Reform Act even increased the relative advantages of home ownership since interest paid on home equity loans could be deducted while consumer installment interest deductibility was phased out. Other major revenue losses stem from employer deductibility of certain employee fringe benefits and the deductibility of state and local taxes, including real estate taxes.

Capital gains continue to be treated relatively favorably in several other respects under the tax code. For one thing, only realized capital gains are taxed. For another, capital gains are not taxed at death. Instead, the heirs are allowed to adjust the cost basis for assets to their estimated value at the time of death. Thus, older wealthy individuals by investing in appreciating assets rather than income-producing assets can escape both the income tax and capital gains taxes.

While gaining consensus on reducing the deficit is difficult, it is not difficult to think of ways to close the deficit. For instance, many economists believe that the rate of taxation on the consumption of energy is too low in the United States. The reason is that the price of energy does not cover the substantial environmental damage stemming from energy consumption, or the problems that result from dependence on foreign sources for oil. Every penny of additional tax on gasoline would raise about $1 billion.[23]

At the same time that the need to close the deficit is stressed, many economists and policymakers are emphasizing the need to stimulate private saving. Previous experience with individual retirement accounts or IRAs, introduced as part of the Economic Recovery Tax Act of 1981, has not been very encouraging. In addition, the coexistence of high real interest rates during the 1980s, a substantial drop in the top marginal tax rates, and a drop in the private saving rate is discouraging from the point of view of designing policies to stimulate the private saving rate. This lends increased importance to reducing the federal budget deficit as the surest way to raise the national saving rate.

The recent thaw in the cold war offers some new hope for a way out of the budget stalemate. If the United States could substantially cut its ground forces in Europe, it could realize large budget savings that could then be used to cut the budget deficit. But some members of Congress want to use any peace dividend to meet other spending priorities, such as improving the infrastructure, cleaning up toxic wastes, conducting research on AIDS, and providing long-term medical care insurance. Thus, if there is a peace dividend, there is certain to be a political struggle over how it is to be used.

Social Security and the Retirement of the "Baby Boom."   Until 1983, the social security retirement program was on a pay-as-you-go system of financing. The current benefits of retirees were paid by tax receipts from the currently working labor force with no intended buildup in reserves. This system worked as long as the labor force was relatively large and growing at roughly the same rate as the retired population. However, as the "baby boom" generation begins to retire early in the next century, the demands on the social security system will grow rapidly. Moreover, because the baby boom was followed by a baby bust, the working population will not grow as rapidly as in the past. As a result, demographers expect a gradual and sustained increase in the ratio of the retired to the working population, reaching a much higher plateau in about 2040. The important thing to note, however, is that the higher dependency ratio is expected to be relatively permanent, not temporary.[24]

After 1983 policymakers put social security on a partially funded basis. Payroll taxes were to be raised substantially in several phases, so that a large surplus would be accumulated in the social security trust funds. These surpluses have, in effect, gone to reduce the federal deficit rather than increase national saving.

Thus, the budgetary treatment of social security trust funds and the financing of the social security system have become controversial issues. At first glance, the issue seems to be about simple accounting changes—whether to include or exclude the social security trust funds from the federal budget. Some individuals argue that the large and growing surpluses in the social security trust funds should be excluded in calculating the budget deficit. Proponents of this change argue that social security surpluses should not be used to finance the deficit in the rest of the government and should not be counted in the budget deficit. If the surpluses are simply used to finance government deficits, they do not add to national saving and contribute to long-run growth, which in turn is needed to support a large increase in the retirement population relative to the working population during the first half of the twenty-first century. Some argue that the overall federal budget, including social security trust funds, should be in surplus by roughly the amount of the trust fund surpluses.

An apparent accounting issue about whether to move social security off the budget masks more substantive issues involving the financing of government in general and the social security system in particular. Using social security to pay for other government functions has implications for the distribution of the tax burden, since the social security system is financed by the payroll tax. In turn, the payroll tax is a basically regressive tax, since wage earnings at the high end of the scale are exempt and nonwage income is exempt. This issue can be related to the trends in the distribution of before-tax income. As discussed earlier, the 1980s were characterized by an increase in inequality, including inequality of earned income.

This situation has prompted some policymakers, such as Senator Patrick Moynihan (D-New York), to propose that the social security tax increases be rolled back and that the system again be put on a pay-as-you-go framework. They argue that it is inequitable for the payroll tax to be financing such a large part of the federal budget, in part because the payroll tax is borne by workers and is a regressive tax. The Bush administration has opposed reducing payroll taxes. Proponents charge that it is doubly unfair of the administration to propose a capital gains tax cut for the rich but to oppose a tax cut for the broad group of working people.

Monetary Policy

In the early 1980s much of the discussion of monetary policy centered on three issues: whether the inflation–unemployment relationship could be significantly influenced by the credibility of monetary policy; which tools the Federal Reserve should use in conducting monetary policy; and the relative independence of the Federal Reserve. The first issue resurfaced at the end of the decade since inflation continued in the 4 to 5 percent rate per year and some policymakers favor reducing it substantially further. The debate on the second issue, however, appears to have abated, for reasons that will be explained below. The third issue on the relative independence of the Federal Reserve is a perennial issue that has also resurfaced.

During the 1970s and early 1980s the monetarists, under the leadership of Professor Milton Friedman, argued that the growth in the money supply was the primary determinant of inflation and of short-run changes in output. They argued, too, that monetary policy should be conducted in terms of a steady but slow rate of growth in the money supply. Monetary policy should not be used as countercyclical policy, because of long and variable lags. In addition, the monetary authorities should not focus on the course of short-term interest rates, because interest rates are an unreliable guide for policy.

Monetary policy from October 1979 to mid-1982 was conducted by focusing primarily on monetary aggregates, and monetary policy was presented and discussed in those terms. Even so, the monetarists criticized monetary policies during the early 1980s on the grounds that the growth in money aggregates fluctuated far too much. However, as the 1980s unfolded, it became increasingly clear that the key assumption underlying the focus on monetary aggregates was not being met. That assumption was that money velocity—the relationship between GNP and the money supply—would remain constant, or at least could be explained and predicted. As a result, the Federal Reserve abandoned the approach of focusing primarily on monetary aggregates in favor of a more eclectic approach.

After abandoning strict money targeting, the Federal Reserve increased the money supply rapidly during the early phases of the economic recovery that began in the fourth quarter of 1982. Many economists of monetarist persuasion argued at the time that such rapid growth in money aggregates was highly inflationary. That did not prove to be the case; instead, velocity or the relation between GNP and money was highly unstable.[25]

The eclectic approach of the Federal Reserve—which describes monetary policy today—includes continual monitoring of the economy, as well as world financial markets, and adjusting monetary policy accordingly. Most observers currently give the Federal Reserve high marks with this policy stance. The Federal Reserve has been trying hard to avoid a common mistake of the past: to wait too long before changing policy direction. In recent years, it has tightened monetary policy before inflation actually showed much acceleration. Beginning in June 1989, monetary policy was again loosened, amid signs that economic activity was slowing.

It is unclear, however, how this policy approach differs from the "finetuning" approach that was much maligned a decade ago. Perhaps the main difference is that the current finetuning is being carried out with more skill and more luck in the sense that there have not been significant shocks to the economy like those that occurred in the 1970s.

In the current context, the Federal Reserve and the administration appear to have same differences over the appropriate growth rate for the economy, although both agree on the advantages of achieving lower inflation. The issues in this "debate" include the near-term strength of the economy and whether current unemployment at slightly above 5 percent is as low as it can get without causing more inflation. In other words, how strong is aggregate demand, and what is the current level of NAIRU? On the second part of this question, most estimates suggest that the economy is currently operating at or somewhat below NAIRU. The Federal Reserve Board, under the chairmanship of Alan Greenspan, has recently been stressing the advantages of a stable aggregate price level and its intention of gradually pursuing that objective.[26]

Legislation has been introduced in Congress that would make price stability or zero inflation the primary goal of monetary policy. This proposed Joint Resolution of Congress (H.J. Resolution 409) instructs the Federal Reserve Open Market Committee to reduce inflation gradually and to eliminate inflation within five years from the date of enactment. The chairman of the Federal Reserve Board and four presidents of Federal Reserve District Banks, including the president of the Federal Reserve Bank of New York, have testified in favor of the legislation.

Again the proposition is being advanced that if a policy of achieving price stability is credible it will have relatively small short-run costs that will be more than outweighed by the long-run advantages of low and stable inflation. However, for the United States there is little evidence to support the argument that inflation can be substantially reduced without creating considerable slack in labor markets. Instances have been cited for other countries in which inflation decelerated markedly without sharp increases in unemployment; it is conceivable that it could happen in the United States. Nevertheless, based on U.S. historical experience to date, there could be substantial transition costs of achieving minimal inflation of, say, 1 percent per year from the current rate of more than 4 percent per year.

At the current time, the Federal Reserve is attempting to walk a very fine line between recession on the one hand and growth slow enough to reduce inflation on the other hand. The Fed is embarked on a policy designed to gradually reduce inflation by maintaining economic growth somewhat below its potential growth rate, while at the same time attempting to avoid a recession. Since the potential rate of growth for the U.S. economy is about 2.5 percent per year, this policy does not leave much room for error. Based on past U.S. history, however, there is not much evidence to suggest that inflation can be lowered substantially while maintaining only marginal slack in labor markets.

Some economists, such as Friedman (1989), are arguing that businesses in the United States have become so heavily leveraged with debt that monetary policy has become heavily constrained. According to this view, the wave of corporate buy-backs of common stock, mergers, and acquisitions in recent years has made the business sector unusually vulnerable to an economic downturn. Since the Federal Reserve knows this, the argument runs, it is unwilling to run a serious risk of a recession. Hence, there is currently an inflationary bias to monetary policy.[27]

To others, however, it seems doubtful that monetary policy is currently severely constrained by corporate debt leveraging. For one thing, the current flat term-structure of interest rates suggests that the market does not believe that higher or lower inflation lies ahead. For another, this thesis was advanced earlier in connection with the threat of insolvent saving and loan institutions, and that situation did not seem to inhibit the Fed's policy. If anything, financial markets and the real economy have come through the S&L debacle relatively unscathed. Thus, even if a recession would cause more bankruptcies than usual, it is not clear that they would have severe implications for the real economy. In addition, not all measures suggest that there is a problem with business debt. While measures of debt service cost relative to income or cash flow are unusually high, the ratio of debt relative to current market value of assets does not signal such cause for alarm (see Bernanke and Campbell, 1988).

Finally, the issue of the independence of the Federal Reserve is being debated once again. In 1989 legislation (H.R. 2795) was introduced in Congress to curb the independence of the Federal Reserve. Proponents argued that monetary policy is too important to leave to officials who are not elected and who serve for long terms. However, others argue that curbing the independence of the monetary authority would cause it to be too subject to short-run political pressures, which could result in a strong inflationary bias.

International Issues

During the 1980s the exchange value of the dollar increased greatly during the first half of the decade—and then declined by as much during the second half (see Figure 2.4). The huge rise in the dollar was a major factor, though not the only factor, behind the deterioration in the U.S. trade balance during the decade. In recent years, the trade deficit has finally begun to decline, but in 1989 this process stagnated as the dollar rallied in foreign exchange markets.

The precise role of the U.S. budget deficit as a contributor to the rise in the dollar and the subsequent deterioration in the U.S. current account has been and is a hotly debated subject among academics (see Evans, 1986 and Feldstein, 1986a). At times, some administration officials have advanced the view that the behavior of the dollar was largely attributable to a tightening of U.S. monetary policy relative to monetary policies in other industrial countries and to an improvement in the climate for investment in the United States relative to the rest of the world, particularly the Third World countries that were struggling with massive foreign debt.

Most economists, however, would argue that the federal budget deficit ultimately played a major role in the U.S. trade deficit and that the most effective policy tool for reducing the trade deficit at the current time is to reduce the fiscal deficit. As discussed earlier, the last half of the 1980s was characterized by a low rate of net national saving in the United States, which in turn was caused in part by a massive increase in government dis-saving. The difference between U.S. domestic investment and saving has been made up by an inflow of foreign capital of major proportions. In turn, the sustained deficit in the current account has transformed the United States from a major net foreign investor at the beginning of the decade to the largest debtor country in the world. It seems likely that the U.S. net foreign debt will reach $1 trillion sometime in the first half of the 1990s.[28]

The rapid accumulation of foreign holdings of U.S. dollar-denominated assets has raised an important sustainability question. How long can this process go on before foreign investors decide that their portfolios are too heavily weighted with U.S. assets? Moreover, foreign investors' opinions on this matter may be highly volatile. One implication is that the lack of external balance on the part of the United States could lead to instability in international stock and bond markets. Some analysts blame the financial tremors in late 1987 on the U.S. twin fiscal and trade deficits.[29]

While intellectually there may be a consensus that the U.S. trade deficits have been caused by macroeconomic forces, the trade deficits have encouraged protectionism as well as heightened concerns about impediments to free trade. Many industries and localities have been severely affected by foreign competition. In

Figure 2.4
Exchange Value of the Dollar and U.S. Current Account

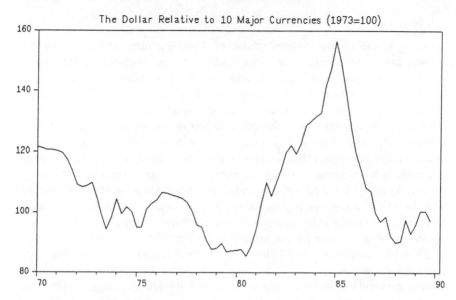

The Dollar Relative to 10 Major Currencies (1973=100)

Source: Federal Reserve Board.

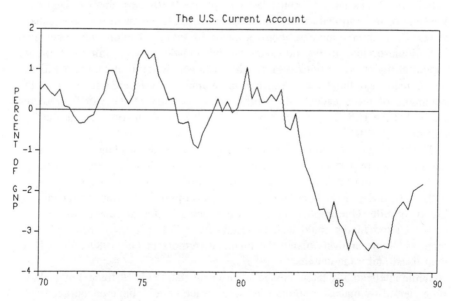

The U.S. Current Account

Source: U.S. Bureau of Economic Analysis.

this climate, it is not surprising that protectionism has been a major factor. In particular, nontariff barriers have been erected against foreign steel, automobiles, and textiles.

In addition, the climate produced by large trade deficits has increased concerns about foreign markets that seem closed to U.S. exports and about foreign dumping in U.S. markets. At the same time, many products from the Third World, such as textiles, face severe restrictions in industrial countries including the United States.[30]

Although the administration opposed many of the protectionist bills in Congress, one of the most important pieces of trade legislation during the 1980s was the Omnibus Trade and Competitiveness Act of 1988. This law expanded the scope of trade remedy laws and increased the likelihood that the executive branch would use them more often. In general, it called for a more activist government role in identifying and attempting to eliminate foreign unfair practices. For example, a new "super 301" provision of the Act requires the U.S. trade representative to identify and seek to eliminate through negotiation key unfair trade practices by major U.S. trading partners. If a trade partner does not eliminate such practices over a three-year period, it will face possible U.S. retaliation. Naturally, these new measures are controversial and are viewed with some suspicion within the international community.

Most economists agree that the outlook for the dollar and the U.S. trade deficit depends heavily on the future of the U.S. budget deficit. A further decline in the dollar will probably be necessary to achieve further progress in reducing the trade deficit. According to a recent report by the Congressional Budget Office (1989a), reducing the federal deficit would be much more effective than monetary policy as a tool for reducing the trade deficit. The main reason that monetary policy is a relatively ineffective tool is that it produces two effects that are largely offsetting in terms of their effects on the trade deficit. For instance, expansive monetary policy might reduce interest rate differentials between the United States and other countries, which could cause the dollar to depreciate. At the same time, easier monetary policy would stimulate economic growth and therefore imports. Yet fiscal tightening would not produce this ambiguous outcome. A common rule of thumb for the United States is that a decline in the budget deficit of one percentage point (of GNP) results in a decline in the current account deficit of about 0.5 percentage point after several years.

MICROECONOMIC POLICIES

The main emphasis of the Reagan administration in the area of microeconomic policies was to reduce the role of government, on the theory that this would free the private sector to be more efficient. Relatively little emphasis was placed on the problems that government policies were originally designed to to address, since government was believed to be "part of the problem and not the solution." At first, much of the national attention and energies in this area were spent on personality-related squabbles. In the beginning, the Reagan administration seemed to go out of its way to appoint individuals who were philosophically opposed to the missions of the agencies they headed and uncompromising.

By the time the Bush administration came to office in 1989, much of the rhetoric had begun to cool. The debates under the Bush administration became more substantive than simply to say that the government was the problem and that less government was better. After considerable neglect, the country once again began to seriously address issues of financial regulation, pollution, anti-trust, competitiveness, and poverty.

Financial Regulation and the S&L Crisis

Beginning in the mid-1970s and continuing in the 1980s, there was a trend toward less regulation of financial markets. In part, this trend was driven by technological change, rapid innovation, and inflation. To an increasing extent, financial markets were becoming linked, and it was increasingly difficult to regulate one segment of the market without regulating other segments—particularly in a volatile and inflationary environment.

The most important development in the regulatory area during the 1980s was the debacle in the regulation of thrift institutions. Because of a failure to close insolvent thrift institutions promptly, the federal agency that insures thrift deposits faced losses of monumental proportions, which in turn have to be paid by taxpayers and by the thrift industry in the form of higher insurance premiums for many years into the future.

To explain these developments, it is necessary to present some background. Traditionally, the savings and loan (S&L) industry had been one of the most heavily regulated of any U.S. industry. In particular, there were strict regulations on interest rates that could be paid on deposits and on the types of investments that thrift institutions could make. In general, savings and loan institutions, or "thrift institutions," were in the business of borrowing short and lending long, primarily for home mortgages. This business was relatively profitable until the era of high inflation and high interest rates of the 1970s and early 1980s. Because of the basic nature of the industry, it suffered massive losses during that period. As a result, regulations on the thrift institutions were gradually loosened, or eliminated. Regulation Q, which put a cap on interest rates that could be paid, was phased out; thrifts were allowed much more latitude on their investments; and capital requirements were reduced. But deposit insurance was left essentially unchanged. In other words, firms in the industry were given more latitude to take risks and make profits, but taxpayers continued to provide the same guarantee. Moreover, in its enthusiasm for less regulation, the Reagan administration in its early years asked for fewer regulators for an industry that was increasingly risky and, at that time, growing rapidly.[31]

In some respects, tax policy exacerbated the problems of the thrift industry.

Under the Tax Reduction and Economic Growth Act of 1981, generous depreciation allowances were introduced for investments in structures, including residential investments. The tax incentives were so large as to stimulate considerable overbuilding—to the point that President Reagan at one point referred to the phenomenon of "see through" office buildings because so many were vacant. Then, in several stages culminating in the Tax Simplification Act of 1986, the tax incentives for structures were drastically curtailed. Thus, inconsistent tax policy contributed to a glut of buildings by the second half of the decade. In turn, many thrift institutions—exercising their new freedoms under deregulation—had made heavy loans on these projects which later went sour.

During the presidential election campaign of 1988, the candidates were strangely silent on the subject of the bankruptcy of the fund that insured the thrift institutions. To its credit, however, one of the first orders of business of the new Bush administration in 1989 was to begin addressing the massive problems of the thrift industry. By midyear, important new legislation had been passed—the Financial Institutions Reform, Recovery, and Enforcement Act of 1989, or FIRREA. Among other things, the new legislation raised capital requirements for the industry and authorized at least $50 billion to be used to deal with unresolved problems of thrift institutions. This would be in addition to approximately $50 billion in costs incurred over the 1980–88 period, making the total estimated cost of dealing with the S&L crisis at least $100 billion. The legislation also placed the responsibility for regulating the thrift industry directly in the Department of the Treasury. The Federal Home Loan Bank Board was thus given a new name—the Office of Thrift Supervision—and transferred under the Treasury. The final compromise also placed a substantial burden on the thrift industry itself in the form of higher depository insurance premiums for many years into the future.

One issue that proved to be difficult to resolve was whether the borrowing to fund the bailout should be included in the federal budget or taken "off budget." The administration argued that the borrowing should be carried out off budget, because to put it on budget would mean that the Gramm–Rudman targets could not be met and that it might alarm financial markets. By contrast, some including the Congressional Budget Office argued that the borrowing should be on budget but that it should not be counted for purposes of the goals under the Deficit Reduction Act. Perhaps the main reason for including these funds in the budget is that the borrowing in that case would be done by the U.S. Treasury at a somewhat lower interest rate than if the borrowing was done by a special agency set up to handle the financing. With respect to the deficit reduction targets, most economists argued that the economic impact occurred when the investments went sour and when the financial institutions failed—not when the government finally recognized its financial liability for deposit insurance at these institutions.

In the end, a compromise was struck by which the bulk of the borrowing was financed off budget by a special agency called the Resolution Trust Corporation.

In any case, the administration's argument that financial markets would be less alarmed if the costs were off budget seems spurious since the financial markets are very able to see through such a distinction.

Another issue was how much of the burden for the bailout should be borne by the thrift industry and how much by taxpayers. Through high deposit insurance fees, the industry is being forced to pay part of the costs. However, there is serious question about whether the industry is profitable enough to pay for a substantial part of the bailout.

Some analysts believe that the legislation did not address the basic problems of the industry (see Kane, 1989). While raising capital requirements and exercising more diligence in closing unprofitable institutions should help, the basic characteristics of the industry remain the same, which raises some fundamental questions. Is there still a need for special financial institutions focused on housing finance and the small saver? Should the deposit insurance be revamped to discourage risk-taking, for example by varying the insurance fees according to asset quality or quality of management?

Finally, the changes that have taken place in financial markets and in the financial services industry prompt some analysts to question whether there is still a need for a specialized thrift industry that caters to the small saver and to financing home purchases. Over time, thrift institutions have gotten more like banks, and banks have lent more for home purchases and mortgage banking activities have grown rapidly. As part of this process, the secondary market for home mortgages has become much more liquid and the holding of mortgages less concentrated in the S&L industry.[32]

The Minimum Wage Issue

In 1989 after several years of debate, the Bush administration and the Congress agreed to raise the minimum wage. The last time the minimum wage had been raised in the United States was in 1981, when it was increased to $3.35 per hour. An equivalent minimum wage in 1989 prices would have been roughly $4.60. This long period in which the real minimum wage was allowed to erode was unusual, because in prior years the minimum wage was periodically raised to keep up with inflation.

In recent years, the minimum wage issue has been among the most contentious. Proponents argue that the minimum wage helps low-income workers and that a worker working full time would make considerably less than the official poverty level of income. Opponents stress that increasing the minimum wage relative to average wages causes a loss of jobs, primarily among teenagers and young adults. In addition, opponents point out that low-wage workers come from a wide range of economic backgrounds and that raising the minimum is an inefficient way to assist the working poor compared with, say, an increase in the earned income tax credit. To the latter point, proponents of a higher minimum wage point out that raising the minimum may be the only realistic way to help the poor because large budget deficits preclude more direct approaches. Essentially, the administration has been opposed to increasing the minimum wage without at the same time introducing a differentially lower "training wage" for teenagers. A differential wage for youths has traditionally been strongly opposed by organized labor, among other groups, on the grounds that it would cause many adults to lose their jobs and that the differential would not be used to provide training regardless of arguments to the contrary by business.

A significant part of the minimum wage debate centered on the size of the job loss from raising the minimum wage and the extent to which the poor would benefit or be harmed. With regard to the employment issue, the debate was more advanced than in earlier decades when proponents frequently argued that the minimum wage increase had no adverse effect on employment because employment increased that year. This time, the debate moved beyond this simplistic framing of the issue to consider how raising the minimum wage affected the baseline for employment—in other words, the effect holding other things constant. However, most of the econometric work on the minimum wage issue had been conducted a number of years before, when the minimum wage relative to average wages was considerably higher. Previous research indicated that the employment effect would in the aggregate be concentrated among teenagers (ages sixteen to nineteen) and young adults (ages twenty to twenty-four). Some mature workers might lose their jobs, but others might gain employment as a result of the job displacement of youths. The rule of thumb that developed around the beginning of the 1980s was that an increase in the minimum wage relative to the average wage would cause a loss of from 1 to 3 percent in teenage employment. The young adult group, ages twenty to twenty-four, would also lose jobs but to a lesser extent.

Proponents of an increase in the minimum wage argued that these estimates were too large for the 1980s. The primary reason was that during the 1980s the minimum wage had declined to an unusual extent relative to average wages. Hence, any given increase in the minimum wage would have a smaller effect than the econometric studies suggested, because a smaller proportion of employment would be affected.

The other set of issues pertained to the importance of the minimum wage for the living standards of the poor. Survey data indicated that the typical minimum wage worker was not poor. On the other hand, many poor individuals worked at low wages, either at the minimum wage or close enough to the minimum to benefit from "ripple effects" as wages somewhat above the minimum were also raised to maintain customary differentials.

Some economists argued that the minimum wage was an inefficient means of helping the poor, because a relatively small proportion of minimum wage workers were poor. According to this view, other approaches such as an increase in the employment tax credit would be a more efficient policy tool. But proponents of the increase in the minimum wage argued that because of the budget deficit such alternatives were unlikely to be pursued. Hence, the minimum wage was the only live option for assisting the working poor.

In late 1989 the Bush administration and the Congress struck a compromise on the minimum wage issue. According to the new law, the minimum wage would increase to $3.80 on April 1, 1990, and to $4.25 a year later. In addition, under certain circumstances, a teenage differential would be permitted. The lower "training wage" for teenagers would be $3.35 the first year and then 85 percent of the regular minimum. A teenager could be paid the training wage for three months; however, to continue for an additional three months for a total of six months, employers would have to certify that the teenagers were receiving training.

Neither side greeted the compromise with any enthusiasm. It was an increase, but not as large as proponents had hoped. Moreover, the teenage differential, or training wage, was viewed as a high price to pay. In the past, organized labor had successfully opposed a differential minimum wage for teenagers on the grounds that it would displace adult workers, with dependents. But business groups complained that the new training wage provision involved too much red tape; they, too, felt that it was a hollow victory.

The battle over the minimum wage may signal future battles to come, not over minimum wages per se but over the regulatory approach to social policy. There may be an increased tendency for policymakers to legislate aid for lower income workers, for instance, by requiring employers to provide health insurance in addition to a minimum wage.

Social Regulation—Environmental Protection

One of the main thrusts of the Reagan administration's economic program was to "get the government off the back of the private sector." Initially, that entailed as much foot-dragging and lax enforcement of the "social regulations" as possible. This was particularly the case for environmental regulations. However, by the mid-1980s the administration's approach became more constructive as it began to emphasize market incentive approaches to social regulation. In addition, the Bush administration has adopted a more sympathetic stance toward the need for environmental protection than the Reagan administration. So far, the main thrust of the Bush administration has been to stress market incentives to environmental problems, rather than the traditional "command and control" approach used in social regulation in the United States. The command and control approach has involved the enactment of laws calling for specific technologies. The market orientation is more flexible, for example, permitting businesses to buy and sell the rights to pollute. However, the Bush administration seems unwilling to take the lead among nations on such crucial issues as global warming due to emissions of carbon dioxide.

Although the United States has not made much progress in rationalizing its programs of social regulation, it has made considerable use of emissions trading in the area of environmental protection. The basic idea of emissions trading is that firms are encouraged to develop less costly ways to control their emissions. The emissions trading policy attempts to take advantage of this situation by creating markets in the right to pollute. Trading of these rights can increase efficiency by concentrating air pollution control efforts on those emission sources that cost the least to control.

The use of market incentives for environmental protection is one of the main frontiers in this area. Potential advantages include more efficient and less costly regulations. The approach, however, is controversial. For example, the information requirements may be severe, and some individuals worry that selling rights to pollute is a roundabout method that could fail to achieve the ultimate objective of preventing environmental damage.[33]

Economic Regulation—Deregulation and Antitrust

The main thrust of economic regulation policies in the last decade has been to reduce government regulation. As such, the direction of policy was established in the late 1970s, and the 1980s can be viewed as a continuation of that trend. Economic sectors that have been affected by this policy stance include the airlines, trucking, and telephone communications.

In addition, the Reagan administration dramatically altered antitrust policies. Traditionally, antitrust policies had been aimed at maintaining competition and limiting monopoly. However, under the Reagan administration there was much less concern about firm size and market share. For one thing, with more international competition, it was important to allow U.S. companies to merge in order to be competitive with their large counterparts abroad. There was also a belief that there was less need to be concerned with concentration because of foreign competition.

Partly as a result of the permissive regulatory climate, merger activity picked up substantially during the 1980s. In addition, many firms attempted to raise the market value of their common stock by buying back their own stock. In some cases, the management would buy the company. Much of this reorganization and takeover activity was carried out through heavy reliance on lower quality debt—known as "junk bonds." The end result was that U.S. business became more highly leveraged with debt and therefore more vulnerable to financial shocks and recessions. As discussed earlier, some analysts believe that this state of affairs would cause the Federal Reserve to back off in its efforts to control inflation if it meant a high probability of causing a recession.

Whether the recent flurry of mergers and acquisitions in the United States has increased economic efficiency is a subject of debate. The prevailing attitude within the Reagan administration was that this activity did improve efficiency. Why else would it have occurred in the free market? On the other hand, research by Ravenscraft and Scherer (1987) raises questions about whether such activity improves economic efficiency. Some in Congress are concerned but are not sure what to do about it, since the cure could be worse than the disease.

Industrial/Growth Policies

In general, the United States does not have an industrial policy in specific terms, although from time to time such a policy stance is debated. The U.S. policy toward growth is primarily broad-based in terms of support for basic research, tax policy designed to encourage investment and constructive risk-taking, and a stable monetary policy—also to encourage investment.[34]

There are a number of exceptions to this general policy stance. For instance, the large defense industry sells its output mainly to the federal government, and the federal government underwrites considerable research in that industry which sometimes has civilian commercial uses. In addition, U.S. trade and regulatory policies sometimes favor a particular industry or set of industries. To cite yet another example, some industries have been specially favored in the tax code, such as the extraction industries with depletion allowances—for example, the oil and gas and timber industries.

As discussed earlier, the Bush administration has argued for a reduction in the capital gains tax on the basis that it would stimulate business investment and growth. The direction of the effect on economic growth is not in doubt; however, there is not much empirical evidence with which to gauge the importance of this factor.

With respect to support for basic research, the Reagan administration was not consistent. At first, it tended to adopt a doctrinaire approach toward government involvement of any kind, including support for basic research. The Reagan administration seemed to feel that government spending was automatically waste-ful—notwithstanding the traditional association between research, productivity, and the well-developed literature on market externalities that justify government support of basic research. After cutting the research budget during its first few years in office, the Reagan administration began to increase its support for research.

CONCLUSIONS

The main policy thrust of the 1980s was to increase reliance on the private sector, competition, and market solutions. A centerpiece of this approach has been changes in tax policy. The dramatic reductions in top marginal tax rates and the broadening of the tax base may have increased economic efficiency. Economic analysis suggests that these benefits could be substantial. As yet, however, the jury is still out, because there is not much indication in the data that the restructuring of the tax system has produced large additions to saving or to the supply of labor. The economy does seem to be less inflation-prone, and productivity has picked up modestly, but the connection between these improvements and tax policy has not yet been conclusively established.

To a large extent, the main policy issues of the 1990s concern the unfinished business of the 1980s. Near the top of the list is the large budget deficit, which exacerbates the low national saving rate in the United States and undermines the renewed emphasis on economic efficiency and growth. Reducing the budget deficit is also promising as a means of reducing the large U.S. current account deficit. In the area of tax policy, the United States continues to grapple with the problem of achieving a more rational tax system, particularly with respect to taxing capital gains and the income from various forms of capital—without adding to inequality.

The problem with inequality and poverty in the United States seems to be getting worse. Its basic causes may lie in major economic trends that would be difficult to alter or affect, but some policy changes during the 1980s made this problem worse—for instance, cutting social programs for the poor and near-poor, raising payroll taxes which are regressive, and lowering the income tax rates on the groups with the highest incomes. Because of budget constraints, policy initiatives to assist lower income workers may emphasize requiring employers to furnish more benefits to their employees.

In the regulatory area, there is a renewed appreciation that laissez faire can lead to a dirty environment and to costly bailouts in the case of deposit insurance for the thrift industry. The future thrust of policy in the environmental area will likely be to develop improved tools of government regulation, which control environmental degradation but preserve a high degree of market flexibility. With respect to financial markets, it is clear that closer supervision of deposit institutions is needed. In addition, regulatory policies may have to adjust further to keep abreast of rapid changes in financial markets and industry structure.

NOTES

Congressional Budget Office, Washington, D.C. The author wishes to thank James Barth, Thomas Lutton, Vito Tanzi, Dominick Salvatore, and Mark Wohar for their helpful comments; Mark Decker for his excellent research assistance; and Verlinda Lewis for her word processing skills. The views expressed in this chapter are the author's and do not necessarily reflect the views of the Congressional Budget Office or its staff.

1. See U.S. Office of the President, *America's New Beginning: A Program for Economic Recovery*, February 18, 1981.

2. For detailed explanation of different views about supply-side economics, see Canto et al. (1983), Feldstein (1986b), and Tanzi (1983).

3. Only toward the end of the decade, when the need had become obvious to most observers, were the Baker and Brady plans introduced. However, these plans may be too little, too late.

4. For some recent assessments of the Reagan economic policies, see Palmer and Sawhill (1984), Blinder (1987), and Boskin (1987).

5. For a summary of the early Bush administration's program, see U.S. Office of the President, *Building a Better America*, February 9, 1989.

6. The concept of the NAIRU is closely related to that of the natural rate of unemployment, which pertains to long-run equilibrium in the labor market. At the same time, it is important to recognize that NAIRU and the natural rate can diverge substantially for extended periods of time.

7. For a detailed analysis of the natural rate of unemployment in the United States, see Gordon (1982) and Adams and Coe (1989), among others.

8. For a recent summary of the literature on the productivity slowdown in the United States, see Fischer (1988) and Jorgenson (1988).

9. For a view of the productivity slowdown that emphasizes the role of government, see Boskin (1987).

10. For a more detailed discussion of the composition of output and interest rates during the 1980s, see Barth, Iden, Russek, and Wohar (1989).

11. For a recent overall assessment of the factors behind the decline in the U.S. private saving rate, see Summers and Carroll (1987) and Eisner (1989).

12. See Lipsey and Kravis (1987) and Eisner (1989).

13. In the United States, poverty is defined in terms of an income of approximately $12,000 for a family of four, in 1988 prices; the poverty level is adjusted from year to year by using the Consumer Price Index. For a recent statistical description of poverty in the United States, see Littman (1989).

14. See, for instance, Tanzi (1980, 1982, 1983, and 1988).

15. For a discussion of the Tax Reform Act of 1986 and the factors leading up to it, see McClure (1987), Pechman (1987), and U.S. Treasury (1977 and 1984).

16. For an assessment of the role of U.S. tax reform in other countries, see Tanzi (1987 and 1988) and Whalley (1989).

17. For recent and contrasting reviews on the evidence on Ricardian Equivalence, see Bernheim (1987) and Barro (1989).

18. For more detailed discussion of the evidence on deficits and interest rates, see Barth, Iden, and Russek (1984–85) and Barth, Iden, Russek, and Wohar (1989).

19. See von Furstenberg et al. (1986).

20. Budget analysts are divided about whether GRH on balance is a constructive budget tool. Some argue that it plays a constructive role in forcing compromise. Others contend that it has led to dishonesty in budgeting and has distorted decision making.

21. Comparisons with other countries suggest that top marginal tax rates are relatively low for income in general but comparatively high for capital gains; see Tanzi (1987) and Walker and Bloomfield (1989).

22. According to the Congressional Budget Office (1988), reducing the capital gains tax rate would cause a significant reduction in tax receipts after the first year. For an overview of this issue, see Auerbach (1988).

23. Each year, the Congressional Budget Office (CBO) prepares a large number of options for reducing the federal deficit; see CBO (1990b).

24. For a recent analysis of the social security issue, see Aaron et al. (1989).

25. For more detailed reviews of monetary policy during the 1980s, see Friedman (1988) and Poole (1988).

26. See, for instance, Greenspan (1989).

27. For an analysis of trends in business debt, see Bernanke and Campbell (1988).

28. Some analysts, such as Eisner (forthcoming), argue that such net debt figures are

highly misleading because U.S. assets are valued at book value rather than market value. The divergence between book and market values of this investment is likely to be substantial since much of the investment was done years ago.

29. For an elaboration of the view that sustainability is a serious problem, see Bergsten (1988) and Krugman (1985). For the contrary view, that U.S. foreign deficits could be sustainable indefinitely, see Mussa (1985).

30. For an analysis of recent protectionism in the United States, see Salvatore (1987a, 1987b).

31. For background and analysis on the crisis in the savings and loan industry, see Barth and Bradley (1989) and Brumbaugh et al. (1989).

32. For a review of the history of the S&L industry and current issues, see Barth and Regalia (1988).

33. For a discussion of market incentive approaches to environmental protection, see the Council of Economic Advisers (1986 and 1989) and the Congressional Budget Office (1985b).

34. For a discussion of the industrial policy debate in the United States, see Norton (1986) and the Congressional Budget Office (1983 and 1989c).

REFERENCES

Aaron, Henry J., Barry P. Bosworth, and Gary Burtless. *Can Americans Afford to Grow Old?* Washington, D.C.: Brookings Institution, 1989.

Adams, Charles, and David T. Coe. *A Systems Approach to Estimating the Natural Rate of Unemployment and Potential Output for the United States.* Working Paper No. 89/89. International Monetary Fund, 1989.

Auerbach, Alan J. "Capital Gains Taxation in the United States: Realizations, Revenue and Rhetoric." *Brookings Papers on Economic Activity,* 1988, vol. 2, 595–631.

Barro, Robert J. "The Ricardian Approach to Budget Deficits." *Journal of Economic Perspectives* 13, no. 2 (Spring 1989): 37–54.

———. "Are Government Bonds Net Wealth?" *Journal of Political Economy* 82 (November 1974): 1095–117.

Barth, James R., and Michael G. Bradley. "The Ailing S&L: Causes and Cures." *Challenge,* March/April 1989, pp. 30–38.

Barth, James R., George Iden, and Frank S. Russek. "Do Federal Deficits Really Matter?" *Contemporary Policy Issues* 3, no. 1 (Fall 1984–85): 79–95.

Barth, James R., George Iden, Frank S. Russek, and Mark Wohar. "Effects of Federal Budget Deficits on Interest Rates and the Compositions of Domestic Output." Paper presented at the conference on The Great Fiscal Experiment of the 1980s, Washington, D.C.: Urban Institute, October 23, 1989.

Barth, James R., and Martin Regalia. "The Role of Regulation in the Savings and Loan Industry." In Catherine England and Thomas Huertas (eds.), *The Financial Services Revolution.* Boston: Kluwer, 1988, pp. 113–61.

Barth, James R., Robin Sickles, and Phillip Wiest. "Assessing the Impact of Varying Economic Conditions on Federal Reserve Behavior." *Journal of Macroeconomics* 4 (Winter 1982): 47–70.

Bergsten, C. Fred. *America in the World Economy: A Strategy for the 1990s.* Washington, D.C.: Institute for International Economics, 1988.

Bernanke, Ben S., and John Y. Campbell. "Is There a Corporate Debt Crisis?" *Brookings Papers on Economic Activity,* 1988, vol. 1, 83–125.

Bernheim, B. Douglas. "Ricardian Equivalence: An Evaluation of Theory and Evidence." With discussion. In Stanley Fischer (ed.), *Macroeconomics Annual 1987.* Cambridge, Mass.: MIT Press, 1987, pp. 263–315.

Blinder, Alan S. *Hard Heads, Soft Hearts: Tough-Minded Economics for a Just Society.* New York: Addison–Wesley, 1987.

Boskin, Michael J. *Reagan and the Economy.* San Francisco: ICS Press, 1987.

Bosworth, Barry P. *Tax Incentives and Economic Growth.* Washington, D.C.: Brookings Institution, 1984.

Bound, John, and George Johnson. "Changes in the Structure of Wages During the 1980s: An Evaluation of Alternative Explanations." Working Paper No. 2983. National Bureau of Economic Research, May 1989.

Brumbaugh, R. Dan, Jr., Andrew S. Carron, and Robert E. Litan. "Cleaning Up the Depository Institutions Mess." *Brookings Papers on Economic Activity,* 1989, vol. 1, 243–83.

Canto, Victor A., Douglas H. Joines, and Arthur B. Laffer. *Foundations of Supply-Side Economics: Theory and Evidence.* New York: Academic Press, 1983.

Congressional Budget Office. *The Economic and Budget Outlook: Fiscal Years 1991–1995.* January 1990a.

―――. *Reducing the Deficit: Spending and Revenue Options.* February 1990b.

―――. *Policies for Reducing the Current-Account Deficit.* August 1989a.

―――. *The Economic and Budget Outlook: Fiscal Years 1990–1994.* January 1989b.

―――. "The Scope of the High-Definition Television Market and Its Implications for Competitiveness." Staff Working Paper, July 1989c.

―――. "Deficits and Interest Rates: Theoretical Issues and Empirical Evidence." Staff Working Paper, January 1989e.

―――. *How Capital Gains Tax Rates Affect Revenues: The Historical Evidence.* March 1988.

―――. *The Changing Distribution of Federal Taxes: 1975–1990.* October 1987a.

―――. *The GATT Negotiations and U.S. Trade Policy.* June 1987b.

―――. *Has Trade Protection Revitalized Domestic Industries?* November 1986a.

―――. *Trends in Family Income: 1970–1986.* February 1986b.

―――. *The Economic and Budget Outlook: Fiscal Years 1986–1990.* February 1985a.

―――. *Environmental Regulation* and *Economic Efficiency.* March 1985b.

―――. *The Economic and Budget Outlook: An Update.* August 1985c.

―――. *The Industrial Policy Debate.* December 1983.

Council of Economic Advisers. *Economic Report of the President.* Washington, D.C.: U.S. Government Printing Office, various years.

Danziger, Sheldon, Peter Gottschalk, and Eugene Smolensky. "How the Rich Have Fared, 1973–87." *American Economic Review* 79, no. 2 (May 1989): 310–34.

Darby, Michael R. "Accounting for Deficit: An Analysis of Sources of Change in Federal and Total Government Deficits." Research Paper No. 8704. Office of the Assistant Secretary for Economic Policy, U.S. Treasury Department, October 1987.

Eisner, Robert. "The Real Rate of National Saving." For presentation to the American Economics Association, Atlanta, December 29, 1989.

―――. *How Real Is the Federal Deficit?* New York: Free Press, 1986.

Eisner, Robert, and Paul J. Pieper. "The World's Greatest Debtor Nation?" Forthcoming in *The Review of Economics and Finance*.

Evans, Paul. "Is the Dollar High Because of Large Deficits?" *Journal of Monetary Economics*. 18 (1986): 227–49.

Feldstein, Martin S. "The Budget Deficit and the Dollar." NBER Working Paper No. 1898. Cambridge, Mass.: National Bureau of Economic Research, 1986a.

———. "Supply-Side Economics: Old Truths and New Claims." *American Economic Review* 76, no. 2 (May 1986b): 26–36.

Feldstein, Martin S., and Douglas W. Elmendorf. "Budget Deficits, Tax Incentives, and Inflation: A Surprising Lesson from the 1983–84 Recovery." Working Paper No. 2819. Cambridge, Mass.: National Bureau of Economic Research, 1989.

Fischer, Stanley. "Symposium on the Slowdown in Productivity Growth." *Journal of Economic Perspectives*. 2, no. 4 (Fall 1988): 3–7.

Friedman, Benjamin M. "Effects of Monetary Policy on Real Economic Activity." (Processed.) Harvard University, July 1989.

———. "Lessons on Monetary Policy from the 1980s." *Journal of Economic Perspectives*, vol. 2 (Summer 1988a): 51–72.

———. *Day of Reckoning: The Consequences of American Economic Policy Under Reagan and After*. New York: Random House, 1988b.

Gordon, Robert J. "The Role of Wages in the Inflation Process." *American Economic Review* 78, no. 2 (May 1988): 276–83.

———. "Inflation, Flexible Exchange Rates, and the Natural Rate of Unemployment." In Martin N. Baily (ed.), *Workers, Jobs and Inflation*. Washington, D.C.: Brookings Institution, 1982, pp. 89–152.

Gravelle, Jane G. "Nonneutral Taxation and the Efficiency Gains of the 1986 Tax Reform Act—A New Look." Working Paper No. 2964. Cambridge, Mass.: National Bureau of Economic Research, May 1989.

Greenspan, Alan. Statement before the Subcommittee on Domestic Monetary Policy of the Committee on Banking, Finance and Urban Affairs. U.S. House of Representatives. October 25, 1989.

Haberler, Gottfried. "The U.S. Budget Deficit and the Strong Dollar." *The AEI Economist*, July 1989, pp. 6–8.

Harrison, Bennett, Chris Tilly, and Barry Bluestone. "Rising Inequality." In David R. Obey and Paul Sarbanes (eds.), *The Changing American Economy*. New York: Basil Blackwell, 1986, pp. 111–34.

Hausman, Jerry A., and James M. Poterba. "Household Behavior and the Tax Reform Act of 1986." *Journal of Economic Perspectives* 1, no. 1 (Summer 1987): 101–19.

Hulten, Charles R., and Isabel V. Sawhill. *The Legacy of Reaganomics*. Washington, D.C.: Urban Institute Press, 1984.

Jorgenson, Dale W. "Productivity and Postwar U.S. Economic Growth." *Journal of Economic Perspectives* 2, no. 4 (Fall 1988): 23–41.

Kane, Edward J. "The Bush Plan Is No Cure for the S&L Insurance Malady." *Challenge*, November/December 1989, pp. 39–43.

Kosters, Marvin A., and Murray N. Ross. "The Quality of Jobs: Evidence from Distribution of Annual Earnings and Hourly Wages." AEI Occasional Paper, American Enterprise Institute, July 1988.

Kotlikoff, Laurence J. "The Deficit Is Not a Well-Defined Measure of Fiscal Policy." *Science* 241 (August 12, 1988): p. 791–95.

Krugman, Paul R. "Is the Strong Dollar Sustainable?" In *The U.S. Dollar—Recent Developments, Outlook, and Policy Options, A Symposium*. Sponsored by the Federal Reserve Bank of Kansas City, August 21–23, 1985, pp. 103–32.

Lipsey, Robert E., and Irving B. Kravis. *Saving and Economic Growth: Is the United States Really Falling Behind?* New York: The Conference Board, 1987.

Littman, Mark S. "Poverty in the 1980s: Are the Poor Getting Poorer?" *Monthly Labor Review* (June 1989): 13–18.

McLure, Charles E., Jr., and George R. Zodrow. "Treasury I and the Tax Reform Act of 1986: The Economics and Politics of Tax Reform." *Journal of Economic Perspectives* 1, no. 1 (Summer 1987): 37–58.

Meulendyke, Ann-Marie. "A Review of Federal Reserve Policy Targets and Operating Guides in Recent Decades." Federal Reserve Bank of New York, *Quarterly Review* (Autumn 1988): 6–17.

Miller, Stephen M., and Orawin T. Velz. "The Influence of Presidential Administrations on Monetary Policy." University of Connecticut, Department of Economics, 1989.

Mussa, Michael L. Commentary on "Is the Strong Dollar Sustainable?" In *The U.S. Dollar—Recent Developments, Outlook, and Policy Options*. A Symposium sponsored by the Federal Reserve Bank of Kansas City, August 21–23, 1985, pp. 133–55.

Norton, R. D. "Industrial Policy and American Renewal." *Journal of Economic Literature* 24 (March 1986): 1–40.

Organization for Economic Co-operation and Development. *OECD Economic Surveys—United States*. Paris: OECD, 1989.

Palmer, John L. *The Reagan Record*. Washington D.C.: Urban Institute Press, 1984.

Palmer, John L., and Isabel V. Sawhill. *The Reagan Experiment*. Washington, D.C.: Urban Institute Press, 1982.

Pechman, Joseph A. "Tax Reform: Theory and Practice." *Journal of Economic Perspectives* 1, no. 1 (Summer 1987): 11–28.

Poole, William. "Monetary Policy Lessons of Recent Inflation and Disinflation." *Journal of Economic Perspectives* 2 (Summer 1988): 73–100.

Ravenscraft, David J., and F. M. Scherer. *Mergers, Sell-Offs, and Economic Efficiency*. Washington, D.C.: Brookings Institution, 1987.

Salvatore, Dominick. *The New Protectionist Threat to World Welfare*. New York: North-Holland, 1987a.

———. "Import Penetration, Exchange Rates, and Protectionism in the United States." *Journal of Policy Modeling* 9, no. 1 (1987b): 125–41.

Schultze, Charles L. "Real Wages, Real Wages Aspirations, and Unemployment in Europe." In Robert L. Lawrence and Charles L. Schultze (eds.), *Barriers to European Economic Growth: A Transatlantic View*. Washington, D.C.: Brookings Institution, 1987, pp. 230–95.

Sheshinski, Eytan, and Vito Tanzi. "An Explanation of Behavior of Personal Savings in the United States in Recent Years." NBER Working Paper No. 3040. Cambridge, Mass.: National Bureau of Economic Research, July 1989.

Summers, Lawrence, and Chris Carroll. "Why Is U.S. National Saving So Low?" *Brookings Papers on Economic Activity*, 1987, vol. 2, 607–35.

Tanzi, Vito. "Forces That Shape Tax Policy." In Herbert Stein (ed.), *Tax Policy in the Twenty-First Century*. New York: Wiley, 1988, pp. 266–77.

———. "The Response of Other Industrial Countries to the U.S. Tax Reform Act." *National Tax Journal* 40, no. 3 (September 1987): 339–55.

———. "The Growth of Public Expenditure in Industrial Countries: An International and Historical Perspective." (Processed.) International Monetary Fund, February 11, 1986.

———. "The Deficit Experience in Industrial Countries." In Phillip Cagan (ed.), *Essay in Contemporary Economic Problems: The Economy in Deficit*. Washington D.C.: American Enterprise Institute, 1985.

———. "The Policy Lessons of Supply-Side Economics: A Very Personal Interpretation." Paper presented at the annual meeting of the Southern Economic Association, November 1983.

———. *The Underground Economy in the United States and Abroad*. Lexington, Mass., 1982.

———. *Inflation and the Personal Income Tax: An International Perspective*. New York: Cambridge University Press, 1980.

U.S. Office of the President. *Building a Better America*. February 9, 1989.

———. *America's New Beginning: A Program for Economic Recovery*. February 18, 1981.

U.S. Treasury Department. *Report to the Congress on International Economic and Exchange Rate Policy*. October 1989.

———. *Tax Reform for Fairness, Simplicity, and Economic Growth*. Vol. I (Overview), November 1984a.

———. *The Effects of Deficits on Prices of Financial Assets Theory and Evidence*. March 1984b.

———. *Blueprints for Basic Tax Reform*. January 17, 1977.

von Furstenberg, George, R. Jeffery Green, and Jin-Ho Jeong. "Tax and Spend, or Spend and Tax." *Review of Economics and Statistics*, May 1986.

Walker, Charles E., and Mark A. Bloomfield. "The Case for the Restoration of a Capital Gains Tax Differential." *Tax Notes*, May 22, 1989, pp. 1019–32.

Whalley, John. "Foreign Responses to U.S. Tax Reform." Paper presented for a conference on the 1986 U.S. Tax Reform Act at the University of Michigan, November 10–11, 1989.

3

FROM CUSTOMS UNION TO ECONOMIC UNION: THE BIRTH OF ECONOMIC POLICY IN THE EUROPEAN COMMUNITY

Antonio Costa

The industrial world is frequently represented as a tripod, with each leg supported by and representing a well-defined group of economies: Europe, North America, and the Pacific Basin. In this tripolar situation, the European Community (EC), with its population of 325 million people, is the largest economic area in the industrialized world. The EC has approximately 80 million people more than the United States and is three times as populous as Japan. In terms of economic strength, the European Community is now also in first place. At the beginning of the 1990s it accounts for roughly one-fourth of world output, the United States about one-fifth, and Japan one-tenth. Furthermore, as the most open economic entity in the world, the EC exports more goods and services than any other competitor (about one-third more than the United States and 10 percent more than Japan). It also imports more than any competitor (the other way around, 10 percent more than the United States and one-third more than Japan).

Surprisingly, for over one-third of a century from its establishment (with the 1956 Treaty of Rome), the European Community has not yet developed into a homogeneous economy with free flow of goods, services, people, and capital (the four fundamental freedoms sanctioned by the Treaty).

As a consequence, the EC has not had a single economic policy since its beginning. Monetary policy has been run separately by the twelve Central banks of member states. Budgetary and fiscal policies have been the results of negotiation between national governments and national parliaments with no concern about Community interests.

This chapter maintains that this policy incongruence and the resulting confusion will soon end as the European Community strives to establish a true unified internal market by 1992, an economic and monetary union soon after, and, eventually, a political union. Indeed, the 1990s will witness the birth of

European Community economic policy with a single currency and a single monetary authority supported by coordinated budgetary and fiscal policies, and with microeconomic management agreed on at the Community level (on the basis of Community legislation sanctioned by the European Court of Justice in case of disputes).

To prove the point, this chapter addresses four questions.

1. It reviews the historical process that is finally forging an economic and monetary union (EMU), among the twelve member states of the EC. Put otherwise, this section addresses the question: Can we now meaningfully talk of European economic policy?

2. Merging a number of previously sovereign states into such a union of a continental scale implies a significant transfer of decision-making power from these states to the Union. The question to be addressed here is: What do the member states have to gain from the economic union in terms of welfare? Are all of these gains worth the effort, given the political tensions likely to emerge as the transition occurs and the zero-sum game of the sovereignty transfer goes on?

3. How will this economic union be accomplished, and how will economic policy be conducted? Namely, what hypotheses can we advance about the likely stages through which the union's birth will go in the years ahead, and what shape will the union itself eventually have?

4. What appropriate monetary and budgetary regimes will make the union work effectively, and what degree of institutional centralization and political framework will likely be required in the longer term?

THE ECONOMIC, INSTITUTIONAL, AND POLITICAL ROOTS OF EMU

History provides important elements for a proper understanding of the present drive toward economic integration in the European Community. In this regard we should study three sets of closely interrelated factors: economic, institutional, and political.

The events of the early 1990s are undoubtedly deliberate responses to the "eurosclerosis" and the "europessimism" of the 1970s and the early 1980s. These terms describe the systemic underperformance of the European economy during that period with respect both to Europe's own past performance and to the performance of its main trade partners (See Tables 3.1 to 3.5).

The European underperformance during that period concerned economic, financial, and monetary issues. Between 1974 and 1985 the European economy performed substantially less well than its international competitors: the EC's economic growth was an average of 1.9 percent per annum compared with 2.4 percent in the United States and 3.8 percent in Japan. This slow growth was combined with high inflation (11 percent for the Community compared with 7 percent for the United States and 6.3 percent for Japan). Even more worrisome (especially in a longer term perspective) was the zero growth in capital formation

Table 3.1
The EC Economy Through the 1980s

	1982–1984	1985–1987	1988–1990
Real GDP (annual avg. % change)	+ 1.6	+ 2.6	+ 3.2
Investment (annual avg. % change)	- 0.1	+ 3.6	+ 6.5
Employment :			
(i) annual average % change	- 0.5	+ 0.8	+ 1.2
(ii) cumulative change over the 3-year period (in thousands)	-1,845	+3,138	+4,700
Inflation (annual average %)	+ 8.7	+ 4.4	+ 4.3
Intra-Community exports (annual average volume % change)	+ 4.0	+ 6.1	+ 7.5

Table 3.2
Principal Budgetary Trends in the Community (EC, general government, percentage of GDP)

	1980	1985	1988	1989	1990	Change 1985–1988	Change 1988–1990
Gross saving	0.3	-1.2	-0.2	0.5	0.4	+1.0	+0.6
Net borrowing/ lending	-3.8	-5.2	-3.6	-2.9	-2.9	+1.6	+0.7
Expenditure	45.1	49.0	47.0	46.3	45.8	-2.0	-1.2
Receipts	41.3	43.8	43.4	43.4	42.9	-0.4	-0.5
Gross Public Debt	41.1	56.8	59.1	58.3	57.7	+2.3	-1.4

that characterized Europe for over a dozen years after the first oil shock in 1973. This "eurosclerosis" could not be allowed to continue, lest the very foundations of the European sociopolitical order be undermined. Indeed, Europe's economic underperformance was not allowed to continue. Governments, which had already changed national policy at the turn of the decade in favor of disinflation and budgetary restraint, adopted a much more Communitarian approach to decision

Table 3.3
Cumulative Changes in Budget Balances and the Mechanical Impact of the Changes in Economic Activity (percentage of GDP)

	1985–1988		1988–1990	
	Actual Balance	Impact of Economic Activity	Actual Balance	Impact of Economic Activity
Community	+1.6	+1.9	+0.7	+1.5
Countries with a budget surplus	+3.4	+2.9	+0.3	+0.3
Countries with a budget deficit below or close to the Community average	+0.8	+1.9	+1.0	+2.0
Countries with a budget deficit above the Community average	+1.7	+1.3	−0.5	+1.4

making (especially in microeconomic areas) tied to the 1992 internal market process. The social partners and society at large supported this dramatic turna-round.

The integration of world financial markets (underway since the late 1970s) started with major political, technological, and legal developments in the United States. The sector itself underwent major structural change, delivering new products, new services, and new approaches to financial intermediation. The process soon spread, fostering systemic changes and increasing liberalization of capital movements, especially in the United Kingdom, West Germany, the Netherlands, Japan, and a few other countries. But Europe as such was not part of the general process. Consequently, it could not influence the process. With a bit of hindsight, we are discovering how troublesome, and possibly ominous, poorly conceived financial liberalization can be.

In the 1980s all that changed. Europeans realized that without full liberalization of capital movements and financial markets (starting with the Community and followed by liberalization of flows negotiated with the rest of the world), Europe could not easily play an active and influential role in this worldwide process. Hence, the drive began toward creating an integrated European financial area on which the monetary and economic union of Europe is being built.

The enormous exchange rate swings that took place between 1980 and 1987 (a period during which the dollar appreciated by about 100 percent, only to return to approximately its starting point) have had consequences for everybody's competitiveness, production structure, and current account balances. These swings also showed the extent to which the currencies of medium and even large countries could be adversely affected by events beyond their control. This in

Table 3.4
General Government Receipts in the Community (percentage of GDP)

	1970	1985	1988	1990
Indirect taxes	13.1	12.9	13.2	13.2
Direct taxes	9.4	12.3	12.3	12.2
Social security Contributions	10.2	14.6	14.5	14.2
Current transfers	3.0	4.0	3.4	3.3

Table 3.5
General Government Expenditure in the Community (percentage of GDP)

	1970	1985	1988	1990
Current transfers	14.6	21.4	20.6	20.0
• to enterprises	1.7	2.5	2.1	1.9
• to households	12.4	17.7	17.2	16.9
• to the rest of the world	0.5	1.2	1.3	1.2
Interest payments	1.9	5.0	4.7	4.8
Public consumption	14.3	18.6	18.2	17.7
Fixed capital formation	4.0	2.9	2.6	2.7
Net capital transfers	0.8	1.1	0.7	0.6
Total	35.5	49.0	47.0	45.8

turn has led to the realization that, whereas policy aiming at currency stabilization worldwide is needed, European monetary cohesion and a less incongruous participation of the Old Continent in international forums where such questions are dealt with (the G7, the G10, the IMF, etc.) is also necessary. Put differently, the Community realized it could not be asked to support world monetary stability without being part of the decision-making process that shapes (or, in any event should shape) such stability. Thus far, there has been "taxation without representation"; that is, the EC countries have been forced to face foreign exchange instability and currency swings without being afforded the capacity to influence events. This could not last.

The background to the EC economic and monetary union process involves more than just the economic, financial, and monetary troubles of the past two decades. There were also significant institutional developments within the Community during the 1980s. To a large extent, the political decisions to go ahead with EMU and the continuing drive toward it were built on the EC's major institutional accomplishments during the 1980s.

Outstanding among the European Community's successes are the European Monetary System (EMS), the European Community Single Act, and the drive toward the internal market.

The EMS. The EMS, now over ten years old, has contributed to disinflation in participating countries as well as to greater stability of exchange rates throughout the Community and beyond. This success has been particularly remarkable given the events on the dollar front and the frequent serious turbulence in foreign exchange and security markets.

The EMS is important for the EMU in that the EMS has stimulated greater monetary cooperation and has shown that such cooperation works. Of course, the EMU is pushing the process one step ahead to its ultimate conclusion, moving monetary cooperation (among twelve monetary authorities and eleven currencies with ten exchange rates) into monetary unification. Put otherwise, it would be much more difficult to prove the economic and business significance of fixed exchange rates (which a monetary union requires) if not for the progressively more stable parities induced by EMS. Indeed, the EMS may be seen as a good, long-term training exercise for both private and public agents regarding behaviors consistent with, and the gains and losses due to, definitive monetary unification.

The European Community Single Act. The first modification of the Treaty of Rome was approved in 1985 and went into effect in 1987. It democratized decision making in the EC by (1) introducing majority voting for much Community legislation; (2) strengthening the roles of elected bodies (the European Parliament); and (3) implementing microeconomic subsidiarity. This act turned the EC system's operations away from the previous antihistoric centralization of decision making toward the more modern mutual recognition of norms and standards. No longer did governments have to agree (quite laboriously and mostly unsuccessfully) on suggestions from the Brussels-based EC bureaucracy. Having tested the validity of this notion at the microeconomic level, the EC now feels more confident of its suitability at the macroeconomic level.

The Drive Toward the Internal Market by 1992. With practically all the legislative acts envisaged for the completion of the single market already approved, the process has now become inevitable. Clearly, the European Community will become a frontier-free economic system, with unrestricted movement of people, capital, goods, and services.

We will now turn to more political issues. The new momentum toward the European construction is a deliberate political reaction to the major geopolitical changes that took place in the 1980s and that the 1990s seem to have accelerated.

The Waning of the Pax Americana. This much discussed development is not taking place in a linear way. Not quite visible during the Reagan administration, it may have accelerated in the late 1980s as the economic situation of the United States has deteriorated. In the early 1990s, with the collapse of the Soviet empire and with the renewal of tensions in the Middle East, the unique U.S. position and role in the world has regained visibility, but probably not on a sustainable basis. Leaving aside the ups and downs of all politico-strategic cycles, it is historically evident that economic, political, and strategic power cannot last in a society that is turning toward overconsumption, overindebtedness, and under-investment.

Japan's Increasing Prominence.   For over a quarter of a century, Japan has been a very powerful trade competitor. Not surprisingly, during the 1980s the country also emerged as an equally forceful financial power. Enormous domestic savings through the trade surplus has given way to massive earnings on foreign-invested capital; the current account surplus has slowly become self-reinforcing.

This large-scale accumulation of a net asset position has acquired political importance in the 1990s. No doubt, it will eventually have a military dimension. To paraphrase what was said above, political and strategic power cannot be avoided as a society turns toward excess saving, overaccumulation, and under-consumption.

The Political and Economic Democratization of Eastern Europe and the USSR.   These striking events have put an end to two circumstances. First, the events in the eight formerly centrally planned economies (the GDR, Czechoslo-vakia, Hungary, Poland, Bulgaria, Albania, Yugoslavia, and Rumania) have terminated a half-century-old artificial separation of the Old Continent into a free and a captive part. Second, the transformation of the USSR into a democratic and market-oriented economy (a very long-term process) will put an end to seventy-five years of Bolshevism.

The relative importance of these events, some of which are still unfolding, is hard to ascertain. None should be dismissed too lightly.

THE COSTS AND BENEFITS OF ECONOMIC AND MONETARY UNION

An economic and monetary union has to be judged on its ability to improve the economic welfare of its citizens. What then are the benefits and costs we could expect from such a union? Academia has divided into two opposing camps on this question.

On one side are those economists who profess a certain amount of agnosticism. Since the analysis of the welfare implications of an economic union is quite complex and not fully amenable to quantification and to hard evaluation, it is argued that economic science is unlikely to give an unambiguous answer. As a consequence, the major benefit to be gained from the process now underway is in fact of a political nature. The EMU is seen as an important forerunner to the European Political Union (EPU).

It is difficult to disagree on the political dimensions of the EMU, given what we have said about the evolving geopolitical situation and the role it played in promoting even greater interest in the EMU. In fact, the political debate con-cerning the possible creation of a federal European political entity is underway. However, the direction of the relationship between "eco-monetary union" and "political union" is far from clear. Historically, economic union has preceded political Union, as happened in Germany during the nineteenth century. The opposite occurred in other places at about the same time. For example, the Italian political unification in 1861 preceded the monetary and economic union by several decades. Also relevant is the case of the United States, whose Federal Reserve was not set up until the early twentieth century, long after the country's political birth.

As an economist, I find it disturbing that our profession declares itself incapable of providing a clear answer as to the costs and benefits of economic union. After all, lots of econometric analysis was done before and since the Common Market was launched. Actually, with the benefit of twenty-five years of hindsight, we can now appreciate the validity of some of those studies.

Agnosticism is therefore unacceptable. Indeed, a growing body of research is now proving that the benefits expected for EC member countries are both quantifiable and perceptible. Our analysis will build on the experience which the European Commission has accumulated in the context of the "Cost of Non-Europe" project (The European Communities, 1989).

If we envisage the monetary union as an optimum currency area (OCA) with irrevocably fixed exchange rates, then both public and private decision making in the Community will undergo enormous changes as the EMU materializes. For analytical purposes, the likely benefits that will accrue to the EC because of the EMU can be grouped under seven sets of issues.

First, the EC economy will achieve a more efficient production structure and stronger economic growth compatible with good macroeconomic management and price stability.

Key to a more efficient economy are the direct, static benefits from the reduction of transaction costs. These advantages, operational in nature and amenable to quantitative estimates, will accrue to the private sector: to producers and traders and, finally, to consumers. At the start of the union, this type of benefit can be estimated at about 0.5 percent of EC domestic production, but this amount is bound to grow. Its importance will increase with the volume of cross-border commercial and financial transactions relative to the total transactions that take place within the Community. Once the EMU has been established, producers and traders will be permanently better off by operating under a much improved regime.

In other words, the economic union will extend the cost reduction and efficiency gains expected from the establishment of the internal market by 1992. Firms will start seeing the European economy as fully integrated as the U.S. economy. This ought to give further momentum to a business climate, which in the second half of the 1980s was already improved relative to the earlier quinquenniums.

More difficult, albeit more promising, is the evaluation of the indirect consequences or dynamic gains of the EMU. What needs to be proved in this regard is that the opinion of European industrialists on the likely impact of monetary union will be positively affected.

Second, the EMU will improve the incentives and expectations of the private sector by abolishing what will be the last major economic barrier separating member countries after the establishment of the internal market, namely, exchange-rate changes. Exchange-rate risks discourage cross-border transactions in trade, investment, and mergers and acquisitions. The longer a business project takes, the more it is affected by exchange-rate risks. Yet, it is precisely the start of major trade and investment decisions that needs to be made on a Communitywide basis if we are to benefit from a better allocation of resources and increased efficiency from the internal market after 1992.

If one is not convinced that the main dynamic benefits of a single currency will be at a microeconomic (cost-benefit) level, just consider the costs that U.S. business would face if the New Jersey dollar were valued differently from the Texas dollar. If we multiply this by 50 (the number of states), we can envision the enormous chaos and welfare losses that would plague the United States.

At the same time, public sectors (both governments and central banks) will compete with each other, aiming to provide the best service at the lowest cost. This should induce a better policymaking environment within the Community.

Third, given that the European monetary policy will be as stability-oriented as the German Bundesbank, countries with poor monetary reputations will gain credibility. Price stability is, per se, always beneficial to an economy. The EMU would make it achievable with greater certainty of success, because some of the competing authorities have excellent track records of monetary discipline. It will also make it possible to realize price stability at a lower cost because countries with a history of relatively poor monetary management will find a sure anchor in the Bundesbank policy. At the same time, Germany will see in EMU the surest way of securing price stability in its partner countries, thus lessening the risk of imported inflation.

Fourth, there will be a beneficial impact on public finances through better management of national budgets. Countries with poor track records of budgetary discipline (like Italy and other Mediterranean countries) and those with huge national debts (Belgium, the Netherlands, Italy, and a few others) will find advantages in lower interest rates. A large part of the budgetary expenditure and, in some cases, a prime cause of the budget deficit are the high interest rates which reflect the exchange risk premium that the EMU can eliminate.

The fifth issue refers to the nature of the costs involved in the economic union. For example, individual countries will have to give up the nominal exchange-rate policy instrument, even in response to real shocks. However, use of the exchange-rate instrument already appears inefficient for European economies open to each other and to the rest of the world. Nonetheless, this will pave the way toward use of existing alternative adjustment policies. Some of these policies are based on the transfer of real resources from richer areas within the EC to the poorer ones. These alternatives will add to the efficiency of each individual economy and further increase the benefit of EMU.

Furthermore, most of these costs will decrease over time as member states' economies converge to common patterns and standards, as has been the case for the United States. The completion of the internal market in 1992 will lead to an increase in the share of intra-Community transactions (compared to the rest of the world), an increase in factor mobility (both capital and labor), and an improvement in the efficiency of markets. Hence, both the different impact of exogenous shocks and the probability of endogenous shocks will decline.

All the above can be encapsulated into the argument that the economic and monetary construction of the Community should and will take advantage of the 1992 goal and become its natural development. The argument could be strengthened by advocating the symbiotic nature of the EMU/internal market relationship. The EMU will contribute value added to the 1992 internal market, increasing its expected benefits. These expected benefits will in turn add stability to the EMS by abolishing the exchange-rate barrier in addition to removing the technical, physical, and fiscal frontiers.

The gains from the EMU in terms of more options in decision making will be felt mostly at the microeconomic level—the firms and the individuals. At the macroeconomic level, the EMU will most likely be a constraint on national decision making. Since governments have time and again shown evidence of significant propensity for major blunders with their systemwide consequences, giving fewer options to the public sector and a few more to the private sector is an acceptable tradeoff.

This loss of economic options is a fundamental question, and it is the sixth issue of concern. Many policy instruments that have been frequently used in the past may not be freely used anymore. Will the loss of freedom to devalue, to print money in order to finance budget deficits, and to tax the banking system through the reserve requirement (which eventually is a tax on savers) be a disadvantage?

From the vantage point of currently sovereign governments, the above amount to a triple loss and a triple transfer of sovereignty to Community decision making. The fact remains, however, that, so far, the freedom to pursue policy instruments has been the freedom to misbehave grossly for quite a number of member states.

1. The loss of freedom to devalue against a strong currency like the Deutsche mark (DM) will be equivalent to an insurance policy contracted by other governments that their own economic policy will be driven by the same general concern for price stability and economic efficiency as Germany. Hence, the transfer of monetary sovereignty to the Community level cannot be seen as a loss. It is actually a good way to import stability.

2. The revenue from seigniorage (printing money to finance the government deficit, thereby causing additional inflation) will no longer be available. Although scientific

evidence shows that revenue from seigniorage has been declining in recent years, this hidden tax remains quite significant in many member states.

3. Similarly, the tendency of governments to tax their banking systems through reserve requirements (held interest-free or well below market rates with the central bank) will end, as will the unnecessary disadvantage to the banking sector.

To conclude, the above triple loss of sovereignty cannot be viewed as a cost. Countries will actually benefit significantly from better economic policy and improved expectations. The switch to a Communitywide economic policy will be likely characterized by stability and sustainable growth.

A final argument concerns the relations between the EC and the rest of the world. The current international monetary system, characterized by a dominant U.S. dollar, emerging worldwide financial integration, and instability in foreign exchange and security markets, is in a shaky state.

The emergence of a monetary union in the European Community will help propagate to the rest of the world the Old Continent's financial stability (as the EMS becomes the EMU), forcing major trade and financial partners to deal with a new reality. A stronger European presence in all forums dealing with international monetary matters will put an end to the "taxation without representation" which Europeans have had to face.

Of course, the overall costs and benefits to be extracted from the EMU, and the nature and shape of Community economic policy, depend on the type, form, and characteristics of the economic and monetary union being set up.

TRANSITION FROM NATIONAL TO COMMUNITY ECONOMIC POLICY

The economic and monetary union binding together the twelve member states of the European Community is based on three principles:

Parallelism: This refers to the integration of the monetary and economic aspects of the union. (See below for a concrete definition of the two types of union.)

Subsidiarity: Subsidiarity is the systemic, macroeconomic counterpart of the principle of mutual recognition of norms and standards. The attribution of competence to the Community in the macro- as well as the micro-domains should be confined to those situations in which collective decision making is necessary to guarantee better results.

Plurality: The Community is made up of twelve member states, each with differing economic, social, cultural, and political characteristics. The preservation of this plurality requires that member states keep control of their own developments to the greatest possible extent. In other words, the specificity of each national situation has to be considered an asset on which to build the EMU, and not an obstacle making the process harder. This gigantic task is the European version of the "melting pot of cultures, races and religions" in the United States.

The blueprint followed by the Community in establishing the *monetary union* is well known in economic literature. Intellectually, this is nothing new: the 1990s will reproduce to some extent a process toward the union and the underlying economic policy quite close to what was sketched out in the 1970s by the Werner Committee—a group of wise men charged with defining the first EMU (which was never accomplished) of the European Community. This time around, the Committee consisted of the twelve EC Central Bank governors, as well as a few experts, and was chaired by the EC Commission president who was charged with the task of drawing up the new EMU blueprint.

The EMU consists of three irrevocable conditions, all of which are necessary and none of which is sufficient alone: (1) convertibility of all currencies; (2) capital liberalization and financial integration; and (3) locking of exchange rates of the currencies of all participating countries.

Once these three irrevocabilities are accepted, three other conditions follow: (1) the adoption of a single currency; (2) the establishment of a single monetary authority charged with managing that currency (the European Central Bank or ECB); and (3) the birth of a Community monetary policy, run by the single monetary authority (the ECB) and concerned with the stability of the single currency.

These conditions will lead to the scrapping of existing currencies and the abolition of exchange rates in the Community. Stopping short of these goals would be like throwing out the baby with the bath water. It will be difficult to tell businesspersons that dealing in currency X or currency Y at some point in time will carry exactly the same foreign exchange risk (as parities among these currencies will be fixed) without adding that at that time the exchange rate between currencies X and Y will be abolished. Furthermore, since dealing with one or another currency will be the same, why should Europeans have to carry different currencies in their pockets instead of a single one, whatever the name, shape, or color?

Former German Chancellor Helmut Schmidt put the case humorously when he said that "unless the EMU is established, from 1993 onward the EC markets will still be more chaotic than the kasbah of Marrakesh, where one single money is used."

Once we accept this consequence, the question of what appropriate single monetary institution within the Community will be charged with issuing the single currency and running the single monetary policy is solved: a single currency must mean a single European Central Bank.

The economic union, a less obvious concept, is described in terms of the 1992 internal market with the freedom of movement for persons, goods, services, and capital. Markets need rules of behavior, however. Hence, the Community's economic policy is being constructed on several building blocks to define what member states can or cannot do in all major economic policy domains:

1. Competition policy and other measures aimed at strengthening market mechanisms
2. Common structural and regional policies
3. Macroeconomic policy coordination, including budget policy. This means developing a system of "safety nets" for constraining sharply divergent fiscal policies and preventing spillover effects from inadequate economic management in other member states

The monetary union process outlined above focuses on three novelties: a single monetary policy, a single currency, and a single central bank. In contrast, the economic union does not require a new economic policy institution. In order to respect the principles of subsidiary and plurality, other-than-monetary policy will remain largely in the hands of national governments. The implications of this circumstance are examined later in this chapter.

The process of creating an EMU in the European Community can be divided into several stages. The first of these stages started in July 1989. A number of important events took place during this period.

On the economic side, the internal market will have to be completed. The legislative process had almost been completed at the time of this writing, and efforts are now being made to incorporate the three hundred pieces of EC legislation into national laws and practices. This task is difficult and long, but per se it is not a threat to realization of the 1992 goal. Given the supremacy of Community legislation over national legislation, the inability of national legislators to issue the required legal texts can in no way stop or obstruct the 1992 process. At the same time, legal texts are necessary to provide a framework for greater coordination of economic policy, especially budgetary policy. This is a Communitywide economic policy in its infancy.

On the monetary side, stage one includes the realization of a single financial area through the already approved liberalization of capital movements; the inclusion of all currencies in the EMS; the removal of all impediments to the use of the ECU (the Community embryo currency); and the agreement on the legal text to strengthen the role of the Committee of Governors of the European Community (the embryo ECB). Stage one also includes the preparation and ratification of the required changes in the Treaty of Rome.

The remaining stages of the process (the Report of the Committee of Governors envisages two additional phases) will witness the actual birth and coming to puberty of EC economic policy. On the economic side, the policy procedures will be coordinated more forcefully to the point of applying a European Court-enforced discipline in case of violation of agreement. In the monetary sphere, the new monetary institution (the ECB) will be established.

When should all of these events take place? There is no specific timetable in the EC for the actual transition to full monetary and economic union; therefore, no birthdate of EC economic policy can be proposed. It is possible to legislate the elimination of physical, technical, and fiscal barriers, as was done in the context of the internal market for which January 1, 1993, was set as the legislative process deadline. However, it is not possible to legislate an appropriate degree of economic convergence to render the EMU process realistic: nobody can dictate the date when the basic EMU conditions will be in place and one stage of the process will lead to the next one.

MONETARY AND BUDGETARY REGIMES

We now turn to a final set of interesting issues: the technical questions concerning the actual implementation and management of economic policy in EMU.

The birth of a European economic policy implies a limitation on the conduct of national policy (particularly budgetary policy), which is politically realistic and economically effective.

All agree that governments should not have access to direct central bank credit or to other forms of monetary financing. This condition, though necessary, is not sufficient for the efficiency of EMU: budget deficits could still have an externality impact throughout the Community. Taxpayers in other countries may be taxed by inadequate policy in any given member state.

Everyone also agrees that the best way to finance public deficits is by means of financial market intermediation, through bonds purchased in the marketplace.

Should this practice be limited, and if so, how? There is no single answer to this question. One answer depends on whether markets or governments are more likely to fail, since we all agree that failures are the reality, both in spontaneous transactions (taking place in competitive markets) and in organized transactions (for example, those run by governments). So it is a question of which type of arrangement is better suited in the new policymaking reality of the European Community.

History is littered with evidence of government failures. The 1970s have provided frequent examples of large-scale budgetary mismanagement, excessive national debts, inefficient resource allocation by political criteria, and costly interference with the allocative mechanism of markets. Most countries have taken ten years to remedy their past excesses. In a number of countries (including some large ones), the adjustment process to excessive budget deficits has not started yet or is only in its very early stage (see Figures 3.1 and 3.2).

Monetary union will be viable only if the Community's future economic policy is run along two parallel tracks. On one of these tracks will be centralized decision making, like the one on monetary matters once the European Central Bank is set up. On the other track will be national decision making like the one on budgetary policy. However, some surveillance of government behavior will be made at the Community level to insure against possibly inadequate policies in some areas and their spillover effects throughout the Community.

Given the well-documented ineffectiveness of multilateral surveillance discharged by the IMF, how can we hope to be successful within the Community? I believe that surveillance should be based on market means, particularly the financial markets. But it would not be wise to rely on it exclusively, since market

Figure 3.1
The EC Economy: The Growth of Public Debt

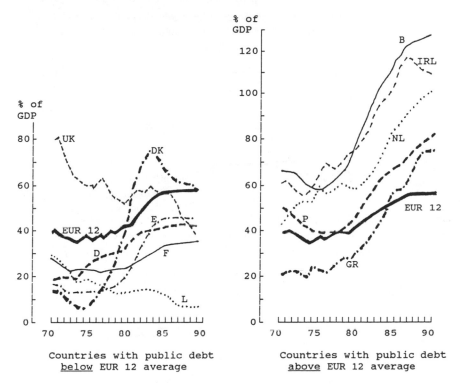

Countries with public debt
<u>below</u> EUR 12 average

Countries with public debt
<u>above</u> EUR 12 average

failures are quite frequent, for several reasons. The economic literature has dealt extensively with market failures in the presence of nonconvex economics (e.g., discontinuities in decision making and binary [zero/one] solutions), in the presence of externalities, or in the presence of public goods. All of these considerations are relevant to the monetary union.

The EMU blueprint pursued by the EC claims (correctly) that market forces alone are too slow and weak or too sudden and disruptive to provide an adequate deterrent to governments' misbehavior and to serve as a remedy to governments' failures. The collapse of New York City's finances and the banks' stampede into and out of lending to LDCs are evocative of market failures, or at least the inefficient self-policing of markets.

All of these issues are related to the problem of institutional centralization and democratic accountability. The final objective of the EMU is irrevocably fixed exchange rates, a single currency, a single monetary policy for the entire Community, and a sole centralized monetary institution (the ECB). What kind of budgetary arrangements need to be devised as a counterpart of centralized monetary management?

Figure 3.2
Public Finances in EUR 12

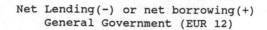

Net Lending(-) or net borrowing(+)
General Government (EUR 12)

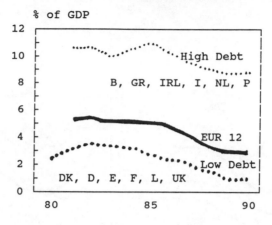

Net Lending(-) or Net Borrowing(+) EUR 12
excluding interest payments

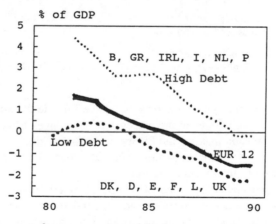

During the past few years, several budgetary regimes have been proposed. Since some of them have made useful contributions to the history of economic ideas, they should be reviewed briefly. We were exposed to

1. a decentralized market-based regime, supported by the exclusion of monetary financing and by the rejection of any bailing out of member states in the Community in case of budgetary mismanagement;

2. multilateral surveillance of national budgetary policy at the Community level, which would combine coordination procedures with a safety net concerning limits on the size of deficits and debts, as well as on the techniques of their financing; and

3. binding mutual guidelines on the size and structures of budget deficits and government debts and on their financing. These would be decided at the Community level, but they would not necessarily require a new institution.

Differences between these schools are a product of political and ideological preferences. They are also the result of alternative approaches to economic science and to the working of economic systems. For example, the *decentralized market-based regime* opposes limits on a country's freedom to run deficits or to build up debts because fiscal policy is considered ill suited based on short-run demand management of the type frequently used in the 1970s and associated with the economic problems of that time. Another reason is that, with fixed exchange rates, fiscal policy is needed to maintain internal balance. Good management of public finances needs to be sanctioned only by the market.

The multilateral surveillance approach, with good decision making supported (and induced) by a safety net, finds its justification in fears that the market discipline is inadequate or disruptive in the way it policies poor policies; and questions about the firmness of political commitment in a monetary union, especially if seen as a first step to political union. Governments, facing electorates reluctant to service debt obligations, may extort solidarity from fellow member states by threatening to default, or to renege on their EMU commitment, or even to opt out entirely on the process toward the EMU.

Those who support *binding budgetary guidelines* see them as a necessary counterpart to a single central banking institution in the Community. The management of society's main asset (stable money) requires certainty about society's main instrument in influencing the performance of that asset (good public finance). There can be no greater certainty than the one provided by ex-ante agreed-upon levels and structure of public spending.

Binding budgetary guidelines are also seen as a necessary counterpart to a single currency. A risk of instability and economic suboptimality may result from maintaining a small Community budget, national budgetary decision making, and centralized monetary policy.

In the final instance, the Community's economic policy will be shaped by centralized monetary management and (nationally run) budgetary policy. The national budgetary policy will respect the principle of subsidiarity. This is to be accomplished by nonmonetary financing of the budget deficit; the use of external borrowing in non-EC currencies; and upper limits on budget deficits in individual member states.

What does the average economist think of these alternative options? For example, what do the average Keynesian economist, the typical neoclassical economist, or the typical Ricardian have to say about them? Of course, there is no such thing as a typical adherent to any of these schools, nor is there a single answer to any of the issues raised. It would depend on the size, degree of openness, and exchange regime of an economy; the causes of a budget deficit, whether brought about by low tax receipts or high expenditure; and the nature of the deficit itself (whether transitory or permanent, expected or unexpected, etc.).

With these qualifications in mind, it would appear reasonable to characterize the thinking of the various economic schools as follows:

A Keynesian economist would probably stress the likelihood of deflationary bias in the EMU if national policy were run independently. Because of the growing import leakages (even more likely in the post–1992 environment and in the EMU regime), countries may refrain from expansionary budgetary policy owing to fears of deficits. (Little increase in real revenue would take place for any added volume of public demand.) Therefore, the Keynesian economist is likely to argue that budgetary policy is a useful instrument to promote domestic demand and to derive output gains if it is accompanied by joint (Community-level) determination of budgetary stances.

For a neoclassicist, the EC budgetary regime ought to be designed to foster convergence toward low public deficits, since permanent deficits crowd out private capital formation and trade higher present consumption for future growth. The negative externality caused by shared monetary conditions throughout the EMU area is to be fought by setting limits on public deficits. The neoclassicist is likely to argue that the EMU will bring about an increased risk of uncontrolled budgetary regimes, that is, for a bias toward fiscal laxity in the EMU (compared to fiscal rigor for the Keynesian). The risk of fiscal laxity will occur because in an EMU regime, increases in the public deficits of member countries would increase interest rates in the whole union and cause a deterioration in the union's balance of payments. This negative externality could become a temptation for member countries to engage in beggar-thy-neighbor budgetary policies.

According to *the Ricardian approach,* the rational private sector can discount future taxes through current budget deficits. The real effects of deficit spending, or variations of it, will be nil. Therefore, the Ricardian would presumably be indifferent to the design of the budgetary regime that accompanied the EMU.

The empirical evidence on the three different views regarding the effects of budgetary policy is rich and quite familiar. We must distinguish between moderate and large deficits. Moderate deficits do not seem to validate the Ricardian school. They do validate the Keynesian approach, since an increase in deficits has a short-term, positive impact on real growth. They also validate the neoclassical paradigm in the longer term, as the increasing public deficit will have a negative impact on savings and investment.

For larger deficits, for example, for the unsustainable situation such as that of one major country, Italy, and many minor countries like Greece and Belgium, aggregate demand is relatively unaffected. To an extent, this seems to lend support to the Ricardian theory of neutrality.

What reasons do we derive from the above in the design of the budgetary side of the monetary union? The following conclusions are offered as food for thought.

1. All economics schools agree that a serious uncertainty exists on how to calculate the most advisable budgetary policy.
2. The principle of subsidiarity should also systematically apply to macroeconomics, to overcome inconsistencies in national budgetary policy and between budgetary and monetary policy within each country.
3. The spillover effects of small changes in budgetary policy may be insignificant. Only if national budgetary policy poses a serious threat to the internal and external balance of the Community at large should they be contested at the Community level and perhaps preceded by Community measures.
4. For Keynesians and neoclassicists alike, the decentralized market-based regime fails to respond to the threat of monetary instability owing to excessive budgetary deficits. In these circumstances, the EC needs to have in its arsenal the means to act against the villain. In contrast, the Ricardian school could live with such a regime.
5. Strict binding guidelines for budgets cannot be in line with the subsidiarity principle. It would be supported by the Keynesian but not by the classicist and the Ricardian.
6. Mutual multilateral surveillance accompanied by a budgetary safety net would not seem to pose major problems either to a reasonable Keynesian or to a moderate neoclassicist.

In conclusion, the practice of multilateral surveillance of fiscal and budgetary management is at the core of the new EC economic policy. Recent legal texts (e.g., the newly approved EC decisions on the role of the Committee of the EC Central Bank governors and on the functions of the Ministerial Council for Economics and Finance) are early institutional building blocks. More will come in the period ahead.

At the outset of the 1990s, the European Community faces several formidable challenges. It must complete the internal market by the end of 1992; enable the less prosperous countries and regions to catch up more quickly, bringing down unemployment rates which remain twice as high as those in the United States and three times the Japanese rate complete the decision making concerning an EMU and begin setting up the new institutions; progress in the discussions concerning Europe's political union; and assist the other half of Europe (the eight countries in the central and eastern part of the Continent) to democratize and prosper.

Views on how to meet these challenges are on the table. Depending on the political will to make them concrete deeds, the economic policy of the European Community will soon become a reality. At that point, the Old Continent will be able to play a role in the tripolar world system commensurate with its economic size and importance. Only at that point will the sinister jargon of the 1970s and early 1980s about europessimism and eurosclerosis become a matter of the past.

APPENDIX: BUDGET POLICY ISSUES IN EC COUNTRIES

The European Community has made significant progress since 1985 in consolidating public finances. There are fears, however, that the movement is tending to weaken. On the basis of the current forecasts, which take into account the measures that have so far been announced, the net borrowing requirement of general government, after falling from 5.2 to 3.6 percent of GDP between 1985 and 1988, fell only slightly in 1989 and stabilized at around 3 percent of GDP in 1990. Government saving was expected to be only marginally positive in 1989 (0.5 percent of GDP) and in 1990 (0.4 percent). Gross public debt as a percentage of GDP was expected to fall slowly. Above all, very significant disparities were expected to remain between the budgetary consolidation programs of member countries.

A Better Contribution of Budgetary Policies to Community Objectives

These insufficiencies are all the more regrettable now that budgetary policies will have to play a greater role in two principal directions in the coming years.

1. The contribution of budgetary policies to the creation of conditions that are favorable to strong, sustainable growth will have to continue and in several member states will have to be strengthened considerably. This orientation is particularly needed in the less prosperous countries in order to permit greater economic and social cohesion and to derive all the gains from the support given to this end by the Community. In these countries, supplementary resources will have to be released in order to comply with the additionality rule governing the structural funds. More generally, over and above the Community measures concerning the approximation of fiscal systems, the completion of the internal market, by increasing competition among the member countries, will impose additional constraints on national public finances. In several countries, measures to adapt the fiscal system have already been taken to prepare for this deadline.

2. Budgetary policies will have to provide a more important support to monetary policies in the pursuit of the stability objective and of greater convergence. These are essential prerequisites for sound, harmonious growth in the Community and for the success of the first stage toward economic and monetary union. In those countries where budget deficits remain very high, the exclusive recourse to monetary policy to achieve this stability objective risks crowding out private investment and, eventually, causing slower growth and employment. On the other hand, the slowdown of inflation obtained in this way is likely to lead, through an increase in interest charges and lower growth, to an unsustainable evolution of public finances.

In order for these objectives to be realized, the Community has established a certain consensus on the necessity to pursue medium-term budgetary policies based on sound financial management principles. A better coordination of budgetary policies does not mean a systematic convergence toward a Community average. On the contrary, it implies taking into account the specific situation of each member state (for instance, the level of national saving, the external balance position, and the need to curb inflation), their structural differences, and the uneven results achieved so far in the consolidation of public finances (see Figures 3.3 and 3.4).

Figure 3.3
Productivity, Real Wages, and Capital/Labor Substitution, EC (5-year moving average of annual growth rates)

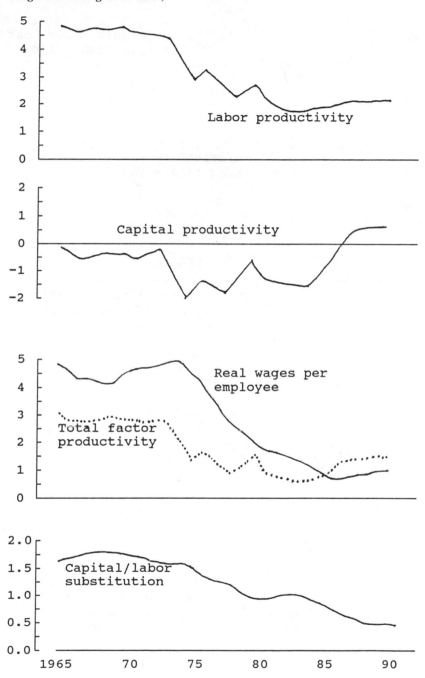

Note: 5-year period ending in indicated year.

Figure 3.4
Real Unit Labor Costs, Profitability, Real Long-Term Interest Rate, Capacity Utilization, and Investment, EC

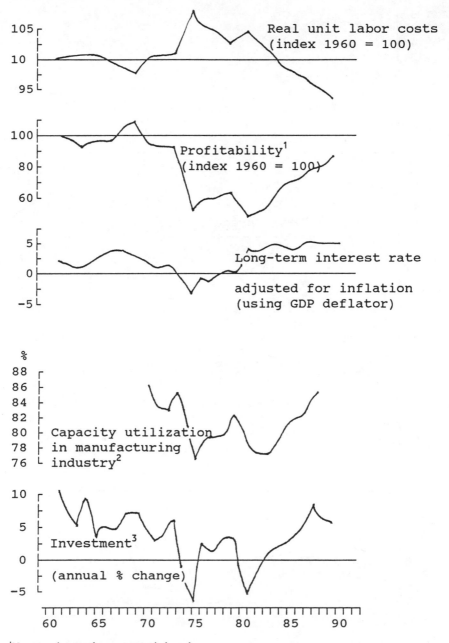

[1]Net operating surplus on net capital stock.

[2]Business surveys.

[3]Gross fixed capital formation at constant 1980 prices.

The implementation of these principles also has to be complemented by an assessment of the possible contribution of budgetary policy, according to the specific situation of each country and the broader framework of the general economic policy mix, to prevent or reduce fundamental disequilibria that eventually lead to exchange-rate adjustments. Such an assessment will also have to be seen in a medium-term rather than a "finetuning" perspective. Periodic multilateral surveillance based on both horizontal and country-by-country examinations, in the course of the first stage of EMU, should allow the criteria and methods of strengthened coordination in this field to be progressively refined.

With respect to sound medium-term management of public finances, the consensus that is building up in the Community rests on four guiding principles: avoiding the monetary financing of deficits, reducing budgetary disequilibria, controlling the share of public finances in GOP, and improving supply conditions.

Avoiding Monetary Financing of Deficits

Respecting this principle involves giving the monetary authorities necessary autonomy in the pursuit of the stability objective. This should at least signify that the budgetary authorities should not have automatic access to credit from the central bank, unless it is for cash advances of limited amounts and repayable within a very short period of time. Currently, the exchequer benefits from an automatic credit line in only four countries—Belgium, Greece, Spain, and Italy. Even then the line of credit is subject to fixed ceilings either in absolute values, as is the case in Belgium, or in the three other member states, as a percentage of the public expenditure of the current year. It should also signify that there should be no obligation on banks to invest in government paper. The banking system is still subject to such an obligation in four member countries (Greece, Spain, Ireland, and Portugal).

In the countries concerned, the borrowing conditions for the state should be progressively aligned with market conditions. This process should accompany the development and decompartmentalization of the national monetary and financial systems, which in any case is being necessitated by greater exposure to the outside world.

Reducing Budgetary Equilibria

The development of budget balances in the medium term should be kept within limits so as to control the debt–GDP ratio, or even reduce it where it is highest and at the same time aiming at a downward convergence of inflation rates. In any event, public finances should not be the original cause of an absorption of private saving by the financing of current expenditure. On these points, despite a sharp improvement at the Community level, the favorable impact of the more sustained growth of recent years has been very unevenly used for reducing budgetary imbalances. The disparities are even widening between two groups of member countries.

In the first group of countries, the budgetary situation can be regarded as consolidated. In three of the countries of this group (Denmark, Luxembourg, and the United Kingdom), the general government budgets are in surplus and the debt ratio is falling sharply. In these countries, the mechanical effects of the economic recovery are being fully utilized to improve the budget balances. In this same group, the budget deficits in Germany, France, and Spain should remain moderate, permitting an almost stable debt–GDP ratio. In addition to a reduction in the budget deficit, the favorable impact of the uptake in activity in these three countries has been beneficially used to reduce receipts in the case of France and particularly in Germany, and to strengthen public investment expenditure in the case of Spain.

In the first group of countries, general government saving will reach 2.5 percent of their GDP in 1989 and 1990, which is equivalent to 8 percent of the Community's gross saving. The contribution which the public finances of these countries will make to savings in the Community is still significantly below where it was at the beginning of the 1970s (5 percent of their GDP and 15 percent of total Community saving on average over the period 1970–73).

In the second group of member states—Belgium, Ireland, the Netherlands, Portugal, and especially Greece and Italy—budget deficits remain at very high levels. Public saving in these countries is expected to continue to be significantly negative in 1990 (more than 5 percent of their GDP on average, or more than 7 percent of total Community saving). In most of these countries, particularly Ireland, important efforts were made between 1985 and 1988 to reduce the budget deficits over and above the effects directly resulting from economic growth. However, in the majority of these countries the maintenance of a favorable economic environment will not result in an equivalent improvement of actual budget balances in 1989 and 1990, according to forecasts. The budgetary balances should even slightly deteriorate on average. In these conditions, the ratio of public debt to GDP should continue to increase with the exception of Ireland and Belgium. In particular, the primary balance (net government lending/borrowing requirement excluding interest payments) in Italy and Greece is expected to deviate by 6 to 7 percentage points of GDP from the level necessary to stabilize the debt–GDP ratio on the basis of current interest rates and nominal growth projected in the medium term.

Controlling the Share of Public Finances in GDP

Even if the government share and role in economic activity are essentially national political choices, it is in the interest of member states and of the Community as a whole to guard against the negative effects of an excessive increase in public expenditure and direct taxes. Between 1970 and 1985 the share of public expenditure in GDP increased by 14 percentage points, following an increase of 6 points during the 1960s. This expansion introduced an element of growing rigidity into the resource allocation mechanism. The corresponding increase in direct taxes heightened the pressures on wage costs and prices. Subsequently, inflation was progressively contained; as a result, this development adversely affected company profitability and thus investment, growth, and employment.

It was possible to reverse the trend from 1985 onward. From that date to 1988, the reduction in public expenditure (2 percentage points of GDP on average) was sufficient to allow a simultaneous significant reduction in budget deficits and a slight fall in the share of receipts in several member states (Belgium, Germany, France, Luxembourg, the Netherlands, and the United Kingdom). Even though, according to forecasts, there should be a slowdown in the reduction of deficits between now and 1990, the tendency for government receipts to fall as a proportion of GDP should increase and affect almost all member states.

Improving Supply Conditions by Restructuring Public Receipts and Expenditures

The budgetary authorities, within the limits imposed by the demands of consolidating public finances, should proceed to a restructuring of expenditure and receipts in order to strengthen economic productivity and growth. These adjustments are generally carried out across a diverse set of particular measures that affect the economy mainly at the microeconomic level, the budgetary implications of which are difficult to measure at the level of the broad expenditure and receipts categories.

When looking at the broad budgetary aggregates, we nevertheless observe that on the receipts side many differences remain between member states in the share and particularly the structure of taxes and social security charges. In 1988 the Community share of public receipts in GDP ranged from a minimum of 35.8 percent in Portugal to a maximum of more than 60 percent in Denmark. At the same time, the largest gap between the Community countries in the level of indirect taxes as a proportion of GDP was in a ratio of 1 to 2. This gap attained a ratio of 1 to 5 for direct taxes and 1 to 10 for social security contributions. It is probable that the completion of the internal market will, by right, gradually result in a certain convergence, following harmonization measures that are directly related to it, or in fact following greater competition between fiscal systems. In general, greater balance ought to be sought, as far as possible, between taxes and contributions that adversely affect the cost of factors of production (direct taxes and social security contributions), which have seen a rapid increase, and those based on consumption (indirect taxes) whose share in GDP has remained almost stable.

On the expenditure side, its reduction as a share of GDP between 1985 and 1990 will have been achieved by a decline in all categories of expenditure, including interest charges. It is important that, in maintaining this trend, training and reconversion programs and economically profitable public investment are preserved, even strengthened, particularly in those countries engaged in the catching-up process where the co-financing of the Community's structural programs must be ensured.

Implications for the Member States

Because of the disparities in the current positions of member states, the implementation of these guidelines would demand different efforts from each member state.

In Greece and Italy, the lack to date of significant improvement in the position of public finances makes the resolute application of a consolidation program very urgent. In the absence of a rapid reduction in the public finance imbalances, the maintenance or uptake in growth in these countries will be seriously compromised, as will the search for more stability and greater cohesion in the Community.

In a second group of countries (Belgium, Ireland, and Portugal), significant progress has already been made in improving public finances. The favorable economic environment should be used to complete the actions already undertaken.

In the other member states, even if a sustainable budgetary position has once again been achieved, in most of them room for maneuver in this area remains constrained by an external position which is in deficit (the United Kingdom and Denmark) or fragile (France and Spain). The growth in public debt in the Netherlands, even though it is slowing down, could become worrisome in the medium term. Germany will use its significant room for maneuver to pursue the tax reform program.

CONCLUSIONS

The prospects for the forthcoming decade are good. The policies that have been pursued since the beginning of the 1980s have allowed an improvement in the factors for sound, employment-creating growth. The completion of the internal market, the catching-up process of the less favored regions and countries, the liberalization of capital movements, and the necessary advance toward economic and monetary union will be the source of new progress and still greater dynamism. They simultaneously pose a challenge to firms, governments, and central banks which, in a situation involving greater competition, must adapt to this new frame of reference.

In order to gain the full benefits from these achievements and opportunities, economic policy efforts need to be pursued in two principal directions:

1. To further improve the fundamental determinants of growth in the medium term. In this way all Community countries will regain a high level of employment. It is

particularly necessary in those countries that need to catch up and will be first to benefit from the structural funds.

2. To further improve the convergence toward monetary stability and the compatibility of macroeconomic performances with sustained and balanced growth. In this way the recovery of the last seven years will not founder on a resurgence of inflation or unsustainable external or budgetary imbalances. Furthermore, greater convergence is necessary to achieve greater stability of exchange rates, which is also a condition for successful completion of the first stage of the EMU.

Three Principles for Better Coordination

The economic policy challenges facing the Community require determined action from individual member states and more effective coordination between them. Coordination of economic policies within the Community has never been an easy task and has not been very successful in the past. Since the early 1980s, however, progress has been made in this area as well, and coordination has become much more effective. At the outset of the first stage of economic and monetary union, the Community must strengthen it further, drawing on the experience accumulated over the years.

Better coordination should rest on three principles: consensus on the way to attain the common economic policy objectives; subsidiarity; and learning-by-doing in a dynamic process.

Consensus on Attaining the Common Economic Policy Objectives. In the industrialized countries, the unsatisfactory experience of the 1970s led in the 1980s to a reorientation of the prevailing economic policy approach toward greater awareness of the importance of stability and supply conditions. In the Community, this trend has been accompanied by a growing recognition of the importance of policy interdependence and the development of a practice of looking for common answers to common problems. Years of cooperation have led to a broad consensus between member states on the fundamental economic policy approach.

The setting up of the EMS represented a quantum leap in this process. The economic policy discussions which went with the relatively frequent realignments at the beginning of the 1980s have been important steps in developing a common approach to economic policy problems. The progressive implementation of the internal market project, with the additional constraints that greater integration and stronger interdependence bring, has also marked an important step in this direction. Since 1985, the Commission, especially in the Annual Economic Reports, has played a more active role in trying to consolidate and develop this consensus not only between member states, but also with and between the social partners.

Member states not only agree on the main objectives of economic policy indicated in the Treaty such as growth, stability, and a high level of employment, but they also share a common view on the best way to attain them. They agree on the objective of job-creating and noninflationary growth with stability, on the framing of policy in the medium term, and on the need to accompany good macroeconomic management with structural reforms, taking into consideration economic and social cohesion in the Community. On several occasions since 1986, the social partners have expressed, in the framework of the social dialogue at Community level, their agreement on the basic principles of economic policy defined in the Annual Economic Reports.[1]

During the 1980s progress was made in this direction throughout the Community, but with different degrees of success. The differences reflect the diversity in the starting points, the specific social situations, and the varying degrees of commitment to achieving this goal.

The success of the first stage of EMU will depend to a large extent on the consolidation and development of this consensus. This is a necessary but insufficient condition; other principles are required.

Subsidiarity and Mutual Engagements. The principle that the Community should seek to act only where a national government cannot be expected to do so satisfactorily is already widely reflected in areas of internal market and microeconomic policies. It should also be applied to the macroeconomic area as the Community progresses toward economic and monetary union.

The creation of the internal market is increasing the economic interdependence between member states and is progressively reducing the scope for independent policy action. The liberalization of capital movements and the approximation of indirect taxes, to mention just two of the internal market measures, will exert a profound influence on policymaking at the national level. In fact, there are already signs that individual governments are responding to these influences or anticipating them by voluntarily taking steps in the direction of the common objectives.

It is sometimes argued that these independent steps taken under market pressure are all that is needed to ensure that member states and the Community as a whole achieve the common goals. Yet, experience shows that the effectiveness of these responses varies widely and that insufficient and/or belated adjustment can be costly. A self-enforced policy coordination based on mutual engagements ensures the attainment of common goals more rapidly at lower adjustment costs. In the first stage of economic and monetary union, an equilibrium (which cannot be defined a priori) will have to be sought in a pragmatic way between market-enforced adjustment and voluntary coordination.

Learning-by-Doing in a Dynamic Process. Over the last decade the Community has accumulated rich experience in dealing with economic policy problems. It can now draw on it to define the actual policies to be implemented and to develop further a common approach. Three examples will give a more concrete idea of the scope of this experience.

First, during the 1980s the Community and the industrialized countries as a whole fought a hard disinflationary battle that has yielded remarkably positive results. The rate of inflation in the Community, in spite of a small acceleration over the last year, is now less than half what it was in 1980.

The most impressive results have been reached in countries that had previously experienced very high rates of inflation rather than in countries such as Germany where a national consensus on the need to maintain price stability had existed for years. In France and Ireland, the present rates of inflation are between a quarter and a third of what they were at the beginning of the decade and are comparable to those recorded by the best performers.

This result has been obtained through a combination of (1) a broadly based national consensus on the need to reduce inflation as part of the efforts aimed at improving growth conditions and eventually reduce unemployment which was at an extremely high level, and (2) a coordinated policy effort that has drawn on all instruments of policy: a stability-oriented monetary policy, a firm exchange rate (both countries have submitted themselves to the discipline of the narrow band of the exchange-rate mechanism of the EMS), and budgetary and wage developments consistent with the stability objective. The experience of these countries now constitutes a useful precedent for the rest of the member states.

Second, visible progress has also been made in the budgetary field. In the Community as a whole, the general government borrowing requirement is now half what it was at the beginning of the 1980s. Three countries are even running a surplus and are therefore reducing the amount of outstanding public debt.

In this area, however, until now some member states have found it difficult to draw on the experience of others, and many worrisome positions still persist. Progress in this area is objectively difficult. Budgetary consolidation, especially if starting from extremely deteriorated conditions, is a painful and politically difficult process. Failure to act does not result in immediately visible negative consequences, but rather permeates the whole economic system and results in a continuous deterioration of structural conditions. The temptation to delay action is difficult to resist. Moreover, the external constraint represented by the exchange-rate discipline takes more time to feed through. It is possible to counter the negative effects of a lax budgetary policy for many years with other means, particularly with a very restrictive monetary policy. This, however, takes its toll on investment and growth.

Reliance on totally independent policy action could be costly, and policy coordination would bring welcome positive results. There are also Community-wide reasons for such coordination. Stability of exchange rates, which is a "common good" for the Community, is eventually undermined by untenable budgetary positions. In addition, the financing of large budget deficits in an integrated system is not without influence on monetary conditions in other member states.

Member states can especially draw on the experience of Ireland and Denmark where the budgetary positions were very precarious and where the amount of public debt represented a serious burden on economic policy. These countries have successfully managed to turn around their budgetary position in a relatively short period and without affecting growth. In Denmark, a general government borrowing requirement exceeding 9 percent of GDP in 1982 was turned into a surplus equal to 3 percent of GDP by 1986 while maintaining an average growth rate of more than 3 percent. In Ireland, the general government borrowing requirement was reduced from 11 percent of GDP in 1985–86 to around 4 percent in 1988–89, while the rate of growth has progressively accelerated to reach over 5 percent this year.

Third, the large and growing imbalances in the external positions of member states show that more effort has to go into the search for a better approach to this policy problem.

In this area as in budgetary policy, other means (essentially monetary policy) can successfully offset the adverse effects of unsound cost, price, and demand developments for many years before eventually giving way to exchange-rate adjustments of policy adjustment. If adjustment is delayed, the structures of production adapted in reaction to incorrect signals and the eventual correction will be all the more painful.

Current account imbalances are often the result of medium-term processes that need several years to be corrected. The timely detection of worrying trends is not easy. By the time symptoms appear, the underlying trend has often acquired a momentum of its own that will be maintained long after the introduction of corrective action. The difficulty of agreeing on a current account balances pattern compatible with all Community objectives, including the strengthening of its cohesion, complicates the problem further.

For the success of the first stage of economic and monetary union, it will be necessary to inject a new spirit into Community macroeconomic coordination on the basis of the principles just outlined.

NOTE

1. In particular, joint opinion on the Annual Economic Report, 1986–87, of November 6, 1986, and joint opinion on the Annual Economic Report, 1987–88, of November 26, 1987, published in *European Economy*, Nos. 30 and 34.

REFERENCES

The European Communities. *The Cost of Non-Europe*. Vols. 1–16. Brussels: The European Communities, Office of Official Publications, 1988.
———. *The Economics of 1992*. Brussels: The European Communities, Office of Official Publications, 1989.
———. *European Economy*. Quarterly. Brussels: The European Communities, Office of Official Publications, 1990.
———. *From EMS to Monetary Union*. Brussels: The European Communities, Office of Official Publications, 1990.
———. *General Report of the Activities of the European Communities: 23rd Edition, 1989*. Brussels: The European Communities, Office of Official Publications, 1990.

————. *Yearbook of the European Communities and Other European Organizations*. Brussels: The European Communities, Office of Official Publications, 1990.

United Nations, Economic Commission of Europe. *Economic Survey of Europe in 1989–1990*. Geneva: United Nations, 1990.

4

NATIONAL ECONOMIC POLICIES IN JAPAN

Ryuzo Sato, Rama Ramachandran, and Elias C. Grivoyannis

THE JAPANESE ECONOMY FROM THE OCCUPATION YEARS TO THE NIXON SHOCK

The Postwar Inflation

The political vacuum that prevailed for a short period in August 1945, between surrender and effective occupation by Allied Command, compounded the dislocation of the Japanese economy from war and defeat. The breakdown of the controls instituted during the war years, the 40 percent increase in the currency circulation from hasty disbursements of the deferred war commitments, the shortfall in coal production with the end of the forced foreign labor in the mines, and the cessation of foreign trade together with a 40 percent fall in rice crops that year, fueled the country's inflation (Schiffer, 1962, p. 29).

The policy of the occupation administration was announced by the Supreme Commander, General Douglas MacArthur, on September 10, 1945. It sought economic demilitarization, promotion of the democratic forces such as the labor unions and agricultural associations, and elimination of industrial concentration including the breakup of the *zaibatsu* (conglomerate of firms). The policy stated that Japan was responsible for its economic plight and must bear the responsibility for reconstruction, including provision of goods and services for the Allied army and repartition as determined by the Allied powers. The occupation administration was more interested in long-term reform of the economic and political system than in immediate stabilization and recovery measures. One of the reasons may have been the widespread belief in Europe that Japan would quickly emerge from the chaos and once more become a competitor (Allen, 1965, p. 15). Whatever the reasons, the policy only impeded the process of normalization.

Another step the government took in 1946 was to cancel the indemnities that still remained and to partially reduce the guarantee of the loans given to finance war production. This was achieved by imposing a 100 percent tax on them with few exceptions; 90 percent of the resulting loss to the industrial corporations was to be borne by shareholders. A special law passed for banks divided deposits into old and new and froze the old. A substantial portion of the large deposits was canceled. Given the abolition of the *zaibatsu* and the monetary reform, it was feared that industry would not receive long-term financing. The government established the Reconstruction Finance Bank in 1947. That year it furnished 72 percent and the following year 69 percent of the funds for the corporate fixed investment (Allen, 1965, p. 50). The government contributed the bank's capital, and the Bank of Japan purchased close to three-quarters of its debentures. The monetization of the bonds sustained the inflation.

Foreign trade was conducted mostly by official trading bodies under a multiple exchange system. Exportable commodities were purchased at a promotional price and sold at international prices abroad. Imported commodities, particularly rice, were purchased at foreign prices and sold at subsidized prices internally. Implied conversion rates for imports ranged from 100 to 300 a dollar, while for exports they varied from 300 to 800. The funds for these hidden subsidies came from the income from the sale of imports that did not need to be paid for (Tsuru, 1955, p. 194). The heavy debit balance in the current account was met by lavish American aid, which amounted to $404 million and $461 million in 1947 and 1948, respectively (Allen, 1965, p. 50).

Rebuilding the Economy

During the first quinquennium after the war, efforts were underway to rebuild the agricultural and industrial sectors and reduce the inflation-generating excess demand through increases in supply. The process was naturally intertwined with the evolution of the new political system.

During these occupation years, the General Headquarters (GHQ) under the Supreme Commander was the effective center of power. The new constitution promulgated in May 1945 established a British type of parliamentary democracy, but, until the Peace Treaty of 1951, the cabinets had to respond to the directives of the GHQ. The GHQ was committed to implementing the policies enunciated by General MacArthur in his statement of September 1945 and pressured the cabinet from time to time to enact legislative and administrative measures that were needed to achieve the goals.

There is a consensus of opinion that, of all the measures of "democratization and demilitarization" programs, the agricultural reform was the one that was most expeditiously and effectively implemented. The process of reform and reconstruction of the industrial sector was complicated by the interplay of many economic and political factors. Like all war-ravaged economies, the industries had to be retooled for civilian production. In addition, Japanese industry was dependent on the import of raw materials like coal, iron, and timber from the outer regions of the prewar empire. Not only were these territories lost, but also international trade during this period practically ceased. A break came in March 1947 when the GHQ agreed to the emergency import of all industrial commodities except steel; however, normal channels of international trade were not restored until 1949.

Next, the Final Reparation Report, prepared by the U.S. Ambassador, Edwin Pauley, required not only financial reparations but also the physical transfer of plants. The objective was to return the standard of living to the prewar levels, and there was concern that it would reduce Japan to an underdeveloped nation. Fortunately, the Pauley plan was never implemented as visualized. With increasing tension between the United States and the Soviet Union and the establishment of the communist government in mainland China, NATO nations began to see Japan as a bulwark against communism in the East. The Draper plan of 1948 sought the reparation of 102 industrial facilities as compared to 990 under the Pauley plan (Nakamura, 1981, p. 31). By the time the San Francisco Treaty was signed in September 1951, most of the Allied nations had joined the United States in renouncing reparations. Payments were committed only to the southeastern nations of the Philippines, Indonesia, Burma, and South Vietnam (Uchino, 1983, pp. 66–67).

Another component of the occupation policy was the breakup of the *zaibatsu* and the reduction in the concentration of industries. Fifty-six designated *zaibatsu* family leaders and eighty-three designated holding companies had to turn their stocks to a government commission for sale to a preferential group of investors. In addition, 325 companies were identified for breakup. Again, the policy was watered down with the beginning of the cold war. Only nineteen companies were split up, and many former *zaibatsu* companies began operating under the old names. Yet there was one profound change. The new *keiretsus*, or association of firms, were centered around banks and were more managerially oriented.

Finally, reconstruction of industry was affected by the evolution of the government's economic policies as the new parliamentary democracy began to take root in the country. The system was characterized by frequent changes in the cabinet. Between 1945 and the middle of 1965, the average life of a cabinet was nine and half months and that of a prime minister who generally presided over many cabinets was twenty-four months. But for a period of nine and a half months in 1947–48, all of them were led by conservative politicians (Ward, 1967, pp. 92–93). Hence, there was a continuity, particularly as policies were decided by developing a consensus among the various factions of the conservative coalitions.

Since inflation persisted during these years, the question has been asked why no efforts were made to adopt a truly effective deflationary policy. The policy adopted during these years partly reflected the economic philosophies of the period, particularly the Japanese interpretation of Keynesian economics. Tanzan Ishibashi of the first Yoshida cabinet was identified with the extreme Keynesian position that monetary expansion was not inflationary as there was still unemployment in Japan. The GHQ also had its share of administrators from the New Deal era. But Uchino (1983, pp. 44–48) argues that a secret committee headed by the Harvard-trained economist Shigeo Tsuru developed a proposal in 1947 for a deflationary program that was abandoned with the fall of the socialist government.

Dodge Disinflation and the Korean War Boom

In 1948 the American government finally became more concerned with the immediate stabilization of the Japanese economy than with long-range reconstruction. It issued a nine-point plan and within two months sent Joseph Dodge, an architect of the German currency reform, to implement it. Debate continues as to whether stabilization would have occurred without Dodge's direct intervention. Given the short period of time between the introduction of his policies and the outbreak of the Korean War, the controversy will, in all probability, never be resolved.

But the Dodge policy did disturb the established pattern of the reconstruction of the industrial sector and necessitated massive retrenchment in the public sector. The problems were complicated by the devaluation of the pound sterling which reduced the competitiveness of the Japanese exports. The Bank of Japan tried to alleviate the problems by loaning out the fiscal surplus, a policy that eventually led to the "overloan" position of the commercial banks. But Dodge resisted the relaxation of the deflationary policy, and the stringent conditions continued into 1950 (Scott et al., 1980, p. 95). The Korean War turned the situation around. As the country nearest to the war zone, Japan received substantial foreign earnings from purchases by the U.S. military. "Special procurement," as it was called, replaced foreign aid.

In 1952 the San Francisco Peace Treaty finally ended the occupation. Japan was free to determine its destiny and soon adopted a number of policies that were to become the cornerstone of the Japanese economy during the boom years. The Japan Development Bank was established to take over the assets and liabilities of the Reconstruction Bank and to provide industry with funds for plant and equipment at low rates. The Japan Export-Import Bank was to encourage exports by providing funds for the same. The four industries—coal mining, iron and steel, electricity, and marine transportation—were chosen for special support and received between 60 and 90 percent of the government funds during the years 1952–54 (Tsuru, 1958, pp. 63–64).

The decline of exports and the increase in internal consumption created a drain on foreign exchange reserves in 1953 which reached crisis proportions in 1954. Monetary and fiscal policies were tightened. The Bank of Japan limited borrowing by city banks through a system of "window guidance" or supervision; the loan increases of each bank were limited on a month-by-month basis with punitive interest rates for exceeding the limit. Prime Minister Yoshida instituted cuts in the government budget. According to Uchino (1983, p. 78), this was the beginning of the "stop-go" measures that would characterize Japan's monetary and fiscal policies for the next two decades. The immediate impact of the new policies was that many firms faced bankruptcies. By the end of the year, however, the recession bottomed out.

The Era of Rapid Growth

Over the next fifteen years, economic growth overshadowed the business cycles (generated by periodic constraints in foreign exchange) and propelled Japan to the ranks of leading industrial nations of the world. During this period, the economy grew at an annual rate of about 10 percent, exceeding even the expectations of the Japanese government. The various government plans increased the growth rate from 5.0 percent in the Five-Year Plan for Economic Independence of 1955 to 10.6 percent in the New Economic and Social Development Plan of 1968. In spite of these revisions, the targets almost consistently fell below the actual growth throughout the period (Uchino, 1983, p. 88). In contrast, between 1952 and 1972 the U.S. economy grew annually at 3 percent and West Germany at 6 percent. Equally impressive were the qualitative changes in the Japanese economy. From an exporter of textile and other inexpensive products, Japan became the leader in automobiles, chemicals, computers, consumer electronics, shipbuilding, and steel. The transformation of a war-torn economy into the second largest industrial economy of the world in a period of fifteen years captured the imagination of the public and professional communities and has been the subject of many popular and scholarly studies.

Behind this smooth facade of reasonably steady growth, the economy went through a radical restructuring. From a country that was subject to periodic balance-of-payment deficits and stop-and-go monetary policies, Japan was about to move into an era of sustained trade surpluses. Simultaneously, it agreed to relax the trade restrictions and move to Article 8 of the General Agreement on Tariffs and Trade (GATT) and join the Organization for Economic Cooperation and Development (OECD) which required relaxed capital controls as well. Japanese government sources claimed that import liberalization reached the 92 percent level by the end of 1963, but this figure was challenged by Western sources (Scott et al., 1980, pp. 160–65).

Another change was that the Bank of Japan accepted, in principle, to move away from direct guidance of the individual banks through "window guidance" to the use of open market operations and the deposit reserve ratios. But the need for tightening the monetary policy in 1964 led to reinstating window guidance with industry targets that interfered with individual banks to a lesser extent. Even more radical, however, was the change in fiscal policy. Breaking from the constraints of Dodge reform prohibiting borrowing through issue of long-term bonds, the government committed itself to countercyclical fiscal policy.

The expansionist trend of the U.S. economy under the domestic policies pursued by the Kennedy–Johnson administrations and the escalation of the Vietnam War led to an export boom for Japan during the second half of the 1960s. It was also a period of rapid increase in investment; the average growth rate of gross domestic capital formation was 15 percent. If that was not impressive in itself, it should be noted that the gross capital formation averaged 32 percent of the gross national expenditure of the second largest economy of the free world. Such massive investments helped Japan avoid the slowdown in productivity that characterized the U.S. economy during this period and to increase the exports at about 17.5 percent per year.

FISCAL POLICY

The main objectives of fiscal policy in Japan during the postwar period were to facilitate control of an excessive aggregate demand, to promote productive investment, to get low-cost financing for strategic sectors of the economy, and to encourage a relatively small budget as a percentage of GNP. At the same time, fiscal policy attempted to assist (through government subsidies) the low-productivity sectors of the economy, such as agriculture and small-scale firms, to adjust income distortions caused by the imbalance of its rapid growth.

Control of Aggregate Demand

The Balanced Budget Years

The 1949 Dodge recommendations enforced a fiscal policy in Japan which adhered to ''sound'' public finance. Despite the popular Keynesian justification for deficit financing, the occupation forces regarded such financing as unsound for Japan, and even government-guaranteed bonds issued by public corporations were unacceptable. The government's operating expenses had to be adjusted to current government revenues, and the Ippan Kaikei (the General Account) always had to be balanced. The Japanese government initially considered the Dodge prescription as unsound because of excess unemployment and a need for industrial reconstruction. Under the circumstances, however, it was accepted, and the government tried to extract as many benefits as it could out of it. It turned out that the imposed balanced budget policy was indeed ''sound'' policy after all.

A small government sector enabled the strong demand for private investment to take full advantage of the existing capital shortage[1] and to gear the economy toward high rates of economic growth. During the rapid growth period of the 1950s and 1960s, Japan experienced a rapid growth of employment. As a result, a large number of new taxpayers were appearing every year. At the same time, rapid growth of income levels was steadily and rapidly moving the old taxpayers into higher income tax brackets. Government receipts were much greater than estimated every year, and the balanced budget principle turned into a superbalanced budget problem. Instead of trying to adjust increasing operating expenditures to stable current revenues, like most governments of growing nations, the government of Japan had to find ways to adjust increasing current revenues to stable operating expenditures. Government expenditures were kept low to avoid deficits, whereas unexpected budget surpluses were shifted forward to subsequent years. Government revenues were growing faster than expenditures, and politicians were happy and confident to promise annual tax reductions. Tax schedules were adjusted downward annually in order to enable the government to reduce receipts and balance the budget! These annual adjustments of tax rates, brackets, exemptions, and deductions became permanent features of fiscal policy and necessary changes in order to keep tax receipts close to 20 percent of GNP in the budgetary process.

The balanced budget principle was necessary during this period because it was releasing resources for capital formation. Business firms were starting their expansionary programs after the war, and their demand for investment funds was eliminating the need for expansionary fiscal policy. The role of fiscal policy during this period was to restrict aggregate demand rather than to promote it. It finally managed to control an excessive aggregate demand by keeping its non-growth-related expenditures low. Social programs, social security, and defense spending were some of the sectors that experienced underspending practices. For fiscal year 1970, the ratio of transfer payments to national income was 5.8 percent in Japan, compared to 11.1 percent in the United Kingdom and 15.5 percent in West Germany. (See Table 4.1 for international comparisons.) For fiscal year 1979, the ratio of defense spending to GNP was 0.9 percent in Japan, compared with 5.0 percent in the United States and 3.4 percent in West Germany (Noguchi, 1982, p. 129). (See Table 4.2 for the social security and defense spending in Japan as a percentage share of GNP.)

Fiscal policy in Japan was restrictive of aggregate demand until the early 1970s. Government expenditure was consistently smaller in Japan than in any other industrialized country relative to the size of the economy and to government revenues (Garin–Painter, 1970, pp. 43–55).

Keynesian Budget Financing

By the early 1960s government expenditures began to rise in response to the country's urgent need for public works and infrastructure projects. During this period, the government undertook 15 percent of the total gross domestic investment in the form of building airports, harbors, roads, and so on. Although the consumption components of government expenditures were kept low, it was obvious that fiscal policy had to allocate more funds to infrastructure projects to support industrialization and rapid economic growth. As a result, the Ministry of Finance started investigating the possibility of budget deficits, and it finally managed to run such deficits with an apparently balanced budget.

In order to satisfy those Japanese who were strongly advocating the "sound budget" strategy of the Dodge plan, the Ministry of Finance transferred some of the capital expenditure items from the General Account Budget into the Fiscal

Table 4.1

General Government Expenditures and Social Security Transfers: Japan and Other Countries, Selected Years, 1955–80 (percent of GNP)

Country	General government expenditures			Social security transfers		
	1955–57	1974–76	1980	1955–57	1974–76	1980
Japan	–	26.6	32.9	3.7	7.0	10.9
France	33.5	41.6	45.7	13.2	19.9	22.9
West Germany	30.2	44.0	45.0	12.0	15.4	15.4
Italy	28.1	43.1	44.3	9.7	19.4	15.8
Sweden	–	51.7	–	7.4	17.1	–
United Kingdom	32.3	44.5	44.3	6.1	11.3	11.7
United States	25.9	35.1	32.7[a]	4.1	10.9	11.1
OECD average	28.5	41.4	–	7.5	13.9	–

Source: Yukio Noguchi, "Public Finance," in Kozo Yamamura and Yasukichi Yasuba (eds.), *The Political Economy of Japan* (Stanford, Calif.: Stanford University Press, 1987), Vol. 1, p. 188.

[a] 1979.

Table 4.2
Selective Items in the General Account Budget, FY 1965–83 (percent of GNP)

Fiscal year	Total budget	Social security	Debt–servicing costs	Defense	National taxes
1965	10.90	1.54	0.07	0.90	9.24
1966	10.93	1.58	0.12	0.86	8.78
1967	10.72	1.56	0.25	0.82	9.13
1968	10.64	1.49	0.37	0.77	9.27
1969	10.39	1.46	0.43	0.74	9.56
1970	10.59	1.52	0.39	0.76	9.99
1971	11.38	1.62	0.39	0.81	9.85
1972	11.89	1.71	0.47	0.83	10.43
1973	12.25	1.81	0.60	0.80	11.74
1974	12.39	2.09	0.62	0.79	11.16
1975	14.02	2.59	0.68	0.87	9.66
1976	14.27	2.82	0.98	0.89	9.48
1977	15.10	3.01	1.24	0.90	9.47
1978	16.59	3.28	1.56	0.92	10.88
1979	17.38	3.43	1.84	0.94	10.97
1980	17.70	3.41	2.21	0.93	11.45
1981	18.43	3.48	2.62	0.95	11.69
1982	18.63	3.41	2.94	0.97	11.71
1983	17.88	3.24	2.91	0.98	11.76

Source: Yukio Noguchi, ''Public Finance,'' in Kozo Yamamura and Yasukichi Yasuba (eds.), *The Political Economy of Japan* (Stanford, Calif.: Stanford University Press, 1987), Vol. 1, p. 202.

Investments and Loans Program (FILP) project which was financed by the government-owned Postal Office Savings Banks. With this accounting maneuver, the General Accounting Budget could remain balanced and even enable government expenditures to increase. Instead of having the government raise funds through the issue of bonds to finance capital expenditures, the government was "borrowing" the funds from depositors in the government-owned Post Office Savings Banks for exactly the same purpose. Eventually, it became irrelevant whether or not the budget was balanced and whether government revenues were coming from taxes or from borrowings. This accounting coverup and deliberate confusion made acceptable the idea of government borrowing, as long as the borrowed funds were used for capital formation.

In 1965 it was the first time in postwar Japan that a deficit in the General Account officially appeared; an issue of short-term government bonds was accepted to cover it. In 1966 the government broke officially with the Dodge principle and accepted Keynesian deficit financing. It officially introduced an open budget deficit and issued long-term government bonds to finance it. The new government borrowing instruments were called constructive bonds and were differentiated from deficit-covering bonds which were still officially considered unacceptable. As Bieda puts it, "bonds are always 'deficit covering,' and if bonds are issued and their proceeds are spent by the Government, no one can be certain what they were spent on, unless one knew which items of expenditure would have been cut if the bond finance had not been available" (Bieda, 1970, p. 109).

These developments had important policy implications. In the mid-1960s the political power of special interest groups started imposing a high degree of downward rigidity on government expenditures and made fiscal policy unoperational as a restrictive economic policy tool. As a result, monetary policy remained the only tool available for restrictive policy while both fiscal and monetary policy could now be used as expansionary tools.

Growth of Budget Deficits

Although deficit financing has been feasible in Japan since 1965, it remained a marginal source of revenue until the mid-1970s. Up to 1974, the average bond dependency ratio (the ratio of bond revenue to total revenue) was close to 10 percent, and all government bond issues were considered a source of funds for capital formation (Noguchi, 1987, p. 192). In 1975, however, the bond dependency ratio increased from an initial budget level of 9.4 percent to 25.3 percent, and it has never declined below 25 percent since. Worse than that, a special law is passed every year to legalize the issuance of *akaji kokusai* (deficit-financing bonds) for noncapital formation expenditures.

As a result, the volume of outstanding government bonds grew from ¥10 trillion in 1974 to more than ¥142 trillion in 1987 (more than 53 percent of GNP). The large government deficits that began in 1975 were funded with ten-year public bonds. Thus, beginning in 1985 vast numbers of these bonds reached maturity. Mass redemption of these bonds reached a peak in May 1988, with an average amount of more than ¥3.6 trillion redeemed daily. In fiscal 1986, an estimated ¥22 trillion of national government bonds were issued, of which roughly half were rollovers to refinance the deficit. In 1987 four issues of twenty-year national bonds, totaling ¥2 trillion, were released. In addition, sixty-day government bills, intended to bridge revenue shortfalls, were also issued when needed and were purchased almost entirely by the Bank of Japan. Japan's market in government debt is the second largest in the world after the U.S. market. In October 1985 a bond futures market opened in Tokyo. By August 1986 volume reached more than 80,175 contracts per day, making the long-term government bond the most actively traded coupon futures contract in the world. As a result, two-way volume in 1986 reached ¥1,870 trillion, roughly 10 percent higher than the volume of trading of U.S. long-term government bond futures on the Chicago Board of Trade (Viner, 1988, p. 167).

By fiscal 1990, the national budget was under the heavy weight of national debt. Costs for government bonds increased in the fiscal 1990 budget to ¥14.29 trillion ($99.93 million), up 22.5 percent compared to fiscal 1989. This is the fastest growth rate ever. The 1990 portion of government bond costs in the general account is also the largest in the postwar period.

Causes of Budget Deficits

The main sources of these sharp, noncapital-related deficits were (1) the government decision to increase social security benefits[2] in the early 1970s, and (2) the substantial reduction in corporate tax revenues, as a result of the oil shock recession of 1975.

Political and economic considerations in the budget-making process introduced significant changes in the social security system[3] in the early 1970s. The introduced changes were a result of fiscal affluence and political pressure from socialist-communist coalitions in many local governments. The fiscal situation was exceptionally favorable during this period because of a remarkable "natural increase" in tax revenues. Revenues from national taxes increased from 9.24 percent of GNP in 1965 to 9.99 percent in 1970 and 11.74 percent in 1973, while total budget expenditures dropped from 10.90 percent of GNP in 1965 to 10.59 in 1970 and then increased to 12.25 percent in 1973 (see Table 4.2). Tax revenues were growing faster than budgeted expenditures. It became politically and economically appropriate, therefore, after two decades of subsidized rapid economic growth, to start allocating fiscal resources to nongrowth- and productivity-related sectors. This new direction in fiscal policy was reinforced by the spread of nonconservatives in many local governments and their slogans for welfare improvements. Free medical care for the aged was one of the programs introduced during this period as a response to nonconservative political pressures.

These trends are still present in the early 1990s. In the fiscal 1990 budget the government allocated ¥11.61 trillion ($81.2 billion), up 6.6 percent, to expenditures for social security in response to Japan's rapidly aging society and the ruling Liberal Democratic party's pledge to spend consumption tax revenues on social welfare. (This new tax was introduced in 1989.) This was the first time in ten years that the increased rate for social security spending surpassed that for defense spending.

Another important factor that contributed to the expansion of welfare benefits was the Ministry of Welfare's theoretical mistake in estimating the required contribution rate for public pensions. This rate is calculated by equating the present value of the future pensions payments to the sum of the present value of future contributions, the present value of future subsidies from the general account, and the value of the existing fund. For this calculation, assumptions have to be made about the future economic growth rate and a discount rate. The Ministry of Welfare assumed a future economic growth of zero percent and a discount rate of 5.5 percent (Japan, Ministry of Welfare, 1981). The discount rate was too high relative to the growth rate, and this wrong assumption led to a serious underestimation of the required contribution rate for the public pensions fund. Had the contribution rate been calculated correctly, it is doubtful that some of the major welfare changes would have been made in the early 1970s (Noguchi, 1987, p. 208).

The advances in the social security system were remarkable during this period. The payment levels in various programs were substantially upgraded, and among the many new programs introduced were the initiation of a children's allowance (1971) and free medical services for the elderly (1972), improvement in medical insurance benefits (1973), initiation for allowances for expensive medical services (1973), and improvements in the old-age pensions (1973) (Noguchi, 1982, p. 132). The ratio of public assistance expenditures to GNP remained almost constant during this period. The ratio of health insurance to GNP and the ratio of public pensions to GNP, however, increased dramatically after 1973. Indeed, fiscal year 1973 is called the first year of the welfare era in Japan because of the new social programs introduced that year (Noguchi, 1987, p. 205). Increased social security expenditures have an accelerating effect on budget deficits because of increasing costs in debt servicing. As indicated in Table 4.2, both social security expenditures and debt-servicing costs are experiencing considerable upward trends. By 1985 the increase in debt-servicing costs (amortization and interest payments on national bonds) surpassed the social security expenditures (Noguchi, 1987, p. 201). They increased from 0.07 percent of GNP in 1965 to 0.39 percent in 1970 and 2.91 percent in 1983. Increased social security expenditures had an accelerating effect on budget deficits because of increasing costs in debt servicing.

As political considerations also are given to international developments, appropriations for defense spending and official development assistance (ODA) have increased as well. The total amount of ODA spending in the 1990 budget reached ¥817.5 billion ($5.72 billion), making Japan the largest ODA donor for the third consecutive year.

On the revenue side, the receipts from national taxes dropped from 11.16

percent of GNP in 1974 to 9.66 percent in 1975 and remained below 11.45 percent until 1980. By 1983 total tax receipts still amounted to 11.76 percent of GNP.

The most important reason for this tax revenue decline was the 1975 recession caused by the oil crisis. Corporate tax receipts dropped from 4.21 percent of national income in 1974 to 2.72 percent in 1975 and remained below 4.00 percent until the mid-1980s regardless of the fact that corporate tax rates were raised two percentage points in 1981.

Increased social security benefits such as health insurance and public pensions have been more important than reduced tax revenues for the post–1975 increase in government deficits.

Attempts to Raise Taxes

The initial effort to reduce deficits focused on increased tax revenues. Until 1974 an average tax reduction of 3 percent of income tax revenues was introduced in most years. After 1975, however, tax schedules were not revised, or, in some cases, they were revised upward. Besides personal and corporate income taxes, various excise taxes were also increased. Higher taxes on liquor, official stamps, and other items raised tax revenue by an additional ¥904 billion in FY 1981, while a 1986 tax revision raised excise taxes on cigarettes by 80 percent.

Zeisei Chosakai (the Tax System Council) expressed the opinion in 1978 that a substantial tax increase was necessary for deficit reduction. It therefore proposed the introduction of a general sales tax, a levy similar to the value added tax of European countries. The Ministry of Finance estimated that adding a 5 percent uniform tax on value for all firms whose sales volume exceeded ¥20 million could have produced ¥3 trillion in additional tax revenues in FY 1980, which would have been enough to cover 21 percent of the expected deficit in that year. In reality, the final report submitted to the Ministry of Finance in 1977 recommended three options: an increase in personal income taxes, an increase in corporate income taxes, and the introduction of a new general sales tax, with emphasis on the last option (Zeisei Chosakai, 1977, pp. 7–26).

A new tax, however, is always a bad tax for the politicians who will have to introduce it. This became very obvious in the 1979 elections. The Liberal Democratic party suffered a serious defeat when it did not oppose the proposal to introduce a general sales tax. The introduction of a sales tax again became an issue in 1985, when the need for tax reform was reconsidered. The bill was withdrawn in 1987 by Prime Minister Nakasone, but Prime Minister Takeshita finally forced it through the National Diet at the end of 1988 and it went into effect on April 1, 1989.

The new tax provides for a 3 percent consumption (sales) tax on almost all goods and services and a new capital gains tax. In return, income, corporate, and inheritance taxes have been reduced. The result is a net tax reduction of ¥2.6 trillion. Moreover, some 70 percent of all corporations are effectively exempt from the consumption tax. Consumers are concerned that businesses will pocket part of the consumption tax instead of giving it to the government, because businesses are not required to issue receipts and maintain a reliable record on sales. It is estimated that businesses may hold back as much as ¥480 billion a year (*The Japan Economic Journal*, Editorial, 1989). The 1988 six-bill national tax reform act has also introduced some kind of confusion and is considered by some as unfinished. Some observers suggest that taxes should be made fairer and that they should be simplified. Before the 1988 revision, the tax system was heavily dependent on income taxes as a source of revenue. The reform is aimed at rectifying this imbalance by taxing consumption and capital gains more heavily. It is expected that the Japanese people will eventually adjust to these new tax provisions.

The public's opposition to the introduction of any new tax forced the Ministry of Finance to adopt a less sweeping approach to raising revenues. One such approach was to raise tax revenues without raising tax rates by enforcing existing laws and trying to reduce tax cheating. The focus of this attempt was on tax revenues from interest income on savings accounts. To avoid taxes on interest income, depositors were opening multiple accounts under fictitious names in the postal savings system which had low restrictions on reporting to tax authorities. The result was a larger number of depositors in postal savings than the population of Japan and a large loss of tax revenue.

This attempt to eliminate tax cheating became known as the green card system under which all savers had to be issued a green card with a unique identification number to be used in the opening of any new tax-qualified savings account. This system would enable the tax authorities to check the total deposits for any household and increase tax revenue. The necessary legislation was incorporated in the 1980 tax reform and was expected to go into effect in 1984. Strong opposition, however, postponed the implementation of the system for 1987. It managed to eliminate it in the tax reform of 1985, but it was finally introduced in the 1987 legislation.

It was also believed that the existing income tax system was unfair. Income from wages and salaries was taxed heavily, while farmers, owners of small businesses, and politicians were cheating heavily. The catchphrase *to-go-san-pin* (10–5–3–1) implied that wage-earners reported 100 percent of their income, small businesses 50 percent, farmers 30 percent, and politicians 1 percent. (See the discussion in Homma, Maeda, and Hashimoto, 1986, pp. 25–26.) This cheating could be reduced by stricter bookkeeping, while the existing unfairness could be eliminated by shifting the weight from direct to indirect taxes. The introduction of the sales tax in 1988 was a move toward this latter direction.

The Administrative Reform Movement and Measures to Balance the Budget

The threat of a potentially big government with higher taxes and more involvement in the economy convinced big business to withdraw its support for growth-oriented policies through deficit spending and to initiate support for administrative reform, small government, and deficit reduction (Shumpei Kumon, 1984, pp. 152, 155).[4] The bond dependency ratio reached a record level of 40 percent in FY 1979, and the Ministry of Finance was planning to reduce deficits by introducing new taxes. Big business was afraid that the new taxes would fall on them, while the beneficiaries from a big government would be small firms and the general public. To protect their interests, they started pressing the Ministry of Finance for administrative reforms and austere fiscal policy. The pressures were coming through Keidanren (the federation of economic organizations), a powerful supporter of big business in Japan, and a number of influential politicians, such as Zenko Suzuki and Yasuhiro Nakasone.

In March 1981 Rinji Gyosei Chosakai (the Ad Hoc Council on Administrative Reform) was established. Its purpose was to review all government activities and to recommend ways of rationalizing government. The Council was headed by Toshio Doko, a business leader and ex-chairman of Keidanren; Keidanren and big business employees largely prepared its reports, with minimum input from government bureaucracy. The main agenda was to reduce the government deficit through fiscal austerity, with a minor emphasis on eliminating government inefficiency. Among the Council's most important recommendations were those to reduce the number of government employees by 5 percent over five years, to revise the social security system, and to privatize three public corporations.[5] The social security system was expected to become a heavy burden in the future, because of the aging population, while one public corporation was already running huge deficits. The annual operating deficit of the Japanese National Railways reached ¥1.7 trillion in FY 1983, and government subsidies covered ¥346 billion of that deficit (Japan National Railways, 1984, p. 123).

By 1982 the number of government employees declined to 1.95 million, from 2.01 million in 1979 (a 3 percent reduction), but the number started rising again and reached 1.99 million by 1985 (Management and Coordination Agency, 1980, p. 51; 1986, p. 73). The growth rate of the government employees' salaries was also cut considerably. The social security system reduced benefits for future recipients in 1985, while the health insurance reform of 1984 reduced the insurance coverage ratio from 100 percent to 90 and the reduction was expected to go down to 80 percent. These reforms were aimed at reducing deficits, but they were not associated with government inefficiency. (An efficient government can run budget deficits, and an inefficient one can have a balanced budget.) Nippon Telegraph and Telephone and Japan Tobacco and Salt were privatized in April 1985 and the Japanese National Railways in the spring of 1987. Government-run services were compared unfavorably with the private sector (Kato, 1984, p. 21), but Nippon Telegraph and Telephone and Japan Tobacco and Salt were consistently generating profits. It was not quite clear, therefore, how their privatization was going to reduce the budget deficit significantly or increase efficiency in the government sector. Public corporations were not included in the general account budget of the central government, and their deficits were financed mainly by borrowing from postal savings through the Fiscal Investment and Loan Program.

Among the other administrative reforms that were implemented during the post–1981 period were the reduction of government support for education, stability in the public works spending programs, and simplification in the procedures for the certification and inspection of manufactured goods. As a result of these policies, the rate of increase in expenditures has fallen significantly since FY 1982 (Noguchi, 1987, p. 211).[6]

The administrative reform movement of the 1980s finally enabled the Ministry of Finance to deal with its main policy objective (the reduction in the size of the government deficits), since its attempt to institute a major new tax in 1979 faced decisive opposition.

Other measures to balance the budget during this period were the Suzuki administration's declaration in 1980 that it would terminate the issuance of deficit-financing bonds by FY 1984. Suzuki's effort turned out to be unsuccessful because of stagnant tax revenues in FY 1981–82.[7] As a result, the Nakasone administration decided to continue the effort by adopting the objective of terminating the issuance of deficit-financing bonds by FY 1990. Indeed, according to the 1990 budget, no additional debt-covering government bonds will be issued in FY 1990, for the first time in sixteen years, in an effort to achieve the current target in the financial reform plan.

Promotion of Productive Investment

The government managed to facilitate promotion of productive investment through a unique system of government-managed financing, the Fiscal Investment and Loan Program (FILP). The principal sources of FILP funds are the substantial net receipts of the government's postal savings and postal insurance systems, and the reserve funds of pensions. The FILP is independent of the General Account Budget and was not subject to the Diet's approval until 1972. The allocation of its funds was not sensitive to political pressures, and they were used exclusively to promote productive investment and economic growth.

The FILP is a byproduct of the balanced budget policy imposed on the Japanese government by the "Dodge line" in 1949. The Japanese government was impelled to terminate subsidies to industry and to balance its budget. Before World War II, subsidies to industry were financed mainly by government bond issues, which were purchased largely by Yokinbu (the Deposit Fund) with funds from postal savings and pension funds. The balanced budget policy eliminated the bond issues and enabled the large amounts of postal savings to flow directly to more than forty government-affiliated agencies[8] for productive investment subsidies and financing. Unyobu Shikin (the Trust Fund) acquired the FILP funds and then preferentially channeled them to heavy and export-oriented industries in the form of low-interest funds through government-affiliated banks such as the Japan Development Bank or the Export-Import Bank of Japan. FILP funds were also channeled to finance the construction of basic infrastructures for economic growth through government-affiliated agencies such as the Japan Highway Corporation and the Japan National Railways. In the early 1950s more than 28 percent of industrial funds were supplied to Japanese industry through FILP channels. In fiscal 1980, the increment of FILP funds allocated to government-affiliated agencies was ¥ 14.9 trillion (almost one-third of the General Account Budget) (Noguchi, 1982, pp. 130–31). (See Table 4.4 for the percentage share of FILP funds to Japanese industry financing from the early 1950s to the mid-1970s.)

Through such financing of productive investment for government and private enterprises, the Japanese government operates like any other financial intermediary. It issues one set of financial liabilities (securities, passbooks, or insurance policies) to the public and uses the proceeds to acquire a different set of financial liabilities—in this case, those of certain government and private enterprises. The net effect of the double transaction is not necessarily to alter the magnitude of aggregate demand, but mainly to change its composition (Ackley and Ishi, 1976, p. 217).

Alterations of fiscal policy in terms of variations in planned expenditure, particularly that financed by the FILP, served as a minor tool of short-run demand management in Japan until the early 1970s. Monetary policy instead played the major short-term role.[9] The Ministry of Finance (MOF) was not feeling any pressure to use fiscal policy for stabilization purposes because it could also dictate the monetary policy of the Bank of Japan (BOJ), which was easier to implement and faster in its impact.[10]

Adjustment of Income Distortions

Income distribution was greatly distorted during the high-growth period. A government attempt to partially adjust for such distortions occasionally took the form of fiscal subsidies to agriculture and small business. These subsidies have been relatively small over the postwar period. The ratio of agriculture-related expenditures to GNP increased during the late 1960s and early 1970s (from 0.31 percent of GNP in 1965 to 0.54 percent of GNP in 1972), but has been falling significantly since then. (It was 0.40 percent of GNP in 1980 and 0.32 percent in 1983.) The subsidies to small and medium firms increased from 0.06 percent of GNP in 1965 to 0.08 percent in 1975 and 0.10 percent in 1982, but they have begun declining thereafter.

The Need for a New Direction in Fiscal Policy

Excess household savings in the postwar period were successfully channeled to the corporate sector for investment and high production purposes. In the mid-1970s, however, the government became a competing source of demand for those funds. By 1978 the government absorbed almost half of household savings. The large household savings have not yet caused any serious economic problems. It is expected, however, that total savings will decrease in the future because of the country's aging population. Such a reduction could result in serious macroeconomic problems and create a need for new reforms in fiscal policy.

MONETARY POLICY

The Bank of Japan

The central banking functions are vested in the Bank of Japan, founded in 1882 and reorganized in 1942 (Suzuki, 1987, pp. 305–34). The Bank is capitalized at 100 million yen, 55 percent of which is contributed by the government and the rest by the private sector. No management participation by stockholders is allowed, and dividends are limited to 5 percent, with the surplus funds (over and above accumulation of reserves) paid to the Treasury. Since 1949 decision making has been vested in the Policy Board; in addition to the governor, the Board has four voting members selected by the cabinet and approved by both houses of the Diet, and two nonvoting members representing the Ministry of Finance and the Economic Planning Agency. The chairman is elected, though customarily the chairman is always the governor. The Ministry of Finance has general powers to issue detailed provisions regarding the objectives, policy, and functioning of the Bank. The Bank generally operates in close cooperation with the government.

Monetary policy objectives are price stability, support of economic growth, and equilibrium in the balance of payments. Until the end of the 1960s, there were no tradeoffs between these objectives. In the period of rapid growth, the Bank and the government followed a stop-and-go policy. Whenever there was a deficit in the balance of payments, it tightened monetary policy, and whenever there was a surplus, the policy was relaxed. By the end of the 1960s, however, monetary inflation and a balance-of-payments surplus began to coexist, creating a need to choose between the goals.

Another qualitative change was that the sole reliance on "window guidance" was eliminated. Other instruments like the discount rate, open market operations, and changes in the reserve requirement played a greater role. As for instruments, the interbank market rates were the only market-responsive interest rates that remained an objective of monetary policy until 1975 when money supply was included in the objectives.

The Exchange Rate Realignment

Toward the end of the high-growth era, the Japanese economy showed a number of contradictions. Even though it had a balance-of-payments deficit as late as 1967, Japan had entered an era of continuous surplus. Overall, surplus

Table 4.3
Inflation in Japan, 1970–88

Year Index	Gross National Expenditure at Constant Prices (GNE)	Percentage Change in GNE	Percentage Change in Wholesale Price Index	Percentage Change in Consumer Price
1970	70,634.5	10.9	14.9	7.7
1971	75,818.4	7.3	-1.0	6.1
1972	82,697.9	9.1	1.6	4.5
1973	90,849.8	9.9	15.7	11.7
1974	89,796.0	-1.2	27.7	24.5
1975	91,968.5	2.4	2.7	11.8
1976	97,499.2	6.0	5.5	9.3
	155,501.8			
1977	163,751.7	5.3	3.4	8.1
1978	172,133.4	5.1	-0.5	3.8
1979	181,136.7	5.2	5.0	3.6
1980	189,787.2	4.7	14.9	7.8
1981	197,462.4	4.0	1.4	4.8
1982	203,908.2	3.1	0.5	2.3
	256,395.2			
1983	264,703.7	3.2	-0.7	1.8
1984	278,140.0	5.1	0.1	2.3
1985	291,806.9	4.9	-0.8	2.0
1986	299,023.9	2.5	-4.7	0.6
1987	312,370.1	4.5	-3.1	0.0
1988	330,098.4	5.7	-0.4	0.7

Sources: *Economic Statistics Manuals*, 1973–89.

Note: GNE = in billions of yen, 1970 to 1976 at constant 1970 prices; 1976 to 1982 at constant 1975 prices; 1982 onward at constant 1980 prices.

hovered around $1 billion from 1968 to 1970 but rose to $7.7 and 4.7 billion in 1971 and 1972, respectively. Another contemporary concern was the emerging divergence between the trend in wholesale prices and that of consumer prices. Because of wide fluctuations in the growth rates, the comparison is very sensitive to the choice of the period. From 1960 to 1964 wholesale prices increased at an average rate of 0.46 percent, while consumer prices increased at the rate of 4.62 percent. During the next quinquennium, the rates were 1.62 and 5.14 percent, respectively, indicating an increase in both rates but no growing divergence. In the two three-year periods, 1966–68 and 1968–70, wholesale prices grew at 1.7 and 2.2 percent, while consumer price inflation increased from 4.7 percent to 6.0 percent. Furthermore, this inflation accelerated in the last three years (see Tables 4.3, 4.4, 4.5, and 4.6 Ohkawa and Rosovsky, 1973, p. 308; Scott et al., 1980, pp. 162, 198; Uchino, 1978, p. 170).

Japanese authorities became concerned about the inflationary trend and decided to enforce a tight monetary policy in September 1969; the discount rate and the reserve ratio were increased, and window guidance was used to restrict the loans to industry. But inflation in wholesale prices was due to the increase in prices

Table 4.4
Growth of the Money Supply in Japan, 1970–88

Year	M1	Percentage Change	M2	Percentage Change
1970	213,595	16.8	542,373	16.9
1971	276,931	29.7	673,982	24.3
1972	345,261	24.7	840,405	24.7
1973	403,115	16.8	981,885	16.8
1974	449,512	11.5	1,094,943	11.5
1975	499,487	11.1	1,253,304	14.5
1976	561,791	12.5	1,422,487	13.4
1977	607,867	8.2	1,580,331	11.1
1978	689,289	13.4	1,787,201	13.1
1979	710,201	3.0	1,937,203	8.3
			1,950,129	9.1
1980	695,727	-2.0	2,089,859	7.2
1981	765,070	10.0	2,320,417	11.0
1982	808,995	5.7	2,504,661	7.9
1983	808,018	-0.1	2,686,928	7.3
1984	863,743	6.9	2,897,142	7.8
1985	889,795	3.0	3,149,388	8.7
1986	982,144	10.4	3,438,875	9.2
1987	1,029,727	4.8	3,808,673	10.0
1988	1,118,440	8.6	4,197,323	10.2

Sources: Economic Statistics Manuals, 1973–89.

Note: Unit for M1 and M2 (M2 + CD from 1979) = 100 million yen.

of imported raw materials at the height of the Vietnam War, and domestic credit tightening did not have the desired effect on prices. Exports began to increase in the second half of 1970 while imports remained flat. This condition contributed to the balance-of-payments surplus. A more effective policy would have been revaluation of the yen which remained at 360 yen per dollar during the postwar years. Unfortunately, the political climate did not make it possible. Monetary policy was relaxed by the fall of 1970 as growth in mining and manufacturing declined substantially and wholesale prices stabilized (Nakamura, 1981, p. 216; Suzuki, 1986, p. 120).

In August 1971, President Nixon announced the New Economic Policy by which the convertibility of U.S. dollars into gold was suspended and tariffs were introduced. The West European countries closed their exchange markets immediately and reopened them only after deciding to float the currencies. The political conviction that any revaluation would lead to a disastrous depression made it politically difficult to revalue the currency, and Japan, unlike European countries, tried to maintain the exchange rate and keep the market open. But the inflow of dollars, about $5 billion in eleven months, made it impractical to continue the policy, and the yen was floated on August 28. The continuing negotiations led to the Smithsonian Agreement which ended with a 16.88 percent upward revaluation of the yen.

Table 4.5
Monetary Policy, Japan, 1970–88

Year	Date	Discount Rate	Year	Date	Discount Rate
1970	01.01	6.25	1979	04.17	4.25
	10.28	6.00		07.24	5.25
1971	01.20	5.75		11.02	6.25
	05.08	5.50	1980	02.19	7.25
	07.28	5.25		03.19	9.00
	12.29	4.75		08.20	8.25
1972	06.24	4.25		11.06	7.25
			1981	03.18	6.25
1973	04.02	5.00		12.11	5.50
	05.30	5.50			
	07.02	6.00	1983	10.2	5.00
	08.29	7.00			
	12.22	9.00	1986	01.30	4.50
				03.10	4.00
1975	04.16	8.50		04.21	3.50
	06.07	8.00		11.01	3.00
	08.13	7.50			
	10.24	6.50	1987	02.23	2.50
1977	03.12	6.00			
	04.19	5.00			
	09.05	4.25			
1978	03.16	3.5			

Sources: *Economic Statistics Manuals*, 1973–89.

In spite of the pessimistic predictions, in 1971 real gross national expenditure (GNE) grew at 7.3 percent, M1 at 30 percent (M2 at slightly lower 24.3 percent), and consumer prices at 6.1 percent, while wholesale prices marginally declined. The strength of the economy was due to the continued growth in exports. Small- and medium-sized firms that depended on exports suffered considerably during this period. Furthermore, Japan's trade balance with the United States increased from $38 million in 1970 to $2,517 the following year (Scott et al., 1980, p. 166). In October 1972 the Japanese government decided to cut the import duty and impose restraints on some exports that showed rapid growth. While exports grew at a lower rate, the increases in gross fixed investment allowed a sizable expansion of the real GNE which grew by 9.1 percent in 1972. Money supply increased at about 25 percent, while prices rose at a moderate rate of 4.5 percent.

In February 1973 the dollar was devalued by 10 percent against Special Drawing Rights, and the yen moved up by 5 percent when floated. Soon the rate moved to 280 yen per dollar, a 22 percent appreciation over two years. Under the impact of the expansionary Tanaka plan (an ambitious plan to rebuild the infrastructure of the country and reorganize the industries) and the worldwide growth of food and raw material prices, inflationary pressures increased in Japan.

Table 4.6
Balance of Payments, Japan, 1970–88

Year	Current Balance	Trade Balance	Long-term Capital (outflow)	Overall Balance
1970	1,970	3,963	1,591	1,374
1971	5,797	7,787	1,082	7,677
1972	6,624	8,971	4,487	4,741
1973	-136	3,688	9,750	-10,074
1974	-4,693	1,436	3,881	-6,839
1975	-682	5,028	272	-2,676
1976	3,680	9,887	984	2,924
1977	10,918	17,311	3,184	7,743
1978	16,534	24,596	12,389	5,950
1979	-8,754	1,845	12,618	16,662
1980	-10,746	2,125	-2,394	-8,396
1981	4,770	19,964	6,449	-2,144
1982	6,850	18,079	14,969	-4,971
1983	20,799	31,454	17,700	5,177
1984	35,003	44,257	49,651	-15,200
1985	49,169	55,986	64,542	-12,318
1986	85,845	92,827	131,461	-44,767
1987	87,015	96,386	136,532	-29,545
1988	79,488	94,789	130,326	-28,982

Sources: *Economics Statistics Manuals*, 1973–89.

Note: Unit = $ million.

There was some hope of moderation in the fall (Uchino, 1983, p. 201), but this hope was shattered by the oil crisis of October. Moreover, the increases in productivity that kept Japanese industries internationally competitive began to slow down while labor costs increased. Unit labor cost increased by 8.7 percent from 1970 to 1973 compared to 2.7 percent during the preceding five years (Lin, 1984, p. 20). The money supply (both M1 and M2) increased by 16.8 percent, but consumer prices increased by 11.7 percent and wholesale prices by 15.7 percent. The discount rate was increased in the first three quarters from 4.25 percent to 7 percent, while window guidance was used to reduce lending by 41 percent. The GNE at constant prices increased at 9.9 percent.

The Two Oil Shocks

The situation worsened in 1974. The increase in oil prices induced an adverse movement in the terms of trade which was estimated to be 25 percent and equivalent to 2.0 percent of the GNP. The adverse change was about twice that of the United States (Lin, 1984, p. 22). Domestic demand declined as a result of a drastic reduction in nonresidential investment and a modest decline in housing. The net effect was that the real GNP declined by 1.2 percent, the first time since the end of the war. Consumer prices increased by 24.5 percent and wholesale prices by 27.7 percent. Both M1 and M2 increased by 11.5 percent. Most disturbing was the trend toward wage increases which amounted to 33 percent. This problem was compounded by the unwillingness of the Japanese industry to reduce labor owing to the commitment to lifetime employment.

The concern about wage cost was behind the caution in relaxing monetary policy in 1975. The discount rate was cut by 0.5 percent in April and June. Further cuts were made only when it became clear that the spring wage offensive had resulted only in an increase of 13.1 percent in basic wages. The discount rate was then cut by another 0.5 percent in August and 0.5 percent in October. Yet at 6.5 percent it was 2 percent above that at the beginning of 1973 (Uchino, 1983, pp. 210–11).

M1 increased by 11 percent and M2 by 14 percent. Consumer price inflation was cut in half, to 11.8 percent, while the decline in the growth rate of wholesale prices to 2.7 percent was even more dramatic. Gross national expenditure increased by 2.4 percent.

The increase in the growth rate of GNE to more than 5 percent in 1976 and 1977 was due mainly to the increase in exports. Components of domestic demand like consumption, government expenditure, and investment grew at a rate lower than that of GNE. In dollar terms, the balance of current transactions moved from a deficit of 682 million in 1975 to a surplus of 3,680 and 10,918 million in 1976 and 1977, respectively. But this was a period of yen appreciation. The average of monthly figures moved from 302.91 yen per dollar in 1972 to 271.14 in 1973; it then increased to 297.25 in 1975 before falling to 266.93 in 1977 and 207.87 in 1978 (Suzuki, 1986, p. 126). The trade friction between Japan and its partners increased during this period as Western nations accused Japan of trying to pull out of the oil recession by an export drive. Japanese writers like Nakamura (1981, p. 240) argue that the appreciating yen created severe economic strains at home. The ratio of current profit to sales remained around 3 percent in Japan compared to 5 percent in the United States (Lin, 1984, p. 29). The Bank of Japan reduced the discount rate three times in 1977. M1 increased by 12.5 and 8.2 percent in 1976 and 1977, while M2 increased by 13.4 and 11.1 percent. Consumer prices increased by 9.3 and 8.1 percent, while wholesale prices increased by 5.5 and 3.4 percent in the two years.

The continuing moderation in wage increases and the growth in productivity led to gradual improvement in economic conditions. In 1978, for the first time after the oil shock, the productivity increase of 8.0 percent exceeded the nominal wage increase of 5.9 percent. Wholesale prices declined, also for the first time since 1971, while the Consumer Price Index rose by a modest 3.8 percent; the discount rate was reduced in steps to the lowest level in postwar years, 3.5 percent. The balance of trade increased by 42 percent to $24,596 million (the current balance by 51 percent to $16,534 million), resulting in a revaluation of the yen. The economy continued to grow by 5.2 percent.

The second oil shock at the end of 1978 added uncertainty to this situation. However, it is now conceded that the Japanese economy absorbed the second shock better than the first one and was more stable in terms of prices and output than the U.S. economy. This state of affairs should be attributed largely to the cost rationalization after the first shock. Unit labor cost, after a decline in 1978, increased by 2.9 percent and 0.9 percent in the next two years, compared to 8.2 and 11.1 percent increases in the United States (Lin, 1984, p. 58). The monetary policy was gradually tightened during the year by increases in the discount rate to 6.25 percent in 1979 and then to 9.0 percent by mid-1980. Thereafter, the rate was reduced, attaining 7.25 by the end of the year. Window guidance was used to reduce loans in 1979. The deregulation of the financial markets began in earnest. Wholesale prices increased by 5 and 14.9 percent in the two years, but the inflation rate was much lower than after the first oil shock. Consumer prices increased even less (3.6 and 7.7 percent). But the trade balance declined substantially to around $2 billion. The economy sustained the 5 percent growth rate.

The Japanese Economy After Financial Deregulation

Although financial deregulation had begun in the 1970s, the passage of the Foreign Exchange and Foreign Trade Control Act at the end of 1980 can be taken as a watershed. It established the general principle that external transactions should not be regulated for influencing the exchange rate. In the aftermath of this legislation and related administrative measures, the inflow and outflow of capital achieved historic heights. The exchange rate was less influenced by the current account and more responsive to capital movements. Moreover, interest rate arbitrage began to be more effective. These liberalization measures remained in spite of the economic weaknesses of the early years of the new decade.

In 1980 and 1981 consumption increased modestly at the rate of about 1 percent. In 1980 imports and exports in dollar values increased at 25 percent. The following year, exports increased by 17 percent, but imports increased at a lower rate, reestablishing the growth in trade surplus. The increase in the discount rate which began with the second oil shock continued in the first part of 1980 when it reached 9 percent. It was lowered to 7.25 percent by the end of that year and to 5.5 percent by the close of the following year. M1 decreased in 1980, while M2 + CD increased by 7.2 percent. In 1981 both increased by about 10 percent. The growth of GNE declined from 4.7 percent in 1980 to 4.0 in 1981.

The picture was even bleaker in 1982. Even though consumption and capital formation picked up, exports in dollar terms contributed to the low growth rate cited earlier. After declining in 1978, the average exchange rate of the yen per dollar had increased by 20 percent by 1982 (Suzuki, 1986, p. 126). Even though wage increases were moderate, the lower growth in productivity contributed to a 1.7 percent increase in costs (OECD, 1984, p. 20). Inflation further moderated, as did the growth in the two measures of money.

The growth rate hardly increased in 1983. The growth rate in consumption moderated, whereas investment in real terms decreased as firms completed the post–shock moderation. Exports in dollar terms increased by 5.7 percent, and imports continued to decline. The discount rate was reduced to 5 percent. M1 declined marginally while M2 + CD increased by 7 percent. Net outflow of capital as inflow and outflow increased under the financial liberalization.

The growth rate recovered to 5.1 percent in 1984 under a double-digit growth in exports. The export growth reflected the boom in the United States and marginally exceeded the growth of exports of the OECD nations. Responding to the expansion of exports, domestic capital formation made a more modest recovery while consumption increased by only 3 percent. The two measures of money supply increased by 7 percent. The wholesale price was flat while the Consumer Price Index rose by 2.3 percent. The balance of trade increased by 40 percent, and current balances rose by about 70 percent. Net outflow of long-term capital increased by 181 percent, reflecting the internationalization of financial institutions.

The growth rate moderated in 1985. Exports increased less than in the previous year, but imports decreased, leading to a further improvement of the balance of trade. From the end of 1979 to the end of 1985 exports in dollar terms grew at a compound rate of 9 percent. This revived the criticism that foreign trade is the engine of growth for Japan. M1 increased by 3 percent, while M2 + CD began to grow faster than in the past three years. Inflation remained at a modest level of 2 percent.

The year 1986 is generally characterized as miserable for Japan's economy. GNE grew at only 2.5 percent, which is lower than in any period other than the years of the oil shocks. The appreciation of the yen reversed the export-oriented boom of the previous two years. Consumer price increases moderated to 0.6 percent, while wholesale prices decreased. The money supply increased by 10 percent, and the discount rate decreased to 3 percent.

Because of government efforts to stimulate domestic demand, the growth rate recovered to 4.5 in 1987. Prime Minister Takeshita sought to implement the Mayekawa Report of 1987. The growth in real consumption increased from 2.7 percent in 1984 and 1985 to 4.2 percent in 1987. The Louvre Accord sought to limit the appreciation of yen. The discount rate was reduced to a low of 2.5 percent.

The stock market crash of 1986 did not lead to the feared recession, and economic growth recovered in 1988 to above the 5 percent level. Reflecting the increases in imports, the trade balance decreased for the first time since the oil shock. M1 and M2 increased at 8.6 and 10.2 percent, while consumer prices increased less than 1 percent.

These developments show that the Japanese economy recovered quickly from the yen appreciation shock, as it did from the oil shocks. Although the growth rate of 4.4 percent in the last four years is greater than the 3.85 percent in the previous four years, the possibility of a downward drift in the growth rate cannot be excluded. Meanwhile, a marginal increase in the growth rate of money supply can be noted. In the five years since the money supply was included among the monetary objectives, M2 increased by 9.46 percent; in the next five years, M2 + CD increased by 8.24 percent, and during the next four years, it increased by 9.25 percent. The decline of wholesale prices with the strengthening of the yen and the increases in productivity kept the price increases at historic lows. This situation has suggested to many observers that Japan can sustain its growth through stimulation of internal demand.

TRADE AND EXCHANGE-RATE POLICIES

Trade Policies

After the postwar industrial reconstruction, the political assumption emerged that unlimited industrial expansion must be Japan's first priority. No essential political decision to change the priority of unlimited industrial expansion has been made since this period. The industrialists continue to expand their market shares, enter new markets with the help of the bureaucrats, and are kept in line by their peers (van Wolferen, 1987, pp. 290–91).

In the early decades after World War II, Japan became accustomed to protecting infant industries and nursing them to international competitive standards. Japanese industrial-sector associations found ways to work with officials in setting standards, allowing fees for pharmaceutical and medical products, restricting procurements of foreign products, and delaying the entry of such goods until domestic markets could make competitive products. Until the 1970s they made it virtually impossible for foreigners to own their own subsidiaries in Japan or to have even indirect economic control over firms in that country. They established vertical linkages between companies that made it very difficult for foreign companies to penetrate Japanese markets even when foreign products had competitive advantages. Japanese officials found ways to slow down the approval process for competitive foreign products because they were convinced that these practices remained in Japan's interest. The Japanese had learned these rules as played by the West since many countries had controlled imports in pursuit of national goals (Vogel, 1986, p. 760).

During this period, Japan's neomercantilistic policies centered on export promotion to acquire needed resources. The problem with this policy in the 1970s and 1980s was not that Japan's exports were more than its imports, but that its exports systematically undermined Western industries. Japan's practices became known as ''adversarial trade'' and were distinguished from ''competitive trade'' whereby a country also imports manufactures of the same kind as it exports. As a result of international friction, since the early 1970s many formal barriers to trade in Japan have been gradually removed. Today the Japanese genuinely believe that they are as open to competitive foreign trade as other powers. They believe that they have fewer tariffs than most other nations and that the ones they do have are among the world's lowest. In their view, the European Economic Community has more barriers than Japan; even the United States has far more barriers than most Americans know about, including various state regulations that make importing difficult.

Japan's unique factor endowments along with trade friction and saturation of commodity markets for standardized consumer products have resulted in drastic changes in its competitive strategy and pattern of trade during the last twenty-five years. Its practical policy choices were to preserve existing jobs and industries within saturated markets and international hostilities, or to move capital and labor to higher value added and more competitive production. The concept of comparative advantage in Japanese trade policy is understood not as a fact of static natural endowments but as an ever-changing quality of social organization and choice over time. It is less a matter of given endowments and more a matter of chosen investments. With this understanding, Japan decided and managed to choose its present comparative advantage. By investing, developing, and deploying human capital, it strategically acquired a comparative advantage in skill-intensive production processes. Its commitment to basic steel, basic petrochemicals, shipbuilding, and simple fibers has been reduced and replaced by capacity expansion in high value added specialized segments of old and new industries. Since technologies are changing rapidly, Japan encourages firms to leapfrog to the next product generation and establish a leading position there. Firms that leapfrog to the next product generation enjoy government subsidies but eliminate the government's need to protect them against imports of the product they aim to surpass.

Japan's success in high-technology products such as consumer electronics, semiconductors, and precision instruments reflect the country's present endowments in skilled labor and its shortages of arable land, oil, coal, gas, and natural resources. Investments in education, training, and group learning define Japan's present comparative advantage and determine the speed and efficiency with which new products are developed and brought to international markets. In the twenty years from 1966 to 1986 real expenditure on R&D grew in Japan at an average annual rate of 8.3 percent (Grossman, 1989). The ratio of current R&D expenditures to GDP grew from 1.55 percent in 1965 to 2.07 percent in 1975 and to 2.61 percent in 1985 (OECD, 1987). During this period, Japan developed extensive capability in industrial innovation. As a result, Japanese researchers seem especially adept at improving the quality of existing products and developing entirely new products for the international markets (Okimoto and Saxonhouse, 1987). Empirical evidence supports the growing importance of R&D in explaining Japan's pattern of trade (Balassa and Noland, 1989).

Exchange-Rate Policies

Japanese authorities have actively intervened in the foreign exchange market in response to exchange-rate movements since World War II. Even under the regime of flexible exchange rates, Japan was unable to leave exchange-rate determination completely to market forces because the flexible exchange rate turned out to be another parameter to be controlled in managing the domestic economy. The main policy measures taken in response to exchange-rate movements have been: (1) discount rate adjustments (Hutchison, 1988), (2) capital controls (Fukao and Okina, 1989; Takagi, 1988), and (3) market intervention (Takagi, 1989).

Adjustments of the discount rate in Japan have been a response to exchange-rate movements in addition to domestic developments. After the shift into the floating exchange-rate regime, in early 1973 the yen began to depreciate. During that year the official discount rate increased gradually from 4.25 percent to 9 percent. The value of the yen was stabilized in 1975 and started appreciating from 1976 to 1978. During this period the discount rate was gradually reduced from 9 percent in 1975 to 3.5 percent in March 1978. From 1979 to 1984 the yen was depreciating and the discount rate increasing. It reached 9 percent by March 1980, but then it started declining in response mainly to domestic considerations (Komiya and Suda, 1983). From 1985 to 1987 the yen kept appreciating, and it remained strong in 1988. During this period the discount rate continued to decline, and by February 1987 it reached 2.5 percent. It remained at this rate until 1989. In 1989 the yen started depreciating and the discount rate increasing. By October 1989 it reached 3.75 percent.

Capital controls have been occasionally used as an instrument of exchange-rate management. Following the depreciation of the yen in 1973, the Japanese authorities liberalized the Japanese financial markets in August 1974. As a result, they managed to encourage capital inflows by allowing foreigners to acquire Japanese securities. Following the appreciation of the yen in 1976, the authorities discouraged capital inflows by setting a 50 percent reserve requirement on the free yen accounts of nonresidents in November 1977 and by raising it to 100 percent by March 1978. At the same time they disallowed the purchase of short-term government securities by nonresidents and restricted the acquisition of Japanese securities by foreigners. Following the depreciation of the yen in 1978, the authorities reversed in February 1979 the restrictions on acquisition of Japanese securities by foreigners and free yen accounts owned by foreigners.

Capital controls as an instrument of exchange-rate management lost their importance with the revision of the Foreign Exchange and Foreign Trade Control Law in December 1980 which liberalized foreign exchange transactions.

With respect to intervention, the authorities followed a policy of "leaning against the wind" by selling foreign exchange when the yen depreciated and purchasing foreign exchange when the yen appreciated (Hutchison, 1984, 1988; Ito, 1987, 1989; Quirk, 1977; Takagi, 1989). When we examine the period of flexible exchange rates (1973–90), we see that the authorities were a net purchaser of foreign exchange as a result of the secular appreciation of the yen.

The Japanese yen began to depreciate in early 1973, dropping from 265 yen to the dollar in 1973 to 300 yen to the dollar by late 1974. In an effort to support the yen, the Bank of Japan kept selling dollars heavily until the middle of October 1973 and sporadically during 1974 (Fukao and Okina, 1989; Komiya and Suda,

1983; Quirk, 1977). From early 1976 to early 1978 the yen began to appreciate, but the Bank of Japan limited intervention to smoothing operations following the agreements of the Group of Seven (G–7) countries in June 1976. The yen began depreciating again in late 1978 and kept declining until early 1985. Although the general attitude of the Bank of Japan during this period was to support the yen, the most significant intervention was in the spring and fall of 1979 (Ohta, 1982). Following the Plaza Agreement in September 1985, the yen kept appreciating until early 1989. As a response, the Bank of Japan kept purchasing dollars with massive-scale interventions in October 1985, through December 1987. Honoring the Louvre Accord of February 1987, the Bank of Japan kept buying dollars during 1988 and 1989 in support not only of the yen but also of the dollar. With agreements such as the Louvre Accord, the Bank of Japan has committed itself to implement systematic currency stabilization in coordination with the central banks of five other countries after more than a decade of uncharted floating exchange rates. Its intervention now will have to be more important and systematic.

THE REGULATORY PROCESS

Regulation is usually understood as a process of curtailing or promoting business activities that are associated with detrimental or beneficial externalities. This makes regulation in many countries an adversarial process, with government officials casting themselves as "regulatory czars" and business representatives as "crying wolves" that always resist regulatory measures. In Japan the regulatory process should be understood as slightly different.

Policies in Japan evolve from intense formal and informal consultations between a ministry and the industrial sectors affected by the policy. Policymaking is a process of consensus formulation coordinated by a ministry. A Japanese tradition of close cooperation between government officials and the business sector goes back to the samurai–merchants relationship in feudal times. This attitude of cooperation makes the regulatory setting and enforcing a friendly and meaningful process rather than an adversarial process where government agencies regulate in isolation, without any input from the industry, and then attempt to impose their regulatory rules against the will of the private sector. The "cooperative" paradigm in Japan works through informal meetings (hearings) between regulatory agencies and industry representatives. The attempt in those meetings is to identify priorities and to achieve consensus between group representatives regarding national goals to be served by proposed regulations. Such attitudes reflect Japan's cultural emphases on self-denial, aversion to conflict, and the primacy of the welfare of the group or community over that of the individual (Pharr and Badaracco, 1988).

Take, for example, the post–World War II history of environmental regulation. During the 1950s and early 1960s environmental regulation was not a national goal. Both government and industry were convinced that their first priority was to promote economic growth, not the environment. The general consensus was to sponsor rather than regulate production. As a result, environmental regulation was collusively avoided. The environment became a national priority issue in Japan in the late 1960s. As a result, the Japanese Environmental Agency was established in July 1971 to coordinate government initiatives on pollution control. Environmental regulations (pollution standards) were slowly introduced; today industry representatives in cooperation with government officials have fully recognized that pollution control is not only unavoidable but also desirable.

This process of interaction enables the government's visible hand to be continuously in touch with the market's invisible hand and permits the government to adopt market-conforming policies. We can safely argue that the main characteristic of Japan's regulatory policies has been their sensitivity to market signals and their discipline to those signals. For example, the policy objectives aim not only to establish favorable conditions for investment, growth, and international competitiveness, but also to slow down investment and growth for industries with saturated markets and high social costs. Government officials have been guided by considerations of economic efficiency, and their policies were in anticipation of market developments.

INDUSTRIAL POLICIES

By industrial policies in Japan, we refer to the policies and methods used by government agencies to increase the productivity of factor inputs and to influence the investment (and disinvestment) decisions of industry (Eads and Yamamura, 1987).

The main industrial policy instruments have been direct industry-specific subsidies and tax incentives, tariffs, de jure and de facto exemptions from antitrust statutes, and various labor market adjustments. One of the most powerful tools, especially during the 1950s and early 1960s, has been the direct control of a large share of national savings by the Ministry of Finance (MOF) and its ability to ration credit. The MOF has direct control over the national postal savings system, and it is rationing postal savings through its Fiscal Investment and Loan Program (FILP). (See Table 4.7.) In addition, in the past it managed to adopt, in cooperation with the Bank of Japan, a "sub-equilibrium interest rate disequilibrium policy" that kept interest rates artificially low and necessitated credit rationing as a result of the excess demand for loanable funds. Another policy instrument has been the power of the Ministry of International Trade and Industry (MITI) to allocate foreign exchange selectively among firms that required imported raw materials and foreign technology. Credit rationing by the MOF and foreign exchange control by MITI enabled the government to direct the flow of national savings and international currency to priority production industries for the achievement of industrial policy goals.

The industrial policies of the 1950s were designed to stimulate fixed investment in important industries through government preferential financing, tax allowances

Table 4.7
Sources of Funds to Industry (percentage share)

	1952–55	1956–60	1961–65	1966–70	1971–75
All Industries					
Capital Market	11.9	21.6	17.8	11.2	12.2
Private banks	59.8	60.7	66.4	73.7	74.2
FILP	28.3	17.7	15.8	15.1	13.7
Four Basic Industries					
Capital Market	6.5	24.9			
Private banks	56.3	53.8			
FILP	37.2	21.3			

Source: A. Ishikawa and T. Gyoten, *Zaiseitoyushi (the FILP), Kinyu Zaisei Jijo* (Tokyo, 1977).

for accelerated depreciation, and special reserve funds for losses due to investment. Industry-specific acts were introduced for petrochemicals (1955), heavy
machines and automobiles (1955), electronics (1957), synthetic rubber (1957),
and aircraft (1958) (Sekiguchi, 1986). At the same time imports were under the
foreign exchange quota system, and tariff escalation was built into the import
tariffs to eliminate international competition in domestic markets.

During the 1960s industrial policies became more selective following MITI's
strategy of heavy and chemical industrialization. Labor-intensive exports, such
as textile products and sundries, were replaced by capital-intensive exports, such
as steel, ships, and electric appliances. In an effort to reinforce international
competitiveness, in 1961 the government announced a liberalization program
for foreign trade and exchange.

The two oil crises of the 1970s necessitated adjustment assistance policies for
refineries, petrochemicals, synthetic fibers, shipbuilding, aluminum firms, and
other declining industries. As a result, MITI organized cartels to scrap excess
capacity; it subsidized capital and labor reallocation, and it protected declining
industries against import competition when factor prices were rigid. In the past,
at the initiative of MITI, adjustment assistance was provided to coal and sulfur
mining and textile manufacturing. In 1978 the Act for Temporary Measures to
Stabilize Specified Structurally Depressed Industries (SDI Act of 1978) was
introduced to provide credit guarantees to firms that dispose of equipment to
reduce capacity and enable manufacturers to form legal cartels to reduce production and capital equipment jointly (Sekiguchi, 1986).

In the late 1970s and during the 1980s industrial policies were oriented toward
managing Voluntary Export Restraint (VER) and promoting R&D investment
for the expansion of frontier industries.

In the 1950s and 1960s the political consensus among all government agencies
was favoring rapid economic growth over all other goals. In the early 1970s,
however, MITI announced a transformation of policy goals from the pursuit of
maximum economic growth to the utilization of economic growth to improve
social and economic performance. It also underlined its intentions to promote a
shift from a capital-intensive, energy-intensive, and environmentally destructive
industrial structure to a knowledge-intensive, energy-conservative, and environmentally sound structure. Market liberalization and international cooperation
have been among the most recently emphasized goals of industrial policy in
Japan (Uekusa, 1987).

NOTES

1. Domestic investment during this period was constrained by the size of domestic
savings. Borrowings of foreign capital were limited because of the overvalued yen
(¥360 = $1 under the Bretton Woods system) and the recurring current-account deficits.
As a result, low government spending, relative to GNP, favored private investment and
economic growth.

2. The main components of the social security system in Japan are public assistance, social insurance, and other welfare programs. The most important component for fiscal policy purposes is the social insurance system which consists of health insurance, public pensions, and unemployment compensation. For a more detailed explanation of the social insurance system in Japan, see Social Insurance Agency, *Outline of Social Insurance in Japan* (Tokyo: Yoshida Finance and Social Security Law Institute, 1981).

3. New programs providing free medical care for the aged and subsidies for expensive medical treatments have been introduced. In addition, health insurance for the self-employed was 50 percent subsidized in the past, and now the subsidy is 75 percent. With regard to the public pension programs, they were offering only 20 percent of the average salary as old-age benefits until 1973; then the ratio of benefits increased to 43 percent with an indexation provision for inflation. The social security system has improved significantly since 1973 because of a growing awareness of the quality of life and because of changes in local politics. (Socialist-communist coalitions gained control of many local governments.)

4. Some forecasts were anticipating government spending to become 60 percent of GNP by the year 2010 because of the aging population and large social security payments. Overtime the government, instead of reducing its weight, was becoming hypertrophous by accumulating liabilities and deficits.

5. These corporations were the Nippon Telegraph and Telephone, the Japanese National Railways, and Japan Tobacco and Salt.

6. The rate of increase in general expenditures (the total budget minus debt-servicing costs and grants-in-aid to local governments) fell to 1.8 percent in FY 1982, to zero in FY 1983, and then to −0.1 percent in FY 1984.

7. For example, the bond dependency ratio, instead of falling, rose in FY 1982 from the initial budget level of 21.0 percent to 30.2 percent at the supplementary budget stage.

8. The most well-known agencies are the Japan Development Bank, the Export-Import Bank of Japan, the Small Business Finance Corporation, the Japan Highway Corporation, and the Japan National Railways.

9. Most Japanese recessions have been the direct and deliberate result of monetary policy actions taken to slow down a rate of growth considered too fast because it has created or threatened to create balance-of-payments problems. When a recession has sufficiently redressed the payments imbalance, monetary policy is shifted toward ease, encouraging growth to resume at its own pace until the need for restriction again becomes clear.

10. The Ministry of Finance is responsible for the overall character of Japan's fiscal policy. The MOF's Budget Bureau, along with the Tax Bureau, prepares the government's expenditure budget and forecasts the government's receipts. The MOF also prepares the FILP and makes plans for bond issues. The entire package is submitted first to the cabinet and then to the Diet to secure their approval. The Bank of Japan is responsible for the monetary policy, but the MOF is always aware of and largely dictates the character of both monetary and fiscal policy in Japan.

REFERENCES

Ackley, Gerdner, and Hiromitsu Ishi (1976). "Fiscal, Monetary, and Related Policies." In *Asia's New Giant: How the Japanese Economy Works*, edited by Hugh Patric and Henry Rosovsky. Washington, D.C.: Brookings Institution.

Allen, G. C. (1965). *Japan's Economic Expansion*. London: Oxford University Press.

Balassa, Bela, and Marcus Noland (1989). "The Changing Comparative Advantage of Japan and the United States." *Journal of the Japanese and International Economics* 3: 174–88.

Bank of Japan (Annual). *Economic Statistics Manual*. Tokyo: Bank of Japan.

Bieda, K. (1970). *The Structure and Operation of the Japanese Economy*. Sydney: Australasia; Wiley.

Cargill, Thomas F., and Shoichi Royama (1988). *The Transition of Finance in Japan and the United States*. Stanford, Calif.: Hoover Institution Press.

Eads, George C., and Yamamura Kozo (1987). "The Future of Industrial Policy." In *The Political Economy of Japan*, Vol. 1, edited by Yamamura Kozo and Yasuba Yasukichi: 423–68. Stanford, Calif.: Stanford University Press.

Fukao, Mitsuhiro, and Kunio Okina (1989). "Internationalization of Financial Markets and Balance of Payments Imbalances: A Japanese Perspective." Carnegie-Rochester Conference Series on Public Policy 30: 167–220 (Spring).

Garin–Painter, Mary (1970). "Public Expenditure Trends." *OECD Economic Outlook*: *Occasional Studies* (July).

Grossman, Gene M. (1989). "Explaining Japan's Innovation and Trade: A Model of Quality Competition and Dynamic Comparative Advantage." National Bureau of Economic Research, Working Paper No. 3194.

Homma, M., T. Maeda, and K. Hashimoto (1986). "The Japanese Tax System." Brookings Discussion Papers in Economics (June).

Hutchison, Michael M. (1984). "Official Japanese Intervention in Foreign Exchange Markets: Leaning Against the Wind?" *Economics Letters* 15: 115–20.

Hutchison, Michael M. (1988). "Monetary Control with an Exchange Rate Objective: The Bank of Japan, 1973–86." *Journal of International Money and Finance* 7: 261–71 (September).

Ito, Takatoshi (1987). "The Intradaily Exchange Rate Dynamics and Monetary Policies after the Group of Five Agreement." *Journal of the Japanese and International Economies* 1: 275–98 (September).

Ito, Takatoshi (1989). "Was There a Target Zone?" In *Monetary Reforms: Introducing the Target Zone*. Tokyo: Japan Center for International Finance: 27–40 (June).

Japan, Ministry of Welfare, Actuarial Division (1981). *Neinkin to Zaisei* [Financing public pensions]. Tokyo: Shakai Hoken Hoki Kenkyukai.

Japan Economic Journal (1989). Tokyo.

Japan National Railways (1984). *Kokutetsu Tokei Daijiesuto: Tetsudo Yoran, 1984* [National Railways Statistical Digest: Railways Survey, 1984].

Kato, Hirochi (1984). "Fiscal Reform Comes First." *Japan Echo* 11 (Winter).

Komiya, Ryutaro, and Miyako Suda (1983). *Gendai Kokusai Kinyuron* [Contemporary international finance]. Tokyo: Nihon Keizai Shinbunsha.

Lin, Ching-yuan (1984). *Japanese and U.S. Inflation*. Lexington, Mass.: Lexington Books.

Management and Coordination Agency (1980 and 1986). *Japan Statistical Yearbook*.

Nakamura, Takafusa (1981). *The Postwar Japanese Economy*. Tokyo: University of Tokyo Press.

Noguchi, Yukio (1982). "The Government-Business Relationship in Japan: The Changing Role of Fiscal Policy Resources." In *Policy and Trade Issues of the Japanese*

Economy: American and Japanese Perspectives, edited by Kozo Yamamura. Seattle: University of Washington Press.

Noguchi, Yukio (1987). "Public Finance." In Vol. 1 of *The Political Economy of Japan*, edited by Kozo Yamamura and Yasuba Yasukichi. Stanford, Calif.: Stanford University Press.

OECD (1984). *Economic Survey: Japan 1983–84*. Paris: OECD.

OECD (1987). "Total Factor Productivity." *OECD Economic Outlook* 42: 39–48.

Ohkawa, Kazushi, and Henry Rosovsky (1973). *Japanese Economic Growth*. Stanford, Calif.: Stanford University Press.

Ohta, Takeshi (1982). "Exchange-Rate Management and the Conduct of Monetary Policy." In *Central Bank Views on Monetary Targeting*, edited by P. Meek. New York: Federal Reserve Bank of New York, pp. 126–31.

Okimoto, Daniel I., and Gary R. Saxonhouse (1987). "Technology and the Future of the Economy." In *The Political Economy of Japan*, edited by K. Yamamura and Y. Yasuda. Vol. 1: *The Domestic Transformation*. Stanford, Calif.: Stanford University Press.

Pharr, Susan J., and Joseph L. Badaracco, Jr. (1988). "Coping with Crisis: Environmental Regulation." in *America Versus Japan*, edited by Thomas K. McCraw. Cambridge, Mass.: Harvard Business School Press.

Quirk, Peter J. (1977). "Exchange Rate Policy in Japan: Leaning Against the Wind." *IMF Staff Papers* 24: 642–64 (November).

Schiffer, Hubert F. (1962). *The Modern Japanese Banking System*. New York: University Publishers.

Scott, Bruce R., John W. Rosenblum, and Audrey T. Sproat (1980). *Case Studies in Political Economy: Japan 1854–1977*. Boston: Research Division, Harvard Business School.

Sekiguchi, Sueo (1986). "Industrial Policy in Japan: Interactions Between Policies and Dualist Structure." In *Japan's Response to Crisis and Change in the World Economy*, edited by Michele Schmiegelow. Armonk, N.Y.: M. E. Sharpe.

Shumpei Kumon (1984). "Japan Faces Its Future: The Political Economics of Administrative Reform." *Journal of Japanese Studies* 10 (Winter).

Social Insurance Agency (1981). *Outline of Social Insurance in Japan*. Tokyo: Yoshida Finance and Social Security Law Institute.

Suzuki, Yoshio (1980). *Money and Banking in Contemporary Japan*. New Haven, Conn.: Yale University Press.

Suzuki, Yoshio (1986). *Money, Finance, and Macroeconomic Performance in Japan*. New Haven, Conn.: Yale University Press.

Suzuki, Yoshio (1987). *The Japanese Financial System*. Oxford: Clarendon Press.

Takagi, Shinji (1988). "Recent Developments in Japan's Bond Money Markets." *Journal of the Japanese and International Economies* 2: 63–91 (March).

Takagi, Shinji (1989). "Foreign Exchange Market Intervention and Domestic Monetary Control in Japan, 1973–89." *IMF Working Papers* 89/101 (December).

Tsuru, Shigeto (1955). "Business Cycles in Post-war Japan." In *The Business Cycle in the Post-war World*, edited by Erik Lundberg. London: Macmillan.

Tsuru, Shigeto (1958). *Essays on Japanese Economy*. Tokyo: Kinokuniya.

Uekusa, Masu (1987). "Industrial Organization: The 1970s to the Present." In *The Political Economy of Japan*, Vol. 1, edited by Yamamura Kozo and Yasuba Yasukichi. Stanford, Calif.: Stanford University Press, pp. 469–515.

Viner, Aron (1988). *Inside Japanese Financial Markets*. Homewood, Ill.: Dow Jones-Irwin, Inc.

Vogel, Ezra F. (1986). "Pax Nipponica?" *Foreign Affairs*: 752–67 (Spring).

Ward, Robert E. (1967). *Japan's Political System*. Englewood Cliffs, N.J.: Prentice-Hall.

Wolferen van, Karel G. (1987). "The Japan Problem." *Foreign Affairs*: 288–303 (Winter).

Zeisei Chosakai (1977). *Kongo no Zeisei no Arikata ni Tsuite no Toshin*.

5

NATIONAL ECONOMIC POLICIES IN OTHER MAJOR OECD COUNTRIES: AUSTRIA, SWEDEN, CANADA, AND AUSTRALIA

Eduard Hochreiter and Aurel Schubert

INTRODUCTION

The countries analyzed in this chapter are small, open, and, with one exception, highly industrialized. Therefore, they are closely integrated into the world economy without being able to exert influence on global trends. An attempt is made in each subsection to describe relative size and openness as well as the development of important economic indicators.

In view of the continuing liberalization, deregulation, and globalization trends, it is expected that economic (and most likely political) integration will significantly expand further in the years to come. Accordingly, economic interdependence will become even closer.

For the management of economic power in small countries, the assumed developments depicted above imply that the structure of domestic economic power can only influence the adjustment path taken, but not increase or reduce international influences over the longer term.

In this context the relative power of fiscal and monetary authorities is decisive. If two targets (internal and external equilibrium) are to be achieved, two independent instruments (fiscal and monetary policy) are required according to the Meade-Tinbergen theorem. However, this principle will apply only if both policies are implemented in an independent way. This will be the more likely the greater the autonomy of the central bank from the government. We will therefore emphasize the relationship between the central bank and the government.

Regulatory and industrial policies may, in a sense, be seen as subsets of the domain of fiscal policy. An analysis of these policies will therefore be restricted to the essentials.

Table 5.1
Selected Economic Indicators, Austria, 1970–89

YEAR	GDP REAL %	CPI %	EXPORTS REAL %	IMPORTS REAL %	CURRENT ACCOUNT % OF GDP	GOVERNMENT DEFICIT % OF GDP
1970	6.4	4.4	7.8	18.6	- .4	- .6
1971	5.1	4.7	3.6	8.4	- .5	- .4
1972	6.2	6.3	11.9	14.8	- .7	- .3
1973	4.9	7.5	8.3	9.5	-1.0	-1.3
1974	3.9	9.5	15.8	5.8	-1.4	-1.9
1975	- .4	8.4	- 9.1	- 9.3	- .5	-4.5
1976	4.6	7.3	15.9	24.1	-2.6	-4.6
1977	4.4	5.5	3.3	9.6	-4.4	-3.8
1978	.5	3.6	7.3	- 2.7	-1.1	-4.2
1979	4.7	3.7	9.5	10.1	-1.5	-3.5
1980	3.0	6.3	2.7	5.3	-2.1	-2.9
1981	- .1	6.8	6.2	- 3.9	-2.0	-2.6
1982	1.1	5.4	.6	- 2.3	1.1	-4.1
1983	2.2	3.3	4.1	7.4	.3	-5.5
1984	1.3	5.7	12.3	11.6	- .3	-4.5
1985	2.6	3.2	12.1	3.3	- .2	-4.5
1986	1.4	1.7	- 3.5	3.9	.3	-5.1
1987	1.5	1.4	3.0	5.3	- .2	-4.7
1988	4.2	1.9	6.9	7.7	- .4	-4.2
1989	3.5	2.8			- .4	-4.0

Sources: International Monetary Fund, *International Financial Statistics*; Organization for Economic Cooperation and Development, Main Economic Indicators; and National Sources.

THE MANAGEMENT OF ECONOMIC POWER IN AUSTRIA

Austria in the World Economy

Austria's economy[1] is small, open, and highly industrialized. It covers an area of 84,000 square kilometers and counts 7.5 million inhabitants. Per capita income in 1987 totaled U.S. $15,500. Austria is closely integrated into the world economy. The share of exports and imports of goods and services in GDP amounts to 40 percent each. The geographical distribution of trade has an important bearing on Austrian politics. The EC takes two-thirds of all Austrian goods exports and accounts for even more of Austria's imports. With 35 percent of total exports and 45 percent of total imports, Germany is by far the most important trading partner. To these already high figures we have to add foreign tourist receipts. They amount to some 7 percent of GDP. Roughly two-thirds of the tourists come from Germany and about 90 percent from EC countries.

Because of current liberalization and deregulation trends, the degree of integration, especially in the financial sphere, will significantly expand in the years to come.[2] The appreciable rise of the share of foreign business in the banks' balance sheet totals from 9.5 percent in 1970 to 25 percent in 1987 gives us some indication about the change in financial sector integration over time.

Table 5.2
Selected Economic Indicators, Austria, 1970–89

YEAR	POPULATION (MILLIONS)	EXPORTS AS % OF GDP	IMPORTS AS % OF GDP	EXPORTS GOODS & SERVICES US$	IMPORTS GOODS & SERVICES US$	GDP BILL US$	GDP PER HEAD US$
1970	7.5	20.0	24.9	29.8	30.4	14	1957
1971	7.5	19.2	25.2	30.0	30.6	16	2252
1972	7.5	19.1	25.4	29.8	30.3	20	2769
1973	7.6	19.3	25.5	30.8	31.4	27	3684
1974	7.6	22.9	28.2	34.1	34.2	33	4394
1975	7.6	20.4	25.0	33.1	33.3	37	4969
1976	7.6	21.4	28.7	34.0	36.5	40	5336
1977	7.6	20.7	29.7	33.8	38.1	48	6364
1978	7.6	21.4	27.6	33.5	36.7	58	7672
1979	7.5	22.9	29.5	37.8	39.5	68	9101
1980	7.5	22.7	31.5	40.7	42.9	76	10182
1981	7.6	24.1	31.5	43.3	45.4	66	8771
1982	7.6	23.6	29.1	43.1	42.0	66	8778
1983	7.6	23.2	28.9	41.6	41.1	66	8857
1984	7.6	25.4	31.5	43.8	44.1	63	8451
1985	7.6	27.4	32.2	46.2	46.5	65	8619
1986	7.6	24.0	28.5	41.3	41.1	93	12329
1987	7.6	23.2	27.5	39.8	40.1	117	15480
1988	7.6	23.9	28.4			126	
1989	7.6						

Sources: International Monetary Fund, *International Financial Statistics*; Organization for Economic Cooperation and Development, *Main Economic Indicators*; and National Sources.

Today national autonomy in economic decision making is quite limited. At a formal level, Austria's new laws are routinely checked as to their conformity with EC standards. Existing laws are adapted. At an economic level, different standards—leading to cost disadvantages with respect to the outside world—will rather quickly spill over and leak out. It is safe to predict that at a macro level national autonomy in policymaking will be further curtailed in the years to come. Monetary policy decisions in the Austrian case are already closely connected with the outside world (the EMS currencies) through the balance-of-payments link, and fiscal policy decisions through the "confidence link."

We can therefore conclude that macroeconomic decisions are very much determined by international developments.[3] The management of economic power therefore ought to be classified as the management of the transmission and domestic distribution of international economic policy decisions.

At the same time, there remains a very important market niche for policymakers at the micro level, the supply side. They are free to deregulate more than international minimum standards require, ease the tax burden further (within certain limits), allow more labor market flexibility, liberalize entry restrictions further, and so on.

The above-mentioned constraints on domestic policymaking have to be kept in mind when we assess what the room for maneuver is for domestic policy decision making. In other words, today, and even more so in the future, domestic decision making in a small country is conditional on international developments. Policy autonomy is shrinking.

The Basic Aims of Economic Policy

It is universally accepted that economic policy should strive to achieve non-inflationary, balanced, sustainable, "full employment" growth securing an "equitable income distribution." In problem cases, priorities are country-specific and variant over time.

Austria has had a long history of giving full employment top priority, the tradeoff being a rising fiscal deficit and mounting restrictions on market forces (for example, on the use and size of the labor force). As a consequence, unemployment could be kept well below the OECD average while public indebtedness rose sharply; it now accounts for some 50 percent of GDP. Only in the 1980s was fiscal consolidation assigned top priority alongside the unchanged importance of price stability.

It is noteworthy, however, that the priority structure has always enjoyed a very broad consensus both among policymakers of the parties represented in Parliament and the public at large. The well-known catchword is social partnership, the essence of which will be dealt with later in this chapter.

The Formal Structure of Economic Management

Austria is a federal republic consisting of nine states (*länder*). The highest public office is that of the federal president. The president holds several important, albeit mostly formal, functions such as the international representation of the Republic, appointment of the federal chancellor, commander-in-chief, and so on. In practice, power resides in the government and, to a lesser degree, in Parliament. Parliament consists of two houses: the Nationalrat (183 seats) and the Bundesrat (63 seats). The Bundesrat's veto can only delay but not thwart legislation passed by the Nationalrat. The Nationalrat is elected by popular vote every four years. (Early dissolution is possible.) The members of the Bundesrat are appointed by the Landtags, the states' parliaments.

The share of the public sector in the Austrian economy reached a peak of 55 percent of GDP (national account basis) in the mid-1980s and has been slowly declining since then. It started to expand appreciably in the mid-1970s, when the authorities tried to cushion the effects of the oil price shock on income and employment. Moreover, this development also reflects the expansion of the welfare state in the early 1970s. Despite efforts to finance these additional expenditures through taxes and fees, a sizable budget deficit evolved, not least because of a significant fall in tax buoyancy (0.8 before the tax reform of 1989).

Only in 1987 did the newly formed grand coalition government between the Socialist and the People's party enter on a medium-term consolidation path.

A large percentage of industry in Austria is publicly owned, mainly because immediately after World War II there was a need to protect basic industries against seizure by the occupation forces.[4] Before the recent privatization and restructuring program, some 20 to 25 percent of Austria's industry measured by industrial labor force or production (nearly 100 percent in mining and basic industry and a great part of energy industry) was nationalized. In the early 1980s nationalized industries produced a maximum of roughly 10 percent of Austria's GDP. Since the mid-1980s the share has been declining steadily.

Economic management in Austria exhibits a very high degree of organization, on the side of both labor and management. Nearly 60 percent of all employees are members of trade unions. Moreover, there is compulsory membership in one of the fourteen chambers covering the employees' and employers' side. This important feature will be discussed in more detail in the subsection on social partnership.

According to the constitution, the legislative power of the federal authorities in economic matters dominates. The power of the states and local authorities is basically restricted to matters closely tied to state and community-related tasks like building and real estate, planning, nature conservation, and environmental protection.

Monetary Policy

According to the Austrian constitution, monetary policy matters are the domain of the federal authorities. Important aspects of monetary policy have, however, been delegated to the Austrian National Bank. In effect, monetary and exchange-rate policy is entrusted to Austria's central bank, which can be considered one of the most independent central banks in the industrialized world.[5] The structure of its shareholders reflects the social partnership principle. The Federal Republic, holds 50 percent of the share capital of 150 mio schilling, with the other half divided evenly among institutions representing the social partners (e.g., trade unions, cooperatives, the federal chamber of commerce, and cooperative banks).

The main responsibilities of the central bank include the issuing of banknotes, the regulation of the circulation of money, the management of foreign exchange reserves, and, most of all, safeguarding the domestic and international value of the schilling. A special feature is the explicit prohibition to finance public authorities against domestic collateral.[6]

The prime task of the Austrian National Bank is to pursue a monetary policy conducive to price stability. The social partners and the government have an agreement that, over the longer term, the economy cannot prosper without a reasonable degree of price stability. It is clear that such a consensus greatly facilitates the task of the Bank, because it fosters the smooth adjustment of the economy to the exchange-rate target.

The Austrian National Bank has pioneered an exchange-rate approach that it terms the hard currency policy. In practice, this policy means the de facto pegging of the schilling to the Deutsche mark. The use of monetary policy instruments is directed at maintaining an adequate interest rate differential with respect to Germany, using either the domestic or the foreign source component (active participation in the foreign exchange market). The longer term success of the policy hinges on the adjustment of the domestic economy (especially wages) to the exchange rate, as pointed out above.

The fourteen-member Governing Board sets the broad overall outlines of monetary policy and supervises the Bank's business. The Board of Executive Directors is responsible for the day-to-day running of the Bank. It reports monthly to the Governing Board. The governor is appointed by the federal president, the two vice governors and five members of the Governing Board are appointed by the federal government, and the remaining six members by the General Meeting. The members of the Governing Board cannot be removed from office.

The Bank does not report to Parliament or to the government. However, the Bank has always made it a point to arrive at a consensus with the government concerning monetary policy. One forum where the Bank voices its opinion about the economy is the "economic policy dialogue" of the social partners.[7] In addition, the Bank regularly informs the public about its policy intentions and interprets its actions.

The Bank administers the foreign exchange law, advises the Federal Ministry of Finance, which is responsible for banking supervision, in matters pertaining to it, and compiles banking statistics on behalf of the Ministry.

The combination of an independent central bank, a social partnership, and equilibrated economic policies has ensured low inflation, high employment, and prosperity for the country.

Fiscal Policy

According to the Austrian constitution, public power is shared among the federal, state, and communal authorities, whereby the power of the federal authorities dominates. The financing of public activities is regulated in the Constitutional Finance Law (Finanzverfassungsgesetz), which also stipulates that the federal authorities decide on tax and fee rights, which amounts to a very centralized solution for a federal state. In this context the Revenue Apportionment Law (Finanzausgleichsgesetz) is of paramount importance. This law regulates the sharing of taxes and fees collected by the federal authorities among the public authorities.

Fiscal policy at the federal level is entrusted to the Federal Ministry of Finance, which leads the budget negotiations and presents the budget to the government.[8] Ten weeks before the end of the fiscal year (December 31), the government (by unanimous vote) has to present the budget bill to the Nationalrat, which then votes on it. The second chamber, the Bundesrat, has no say in the budget process and cannot veto a budget passed by the Nationalrat.

Most of the taxes are collected at the federal level and are then divided among the public authorities as has been noted above. At present about one-third of the gross tax receipts is transferred to the states and communities whose right to levy their own taxes is extremely limited. Only 1.5 percent of the states' expenditure and 8 percent of the communities' expenditure can be financed by own taxes. Furthermore, certain tasks under the constitutional responsibility of the states (for example, housing) are financed by funding specifically assigned by the federal authorities for this purpose. Such a setup forces the states and communities to adjust their expenditures according to fund availability and not according to their own priorities.

It is an Austrian peculiarity that indirect taxes generate more revenue than direct taxes.[9] The personal income tax and the value added tax are the most important sources of revenue. Furthermore, social security contributions constitute an important form of taxation. The 1989 tax reform significantly reduced tax progression with regard to both personal and corporate income taxes. At the same time average taxation was lowered.

On the expenditure side, outlays for social security, health, and housing construction approach 25 percent of all expenditures by the central government. In addition, contributions to the national railways and agricultural subsidies place heavy demands on the budget. At present, nearly 90 percent of all expenditures are predetermined by regulations stipulated by law, severely limiting the government's discretionary room for maneuver to reduce the budget deficit.

Austria's public debt (which at the end of 1989 was some 50 percent of GDP) is managed by the Federal Ministry of Finance. Borrowing may be either domestic or foreign, but not through the central bank.[10]

The Economic and Social Partnership (ESP)

The ESP is a unique Austrian institution. It encompasses the major social groups and constitutes an informal and voluntary institutional forum not regulated by law. Its main function is to work out solutions to economic and social questions. The ESP is therefore much more than incomes policy. It has sometimes even been called a second government. In matters affecting the social partners, the government lets the ESP draw up legislation (e.g., the Foreign Workers Employment Act), or, alternatively, the government passes the framework legislation and lets the social partners work out the details (e.g., the regulation of the food market).

The ESP is embodied in the Joint Commission for Wages and Prices (the Parity Commission) and its three subcommittees for prices, wages, and the Economic and Social Advisory Board.[11] In each body the four major social groups[12] are represented, guaranteeing parity between employers and employees as well as between the Socialist and People's party. Participation is strictly voluntary. Decisions are taken unanimously, with the government representatives having no voting rights.

The Parity Commission endorses the decisions made by the subcommittees or takes a decision when agreement cannot be reached at the lower, more technical level. It also discusses major economic questions in an economic policy context.

The price subcommittee oversees the development of prices for domestically produced goods[13] (currently less than 20 percent of the goods and services included in the Consumer Price Index) and endorses price increases if "unavoidable" cost increases can be proven. Producers who want to raise prices may voluntarily place their application with the price subcommittee, which, after examining the claim, endorses it. In recent years the committee's importance has been declining because of the general liberalization and deregulation trends and because of decreasing inflation. In addition, cost-related pricing tends to shield producers from competition rather than protect consumers from demand-related price rises as was the original intention.

The wage subcommittee oversees the development of wages (and working time). Although the fifteen specialized unions are in principle free to set their wage claims independently, in practice there is a certain check on their levels. This is so because the unions are required to obtain "permission" from the subcommittee to open wage negotiations. Moreover, only the Trade Union Federation, and not the single union, can apply for the opening of negotiations. This peculiar procedure ensures the coordination of wage claims with regard to both their level and duration, as well as a certain check as regards their conformity with overall economic developments.

The Economic and Social Advisory Board's task is to scientifically explore important economic and social questions and to make recommendations to the government. As these recommendations are based on unanimous decisions by the social partners, Parliament usually endorses them.

Trade Policy

Austria is a member of the General Agreement on Tariffs and Trade (GATT) and the European Free Trade Association (EFTA), has concluded free trade arrangements with the EC, and in July 1989 applied for membership in the EC. Within these international arrangements, Austria's trade policy for industrial goods and services is the responsibility of the Federal Ministry of Economics, whereas trade with agricultural products is the responsibility of the Federal Ministry of Agriculture. Over the years import duties have been lowered, but they remain at a level (somewhat less than 5 percent on average for industrial goods) higher than, for example, that of the EC. The Oesterreichische Kontrollbank administers Austria's export promotion scheme. In addition, the Federal Economic Chamber maintains more than ninety foreign trade missions designed to promote Austrian exports.

Austria's possible future EC membership will merge Austria's trade policy with that of the EC; that is, there will be no room for an autonomous policy left. In the meantime, Austria's policy will have to be harmonized with that of the EC.

THE MANAGEMENT OF ECONOMIC POWER IN SWEDEN

Sweden in the World Economy

Sweden covers an area of 450,000 square kilometers and is the fourth largest country in Europe. With its 8.5 million inhabitants, however, it is only slightly more populated than Austria, while Australia has twice and Canada three times as many inhabitants. With only nineteen inhabitants per square kilometer, Sweden is rather sparsely populated compared to about ninety in Austria. This vastness of the country coupled with the low population density has repercussions on the distribution of economic power: it is a very decentralized economy.[14]

With almost U.S. $19,000, Sweden's per capita gross domestic product (GDP) is one of the highest in the world, about 20 percent above that of Austria and Canada and almost 60 percent above that of Australia. Its wealth and its high level of employment are very trade dependent, with its exports of goods and services accounting for more than a third of GDP. In our sample of small OECD countries, only Austria is somewhat more open. (Forty percent of GDP results from exports.) In Australia, in comparison, the share of exports in GDP is only about half as high as that in Sweden. Given this openness, considerable attention is attached to the foreign sector and its international competitiveness. Devaluations of the Swedish krona have repeatedly been used (the last time in October 1982) to improve, at least temporarily, the competitive position of the Swedish export industry. More than half of Swedish exports go to the European Community and almost 90 percent to OECD countries. Germany is Sweden's most important trading partner. In contrast, The Comecon countries are of only limited importance for Swedish foreign trade: only about 2 percent of all exports go there and about 4 percent of all imports originate from there.

The Basic Aims of Economic Policy

The objective of full employment has always been given very high priority in Swedish economic policy, independently of the party (or parties) in power. As the governor of the Sveriges Riksbank defined it (*Financial Times*, October 2, 1989):

For Swedes the commitment to full employment amounts to the same kind of political obsession as inflation does for the West Germans. The experience of the 1930s never dies. And this commitment to the cause covers every segment of the Swedish political scene.

Table 5.3
Selected Economic Indicators, Sweden, 1970–89

YEAR	GDP REAL %	CPI %	EXPORTS REAL %	IMPORTS REAL %	CURRENT ACCOUNT % OF GDP	GOVERNMENT DEFICIT % OF GDP
1970	6.5	7.6	8.8	11.2	- .8	-1.8
1971	.9	7.8	5.7	- 1.2	.6	-1.3
1972	2.3	5.4	9.8	4.3	.6	-1.2
1973	4.0	6.8	10.6	5.8	2.3	-1.4
1974	3.2	9.7	1.3	11.7	-1.6	-3.1
1975	2.6	9.8	- 5.7	- 2.5	0.0	-2.5
1976	1.1	10.8	5.6	3.7	-2.2	- .3
1977	-1.6	11.2	1.4	- 4.2	-2.7	-1.6
1978	1.8	9.9	8.1	- 4.7	- .4	-5.0
1979	3.8	7.2	7.8	12.4	-2.3	-7.2
1980	1.7	13.8	- 1.8	- .7	-3.7	-8.2
1981	- .3	12.1	2.0	- 7.2	-2.5	-9.0
1982	.8	8.5	3.7	4.1	-3.6	-8.4
1983	2.4	9.0	11.7	2.1	-1.0	-8.5
1984	3.9	8.2	7.1	3.5	.1	-6.1
1985	2.1	7.1	3.1	8.6	-1.2	-5.4
1986	1.1	4.4	1.1	5.9	.7	-2.8
1987	2.4	4.2	2.3	8.3	- .7	1.8
1988	2.1	5.8	3.0	5.2	-1.4	
1989	1.7				-1.6	

Sources: International Monetary Fund, *International Financial Statistics*; Organization for Economic Cooperation and Development, *Main Economic Indicators*; and National Sources.

As a consequence, labor market performance and policy in Sweden have been "distinctly different" from performance and policy in other OECD countries.[15] The emphasis on low unemployment figures made sure that unemployment rates did not rise significantly after the two oil price shocks of the 1970s—contrary to the developments in most other OECD countries. The mirror image of these low jobless rates was, however, strong growth in public sector employment during the last twenty years, from 21 percent of the total labor force in 1970 to 32 percent in 1987.[16] This indicates that the public sector has at times taken the role of an employer of last resort. Early retirement and longer education periods also contributed to lower labor force growth in the 1980s and, therefore, to lower recorded unemployment. On average, recorded unemployment amounted to only 2.2 percent during the 1978–87 period. This put it far below the average of all OECD countries.[17]

Low wage differentials are another characteristic feature of the Swedish economy, based on the concept of social justice and solidaristic attitudes. Therefore, in an international comparison, both intersectoral and interprofessional wage dispersion are very low, although the OECD observes signs that this dispersion has started to widen. Nevertheless, labor markets are perceived as typifying more than anything else the Swedish way of economic policymaking.

Table 5.4
Selected Economic Indicators, Sweden, 1970–89

YEAR	POPULATION (MILLIONS)	EXPORTS AS % OF GDP	IMPORTS AS % OF GDP	EXPORTS GOODS & SERVICES US$	IMPORTS GOODS & SERVICES US$	GDP BILL US$	GDP PER HEAD US$
1970	8.0	20.3	21.0	24.8	25.1	33	4140
1971	8.1	20.5	19.4	25.2	23.7	36	4492
1972	8.1	20.5	19.0	25.2	23.2	42	5269
1973	8.1	23.4	21.0	28.6	25.2	51	6378
1974	8.2	27.5	28.8	33.2	33.4	57	7070
1975	8.2	23.9	24.9	29.0	28.6	72	8844
1976	8.2	23.6	24.5	28.7	29.8	78	9501
1977	8.3	23.2	24.4	28.3	29.9	82	10007
1978	8.3	23.8	22.5	29.7	28.6	91	11024
1979	8.3	25.6	26.6	32.5	33.7	107	13008
1980	8.3	24.9	26.9	31.7	34.2	124	14939
1981	8.3	25.3	25.5	32.8	34.4	113	13602
1982	8.3	26.8	27.7	35.3	37.7	99	11993
1983	8.3	29.8	28.4	38.3	38.4	92	11044
1984	8.3	30.8	27.7	39.0	37.8	95	11445
1985	8.3	30.3	28.4	38.4	38.9	100	11982
1986	8.4	28.5	25.0	35.7	34.6	130	15627
1987	8.4	28.0	25.6	35.2	35.1	158	18874
1988		27.8	25.5			178	
1989							

Sources: International Monetary Fund, *International Financial Statistics*; Organization for Economic Cooperation and Development, *Main Economic Indicators*, and National Sources.

Compromise, consultation, and cooperation form the basis of an approach that combines economic growth and social redistribution. Labor market policy has provided Swedes with a policy ideology that exemplifies a belief in action produced through the consent of extensively organized and centrally coordinated interests.[18]

It is not only the labor market organization in Sweden that shows considerable similarities to the one in Austria; so does the result, namely, the extremely low level of industrial strife.

The need for external equilibrium has traditionally been a constraint on Swedish economic policy, and it remains so. The current-account deficit doubled between 1987 and 1988 and reached about 1-1/4 percent of GDP. As noted earlier, in the past Swedish policymakers have repeatedly used devaluations of the krona in attempts to improve the foreign balance. As a result of two devaluations in 1981 and 1982, the effective exchange rate of the krona was reduced by 20 percent and market shares improved sharply. Deteriorating trends in cost competitiveness reversed the gains, and by 1988 relative unit labor costs were more or less at the level observed before the 1982 devaluation.[19] High domestic wage increases were the main factor behind these developments. Despite the very centralized wage negotiation system with one of the most centralized wage formation processes in the OECD area, the potential gains in competitiveness created by the large devaluations could not be preserved over a longer time period.

Sweden has had a long tradition of being closed to foreign financial influence. A plethora of restrictions have been used to impede the inward movement of foreign investment and foreign ownership of Swedish industry and services. Share ownership in Swedish banks and other financial institutions, for instance, was completely closed to nonresidents until the end of 1989 (and even now is subject to an upper limit). At the same time, foreigners were not allowed to invest in Swedish government bonds until the late 1980s.

The Formal Structure of Economic Management

Sweden is a constitutional monarchy with a parliamentary system. The king has only ceremonial functions; the formal decision-making power lies with the Parliament (the Riksdag) and the government. The task of governing is entrusted by Parliament to the government. Parliament consists of one chamber, whose members are elected every three years in general elections. Parliament designates the prime minister, who then appoints the other ministers. About a dozen different ministries prepare government bills for submission to the Riksdag. The execution of the laws rests with about one hundred relatively independent central administrations and more than twenty provincial governments. Each of the provinces has its own elected provincial government, which has the power to raise taxes and is mainly in charge of health care services. In addition to the provinces, there are 284 municipalities, each with its own elected municipal government. These are empowered to raise their own income taxes and to provide a wide range of public services.

Swedish government administration is divided into ministries and boards or agencies. The ministries are primarily responsible for policy matters, whereas the enforcement of government decisions, current legislation, and regulations is entrusted to a number of central administrative boards or agencies that function independently of the ministries. These agencies or boards (ämbetsverk) are normally central administrative authorities responsible directly to the government and have a national field of operation. These include such central agencies as the Central Bureau of Statistics, the National Institute of Economic Research, the National Audit Bureau, the National Tax Board, or the National Price and Cartel Office.

The Swedish economy is characterized by a very large share of the public sector—a share that has continuously increased since World War II. If we include all transfer payments, about two-thirds of GDP passes through the public sector, compared to about one-third one generation ago.[20] This large and increasing government involvement in the economy and the government's role as an employer of last resort resulted (despite the very high level of taxation) in large government deficits, especially between 1978 and 1985. At its highest point (in 1981), it reached 9 percent of GDP. Since 1982 the government has embarked on a new medium-term economic policy strategy, and progress has been made, leading initially to declining budget deficits and next to public sector surpluses.

Despite the government's large involvement in the economy, about 90 percent of industry is in private ownership and only 10 percent is either government owned or in the hands of cooperatives.

Sweden's economic management is characterized by a very high degree of labor as well as management organization. Of the almost 4.5 million employees, roughly 80 to 85 percent are unionized. Among blue-collar workers, the share reaches 90 percent, and among white-collar employees and civil servants, still about 75 percent. Most of the employers are equally organized in the Swedish Employers Association. Most of the regular wage negotiations take place between the respective organizations with little or no interference by the government. But the power of these and the many other special interest organizations goes far beyond wage negotiations, leading scholars of the system to speak of administered politics, corporate pluralism, or societal corporatism.[21] As Heclo and Madsen (1987, p. 19) point out,

[T]he unions and their private management counterparts are more than mere interest groups in a particular area. They are powerful social actors whose scope of concern and influence has become almost as broad as that of any political party.

For Sweden, just as as for Austria, the formal structure of economic management is dominated by the overriding goals of stability and predictability. The pressures in the political system are organized and channeled in quite stable, predictable, and orderly ways.

Monetary Policy

Monetary and exchange-rate policy in Sweden is in the hands of the Bank of Sweden (the Riksbank), the country's central bank. It is considered to be the oldest existing central bank, its origins dating back to 1668. Like the Austrian National Bank, it issues banknotes, administers the gold and foreign exchange reserves of the country, and functions as the bank for the country's banking system. In contrast to the Austrian central bank, however, it also performs the role of bank for the central government.

The Riksbank manages liquidity in the banking system, interest rates, and the exchange rate in accordance with the goals of stabilization policy. It is at present committed to a stable exchange rate.[22] It implements monetary policy by means of direct interventions in the money market. It influences the level of liquidity in the banking system and the short-term interest rates by dealing in government securities (either through purchases, sales, or repurchase agreements) and by changing the cash reserve requirements. Its goal is to steer the general interest level, especially the shorter rates in the money market. The overnight rate—

which can be steered by the Bank with considerable precision—is used as a lever for this purpose.[23]

Responsible for the central banking policy of the Bank of Sweden is its Governing Board, which usually meets weekly (at least biweekly). It is made up of eight members, seven of whom are appointed by the Riksdag. The eighth, the governor, is appointed by the other Board members.[24] Neither a cabinet minister nor a member or deputy member of the board of a credit institution can serve on the Governing Board. The governor is the chairman of the Board of Directors and is responsible for the day-to-day management of the bank. His tenure lasts five years. The Board of Directors consists of the governor, the (two) deputy governors, one member of the Governing Board as a permanent member, one other of the members of the Governing Board appointed by Parliament on a rotating basis, and the director of the bank whose area covers the question to be discussed. The main functions of the Board of Directors center on administrative matters.

The chief monetary policy function of the Governing Board is similar to that of the Board of the Austrian National Bank: to change the discount rate. The main policy instruments are, however, open market operations, and their implementation does not require any decisions by the Governing Board.

This setup of the decision-making bodies in the Bank of Sweden reflects the very different relationship between the central bank and the political representatives, Parliament and the cabinet, that exists in Sweden compared to Austria. As mentioned above, the Austrian National Bank enjoys rather far-reaching independence from the political bodies. The Riksbank, however, is subordinated to the Swedish Parliament. As the Swedish constitution states unambiguously, the Riksbank is a parliamentary agency.[25]

One sign of the influence of Parliament on the central bank is its right to appoint seven of the eight members of the Governing Board, with the eighth, the governor, appointed by the other board members. Since every year two members of the Governing Board have to be (re)appointed, any majority party in Parliament can slowly achieve a majority in the Board, and this majority can elect a governor of its (political) choice. Moreover, some of the members of the Board of Directors are either members of the Governing Board or appointed by it.

Only Parliament is empowered to give orders to the Governing Board of the Riksbank, and the Board is responsible solely to Parliament and to the auditors appointed by the Parliament. Section 42 of the Riksbank Act states that "before the Riksbank makes a decision of major importance in terms of monetary policy, consultation shall take place with the Cabinet Minister designated by the Government." The Governing Board has to submit an annual report to the Committee on Finance, a standing committee of Parliament, which deals with monetary, credit, and foreign exchange matters. After careful scrutiny and discussions, and supplemented by its comments, this committee forwards the report to Parliament for approval. The Riksbank's profit and loss account and balance sheet have to be adopted by the Riksdag, which determines how the Bank's profits are to be utilized. The Riksdag decides on the discharge of the members of the Governing Board from liability for their administration of the Riksbank.

Even without an explicit provision in the law, the Bank has to coordinate its policies with the economic policies of the government. In the case of a major disagreement between the two, it is the Bank that has to accommodate.

Sweden has a long tradition of exchange controls. In charge of those controls is the Foreign Exchange Control Board, which is directly responsible to the Governing Board of the Riksbank. It is led by one deputy governor of the Riksbank and has seven members on its board. All are appointed by the Governing Board. The Riksbank is represented by one deputy governor, one member of the Governing Board, and one director of the Bank. Four members are from outside the Bank, two represent the banking sector, industry, and commerce, and two represent the employees. At present, the government has committed itself to abolishing all the remaining exchange controls by mid-1990.

Clearly, the Swedish Riksbank, in pursuing monetary policy, is largely dependent on Parliament and the cabinet.[26] By no means does it enjoy a degree of independence comparable to that of the Austrian National Bank or the German Bundesbank.[27] Consequently, the Swedish Parliament controls both tools of macroeconomic policy, fiscal policy (together with the local governments) and monetary policy. Only to a limited degree does it share its economic power with the central bank.

Fiscal Policy

Parliament decides on taxes and determines how the central government's funds are to be used. Every year the government submits its program of action for the coming fiscal year to Parliament. This budget bill includes not only the government's projected revenues and expenditures, but also, in a number of appendices, a detailed account of the cabinet's economic policies. It is compiled by the Ministry of Finance, based on the recommendations and requests of the individual ministries. The annual budget bill is the product of an exhaustive process that lasts about one and a half years. The actual discretionary fiscal possibilities are, however, rather limited (at least in a contractionary direction) since about 85 percent of central government expenditure is determined by various forms of automatic regulations.[28]

The most important direct taxes are the central (very progressive) and the local (flat rate) income taxes and the central wealth tax.[29] Smaller direct taxes are the inheritance tax and an extensive system of employer contributions to social security. The Riksdag has the power to decide on both central and local taxes, but the local administrations can then set the specific tax rates according to their own preferences.[30] The major indirect taxes include the value added tax and the sales tax on certain goods. The proceeds of both go almost exclusively to the central government.

The Swedish constitution explicitly forbids the government from borrowing without the approval of Parliament. It places the central government's borrowing and the administration of the national debt in the hands of a separate institution, the National Debt Office.[31] This body is headed by seven commissioners and is responsible to Parliament. Members of Parliament are not allowed to serve as National Debt commissioners. In addition, in 1984 the Riksbank and the Ministry of Finance decided that there should be no more government borrowing abroad. All deficits on current account have to be balanced by private sector borrowing abroad.

Although the cabinet is the highest planning and administrative authority, it governs the country on behalf of Parliament and is responsible to this institution. The actual balance of power between cabinet and Parliament depends on the parliamentary situation, that is, the number of seats held by the different parties. With a clear majority of the governing party (parties) in Parliament, the focus of political power is in the government. If, however, there is a close balance between government and opposition, the focus shifts toward Parliament.

Sweden has a long tradition of local self-government and as already mentioned, is a very decentralized country. The country has twenty-three counties (*landstingskommun*) and 284 municipalities (*kommun*). Over the years the local sector has gained increasing economic importance, and today local governments account for about 70 percent of government spending, consumption as well as investment. In 1985, for instance, central government expenditures reached only about 9.5 percent of GNP compared to 22.5 percent for local government expenditures. Of the latter, two-thirds are due to the 284 municipalities. Consequently, fiscal policy in Sweden, at least as far as the expenditure side is concerned, is largely decentralized.

Local governments handle their own affairs, with their largest source of income being direct taxation of individuals. Municipalities have the right to collect income taxes (the rates are set annually by each Municipal Council) and to receive the revenues of a rather low land tax. In addition, they can charge levies for the public services they offer. Those amounted to almost 20 percent of their overall income in 1986. Most of the municipalities, as well as the counties, also receive subsidies from the central government, giving the central authorities additional influence over the local authorities. One part of those subsidies is for very specific projects and expenditures; the rest is without strings attached. In 1986, for instance, the central government's subsidies to the municipalities accounted for about 25 percent of their overall receipts. Counties can also raise an income tax in order to cover their expenditures. (The rates are set annually by each County Council.) In addition, they receive subsidies from the central government amounting to nearly 20 percent of their overall income.

The division of labor between municipalities and counties is based on the idea of subsidiarity; that is, those tasks that require the cooperation of a larger share of the population are supplied by the counties and all others by the municipalities. The major responsibilities of municipalities (which in an international comparison offer a very wide range of services) are education, social welfare, water and electricity supply, canalization, road building, cultural activities, and child care, whereas the counties are in charge mainly of health care and some educational services. Municipalities and counties together employ more than 1.1 million people, roughly a fourth of the Swedish labor force. The respective decision-making power rests with municipal and county councils, both of which are elected directly by the public every three years. There are about seventy thousand elected officials in the municipalities and counties. The autonomy of the local authorities, though rather extensive, is nevertheless restricted by federal laws–sometimes rather generally, at other times very specifically. The central government sets the framework within which the local governments can work very freely depending on the perceived local needs. The division of labor between the local and central authorities changes constantly.

Trade Policy

As indicated above, Sweden is a very open economy, highly dependent on international trade. Therefore, the country has always placed great emphasis on trade policy. Sweden is a member of EFTA and GATT. The ultimate responsibility for shaping trade policy lies with Parliament, but in practice it is largely shaped and implemented by government ministries and the national civil service. The Foreign Trade Department in the Ministry of Foreign Affairs is in charge of trade matters within the Swedish government. Moreover, because of the importance of trade for the Swedish economy, there are a number of trade-related government agencies, such as the National Board of Trade and the Export Credits Guarantee Board.

Industrial Policy

Since 1969 Sweden has had a Ministry of Industry which among other things is responsible for setting general guidelines for industrial policy, regional policy, the majority of state-owned enterprises, and structural and sectoral measures within industry. The major guidelines for Swedish industrial policy, as adopted by the Parliament, stress that industrial policy should promote long-term industrial growth based on favorable international competitiveness. In order to strengthen competitiveness, industrial policy should promote growth and structural adjustment in the manufacturing and service sectors. In addition to the Ministry of Industry, a number of boards or agencies enforce the government decisions and regulations in the field of industrial policy. On the initiative of the minister of industry, a number of advisory councils and other consultative bodies for different sectors of industry and business have been established.

THE MANAGEMENT OF ECONOMIC POWER IN CANADA

Canada in the World Economy

Compared to the other OECD countries discussed in this chapter, Canada is by far the largest economy.[32] In terms of overall GDP, its economy is almost four times as large as Austria's and still two-and-a-half times as large as the Australian economy. Canada covers an area of almost 10 million square kilometers, making it the second largest country in the world. It is one of the seven largest industrialized countries in the world. With almost 26 million inhabitants, it is more than three times as populated as Austria or Sweden. Its per capita GDP, however—about U.S. $16,000—is far below that of Sweden (U.S. $18,900) and only slightly higher than Austria's (U.S. $15,500). Its trade dependence is considerably smaller than that of the two previously discussed countries. Only about 26 percent of its GDP is accounted for by exports of goods and services, compared to 40 percent for Austria. But its trade is very concentrated on one single country, namely, the United States, which takes about three-quarters of Canada's exports. In comparison, only about one-third of Austria's exports go to its most important trading partner, Germany.

The Basic Aims of Economic Policy

The strong geographical concentration of Canada's exports links the country's economy very closely to that of the United States. Recognizing this dependence, Canada has made great efforts to reach a free trade agreement with its southern neighbor. The basic goals were to enhance Canada's access to the U.S. market and to make Canada's domestic market more competitive by eliminating all tariffs, reducing the nontariff barriers, and liberalizing the investment flows between the two countries. The basic aims of economic policy in Canada during the second half of the 1980s were set out in the government's Agenda for Economic Renewal of November 1984. In order to create conditions for sustained economic growth, a mixture of microeconomic reforms and macroeconomic stabilization policies was put together. The main ingredients are deregulation of the economy (especially of the energy, transportation, and foreign investment areas), tax reform, budget deficit consolidation, and stimulation of private sector growth.

The Formal Structure of Economic Management

Canada is one of five federally structured members of the OECD. Relationships between the central government in Ottawa and the ten provincial governments are basically determined by the British North America Act (BNA) of 1867[33] which, while specifying both exclusive and shared areas of competence, leaves residual powers to the federal government. In contrast, in other federally struc-

Table 5.5
Selected Economic Indicators, Canada, 1970–89

YEAR	GDP REAL %	CPI %	EXPORTS REAL %	IMPORTS REAL %	CURRENT ACCOUNT % OF GDP	GOVERNMENT DEFICIT % OF GDP
1970	2.6	3.4	9.6	3.1	1.2	-1.1
1971	5.8	2.8	5.1	9.9	.4	-2.0
1972	5.7	4.8	9.2	16.9	- .3	-1.6
1973	7.7	7.7	10.7	16.1	.2	-1.3
1974	4.4	10.8	- 3.7	10.3	- .9	-1.3
1975	2.6	10.8	- 7.3	- 5.5	-2.7	-3.4
1976	6.1	7.5	12.7	7.4	-2.1	-3.2
1977	3.6	8.0	8.8	.8	-2.0	-4.4
1978	4.6	8.9	9.7	4.3	-2.0	-5.0
1979	3.9	9.1	2.1	9.8	-1.8	-3.9
1980	1.5	10.2	- .4	- 6.0	- .4	-3.5
1981	3.7	12.5	3.5	3.7	-1.7	-2.4
1982	-3.2	10.8	- .1	-17.7	.8	-5.6
1983	3.2	5.8	7.1	10.8	.8	-6.3
1984	6.4	4.4	18.6	19.1	.8	-6.5
1985	4.6	3.9	4.5	5.9	- .2	-6.0
1986	3.1	4.2	4.6	9.1	-2.1	-4.0
1987	4.0	4.4	2.9	3.6	-1.9	
1988	4.5	4.0			-1.9	
1989	3.2				-1.9	

Sources: International Monetary Fund, *International Financial Statistics*; Organization for Economic Cooperation and Development, *Main Economic Indicators*, and National Sources.

tured countries such as Australia, Austria, Switzerland, or the United States, the residual powers rest with the states. The federal government was accorded specific authority over, among others, banking, the currency (including note issue), and the regulation of trade and commerce, and was given the power to impose taxation in any form. Provinces were given specific authority over public lands belonging to the provinces (natural resources), hospitals, education, municipal institutions, and property and civil rights. Their taxing powers were limited to direct taxation within the province.[34] Recent developments concerning the balance of power, based on judicial interpretations of the Act as well as social and industrial developments, have, on balance, been favorable to the provinces. The provincial-local sector has therefore assumed increasingly more importance.

Canada has strong regional differences in economic developments, for the economic structures of the regions are very different. International developments and shocks affect the provinces very differently. These regional differences in economic performance mirror the diversity of the Canadian economy. Nevertheless, it has a unified national monetary policy on the basis of national levels of economic activity and inflation run by the one and only central bank, the Bank of Canada.

Fiscal policy, however, is regionally different. The federal government, as well as all the ten provincial governments, have their own budgets.

Table 5.6
Selected Economic Indicators, Canada, 1970–89

YEAR	POPULATION (MILLIONS)	EXPORTS AS % OF GDP	IMPORTS AS % OF GDP	EXPORTS GOODS & SERVICES US$	IMPORTS GOODS & SERVICES US$	GDP BILL US$	GDP PER HEAD US$
1970	21.3	19.0	15.8	24.0	23.2	84	3960
1971	21.6	18.5	16.2	23.0	23.1	95	4428
1972	21.8	18.7	17.3	22.8	23.4	108	4987
1973	22.1	20.1	18.5	24.3	24.5	126	5727
1974	22.4	21.5	21.0	25.8	27.2	154	6890
1975	22.7	19.6	20.4	23.8	26.8	167	7357
1976	23.0	19.6	19.1	23.3	25.7	199	8644
1977	23.3	20.6	19.6	24.5	26.7	203	8728
1978	23.5	22.2	20.9	26.5	28.5	210	8941
1979	23.7	23.9	22.9	28.4	30.3	234	9872
1980	24.0	24.7	22.5	29.6	30.3	263	10984
1981	24.3	23.7	22.5	28.5	30.6	294	12112
1982	24.6	22.7	18.2	27.5	27.1	301	12236
1983	24.9	22.5	18.8	27.1	26.6	326	13112
1984	25.1	25.5	21.6	30.0	29.6	340	13560
1985	25.4	25.1	22.0	30.0	30.6	347	13718
1986	25.6	24.0	22.4	28.8	31.2	361	14114
1987	25.6	23.0	21.3	27.8	30.1	410	16019
1988		23.4	22.1	28.3	30.9	482	
1989							

Sources: International Monetary Fund, *International Financial Statistics*; Organization for Economic Cooperation and Development, *Main Economic Indicators*, and National Sources.

Because of its federal system, Canada's economy is characterized by the existence of overlapping federal, provincial, and local levels of supervision and regulation. As the OECD once remarked, "this broadens the scope for both conflict and duplication."[35] For policymakers the continuous challenge is to limit the economic costs of these overlaps and this lack of uniformity within the country.

The strong provincial control over specific sectors results in considerable limitations to the free flow of goods, services, and production factors within the country. With regard to the circulation of goods and services, provincial governments generally accord special preferences to local suppliers in their procurement policies. At the same time, the mobility of personnel is restricted, and Canada is the only federal state in the OECD that does not guarantee freedom of labor mobility within its borders.[36] However, as the OECD continues to remark, the federal powers over money and banking have paved the way for a national banking system and a relatively freely operating capital market.[37]

The barriers to interprovincial trade which shield certain industries from rationalization pressures also have been identified as a possible reason why Canadian productivity growth has lagged behind that of other countries.

Monetary Policy

The conduct of monetary policy in Canada is in the hands of the Bank of Canada. Its main functions are to implement monetary policy and to act as fiscal agent of the government of Canada. The Bank of Canada began its operations in 1935, considerably later than the central banks of most other Western industrial economies.[38] That does not mean that the functions of a central bank were not provided in Canada before 1935. As Bordo and Redish (1987) point out, virtually all the elements of traditional central banking had emerged by the beginning of the twentieth century, undertaken either by private institutions or directly by the government. Therefore, the emergence of the Bank reflected political, rather than economic, imperatives.

Canada has an efficient, unified financial system without barriers to the movement of funds across the country. Therefore, interest rates will always be the same across the country. The Bank of Canada's policy is also implemented on a national level. Its policy does not differentiate by regions, although the economic conditions might diverge considerably among the ten regions. The Bank of Canada gears its actions to the needs and circumstances of the country as a whole. As a sign of this national orientation, the Board of Directors of the Bank is made up of Canadians from all provinces of the country.

The preamble of the Bank of Canada Act outlines the main functions of the Bank as (1) to regulate credit and currency in the best interest of the economic life of the nation; (2) to control and protect the external value of the national monetary unit; (3) to mitigate by its influence fluctuations in the general level of production, trade, prices, and employment, and generally (4) to promote the economic and financial welfare of the dominion.

Through the Bank of Canada Act, Parliament has vested responsibility for the affairs of the Bank in its Board of Directors, composed of a governor, a deputy governor, twelve directors, and the deputy minister of finance; however, the Board does not have a right to vote.[39] Therefore, there is a direct formal link between the central bank and the Ministry of Finance. However, the minister's influence on the bank goes far beyond the membership of his deputy on the Board of Directors. He appoints the directors on the Board with the approval of the governor in Council, and those directors in turn appoint the governor and his deputy.

The Bank of Canada Act states further that the minister and the governor shall consult regularly on monetary policy and on its relation to general economic policy. This provision underlines the fact that the Bank of Canada is part of the broad public policy structure. But if there is

a difference in opinion between the Minister and the Bank concerning the monetary policy to be followed, the Minister may, after consultation with the Governor and with the approval of the Governor in Council, give the Governor a written directive concerning monetary policy, in specific terms and applicable for a specified period, and the Bank shall comply with such directive. (Bank of Canada Act, §14 [2])

This rule states very clearly that the *ultimate* responsibility for monetary policy in Canada lies with the minister of finance, although the Bank of Canada has sufficient independence to take direct responsibility for the monetary policy pursued. However, no such directive of the government to the Bank has yet been issued, and each successive governor has announced that he or she would resign if such a directive were ever issued.

The long-run objective of the Bank of Canada is overall price stability. For that purpose, the Bank used different indicators at different times. Before 1982 explicit monetary targeting was the policy guide, followed by a monitoring of a number of money and credit aggregates, with special emphasis on exchange-rate developments. More recently, the Bank has paid increasing attention to broader monetary aggregates as indicative policy guides. These aggregates have been less affected than narrower ones by shifts resulting from financial innovation and have proved to be most closely related to aggregate spending and prices in Canada. The Bank sees interest rates and exchange rates as the main channels of transmission of monetary policy. The Bank maintains its leverage over monetary policy conditions by influencing the very short-term interest rates directly by determining the settlement balances available to the major deposit-taking institutions.

Generally, we can say that the Bank of Canada follows a rather pragmatic approach to monetary policy, always considering external influences, especially those emanating from the United States.

Fiscal Policy

According to OECD estimates, the size of the government sector in Canada appears to conform rather closely to the OECD average. The ratio of government expenditures to GDP in Canada is at an intermediate position between the European economies with their comprehensive welfare systems and Japan and the United States, Canada's most important trading partners.

Compared with the average OECD tax structure, Canada makes relatively heavy reliance on direct taxes but less on social security contributions. The role of indirect taxes is very close to the OECD average. Tax receipts represent by far the largest part of government revenue raised to finance expenditure. Income tax rates are moderate and social insurance contributions low by international comparisons.[40]

The public sector in Canada consists of the federal government and the provincial/local/hospital (PHL) sector. The federal government, with major responsibility for the provision of traditional public goods, such as defense or justice, accounts for only about one-quarter of public spending on goods and services but is a major source of income transfers to other levels of government and individuals. The most important responsibilities of the provinces—which account for somewhat larger expenditures on goods and services than the central government—are in the areas of social security (shared with the federal government), welfare, housing, community services, education, and health. Local governments (including hospitals) account for almost one-half of public sector goods and services expenditure. They are extremely dependent on transfers chiefly from provincial governments.

Since 1947 fiscal relations between the federal and provincial governments have been determined primarily by a series of five-year agreements that have successively incorporated significant on-going modifications.

The recent expenditure trends have been toward a strong increase in the outlays of the combined provincial/local sector relative to those of the central government. At the same time, especially during the late 1970s, there has been an increasing divergence in revenue trends, with provincial/local government income growing strongly owing to revenues flowing from exploitation of Canada's natural resources while federal income growth was reduced by a series of discretionary tax measures.

The general government deficit in 1987 was 4.5 percent of GDP, which is rather high by international standards. Of that, the nonfederal government deficit (including local governments, hospitals, and public sector pension funds as well as provinces) amounted to only 0.8 percent of GDP.

The Bank of Canada is closely involved in public debt management in its capacity as fiscal adviser to the government of Canada. However, public debt management and monetary policy management are separate areas of operation. (Public debt management operations used to interact in an important way with monetary policy actions by exerting a strong impact on credit conditions.) The Bank advises the government and administers marketable bond issues that are allocated to a network of commissioned dealers about seven times a year. The Bank is also prepared to purchase government securities from authorized dealers who agree to repurchase them at a later time.

Public ownership in Canada, largely an inheritance of the past, is considerably more widespread than it is in the United States, where control over natural monopolies has typically been exercised via regulatory commissions rather than public ownership. In 1986 Canada had about 1,300 government enterprises (including subsidiaries)—330 federal, 450 provincial, and 520 local—accounting for about 15 percent of total corporate assets (OECD, 1986). In the meantime public ownership has been reduced considerably, and plans are to reduce it further. Federal ownership includes such activities as railways, telephones, petrol retailing[41] and atomic energy, while provincial enterprises cover inter alia electrical utilities, telephones, natural resource exploitation, banking, car insurance, and railways. Local government enterprises are generally responsible for local utility services and urban transportation. Gas supply and telecommunications, two "usual" candidates for public ownership in European economies, are primarily in the private domain in Canada, subject to regulatory control.

Trade Policy

Canada is a contracting party of GATT and, like Australia a member of the so-called Cairns Group, a collection of thirteen agricultural exporting nations that have pooled their resources to fight for common goals in the field of international trade in agricultural goods. Besides these memberships which underline its basic commitment to free trade, Canada is also a signatory to the Multifiber Agreement (MFA) which puts quantitative limits on trade in textiles and clothing. In addition, it has repeatedly negotiated voluntary export restriction arrangements with Japan in order to limit the number of Japanese cars exported to Canada. The goals of both, the MFA and the car export arrangements, were to maintain employment in declining and trade-sensitive industries, but, as has been repeatedly shown, the cost of these protective arrangements has been very high for Canadian consumers.[42]

As mentioned above, about three-quarters of Canada's exports go to the United States. These account for about 20 percent of Canada's GDP. In view of this dependence, Canadian governments—on the federal as well as on the provincial level—have always given special attention to trade relations with the southern neighbor. Therefore, it is no surprise that Canada devoted so much effort to reaching a free trade agreement with the United States. The U.S.–Canada Free Trade Agreement which was signed in 1988 is seen as a watershed in the history of Canada's commercial relations. There are widespread expectations that this agreement will enhance Canada's access to the U.S. market and make its domestic market more competitive. Its main features are the elimination of all tariffs between the two countries by the end of the century, the reduction of nontariff barriers to trade, the liberalization of investment flows, and the establishment of trade-dispute settlement procedures. In particular, the possibility of exploiting the advantages of economies of scale should prove very beneficial for the Canadian economy.

The free trade agreement has already stimulated certain provinces to sign trade and tourism agreements with the U.S. and Canadian states (e.g., Manitoba with Kansas, or British-Columbia with Washington State). This is another sign of the growing importance of Canada's provincial powers.

As mentioned above, considerable interprovincial barriers to trade remain, including transport regulations, marketing boards, and product standard regulations.

THE MANAGEMENT OF ECONOMIC POWER IN AUSTRALIA

Australia in the World Economy

Australia covers 7.7 million square kilometers and has over 16 million inhabitants. With only 2.1 inhabitants per square kilometer it is extremely sparsely populated. Compared to Austria, its geographical extension is ninety times larger,

Table 5.7
Selected Economic Indicators, Australia, 1970–89

YEAR	GDP REAL %	CPI %	EXPORTS REAL %	IMPORTS REAL %	CURRENT ACCOUNT % OF GDP	GOVERNMENT DEFICIT % OF GDP
1970	6.1	3.9	15.0	7.9	-2.1	- .8
1971	5.9	6.1	7.9	- 3.7	-2.0	- .2
1972	3.9	5.9	3.0	- 9.9	.9	.3
1973	5.9	9.5	- 3.6	24.6	.6	- .8
1974	1.4	15.0	- .6	15.1	-3.3	.2
1975	2.6	15.1	11.1	-22.0	-1.2	-3.6
1976	0.0	13.5	8.1	10.3	-2.0	-4.4
1977	3.6	12.4	- .3	.9	-3.1	-3.0
1978	.8	7.9	.9	5.0	-3.9	-3.3
1979	3.4	9.1	9.3	- 1.6	-2.1	-3.0
1980	3.4	10.2	- .2	- 4.9	-2.8	-1.6
1981	2.0	9.6	- 3.4	13.7	-5.0	- .7
1982	3.1	11.1	7.6	6.0	-5.1	- .3
1983	.4	10.2	- 1.3	-18.5	-3.7	-2.6
1984	6.7	4.0	17.9	23.0	-4.8	-4.0
1985	5.5	6.7	9.9	7.9	-5.5	-3.0
1986	1.8	9.1	2.4	- 1.2	-5.9	-2.4
1987	4.3	8.5	7.7	1.6	-4.6	-1.2
1988	3.8	7.2	- 1.5		-4.4	
1989	3.3				-4.5	

Sources: International Monetary Fund, *International Financial Statistics*; Organization for Economic Cooperation and Development, *Main Economic Indicators*, and National Sources.

but its population is only somewhat more than twice the Austrian. About 61 percent of the country is used for agricultural purposes, but only about 400,000 Australians are employed in this sector of the economy.[43]

Today Australia accounts for about 1.2 percent of world exports (compared to about 1.7 percent in 1970). This loss of market shares is related to the fact that its exports are heavily weighted toward primary commodities. Its most important group of export goods are agricultural exports, which account for about 37 percent of the goods sold abroad. Among these exports the predominant categories are the sales of wool and sheepskins (amounting to about 14 percent of exports). Basic materials, such as metal ores, minerals, and mineral fuels, account for another 31 percent. The geographical orientation of its exports is shifting increasingly from Europe toward the Pacific Region, especially Japan. About a quarter of its exports go to Japan compared to about 15 percent to the European Community and another 10 percent to the United States. On the import side the European Community accounts for about one quarter and Japan and the United States for one-fifth each.

The Basic Aims of Economic Policy

The basic goal of Australian economic policy is to attain economic growth and an equitable income distribution under conditions of internal and external equilibrium. There is a strong belief in comparative wage justice.

Table 5.8

Selected Economic Indicators, Australia, 1970–89

YEAR	POPULATION (MILLIONS)	EXPORTS AS % OF GDP	IMPORTS AS % OF GDP	EXPORTS GOODS & SERVICES US$	IMPORTS GOODS & SERVICES US$	GDP BILL US$	GDP PER HEAD US$
1970	12.5	12.8	11.9	15.3	17.4	37	2979
1971	12.9	12.3	10.9	14.8	16.7	42	3272
1972	13.2	13.0	9.1	15.6	14.5	49	3763
1973	13.4	13.6	9.6	16.1	15.3	70	5265
1974	13.7	13.0	12.9	15.9	18.9	84	6199
1975	13.9	13.0	10.6	15.7	16.4	92	6636
1976	14.0	13.0	10.9	15.3	17.1	101	7233
1977	14.2	13.2	12.1	15.7	18.5	101	7129
1978	14.4	12.4	12.2	15.0	18.7	115	8063
1979	14.5	14.5	12.8	17.6	19.4	128	8815
1980	14.7	14.6	13.6	17.7	20.5	148	10109
1981	14.9	12.7	13.9	15.5	20.5	169	11356
1982	15.2	12.9	14.2	15.6	20.6	166	10966
1983	15.4	12.6	11.6	15.4	19.2	160	10410
1984	15.6	13.1	12.8	16.1	20.9	177	11410
1985	15.8	14.5	14.7	17.4	23.3	157	10014
1986	16.0	13.7	14.5	16.9	23.2	165	10365
1987	16.3	13.7	13.9	17.5	22.6	193	11913
1988							
1989							

Sources: International Monetary Fund, *International Financial Statistics*; Organization for Economic Cooperation and Development, *Main Economic Indicators*, and National Sources.

In the postwar period, the Australian economy developed around a framework of significant government intervention. The creation of a large and diverse manufacturing base was a high priority of successive governments. This strategy was pursued through an import-substitution policy, supported first by import licensing and then by various tariffs. Since the early 1980s the government has reduced reliance on protection and has moved away somewhat from using tariffs.

In Australia, immigration policy has been traditionally used as a tool for economic development.

The Formal Structure of Economic Management

Australia, or as it is officially named, the Commonwealth of Australia, is a federally structured state that resulted from the union of six British colonies—New South Wales, Victoria, Queensland, South Australia, Western Australia, and Tasmania—in 1901. The former colonies are now the states of the Commonwealth, each with its own government and Parliament. The federal Parliament comprises the queen (represented by the governor-general), the Senate (with ten senators per state), and the House of Representatives (with 125 members). Elections for the Senate take place every six years, and for the House of Representatives every three years. The executive power is with the government, consisting of the prime minister and the ministers, appointed by Parliament.

The constitution states the areas in which the federal authorities have the legislative power and leaves all other areas to state legislation. The constitution assigns to the Commonwealth responsibility for defense, foreign affairs, international and interstate trade and commerce, maritime activities, currency and banking, and social security payments. In the area of banking, the constitution gives the Commonwealth power over "banking, other than State banking; also State banking extending beyond the limits of the State concerned, the incorporation of banks and the issue of paper money." The states are responsible for most other areas, especially for education, health, transport, public safety, and community and social services. Local authorities operate some of the road systems, recreation and cultural services, and services to property.

Australia has a considerably unionized workforce (about 42 percent of employees are members) built mainly along craft occupational lines. There are 153 unions affiliated with the Australian Council of Trade Unions. If the state-registered unions are counted separately, there are more than three hundred unions, but only about eighty-five of them have a membership of more than five thousand. This has led to a decomposition of the workforce into a large number of skill and occupational groups. Contrary to most other OECD countries, relationships between employers and unions are not governed by collective agreements but by so-called awards that are a combination of agreements between the parties and subsequent decisions by federal and state industrial tribunals. The resulting awards, according to OECD estimates, cover about 85 percent of the workforce and even include nonunionized firms.[44]

Australia's financial system was highly regulated until the end of the 1970s, leading to a strict segmentation of the financial markets. Regulation took several forms: interest rate and maturity controls, portfolio restrictions, entry controls, and, finally, exchange controls. One result of these controls was that by the early 1980s the Australian banking sector had developed into a highly concentrated sector; four trading banks accounted for more than 85 percent of all trading bank assets. The system of regulatory measures in force at that time was constructed not only to protect investors and to maintain confidence in the stability of financial markets and institutions, but also to assist in implementing monetary policy and to aid the sale of government securities.

In 1979 a reform process was initiated and progressive liberalization started leading to a lifting of exchange controls by 1983, abolition of interest rate controls, introduction of a tender system for selling Treasury notes, and establishment of a considerable number of new banks. Deregulation has transformed the Australian financial sector from a highly regulated and uncompetitive one into one in which market forces are the dominant determinants of financial and credit flows. As a result, the government has lost some of its economic power.[45]

Monetary Policy

Monetary policy in Australia is in the hands of the Reserve Bank of Australia, but it involves both the government and the central bank. The Reserve Bank's charter is set out in the Reserve Bank Act. It enjoins the Board of the Bank, "within the limits of its power," to ensure that monetary and banking policy is directed "to the greatest advantage of the people of Australia." The relevant powers are to be "exercised in such a manner as, in the opinion of the Board will best contribute to the stability of the currency of Australia; the maintenance of full employment in Australia; and the economic prosperity and welfare of the people of Australia." The Reserve Bank was established in 1959 and started to operate in 1960. However, its functions had been performed by other institutions before.

The ultimate goal of monetary policy in Australia has always been noninflationary growth of the economy. The policy seeks to achieve monetary and credit conditions consistent with that objective. As a secondary objective, the Bank operates to smooth major seasonal and other short-term fund imbalances in the market. These arise mainly from the pattern of Commonwealth government transactions, particularly tax collections.

The Reserve Bank Act puts the duty on its Board to formulate and carry out its monetary policy—not as agent for, or adviser to, government, but on its own responsibility. Based on the Reserve Bank Act, the Bank Board consists of the governor, the deputy governor, the secretary of the Department of the Treasury, and seven other members, who are appointed by the governor-general. Of these seven other members of the Board, at least five cannot be officers of the Bank or of the Public Service of the Commonwealth.[46] The governor is the chairman of the Board, and his deputy is the deputy chairman. The governor and the deputy governor are appointed by the governor-general for a period not exceeding seven years and are eligible for reappointment. The seven other members are also appointed by the governor-general but only for five years each.

The Bank has twin roles: power over monetary policy and supervision of banks' competence and performance. The Reserve Bank attempts to control the liquidity of the overall financial system, thereby influencing interest rates, and lending and monetary growth, in a way that does not discriminate against banks.

Since the late 1970s and early 1980s open market operations have become the principal instrument of monetary policy. (Before that time, the Reserve Bank relied mainly on changes in the statutory reserve deposits ratio of the banks with the Reserve Bank[47] and informal controls on the level of bank lending.) With the floating of the Australian dollar in December 1983 and with the removal of most interest rate and deposit-taking restrictions, the environment was created within which monetary policy could be far more market oriented in its operations and monetary authorities could exercise greater control over prime liquidity in the system.

The major aim of the Reserve Bank's domestic market operations is to maintain the official market interest rate at a level consistent with the objectives of monetary policy. This type of policy, which uses the interest rate as an operating instrument, has been implemented since the floating of the exchange rate in December 1983. The Reserve Bank tries to maintain interest rates within some desired band while it does not try to peg them.[48]

The bulk of the Reserve Bank's market operations are with the (nine) authorized dealers (whose ownership is strictly controlled as to prevent other than minority holdings by Australian banks or by nonresidents). The dealers act as the intermediaries between the Bank and the financial system, as banks do not hold liquid deposits of any size with the Reserve Bank. By trading in securities with the dealers, the Bank can influence the dealers' funding needs in the market more generally. Only in unusual situations will the Reserve Bank transact directly with banks when implementing its open market operations.

The Reserve Bank exercises what is generally known as prudential supervision over the standards of control and operation of banks that are authorized under Commonwealth law. Although state banks are not within the same Commonwealth authority, each state bank has voluntarily entered into parallel arrangements with the Reserve Bank. The Reserve Bank has installed a comprehensive system for the prudential supervision of banks. With the deregulation of the banking system in the mid-1980s, the substantial growth in the number of banks, and the rapid diversification of bank activities both in Australia and abroad, the Reserve Bank has strengthened its prudential supervision. Each new authorization to open a bank carries conditions that the new bank will consult with the Reserve Bank on prudential matters and will operate within prudential standards determined by the Reserve Bank. The Reserve Bank is also in charge of note issuing and for this purpose has a Note Issue Department.[49]

The Bank is the banker and financial agent of the Commonwealth and of several state governments. It keeps all the accounts of the Treasury, performs the usual banking activities for these customers, and advises and supports the central government with respect to its short- and long-term financial needs. It sells and administers the government notes and bonds.

The Bank is required to keep the government informed of its policy. If there are differences of view about the appropriateness of that policy, then the treasurer and the Board must confer and seek to resolve the differences. If they fail to do so, then the governor-general determines the policy which the Bank must adopt, but he receives a recommendation from the treasurer. When such a direction is given, the treasurer is required to inform Parliament and to table statements by the government and the Board, setting out their respective views on the issues involved. But these provisions have never been used. Therefore, there are good grounds for the central bank to try to understand the policies and aspirations of the government of the day and, so far as its own statutory duties permit, to cooperate with the government. In return, the government ought to allow the central bank freedom to operate in its own field within the limits of its charter. The net profits of the Bank in each year are divided between the Reserve Bank Reserve Fund and the Commonwealth.

Fiscal Policy

The structure of public finances in Australia reflects the federal system of government. It comprises three tiers, namely, the Commonwealth, the states, and local governments. The Commonwealth sector comprises the transactions of the Commonwealth budget and those of a number of public enterprises that operate outside the budget, including the Australian Postal and Telecommunications Commissions, the Australian Shipping Commission, the Australian Wool Corporation, Quantas Airways, and Australian Airlines. The budget accounts for the great bulk of Commonwealth sector outlays and receipts (both about 95 percent in 1985–86), although the nonbudget sector undertakes most of Commonwealth direct capital spending (86 percent in 1985–86).

In addition to the Commonwealth sector, the public sector includes the state and local sector, which comprises the budget and nonbudget authorities of six states and the Northern Territory, as well as numerous local authorities. The state and local sector is an important part of the public sector; its outlays, which amounted to about 22 percent of GDP in recent years but declined to 18.5 percent in 1988–89, represent more than half the total outlays of the public sector.

The composition of outlays differs markedly between the Commonwealth and the state and local sector. The state and local sector accounts for almost 70 percent of total public spending on goods and services, while the Commonwealth sector provides most of the transfer payments from the public to the private sector (about 75 percent). The differences in the composition of outlays reflect the distinct constitutional responsibilities of the different levels of government (which have already been mentioned above).

The Commonwealth raises almost 75 percent of total public sector receipts. Taxes collected by the Commonwealth approach about 80 percent of total tax revenues. The constitution gives the Commonwealth the exclusive right to impose customs and excise duties as well as most sales taxes. By agreement with the states, the Commonwealth also collects income taxes on companies and individuals. The states and local governments raise taxes only through payroll taxes, and various narrowly based taxes, such as property taxes, stamp duties, and motor vehicle taxes.

In an international comparison, both payroll taxes and taxes on property are comparatively important revenue raisers in Australia, reflecting their significance to the states and the local authorities. Motor vehicle license fees are another important source of revenue to the state and local sector.

Because of the limited tax authority, the state and local sector has to rely heavily on transfer payments and net advances from the Commonwealth. More than 40 percent of the outlays of the state and local government sector are covered by transfer payments and net advances. The main forms of Commonwealth payments to state governments are (1) general revenue grants, (2) specific purpose payments, and (3) general purpose capital assistance.

General revenue grants are mainly in the form of financial assistance grants and identified health grants. They are normally determined at annual Premiers' Conferences and assist states in financing current spending. Their use is at each State's discretion. They amount to more than half of the total payments from the Commonwealth to the state and local government sector. The Commonwealth

Grants Commission (CGC), an independent statutory body, determines the distribution of the major general revenue grants among the states and the Northern Territory in accordance with the principle of fiscal equalization. The goal is to enable each state to provide government services at about the same standards as in the other states without imposing taxes and charges at levels very different from those in the other states.

Specific purpose payments are tied; that is, the Commonwealth sets conditions on how they are to be used. Specific purpose grants can be for either current or capital purposes.

The third major form of Commonwealth payment to the states—general purpose capital assistance—is determined by the Loan Council, which comprises the representatives of the Commonwealth and each state government. It usually meets in conjunction with the Premiers' Conference.[50]

In Australia government borrowing from the central bank used to be guaranteed by the issue of "public" Treasury bills, not available for public subscription. The government was able to borrow from the central bank by issuing low-interest Treasury bills. These arrangements fell into disuse during the 1980s when borrowing in the market replaced borrowing at the central bank. Now, the government no longer borrows from the central bank by way of Treasury bills but has short-term borrowing facilities with the Bank and draws against this account whenever it needs money to bridge unforeseen gaps between net government spending and the receipt of funds via the issue (by tender) of government securities. These borrowings are at market-related rates and are for very short terms. They serve as emergency measures and are not part of the government's normal funding arrangements.

The Treasury, subject to the approval of the Australian Loan Council, is responsible for financing the Commonwealth government's budget. The terms of borrowing by the Commonwealth government are fixed by the Council in the light of market conditions, with advice received from both the Treasury and the Reserve Bank.

Incomes Policy

During most of the 1980s the wage determination process in Australia was dominated by the bilateral Accord between the Australian Council of Trade Unions (ACTU) and the Labor party. As a consequence, wage determination has been a very centralized process. Negotiations between government and union regarding the required size of the wage adjustment have tended to be long and the outcome uncertain. In 1987 the OECD observed that this long, uncertain process might sometimes have had negative repercussions on business and foreign investors' expectations, leading to hesitancy in investment decisions and exchange market pressure. To the extent that monetary policy had to be tightened to support the currency, interest rates were higher than would otherwise have been the case. In this respect the wage negotiation process in Australia has potential repercussions on monetary policy and reduces the central bank's power and degree of freedom.

Trade Policy

Australia has a long history of intervention in product markets, especially through the use of border protection of various forms. For many years, trade protection constituted the principal instrument of industrial policy in Australia. In terms of nominal tariff levels, Australian protection of manufacturing is among the highest in the developed world. The OECD estimated that in 1983 about 44 percent of all imports entering Australia were subject to nontariff barriers, compared, for instance, to only 7.5 percent in the case of Austria. Australia is a member of GATT and of the Cairns Group of exporters of agricultural goods.

NOTES

We are indebted to Gerhard Lehner, Doris Grünwald, Ake Törnquist, Winfried Lang, Bruce Montador, John Murray, Chris Ryan, and Peter Zdrahal for helpful comments. Any remaining errors are, however, our own responsibility. The views expressed are those of the authors and not necessarily those of the Austrian National Bank.

1. See Tables 5.1 and 5.2.

2. Liberalization is defined as the cross-border dismantling of controls (foreign exchange controls), and deregulation refers to the abolition of domestic impediments to market forces. Note, however, that a "fully" liberalized and deregulated economy will also have a set of broad regulations ("rules of the game") within which markets are free to operate.

3. For example, both monetary policy and fiscal consolidation measures are "caused" by international trends.

4. Note that the nationalization laws were not passed for ideological reasons.

5. See Hochreiter (1989b).

6. There is an exception insofar as the Bank may discount federal Treasury certificates up to 5 percent of the Federal Republic's gross annual tax receipts according to the latest published provisional budget results (Art. 41, Austrian National Bank Act).

7. At irregular intervals the Parity Commission meets as the "economic policy dialogue" and discusses the state of the economy as presented by the Austrian Economic Research Institute, the Ministry of Finance, and the Austrian National Bank.

8. The power of the Ministry of Finance is extraordinarily large. Apart from responsibility for the budget, the ministry also supervises banking and insurance operations, serves as the ownership representative in the (partly) state-owned banks, controls the issue of securities, and handles debt management.

9. The figures are 52 percent and 40 percent of total revenue, respectively. The rest is made up of fees and import taxes.

10. See the subsection Monetary Policy above.

11. The Parity Commission was set up in 1957, and the subcommittees in 1957, 1962, and 1963, respectively.

12. The Federal Economic Chamber, the Austrian Chamber of Labor, the Presidential Conference of Agriculture, and the Trade Union Federation.

13. There are the following important exceptions: new products, technical products, goods exposed to fashion trends, and most services.

14. See Tables 5.3 and 5.4.

15. OECD, *Economic Surveys, Sweden,* 1988–89 p. 55.

16. About 7 percent in the central administration and more than 25 percent in the regional and local administrations.

17. But as the OECD (1989) points out, the Swedish unemployment statistics do not include workers who take part in labor-market programs. Inclusion of these workers would raise the unemployment ratio by about 3.5 percentage points. At the same time early retirement pensioners, another large group amounting to about 3.5 percent of the labor force, is also not counted. Finally, part-time workers who would want to have full-time jobs are also not part of the statistics.

18. Heclo and Madsen (1987), p. 109.

19. See OECD, *Economic Surveys, Sweden,* 1988–89, p. 14. See also Hochreiter (1989a) for a comparison of Austrian and Swedish monetary policy.

20. The general government's current revenues amount to 63 percent of GDP and public consumption 27 percent (1987).

21. See Heclo and Madsen (1987), p. 9.

22. As the Bank states in its Annual Report, 1988, "the primary goal for monetary policy is the maintenance of a fixed exchange rate with a trade-weighted basket of foreign currencies."

23. See Bank of Sweden, *Quarterly Review,* I/1988.

24. The members of the Governing Board elect from outside their own number no more than two deputy governors of the Riksbank.

25. As is the National Debt Office which administers the national debt.

26. The new Riksbank Act which came into force in 1989 has reduced the dependence of the Riksbank on the Parliament somewhat by, for example, extending the term of the governor, but, as we tried to show, the degree of independence is by no means comparable to that in some countries in Central Europe.

27. One likely consequence of this different approach to central bank independence is the fact that inflation in Sweden has been consistently higher than that in Austria— usually two to three times as high during the 1980s.

28. Heclo and Madsen (1987), p. 105.

29. In November 1989, however, an ambitious tax reform package was adopted with the goal of encouraging hard work and saving by lowering income tax rates considerably.

30. However, there is the rule that central and local income taxes are not allowed to surpass 80 percent in any income bracket.

31. Swedish Constitution of 1974, Chapter 9, Article 10.

32. See Tables 5.5 and 5.6.

33. In 1982 the patriation of the British North American Act occurred, but because of disputes among the provinces the constitution has not yet been implemented. In April 1987 an accord was reached between the federal government (prime minister) and the provincial premiers, the so-called Meech Lake Accord, characterized by a certain degree of decentralization. The formal ratification by the ten provincial legislatures, however, had not yet occurred by the end of 1989.

34. OECD, *Economic Surveys, Canada,* 1980–81, p. 18.

35. OECD, *Economic Surveys, Canada*, 1985–86, p. 41.

36. OECD, *Economic Surveys, Canada* 1980–81, p. 32.

37. Ibid., p. 31.

38. For a detailed description of the reasons for the establishment of the Bank of Canada, see Bordo and Redish (1987).

39. The twelve outside members of the Bank of Canada's Board of Directors are intended to bring a wide range of backgrounds and a good balance of regional representation to the formulation of the Bank's policies.

In practice, the governor and senior deputy governor, with the assistance of their senior officers, formulate and conduct monetary policy and report to the Board. The directors, who are expected to devote only a small part of their time to the affairs of the Bank and are not required to be experts in the field of monetary policy, are concerned almost exclusively with administrative questions.

40. OECD, *Economic Surveys, Canada*, 1985–86, p. 47.

41. Public ownership of petrol retailing is about to be terminated.

42. See OECD, *Economic Surveys, Canada*, 1987–88, p. 70.

43. See Tables 5.7 and 5.8.

44. See OECD, *Economic Surveys, Australia*, 1987–88, p. 71.

45. See Swamy and Tavlas (1987).

46. In practice, none of the seven members has ever come from within the Bank or public service.

47. The last change occurred in 1981.

48. See Dotsey (1987).

49. Its accounts and transactions used to be kept separate from the other accounts and transactions of the Bank, but they are no longer separated.

50. The Loan Council was established in 1927 under the Financial Agreement between the states and the Commonwealth, with a view to coordinating the borrowings of the Commonwealth and the state governments. It consists of the prime minister of the Commonwealth and the six state premiers, or their representatives. Under the Financial Agreement, state governments gave up the right to borrow by issuing their own securities. The Commonwealth issued securities on their behalf (the last time in 1986–87), the amount being determined by the Loan Council. The funds borrowed were then lent to the states for spending at their discretion on capital works. The Loan Council set global limits on borrowings by state and territory, semigovernment and local authorities, and government-owned companies and trusts. The Commonwealth authorities' borrowings are also subject to global borrowing limits.

REFERENCES

Austrian National Bank Act, 1984.

Bank of Canada Act.

Bank of Sweden (1988). *Quarterly Review* 1 (1988).

Bordo, M. D., and Redish, A. "Why Did the Bank of Canada Emerge in 1935?" *Journal of Economic History* (June 1987): 405–17.

Breuss, F. "Österreichs Aussenwirtschaft 1945–1982." Wien: 1983.

Clement, W., and Socher, K. (eds.). *Stephan Koren—Wirtschaftsforscher und Wirtschaftspolitiker in Österreich*. Wien: Orac, 1989.

Crow, J. W. "The Work of Canadian Monetary Policy." Eric J. Hanson Memorial Lecture, January 18, 1988.

Dotsey, M. "The Australian Money Market and the Operations of the Reserve Bank of Australia: A Comparative Analysis." *Federal Reserve Bank of Richmond Economic Review* (September/October 1987): 19–31.

Farnleitner, J. and Schmidt, E. "The Social Partnership." In *The Political Economy of Austria*, edited by S. W. Arndt. Washington D.C., and London: American Enterprise Institute, 1982, pp. 87–98.

Gantner, M. "Die öffentliche Finanzwirtschaft." In *Handbuch der österreichischen Wirtschaftspolitik*, 3, edited by H. Abele et al. Auflage, 1989, pp. 221–46. Wien: Manz.

Hochreiter, E. "Austria's Monetary and Exchange Rate Policy—Some Comparative Remarks with Respect to Sweden." Paper prepared for a talk at the Sveriges Riksbank, April 5, 1989a.

———. "The Austrian National Bank Act—What Does It Say About Monetary Policy?" 1989b.

Johnston, R. A. "Address to Australian Business Economists." Sydney, July 14. Reprinted in *BIS Review* (September 1, 1989): 1–4.

Lehner, G. *Steuerpolitik in Österreich*. Wien: 1987.

Lindström, E. *The Swedish Parliamentary System*. Stockholm: The Swedish Institute, 1983.

Nowotny, E. "Institutionelle Grundlagen, Akteure und Entscheidungsverhältnisse in der österreichischen Wirtschaftspolitik." In *Handbuch der österreichischen Wirtschaftspolitik*, 3, edited by H. Abele et al. Auflage, 1989, pp. 247–70. Wien: Manz.

OECD. *Economic Surveys. Australia*. Various issues. OECD: Paris.

———. *Austria*. Various issues. OECD: Paris.

———. *Canada*. Various issues. OECD: Paris.

———. *Sweden*. Various issues. OECD: Paris.

Reserve Bank Act, 1959.

Reserve Bank of Australia. "The Reserve Bank's Domestic Market Operations." *Bulletin* (June 1985).

———. "Monetary Policy from the Inside." *Bulletin* (November 1985).

———. "Recent Developments in Regulatory and Supervisory Arrangements in Australia." *Bulletin* (September 1989).

———. *Report and Financial Statements*. Sydney: 1989.

Swamy, P.A.V.B., and Tavlas, G. S. "Financial Deregulation, the Demand for Money, and Monetary Policy in Australia." International Monetary Fund, Working Paper WP/87/74, 1987.

Vincent, B. "New Baby Is Causing Concern." *Financial Times*, November 9, 1989, Section 3, p. 4.

Winckler, G. "Geld und Währung." In *Handbuch der österreichischen Wirtschaftspolitik*, 3, edited by H. Abele et al. Auflage, 1989, pp. 247–70. Wien: Manz.

Winckler, G., and Amann, E. "Exchange Rate Policy in the Presence of a Strong Trade Union." *Zeitschrift fur Nationalökonomie* 5 (1986): 259 ff.

SUGGESTIONS FOR FURTHER READING

Abele, H., Novotny, E., Schleicher, St., and Winckler, G., eds. (1989). *Handbuch der österreichischen Wirtschaftspolitik*. Auflage, Wien: Manz.

Arndt, Sven W., ed. (1982). *The Political Economy of Austria*. Washington, D.C., and London: American Enterprise Institute for Public Policy Research.

Courchene, Th. J. (1986). *Economic Management and the Division of Powers*. Toronto: University of Toronto Press.

Doern, G. B., and Phidd, R. W. (1983). *Canadian Public Policy: Ideas, Structure, Process*. Toronto: Methuen.

Hadenius, St. (1988). *Swedish Politics During the 20th Century*. Stockholm: The Swedish Institute.

Heclo, H., and Madsen, H. (1987). *Policy and Politics in Sweden*. Philadelphia: Temple University Press.

Howitt, P. (1986). *Monetary Policy in Transition: A Study of Bank of Canada Policy 1982–85*. Scarborough: Howe Institute.

OECD. *Economic Surveys, Australia*. (Yearly.) Paris: OECD.

OECD. *Economic Surveys, Austria*. (Yearly.) Paris: OECD.

OECD. *Economic Surveys, Canada*. (Yearly.) Paris: OECD.

OECD. *Economic Surveys, Sweden*. (Yearly.) Paris: OECD.

Reserve Bank of Australia. *Bulletin*. (Monthly.)

Reserve Bank of Australia. *Report and Financial Statements*. (Yearly.)

Sargent, J. (1986). *Fiscal and Monetary Policy*. Toronto: University of Toronto Press.

PART III

NATIONAL ECONOMIC POLICIES
IN DEVELOPING COUNTRIES

6

NATIONAL ECONOMIC POLICIES IN NEWLY INDUSTRIALIZED COUNTRIES

Sung-Tae Ro

INTRODUCTION

In the modern history of economic development, the rise of newly industrial countries (NICs) in Asia is unparalleled. As a result of rapid economic growth, per capita income in Korea, which is the lowest among the Asian NICs, reached U.S. $5,000 in 1989, a big jump from the meager U.S. $87 in 1962. The performance of the four NICs namely, Hong Kong, Singapore, Taiwan, and Korea, has been especially remarkable in recent years. During the period 1986–89, their economy as a whole grew at an average annual rate of almost 10 percent. Prices were stable; in Taiwan, wholesale prices declined around 10 percent during the period. The balance-of-payments surplus snowballed until 1989, with the surplus/GNP ratio in Taiwan surpassing 20 percent in 1986.

The economic success of these countries depends heavily on prudent economic policies. Other developing countries which are endowed with richer natural resources and had a head start in their development efforts are falling far behind. This chapter discusses the major economic policies of the Asian NICs, focusing mainly on Korea. Korea was chosen because it was the biggest economy among the four (see Table 6.1) and the limited space available to us did not allow us to go into policy details for each country. In addition, the Korean government has had strong control over the economy and has experimented with various types of economic policies at various stages of economic growth. Therefore, it deserves special attention.

FISCAL POLICY

The fiscal policies of the Asian NICs have traditionally been quite conservative, with budgets normally showing a slight surplus, especially in the 1980s. From

Table 6.1
Economic Performance of Asian NICs, 1986–89 (annual average, in percent)

	Real GDP Growth	Inflation Rate(WPI)
Korea	10.5	0.8
Taiwan	9.9	-2.2
HongKong	8.7	6.7
Singapore	7.9	-1.7

Source: Bank of Korea, Economic Indicators of Major Countries, 1990.

Note: The inflation rate for Hong Kong is in terms of the Consumer Price Index.

the early stages of development, they have had well-organized tax systems, and the principle of a small government prevailed in determining the size of the budget. Even in countries like Korea and Taiwan, which could not help spending a large amount of money for defense purposes, total government spending has been constrained not to increase at a higher rate than the expected nominal GNP growth rate.

In Korea, fiscal policy was formulated in consideration of a development strategy: a high level of savings and investments on the one hand, and export-led growth on the other. Both tax and expenditure shares of GNP are relatively low. Reliance on indirect taxes is quite high. The fiscal policy appears to have done well in view of Korea's rapid economic growth. Yet, it has created serious disparity in income and wealth with less emphasis on social welfare. Recently, some efforts have been made to improve the situation with an increasing share of social services expenditures and of direct taxes.

Tax Policy

Korea's tax policy has been devoted to economic growth. Its major concern is simply to secure more revenue and to increase government savings. The general assessment is that the policy has been quite successful in meeting the government's revenue requirements needed for economic development. Yet, it has contributed to the unfair distribution of the tax burden and the inefficient allocation of economic resources, together with preferential loans and industrial promotion measures. As the economy matures, more attention is being paid to an equitable tax system, and the portion of direct taxes is increasing.

The Tax System

The tax-raising authority in Korea is highly centralized to the central government.[1] In 1966 the government modernized the tax system and created the Office of National Tax Administration (ONTA), a tax collection agency, in an attempt

Table 6.2
Tax Structure, 1989

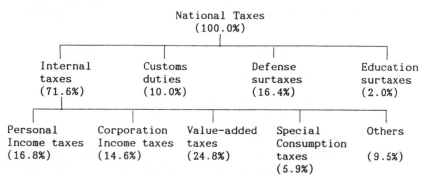

National Taxes
(100.0%)

Internal	Customs	Defense	Education
taxes	duties	surtaxes	surtaxes
(71.6%)	(10.0%)	(16.4%)	(2.0%)

Personal	Corporation	Value-added	Special	Others
Income taxes	Income taxes	taxes	Consumption	
(16.8%)	(14.6%)	(24.8%)	taxes	(9.5%)
			(5.9%)	

Sources: Economic Planning Board, *Korean Economic Indicators*, 1990; Bank of Korea, *Monthly Bulletin*, April 1990.

to increase tax revenues. It also introduced a value added tax, a defense surtax, luxury consumption taxes in the 1970s, and an education surtax in 1981. Tax receipts (national taxes) accounted for 83 percent of government revenues and about 18 percent of GNP in 1989. As shown in Table 6.2, central government taxes are divided into internal taxes, customs duties, defense surtaxes, and education surtaxes. Internal taxes account for 71.6 percent of the government's total tax revenues. Internal taxes include individual income taxes, corporation income taxes, value added taxes, special consumption taxes, and others (liquor, telephone, stamp, inheritance and gift, assets revaluation, securities transaction taxes, and other miscellaneous receipts).

Currently, there are eight tax brackets for personal incomes from 5 to 50 percent.[2] Including the defense surtax, personal incomes are actually taxed in the range of 5.5 to 60 percent. Capital gains from securities sales are exempt from taxation, whereas capital gains from other assets sales are taxable but hard to capture. Personal income taxes account for only 16.8 percent of national taxes. The portion is very low compared to that in developed countries.[3] The nominal corporate tax rate varies from 20 to 33 percent. With the inclusion of defense surtaxes, the effective tax rate ranges from 24 to 41.25 percent. Corporation income taxes account for 14.6 percent of total tax revenues.

The value added taxes introduced in 1977 are the biggest portion of internal taxes, accounting for 24.8 percent of total tax receipts. It has a uniform tax rate of 10 percent. A defense surtax was adopted in 1975 and has put additional taxes of 2.5 to 30 percent on almost all types of income, commodities, services, and imports. This surtax accounts for 16.4 percent of total tax receipts and has been used to establish a self-reliant national defense. It expires at the end of 1990. In 1981 the Korean authorities introduced an education surtax to secure expenditures on school facilities and compensation for teachers. The education tax is levied at the rates of 0.5 to 10 percent on interest and dividend income,

Table 6.3
Ratios of Direct and Indirect Taxes to Total Tax Receipts

	1980	1984	1987	1988	1989
Direct taxes	26.0%	38.1%	41.1%	44.9%	49.8%
Indirect taxes	74.0%	61.9%	58.9%	55.1%	50.2%

Source: Ministry of Finance, *Financial and Monetary Statistics*, various issues.

liquors, cigarettes, and the gross receipts from the finance and insurance business. It accounts for 2 percent of total tax revenue. This education surtax will be replaced by a research surtax after 1991. Customs duties account for 10 percent of tax revenue. However, its share continues to decline as the Korean economy becomes an international open market with lower tariff rates.

Tax Burdens

As discussed above, Korea relies heavily on indirect taxes in order to support government expenditures, whereas the majority of government revenues in developed countries is in the form of direct taxes such as income taxes. Although this Korean tax system was effective for the export-led industrialization policy, it resulted in an unfair distribution of tax burdens and aggravated the social tension between haves and have-nots. Recognizing this problem, the government has recently tried to improve the situation. As a result, the direct tax share in the total national tax revenues increased continuously from 26.0 percent in 1980 to 49.8 percent in 1989, while the weight of indirect taxes decreased from 74.0 to 50.2 percent during the period (see Table 6.3).

During the 1970s the Korean government gave export-oriented companies tax favors such as accelerated depreciation and investment tax credits. The accelerated depreciation is still in effect, whereas investment tax credits were abolished in 1981. The economic recession of the early 1980s resulted in many bankruptcies. As a remedy, the government gave acquiring firms financial benefits such as tax exemption on capital gains from the sales of acquired assets and loans with low-interest rates. The government also cut tax rates for capital gains on real estates and for selected consumption items to encourage construction and consumption activities.

Overall, the tax policy in Korea has played a successful role in achieving economic growth and stability for the last two decades. Yet, it has also produced side effects such as an unfair and inefficient distribution of economic resources by giving many favors to powerful conglomerates. Although the current tax system is favorable to the rich, the tax burden of 18.3 percent in 1988 when the per capita GNP of Korea exceeded $4,000 is quite low compared to the tax burdens of developed countries in the years with a similar level of per capita GNP (see Table 6.4).

Table 6.4
Tax Burden Ratio to GNP

	Korea	Japan	USA	UK	W Germany
Year	1988	1975	1970	1975	1970
Per capita GNP	$4,040	$4,466	$4,841	$4,221	$3,041
Tax burden ratio	18.3%	14.9%	23.0%	29.7%	22.6%

Source: Ministry of Finance, *Financial and Monetary Statistics*, May 1989.

Expenditure Policy

The Korean government has pursued economic progress and efficiency but did not pay much attention to social welfare until recently. As a consequence, the portion of welfare spending is very small in government spending compared to defense expenditures. However, Korea has achieved phenomenal economic success. Thus, the government is looking for a gradual turnaround in the direction of spending, with more stress on social welfare.

The Budgetary Process

The Economic Planning Board (EPB), whose minister is also the deputy prime minister of the Korean government, monitors the budgetary process.[4] The system has been in effect since the 1960s. Government ministries and agencies are requested to submit their plans for new projects for the following fiscal year by the end of February. The budget office of the EPB promulgates budget guidelines to all ministries and agencies by the end of March. Their formal budget outlines are submitted to the EPB by the end of May. After discussions with various ministries, the EPB prepares a draft budget and submits it to the president by the end of August. During September adjustments are made in response to pleas by ministers or the ruling party. The final draft is turned in to the National Assembly in early October.

The National Assembly should discuss and revise the budget by December 3. The Congress may reduce the budget amount, but it may not increase it without presidential approval. If the budget is not approved on time, operating expenditures at the level of the current year are automatically approved. Within statutory limits, some existing tax rates may be increased or reduced without the approval of the National Assembly.[5] Supplementary budgets are usually submitted in the late summer or early fall for congressional approval.

The EPB is also responsible for monitoring budget expenditures during the course of the year. Ministries should report their spending quarterly. In general, Korean officials adhere to the approved budget. The EPB may advance or retard expenditures, especially the inauguration of new projects, by issuing guidelines. This powerful role of the EPB was effective during the past years of the government-led economic development.

Table 6.5
Composition of Government Expenditures as Proportion of GNP

	1975	1980	1985	1988
General Account	15.1%	17.6%	15.9%	14.3%
	(100.0%)	(100.0%)	(100.0%)	(100.0%)
General administration	1.7%	1.7%	1.6%	1.4%
	(11.3%)	(9.7%)	(10.1%)	(9.9%)
Defense expenditures	4.4%	6.3%	4.9%	4.4%
	(28.8%)	(35.6%)	(30.6%)	(30.7%)
Social development & education	2.9%	4.3%	4.3%	4.0%
	(19.4%)	(24.1%)	(26.9%)	(28.3%)
Economic development	4.0%	3.8%	2.6%	2.1%
	(26.7%)	(21.5%)	(16.1%)	(14.6%)
Others	2.1%	1.6%	2.6%	2.3%
	(13.9%)	(9.0%)	(16.2%)	(16.4%)
Special Account	5.8%	5.9%	3.3%	3.6%
Total	21.0%	23.5%	19.2%	17.8%

Source: Economic Planning Board, *Korean Economic Indicators*, 1990.

Government Expenditures

As shown in Table 6.5, as a proportion of GNP, total central government spending ranged from 23.5 percent in 1980 to 17.8 percent in 1988. This expenditure level is lower than the average government spending level of developed or developing countries. Military spending takes the biggest chunk of the pie, ranging from 4.4 to 6.3 percent of GNP. A high level of defense expenditures has probably contributed to less spending on social welfare or income redistribution. However, the share is expected to decrease in the future owing to the worldwide detente.

The second largest part of the budget goes to social services which cover education, health, housing, social security and welfare, and community services. Notably, more than half of this money was allocated to education. Education opportunities for have-nots appear to have helped reduce wage and salary differentials as well as forming human capital for economic and social progress. As the Korean economy grows and matures, the share of expenditures for social services is also growing—from 2.9 percent of GNP in 1975 to more than 4 percent in later years. This share is still very low compared to that in developed countries, but is expected to grow very fast in the coming years.

The portion of economic development expenditures, which was once the biggest budget item, is gradually declining from 4 percent of GNP in 1975 to only

2.1 percent in 1988. This reflects a shift in the Korean government's expenditure priorities from economic to social services. Special funds, in addition to the general account, are established mainly to support investments in infrastructure projects. The share of these funds is also decreasing—from about 6 to 3 percent of GNP in recent years.

MONETARY POLICY

The environment under which the monetary policy is implemented, namely, the central banking system and financial markets, is substantially different among Asian NICs. Hong Kong has no central bank, whereas in Singapore the Monetary Authority of the government actually implements the role of central bank. Both Taiwan and Korea have legitimate central banks—the Bank of Taiwan and the Bank of Korea.

Even in Korea and Taiwan, the power and degree of independence of the central bank differs. The Bank of Taiwan is relatively strong in terms of executing monetary policies and supervising the activities of banking institutions. Originally, the Bank of Korea also was assigned a high degree of independence when it was established in 1950 under the Bank of Korea Act. However, starting in 1962, a series of amendments of the Act have strengthened government control over monetary policy, and the independence of the central bank has accordingly weakened.

In terms of financial market development, Hong Kong and Singapore are far ahead of Korea and Taiwan. Hong Kong and Singapore have a liberalized and quite sophisticated financial system, whereas the financial development was relatively slow in Korea and Taiwan owing to government control and intervention. In response to the rapidly changing financial environment, both external and internal, a broad range of financial reform and liberalization efforts have been made in both Taiwan and Korea.

Notwithstanding the differences in financial system, the four countries have one common feature: they have successfully controlled the money supply and thereby contained inflation. After the second oil shock, they were able to restore price stability in a short period of time. This success can be largely attributed to these nations' appropriate execution of monetary policies.

Korea's Financial System

Monetary Authorities

The monetary authorities in Korea are the Bank of Korea and the Ministry of Finance. The country's central bank, the Bank of Korea, which was established in June 1950 under the Bank of Korea Act, aims to maintain the stability of the value of money and to further the efficient utilization of national resources through the sound operation and functional improvement of the nation's banking system.

The country's policymaking organ, the Monetary Board of the Bank of Korea, has formal responsibility for formulating and executing monetary policies as well as supervising the activities of banking institutions. However, the minister of finance has actually had ultimate responsibility over monetary policies since the Amendment of the Bank of Korea Act in 1962. With the start of political democratization in 1987, the rivalry between the central bank and the Ministry of Finance has become more visible, erupting in a series of heated debates on the independence of the Bank of Korea. The problem remains unsettled, hampering the liberalization and internationalization of the financial system.

Financial Institutions

Korea's financial institutions consist of both banking and nonbanking institutions. The banking institutions are the commercial and specialized banks. Under the provisions of the General Banking Act and regulations of the Monetary Board, commercial banks are regularly and systematically engaged in short- and long-term financing, sales of commercial bills, securities investment, foreign exchange business, and other financial services, with funds acquired by offering liabilities in the form of deposits, securities, or other evidence of debt (see Figure 6.1).

As of (1990), the commercial banks included eight nationwide banks, fifteen regional banks, and sixty-five branches of foreign banks. The financial structure of regional banks is similar to that of the nationwide commercial banks except for the relatively small proportion of loans in foreign currencies and foreign exchange holdings. Even though foreign banks were allowed to open branches in Korea in 1967, until recently their business activities were subject to various discriminatory restrictions. The number of regulations imposed on them, however, has been significantly reduced. In addition, the Monetary Board permitted them to have access to the rediscount facilities of the Bank of Korea as of March 1985. Commercial banks, excluding foreign bank branches, have adopted the nationwide or provincewide branch bank system and borrow heavily from the Bank of Korea to partially cover persistent excess demand by the public for banking funds.

Most specialized banks were established during the 1960s in order to provide funds to particular sectors that did not have access to commercial banks because of insufficient banking funds and/or their low profitability. They rely heavily on deposits from the public for their sources of funds, in addition to the issuance of their own debentures and borrowing from the government. Thus, they engage in business similar to that of commercial banks and compete with them for the acquisition of deposits. As of the end of June 1989, specialized banks held 47.1 percent of the assets of the total banking institutions. Loans and discounts made up 62.2 percent of their total assets, while deposits accounted for 66 percent of total liabilities (see Table 6.6).

Nonbank financial intermediaries were introduced mostly in the 1970s to attract curb market funds into the organized market, thereby helping finance the eco-

Figure 6.1
Financial Institutions (as of the end of 1989)

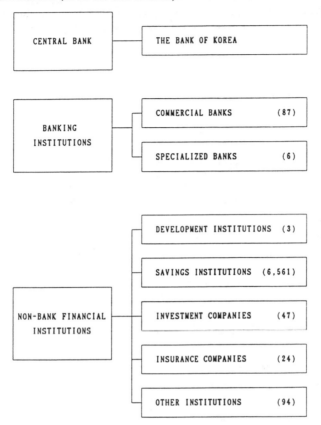

Note: Numbers in parentheses indicate the number of institutions.

nomic development plans. Their numbers and the volume of funds held have increased rapidly, and, recently, their share in total deposits held at financial institutions outstripped that of deposit money banks.

Nonbank financial institutions can be broadly classified into five categories according to their business activities: development, savings, investment, insurance, and other institutions. Development institutions provide medium- and long-term loans or credit for development of key sectors such as the export of heavy and chemical industry with government funds and funds financed by the inducement of foreign capital or the issue of special bonds. Savings institutions grant various small loans, with funds financed by special deposit-taking in the form of time deposits. The principal services of investment companies are short-term financing business such as purchases and sales of commercial paper issued by business firms, with funds raised through the issuance of their own paper or debentures and handling the Cash Management Account (CMA). In addition,

Table 6.6
Market Share of Financial Institutions (the end of period, in percent)

	'75	'80	'85	'89
Deposits				
Commercial Banks	54.6	43.8	31.4	23.9
Specialized Banks	24.3	26.4	22.3	18.3
N.B.F.I	21.1	29.8	46.3	57.8
Total	100.0	100.0	100.0	100.0
Loans & Discounts				
Commercial Banks	47.2	39.6	34.4	29.4
Specialized Banks	25.9	25.0	24.4	23.1
N.B.F.I	26.9	35.4	41.2	47.5
Total	100.0	100.0	100.0	100.0

Source: Bank of Korea, *Economic Statistics Yearbook*, 1990.
Note: NBFI = nonbank financial institutions.

insurance companies and other institutions such as securities companies and lease companies function as supplementary financial institutions, although they do not act as financial intermediaries.

In recent decades enormous changes have taken place in the structure of the financial system; these changes are reflected in the market share of different institutions. The market share of banking institutions has shrunk considerably, while that of nonbank financial institutions has grown rapidly.

The market share of banking institutions in terms of deposits in won currency contracted from about 79 percent in 1975 to around 42 percent at the end of 1989, while that of nonbank financial institutions increased from about 21 percent to around 58 percent during the same period. Among them, the share of investment companies has risen rapidly. As for loans and discounts, the market share of banking institutions dropped sharply from about 73 percent to about 53 percent during the same period.

These rapid changes in market share were caused largely by differences in regulatory treatment: nonbank financial institutions have been allowed greater freedom in their management of assets and liabilities and, most importantly, have been permitted to apply higher interest rates on their deposits and loans than those of banking institutions.

The supervision of financial institutions in Korea is shared by the Ministry of Finance and the Bank of Korea. The Bank is responsible for the supervision of banking institutions, and the Ministry supervises nonbank financial institutions.

The Monetary Board of the Bank of Korea authorizes changes in the paid-in capital and business scope of banking institutions. Most of the Board's power is delegated to the superintendent of the Office of Bank Supervision and Examination.

As for the supervision of nonbanking institution, the minister of finance directly controls the entry of the industry and indirectly supervises changes in paid-in capital and establishment/closure of branches.

Monetary Policy

Objectives and Intermediate Targets

As in other countries, income expansion through economic growth, attainment of full employment, and efficient allocations of national resources represent the ultimate goals of monetary policy in Korea. Stabilization of the overall price level, maintenance of external balance, and adjustments of cyclical fluctuations can be added as short-run goals or economic constraints.

In general, policies designed to achieve these objectives inevitably involve some tradeoff. Therefore, it is necessary to assign priorities among competing goals by judging the overall condition of the national economy.

The monetary authorities choose their instruments that will bring about desirable values for the ultimate goal variables. However, the transmission mechanism through which changes in policy instruments affect the ultimate goals is still in dispute and, in addition, involves operational lags of uncertain length. For this reason, the authorities generally choose to control particular financial variables—monetary aggregates or market interest rates—which are thought to be reliably linked to the ultimate goals. These financial variables are called intermediate targets.

The desirability of intermediate targeting is an unsettled issue in terms of the definition of intermediate targets and their reliability and controllability.

In Korea, the monetary authorities have focused on the management of different monetary aggregates since 1957, their main purpose being to grapple with the persistently high inflation accompanying rapid economic growth. Since 1979, M2, the sum of currency in circulation and total deposits of banking institutions, has served as the principal target of monetary control.[6] At present, the target rate of money growth is determined according to the following equation: target rate of money growth (annual average balance of M2) = the expected growth rate of real GNP + the anticipated inflation rate − the predicted rate of increase in the velocity of money.

Instruments of Monetary Policy

To keep monetary growth on target, Korea's monetary authorities implement their monetary policies principally through three related and complementary instruments: changes in the terms and conditions of rediscounts, open market operations in specified securities, and changes in reserve requirement ratios.

In addition to these policy instruments, the monetary authorities are also empowered with such policy instruments as setting and altering maximum interest rates on each type of deposit and directly controlling the volume of bank credit in periods of pronounced monetary expansion.

Open Market Operations. The Bank of Korea is authorized to buy or sell securities representing government obligations, other securities fully guaranteed by the government, and special negotiable bonds of the Bank of Korea called Monetary Stabilization Bonds (MSBs) in the open market. Because of the shortage of marketable instruments such as Treasury bills, the Bank of Korea's main operations involve the issuance and repurchase of Monetary Stabilization Bonds.

During 1986–89, the years of the rapidly rising current-account surplus, the Bank of Korea absorbed a sizable amount of the liquidity supplied through the foreign sector largely by the issuance of MSBs. The issuance of MSBs reached its peak at a net value of 7,199 billion won during 1988 when the balance-of-payments (BOP) surplus recorded $U.S. 14.2 billion. In 1989 the net issuance of MSBs decreased to a value of 1,148 billion won in accordance with the shrinkage of the BOP surplus to U.S. $5.1 billion.

The bond usually carries the market interest rate, but it is still not attractive to investors compared to the interest rates of the other market instruments or curb market loans. Therefore, in many cases, the bond was allocated among financial institutions.

Reserve Requirement Policy. The Bank of Korea fixes and alters the minimum reserve requirements against the deposit liabilities of banking institutions. The ratios may not exceed 50 percent, but in a period of pronounced monetary expansion, the Bank is authorized to impose marginal reserve requirements of up to 100 percent of any increase in deposits.

The minimum reserve requirement ratio for bank deposits gradually rose from 4.5 percent in 1987 to 11.5 percent, effective March 8, 1990, in response to the expansionary pressure in the money supply through the foreign sector.

Rediscount Policy. The rediscount policy of the Bank of Korea plays an important role in monetary control in Korea where commercial banks rely heavily on loans from the Bank.

The Bank of Korea supplies credit to banks through two channels, policy loans and general loans. Policy loans (rediscount of commercial bills and loans for export financing, agriculture, and fisheries) are extended to encourage banks to make loans to specific sectors. The Bank can affect the availability and cost of funds for banks by changing the loan ratios or rediscount rates. General loans of Type A are available to banks that have participated in some preferential financing. Type B general loans are frequently used to control the banks' reserve positions. For instance, loans are available with penalty rates to banks that have temporarily fallen short of reserve funds.

Direct or Selective Credit Control.   In addition to these indirect instruments, the Bank fixes ceilings on the aggregate volume of loans for each banking institution and approves in advance individual loan applications made to banks in excess of a specified limit in periods of excessive monetary expansion. The Bank may also establish general guidelines on the allocation of banking funds in order to direct loans to essential sectors.

Interest Rate Policy.   Until late 1988 interest rates for loans and deposits had been determined following the guidelines of the monetary authority. In retrospect, interest rates have been fixed artificially below the market equilibrium level, giving birth to the prosperous curb loan market. In many years real interest rates, which are the nominal rates adjusted by the inflation rate, were negative.

On December 5, 1988, however, the minister of finance removed ceilings on the major lending rates of financial institutions as well as those on a few long-term deposit rates in order to strengthen the price mechanism of interest rates and to promote the liberalization and internationalization of the financial sector (see Table 6.7).

Monetary Policy in Korea (1960–90)

Monetary Policy in the 1960s and 1970s

Economic policies in the 1960s and 1970s placed high priority on high economic growth and the creation of new employment opportunities. Accordingly, the major aim of monetary policies in these years was to help finance economic development plans.

Given the low level of capital accumulation and the lack of well-organized money markets, the monetary authorities undertook several measures aimed at a more effective mobilization of private savings in the financial markets (1) In addition to the existing nationwide commercial banks, specialized banks and regional banks were established; (2) foreign banks were allowed to open branches in Korea, largely to help induce foreign capital, thereby bridging the investment–savings gap; (3) non-bank financial institutions were introduced in an attempt to induce funds from the curb market into the organized financial market; and (4) to secure long-term investment funds for business enterprises, the government took various steps to develop the securities market.

Despite these measures, the shortage of funds persisted and usually had to be solved by expanding the money supply or by inducing an inflow of foreign capital. As a consequence, chronic inflation dogged the pursuit of rapid economic growth.

Table 6.7
Nominal and Real Interest Rate, 1970–89 (percent per annum)

	Deposit Rate (A)	Inflation Rate (B)	Real Interest Rate (A-B)
1970	22.8	15.9	6.9
1971	22.8~20.4	13.5	9.3~6.9
1972	16.8~12.0	11.7	5.1~0.3
1973	12.0	3.0	9.0
1974	15.0	24.3	-9.3
1975	15.0	25.3	-10.3
1976	15.0~16.2	15.3	-0.3~ 0.9
1977	16.2~14.4	10.2	6.0~ 4.2
1978	14.4~18.6	14.5	-0.1~ 4.1
1979	18.6	18.2	0.4
1980	24.0~19.5	28.7	-4.7~-9.2
1981	19.5~16.2	21.3	-1.8~-5.1
1982	15.0~ 8.0	7.3	7.7~ 0.7
1983	8.0	3.4	4.6
1984	9.0~10.0	2.3	6.7~ 7.7
1985	10.0	2.5	7.5
1986	10.0	2.8	7.2
1987	10.0	3.0	7.0
1988	10.0	7.1	2.9
1989	10.0	5.7	4.3

Source: Bank of Korea, *Monthly Bulletin*, 1971–90.

Note: Deposit rate is the rate on the time deposit with the maturity of one year, while the inflation rate is the change in the Consumer Price Index.

Policy instruments for monetary control, both orthodox instruments and direct controls of bank credit, could not function effectively because of factors such as the immaturity of the financial structure, the existence of persistent excess demand for banking funds, the commercial banks' heavy borrowing from the Bank of Korea, and large government deficits. Open market operations were utilized only sporadically because of the shortage of marketable instruments, as the government depended largely on borrowing from the Bank of Korea to finance its fiscal deficit rather than on the issue of government securities. Discount policy remained essentially passive and was carried out principally by reliance on adjustments of rediscount ratios and the availability of funds.

Table 6.8
Money Supply and Inflation, 1981–89 (rate of increase, in percent)

	81	82	83	84	85	86	87	88	89
M2 (Average)	25.0	27.0	15.2	7.7	15.6	18.4	19.1	21.5	19.8
CPI	21.6	7.1	3.4	2.3	2.5	2.8	3.0	7.1	5.7

Monetary Policy in the Early 1980s

Chronic inflation accompanying high economic growth in the 1970s distorted income distribution and weakened the economy's long-term growth potential by deteriorating the country's international competitiveness. Moreover, the rapid expansion of the national economy created conditions whereby direct intervention by the authorities was no longer feasible, nor indeed desirable.

Recognizing the seriousness of these problems, the monetary authorities have undertaken financial reforms aimed at bolstering reliance on the market mechanism and consolidating economic stabilization since 1981. To cope with the persistently high rate of inflation, the monetary authorities adopted a relatively tight monetary policy. The annual growth rate of the money (M2) supply, which had averaged over 30 percent in the 1970s, has tended to increase at an average level of well below 20 percent since 1983. The rate of inflation, which had reached as high as 20 to 30 percent per annum in the early 1980s, has been stabilized since 1982 at a low level of 2 to 7 percent per year (see Table 6.8).

To promote mutual competition in the financial market and thereby enhance the stabilizing function of the market mechanism, the following measures for adjusting the financial market structure were undertaken in the 1980s: privatization of commercial banks, lowered entry barriers to the financial market, greater autonomy in the management of financial institutions, reduced application of preferential interest rates on policy loans, liberalization of money markets, and gradual liberalization of foreign ivestment.

Current-Account Surpluses and Monetary Policy

During the long period of current-account deficits, the foreign sector served to siphon off liquidity. Hence, the monetary authorities relied mainly on direct controls of bank credit to the private sector so as to contain the growth of the money supply within the annual target range. With the shift of the current account into surplus since 1986, however, the excessive supply of money through the foreign sector has caused great difficulties in controlling the monetary aggregates (see Table 6.9).

Since this turnaround, the monetary authorities have made strenuous efforts

Table 6.9
MSB Outstanding and BOP Surplus, 1986–89 (billion won)

	86	87	88	89
MSBs issued (Net)	2,754.5	4,915.9	7,199.0	1,148.6
MSB outstanding	3,258.6	8,174.5	15,375.5	16,522.1
Interest on MSBs	252.1	735.9	1,469.8	2,407.0
BOP Surplus(mil US)	4,617.0	9,853.9	14,160.7	5,054.6

Source: Bank of Korea, *Economic Statistics Yearbook*, 1990.

Note: MSB = Monetary Stabilization Bond; BOP = Balance of payment in current account.

to keep the money supply within the target level: restricting the inducement of foreign capital and encouraging overseas investments and early repayment of foreign debts, a tighter control of bank credit to large enterprises via the adjustment of rediscount rates and ratios, and a substantial reduction in policy loans for export finance.

These measures had only limited effects in absorbing excess liquidity. Therefore, the Bank of Korea depended increasingly on the issuance of large amounts of Monetary Stabilization Bonds to alleviate the pressure of monetary expansion through the foreign sector.

The expansion of bond issuance and the assignment of these bonds to nonbank financial institutions hindered the proper operation of the financial market. Moreover, the increasing interest payments on MSBs themselves served to cause additional increases in the money supply, which limited the effectiveness of the issuance of MSBs as a monetary control instrument.

Realizing the need for more effective monetary control, the monetary authorities undertook an extensive deregulation of interest rates in December 1988 to make better use of the price function of market interest rates. In addition, the Bank of Korea has attempted to move gradually from a direct credit control system that imposed credit ceilings on individual banks to an indirect system whereby credit is controlled through orthodox policy instruments.

TRADE AND EXCHANGE RATE POLICIES

The NICs share a high degree of openness. As they have depended on trade for economic growth, the trade/GNP ratio is extremely high. In Singapore the ratio was over 300 percent in 1988, and even in Korea, which had the lowest among the four, it was 65 percent.[7] (See Table 6.10.)

Table 6.10
Proportion of Trade to GNP, 1981–89 (in percent)

	1981	1982	1983	1984	1985	1986	1987	1988	1989
Korea	71.0	64.7	63.6	68.9	68.5	64.5	68.5	65.1	58.9
Taiwan	91.3	85.3	87.8	90.1	83.1	86.0	89.4	92.3	78.9
HongKong	157.6	145.0	161.4	178.9	178.8	184.4	205.5	232.2	–
Singapore	365.4	331.1	289.0	276.4	268.3	263.7	296.1	335.5	–

Sources: Economic Planning Board (Korea), *Major Statistics of Korean Economy*; The Central Bank
of China, *Financial Statistics*; Census and Statistics Department, (Hong Kong) *Monthly Digest
of Statistics*; and International Monetary Fund, *International Financial Statistics*.

Table 6.11
Export Growth Rates, 1960s–1980s (in percent)

	1960's	1970's	1980's
Korea	40.8	39.2	15.8
Taiwan	24.2	32.6	15.7
HongKong	–	20.5	17.9
Singapore	4.6	22.15	13.0

Sources: Economic Planning Board (Korea), *Major Statistics of Korean Economy*; The Central Bank
of China, *Financial Statistics*; Census and Statistics Department (Hong Kong) *Monthly Digest
of Statistics*; and International Monetary Fund, *International Financial Statistics*.

Note: 1960s = 1962–69; 1970s = 1970–79; 1980s = 1980–89 (in the case of Hong Kong and
Singapore, 1980–88).

High dependence on trade is a natural result of these countries' export promotion policies. Export growth has been remarkable; in the 1960s export in U.S.
dollars had been growing at an average annual rate of 40 percent in Korea. In
the 1970s, the export growth rates of Asian NICs ranged from 39.2 to 20.5
percent. In the 1980s they ranged from 13.0 to 17.9 percent. (See Table 6.11.)

In the mid-1980s, thanks to both rapid export growth and declining oil prices,
Asian NICs started to record a large amount of balance-of-payments surpluses.
In Taiwan, the surplus/GNP ratio reached 20.8 percent in 1986, and the foreign
assets held snowballed (See Table 6.12.) The United States, suffering from its
ever-growing trade deficit, strengthened its pressure on NICs to open their markets and to appreciate their currencies. With the introduction of adjustment
policies, the current-account surplus has begun to shrink in these countries,
notably in Korea.[8]

Table 6.12

Proportion of Trade to Surplus or Deficit to GNP, 1981–89 (in percent)

	1981	1982	1983	1984	1985	1986	1987	1988	1989
Korea	-7.3	-3.4	-2.1	-1.6	-1.0	2.2	4.9	5.2	0.4
Taiwan	2.9	6.8	9.3	14.4	17.3	20.8	18.6	8.3	9.1
HongKong	-9.8	-8.5	-7.0	-0.6	1.5	0.3	0.0	1.3	-
Singapore	-49.6	-50.0	-36.4	-24.1	-19.1	-16.5	-18.8	-18.5	-

Sources: Economic Planning Board (Korea), *Major Statistics of Korean Economy*; The Central Bank of China, *Financial Statistics*; Census and Statistics Department (Hong Kong) *Monthly Digest of Statistics*; and International Monetary Fund, *International Financial Statistics*.

Note: + = trade surplus; – = trade deficit.

TRADE POLICY

Export

The governments of Asian NICs have provided exporters with various types of incentive, which have played a major role in export expansion. In the case of Korea, in the 1960s when government promoted exports in full force, one of the most favorable treatments for exporters was the export loan. Since the government had adopted a low-interest rate policy, there was excess demand for bank credits. Exporters, however, had access to bank loans, and as long as certain conditions were met, their applications were almost automatically approved. The interest rate on the export loan was much lower than that of other types of bank loans, which was quite low when compared to unorganized financial market rates. For example, in 1969 the curb market loan rate was about 50 percent per annum and the general bank loan rate was 24 percent per annum, whereas the export loan rate was only 6 percent.

In Korea, export incentives introduced up until the early 1970s included a commodity tax exemption, export financing, a foreign exchange deposit system that insured exporters against exchange risk, trade licensing based on export performance, the deduction of corporation and income taxes, tariff exemptions of raw material imports for export promotion, a business tax exemption, and an accelerated depreciation allowance for exporters.

The Korean government specified the long-term export target in the Five-Year Economic Development Plan. In addition, at the beginning of each year the Ministry of Commerce and Industry announced its annual export goal; sometimes it was a modified one in response to a change in economic conditions. Every month, to encourage exports, the president presided over "Expanded Meetings for Export Promotion," where major exporters as well as cabinet members participated. The Korean government established "general trading companies" to promote large-scale export and provided preferential treatment for them. Exporters who performed very well in the export arena received a variety of privileges and presidential awards.

Around the end of the 1970s it became evident that Korea's export policy was causing serious problems both at home and abroad. Domestically, resources were allocated inefficiently owing to an excessive dependence on export, and price instability resulted from supply shortages within a home market. Internationally, as the volume of export expanded, Korea's export policy became more noticeable to its trading partners and was criticized. Thus, the Korean government started to abolish a variety of export assistance schemes in the late 1970s. The export financing system, which was the most powerful incentive, became practically nonexistent.

Import

Until the beginning of the 1980s various types of import restrictions had been imposed in both Korea and Taiwan, whereas the markets of Singapore and Hong Kong were open even by an advanced country's standard. Korea's restrictive import policy was justifiable because it had been a chronic trade deficit country. Only in 1986, for the first time in its modern history, did Korea record a trade surplus. In the meantime the foreign debt accumulated and reached US $46.8 billion, or 40 percent of GNP, in 1985. Korea was the fourth largest debtor country among developing countries at that time.

In addition to reducing the trade deficit, the import restrictions protected the domestic infant industries. The restrictions included high tariff rates on imports for domestic uses and nontariff barriers, such as quotas, import licensing, an import surveillance system, and other restrictions specified in special laws.

Since the early 1980s the Korean government has introduced ambitious import liberalization measures in response to changing circumstances.[9] The major objectives of the measures were to reduce the pressure from Korea's trading partners (especially the United States) and to strengthen the international competitiveness of Korean industries by abolishing overprotection.

One of the major import liberalization policies was the gradual abolition of restrictive licensing. As we see in Table 6.13, the import liberalization ratio, which shows the ratio of imports that does not need government approval to total commodities, rose from approximately 75 percent in 1981 to 96 percent in 1990. Thus, there was almost complete liberalization of manufactured goods. For agricultural products, livestock, and fishery goods, the government plans to pursue import liberalization according to the international norms of trade, or the agreements of the Uruguay Round.

Another major import liberalization effort was tariff reduction. The Korean government has gradually reduced tariffs according to the five-year plan for tariff reduction, established in 1984. As a result, the overall average tariff rate was reduced from 23.7 percent in 1983 to 11.4 percent in 1990 (see Table 6.14). During the same period, the average tariff rate on manufactured goods decreased

Table 6.13
Trend of Import Liberalization, 1981–90 (in percent)

	Total Number of Itmes (A)	Number of Non-Restricted Itmes (B)	Number of Restricted Items	Import Liberalization Rate (B)/(A)
1981	7,465	5,576	1,886	74.7%
1982	7,560	5,791	1,769	76.6%
1983	7,560	6,078	1,482	80.4%
1984	7,915	6,712	1,203	84.8%
1985	7,915	6,945	970	87.7%
1986	7,915	7,245	670	91.5%
1987	7,911	7,408	503	93.6%
1988	10,241	9,694	547	94.7%
1989	10,241	9,776	465	95.5%
1990	10,274	9,898	376	96.3%

Source: Economic Planning Board (Korea), *Major Statistics of Korean Economy*.

Table 6.14
Trend of Average Tariff Rates, 1983–90 (in percent)

	Manufactured Goods	Agricultural Goods	Overall
1983	22.6	31.4	23.7
1984	20.6	29.6	21.9
1985	20.3	28.8	21.3
1986	18.7	27.1	19.9
1987	18.2	26.4	19.3
1988	16.9	25.2	18.1
1989	11.2	20.6	12.7
1990	9.7	19.9	11.4

Source: Economic Planning Board (Korea), *Major Statistics of Korean Economy*.

from 22.6 percent to 9.7 percent, and the average tariff rate on agricultural goods was reduced from 31.4 percent to 19.9 percent.

Because of the liberalization policies and booming economy, imports started to grow by leaps and bounds. In U.S. dollars, they increased by 29.9 percent and 26.3 percent in 1987 and 1988, respectively.

Table 6.15
Trend of Appreciation Rates in Asian NICs, 1981–89 (in percent)

	Korea (W/$)	Taiwan (NT$/$)	Hong Kong (HK$/$)	Singapore (S$/$)
1981	-5.8	-4.8	-11.0	1.3
1982	-6.5	-5.2	-7.9	-1.3
1983	-5.9	-0.9	-16.5	1.3
1984	-3.9	2.0	-7.0	-0.9
1985	-7.1	-1.0	0.3	-3.1
1986	3.3	12.3	-0.2	1.0
1987	8.7	24.3	0.1	3.4
1988	15.8	1.3	-0.1	4.7
1989	0.7	7.7	-	3.2

Sources: Economic Planning Board (Korea), *Major Statistics of Korean Economy*; The Central Bank of China, *Financial Statistics*; Census and Statistics Department, (Hong Kong) *Monthly Digest of Statistics*; and International Monetary Fund, *International Financial Statistics*.

Exchange Policy

Until 1980 Korea had a fixed exchange-rate system, pegging the won to the U.S. dollar. Policymakers, worried about the inflationary effects of devaluation, both real and psychological, made special efforts to maintain the current nominal exchange rate even when inflation was running wild and the competitiveness of Korean goods was declining steeply. They learned a hard lesson in the late 1970s. Only after a reduction in the volume of export in 1979, for the first time in almost twenty years, did they make a major turnaround.

In January 1980 the won was devalued by 20 percent against the dollar, and the next month the pegging system was replaced with a new managed-floating, "double basket system." Under the new regime, the exchange rate of the won to the U.S. dollar was to be determined in principle on the basis of movements of the nominal exchange rates and the prices of major trading partners.

Two characteristics of the management of exchange rates afterward deserve mention. First, with the new system, the exchange rate changed more flexibly to maintain external competitiveness. Therefore, real effective exchange rates varied conspicuously less in the 1980s than they did in earlier periods. Second, when adjustment was needed, it was made gradually. Earlier, the exchange-rate adjustment was abrupt and large, and it was harmful to the economy. The policymakers may have wanted to avoid a repetition of past mistakes.

Because the January 1980 devaluation was not sufficient to restore the competitiveness of Korean exports, gradual depreciation continued until 1985 (see Table 6.15). As the Korean economy recorded its first-ever trade surplus, helped by the exchange-rate adjustment among major currencies and oil price collapse, U.S. pressure for the appreciation of the won intensified.

At that time the Korean government was opposed to the drastic appreciation of its currency for at least four reasons. First, the Korean won was not greatly overvalued, and the surplus was largely due to the decline in oil prices. Second, the effects of exchange-rate changes on the economy are uncertain and controversial. Third, rapid real appreciation might aggravate Korea's bilateral imbalances with Japan. It was quite possible that most benefits of appreciating the won would go to Japan, widening Korea's deficit with Japan even further without contributing to the reduction of the deficit on trade with the United States, the country pressing for appreciation. Fourth, labor disputes which erupted with the acceleration of democratization have made policymakers very cautious about exchange-rate management.

In 1986 the value of the Korean won rose 3.3 percent against the U.S. dollar. Appreciation accelerated in 1987 and 1988 as the current-account surplus increased. Starting in 1989, the surplus began to shrink as the country was losing its competitiveness owing to the appreciation and high wages. Even with the reduced deficit and a large appreciation, that year the United States designated Korea as an exchange-rate manipulating country.

In an effort to wipe off the stigma on the one hand and as a first step in liberalizing the foreign exchange market on the other, the Korean government adopted the market average exchange-rate system in March 1990. Under the new system, the exchange rate freely fluctuates within a certain range around a base rate. This rate, called the central rate, is determined on the basis of the weighted average interbank market rate obtained on the previous day. The market average exchange-rate system is an intermediate step, and, eventually, the Korean exchange-rate system is expected to be a free-floating regime.

REGULATORY POLICIES

Evolution

In some Asian NICs, especially Korea and Taiwan, government intervention prevailed in the early stage of economic development. In fact, government intervention in its economy boosted economic growth in both countries. However, it remains unanswered whether excessive government intervention in the economy is still effective and desirable when the economy grows big.

Evolution of Governmental Regulations

In the 1960s the Korean government launched its first five-year economic development plan. To expedite economic growth, the government strategically selected a few industries and intensively supported them with favorable bank credits and tax breaks. In addition, the government adopted such protective regulations as entry barriers and price regulations to promote the selected industries. This was the beginning of the history of government regulations in Korea.

In the 1970s the government decided to develop the chemical and heavy industries, and so it encouraged firms to invest lots of money in these industries. In addition, the government decided which firms could enter certain industries, including chemical and heavy industries, and deliberately discouraged competition from other firms (both domestic and foreign) in the industries in the name of industry promotion.

Beginning in the late 1970s, however, cautious talks were held regarding the reduction of government regulations and the promotion of competition, because the side-effects of these regulatory policies began to be visible and exerted an adverse effect on economic development. As the Korean economy became larger and more complex, the cost of policy failure became greater and the government could not cure all the economic problems.

At last, the government enacted the Antitrust and Fair Trade Act in 1980 and the Industry Development Act in 1986. The Industry Development Act was a merger of seven preexisting laws that had been designed to promote and support specific industries. In the 1980s, such social regulations as environmental, consumer, and worker protection were reinforced. However, the Fair Trade Act still allows exceptions to the general principles of antitrust and promotion of competition, and the Industry Development Act gives the government the authority to limit new entries into certain industries and to regulate the production capacities of the firms in the industries under the name of industry rationalization.

Characteristics of Regulations

Most government regulations in Korea were introduced in order to achieve such industrial goals as protection and promotion of domestic industries. This type of regulation usually took the form of protective regulations and resulted in a suppression of market competition. At the same time, many regulations were adopted to prevent ''excessive competition'' and to maintain ''market order.'' The industries frequently requested this kind of regulation, and in many cases the result was an arbitrary distribution of economic privileges (economic rents).

Many business activities have been subject to government permits or licenses. In many cases, however, the issuance of permits (or licenses) has been decided based on the subjective judgment of government officials. Consequently, the bureaucrats somewhat abused their discretionary power in the past. On the other hand, some business activities were required only to notify the government or to register with the government. However, the government sometimes refused to accept registrations and, in effect, made the registration procedure a licensing one.

There have been many unlawful regulatory practices. For example, the government has regulated many business activities through unofficial interventions and recommendations often called administrative directives. Although no legal penalties were in place for not following such directives, Korean businessmen could not violate such directives.

Current Regulations in the Manufacturing Sector

Overview

According to a survey conducted by the Federation of Korean Industries, there are 1,013 regulations in sixty-four laws on business activities in the manufacturing sector. These regulations are classified into five categories, and the regulations on production activity account for the largest proportion of the regulations. The most common type of regulations has to do with setting standards.

In terms of the number of individual regulations, there are more social regulations than economic regulations, because most social regulations consist of individual purpose-specific laws.

Entry Regulations

There are about forty markets for which a firm's entry must be approved by the government. Ginseng and tobacco production are legal monopolies operated by public enterprises. In addition, new products, which are in the areas of food, drugs, food additives, fertilizer, liquor, pesticides, petrochemicals, and so on, require government approval. Some of the entry regulations are introduced especially to protect such industries as aviation, fertilizer, reeling and the silk-reeling industries. For the purpose of stabilizing supplies and prices, the new entry is limited in the oil refinery, coal processing, and grain processing industries.

In addition to these industry-specific entry regulations, as mentioned earlier, the Industry Development Act enables the government to impose entry restrictions on certain industries by designating them ''the industries to be rationalized,'' when the government views them to be either declining industries or promising infant industries.

To protect and promote small businesses, the government can also prohibit the new entry of large firms into 205 markets: wig, baggage, heater, umbrella, electric shaver, tent, towel manufacturing, and so on. This regulation, however, has aroused controversies over whether it is effective and desirable (see Table 6.16).

Production Regulations

Most quantity regulations are introduced to secure supplies and to stabilize the prices of important products (e.g., oil refinery), but some are introduced to protect agriculture and the fishing industry (e.g., fertilizer, agricultural machinery, fishing boat), to protect general safety and health (e.g., weaponry and explosives), and to secure tax revenue (e.g., liquor).

Table 6.16
Regulations on Business Activities and by Type

Business Activities			Type	
Entry/Exit	220	21.7%	Standards	53.9%
Production	420	41.5%	Licensing/Permit	19.8%
Purchase/Sales	163	16.1%	Prohibition	10.2%
Personnel/Labor	210	20.7%	Order/Decree	8.8%
			Inspection	6.4%
Total	1,013	100.0%		100.0%

Regulations also cover production methods and technologies (e.g., food, food additives, medicine, toys), and product specifications (e.g., medical equipment, electric devices, processed food). In particular, regulations covering workers and consumer protection have recently increased, reflecting the social trend in Korea. In addition, energy conservation measures have been in effect since the oil crisis of 1973.

Price Regulations

Two important laws regulate a firm's pricing decisions: the Price Stabilization and Fair Trade Act and the Antitrust and Fair Trade Act. The Price Stabilization and Fair Trade Act provides a comprehensive legal framework through which the government regulates prices in any market when the government considers it essential to stabilize prices. The prices of utilities such as electricity, gas, and water, and the rates of telephone and postal services are under government control. This law also regulates transportation fares (railroad, airline, taxi, highway tolls), tuition for all schools and universities, and medical insurance premiums.

The Antitrust and Fair Trade Act gives the government the authority to regulate the product prices of firms that are "dominant" in their own markets. If these firms change their prices in a predatory or an abusive manner, the government can order them to correct such practices. The "dominant" firms are defined by the law as follows: among the firms whose annual sales exceed 30 billion won (approximately U.S. $420 million) in a market, the one whose market share exceeds 50 percent, or the two or three largest firms whose market shares exceed 75 percent jointly and 10 percent individually.

Reform of the Regulations

Background

Since the early 1980s regulatory policies in Korea have experienced substantial changes for several reasons. First, beginning in the 1980s businesspeople in particular began to realize the limits of the government's ability to control the economy. As the economy became larger, it became very difficult for the government to manage it as effectively as before.

Second, there has been a change in the people's perception of the government's role in the economy. The Korean people began to realize that the government's role in the economy was not just to expedite economic growth but to improve living standards. Thus, the people wanted the government to switch from export-oriented (or growth-oriented) to welfare-oriented policies.

Third, the private sector's attitude toward government regulations changed. Until the early 1980s most big firms in Korea enjoyed the government's export-oriented protective policies and regulations. After the early 1980s, however, when the firms became more independent and internationally competitive, they realized that the government's intervention, far from always being a blessing, was sometimes even a burden.

To implement these changes, in 1982 the government formed a task force that studied the potential reform of economic regulations. This early attempt did not bear much fruit because it was not accompanied by changes in the political system and social structure. A significant social and political change has taken place in Korea since 1986, and it has become easier to reform the economic regulations.

The Current State of Reform

First, the government is expected to privatize eleven public enterprises by the early 1990s by selling the companies' stocks. Moreover, the government plans to give the management of the public enterprises more freedom in their business decisions.

Second, an interministry working group, which was formed to coordinate the interests of the government agencies, discussed ways to promote competition and reform the regulations. The group finalized the reform in March 1989. The new government regulations include eighty-seven provisions to reduce government intervention and promote competition in a market (see Table 6.17).

INDUSTRIAL POLICY

The emergence of NICs in East Asia is one of the most notable events in the development history of the last three decades. By pursuing an export-oriented development strategy, these economies have achieved rapid growth of exports and income. The development of the Korean economy in a relatively short period

Table 6.17
Regulations by Purpose

Economic Purpose		Type	
Promotion of Competiton	21.7%	Safety and Health	38.4%
Promotion of Industry	41.5%	Environmental Protection	11.1%
Stabilization of Supply / Price	16.1%	Cousumer Protection	11.3%
Promotion of R & D		Worker Protection	15.6%
Total	23.4%		76.6%

Table 6.18
Korea's Industrial Structure

	1962	1972	1979	1983	1988
Agriculture, Forestry and Fishery	43.3	26.5	17.5	16.3	10.8
Mining and Quarrying	2.0	1.8	1.4	1.4	0.8
Manufacturing	9.1	16.9	27.6	29.0	31.6
Services	45.6	54.8	53.5	53.3	56.8
Total	100.0	100.0	100.0	100.0	100.0

Source: Economic Planning Board, *Major Statistics of Korean Economy*, 1989.

Note: Figures denote percentage distribution of the GNP in constant prices, but the 1988 figures denote percentage distribution of the GDP in current price.

of time also has been brought about by outward-looking policies, which emphasize industrial development mainly along the lines dictated by the nation's comparative advantage.

As a result of the concerted efforts of business, labor, and government, Korea has achieved rapid industrialization. The agriculture, forestry, and fishery sectors, which accounted for 43.3 percent of GNP in 1962, were responsible for only 10.8 percent of GNP by 1988, while the share of the manufacturing sector increased from 9.1 to 31.6 percent (see Table 6.18).

Promoting exports on the basis of abundant labor during the initial development stage was broadly in line with Korea's resource endowment. After some fifteen years of impressive growth, however, the Korean economy began to show severe macroeconomic imbalance and industrial inefficiency in the latter half of the

1970s, undermining the economy's growth potential. The strong government initiative in developing heavy and chemical industries (HCIs) was based on a government-imposed factor price structure inconsistent with the market situation. Excessive and duplicative investment in the favored HCIs was financed with the rapid expansion of subsidized bank credit, resulting in inflationary pressure, financial repression, protection of domestic industries, and underinvestment in other industries.

Korea's structural adjustment efforts in the 1980s were designed mainly to correct these imbalances and inefficiency. However, the need for structural adjustment arises not only from irrational government intervention in resource allocation but also from major changes in the market environment. In the following section, we briefly review the industrial policies followed by the Korean government from 1962 to 1989. We differentiate three distinct periods of differing policy emphasis: 1962 to 1972, 1973 to 1979, and 1980 to the present.

Economic Planning and Export Promotion (1962–72)

For countries like Hong Kong and Singapore, their small size and lack of natural resources made necessary the choice of an export-oriented strategy. In Taiwan and Korea, however, the choice was not so obvious. Not only were their domestic markets much larger than those of the city states, but also their policymakers were influenced by the popular postwar belief in import substitution. In the late 1950s in Taiwan and in the mid-1960s in Korea, an export-oriented strategy was adopted after these countries had suffered from economic stagnation under a protective import regime. In 1962 Korea launched its First Five-Year Economic Development Plan. The Plan adopted an outward-looking development strategy and identified the development of basic infrastructure, the modernization of the nation's industrial structure, the development of several key raw material-supplying industries, and the growth of exports as its major goals.

To achieve these objectives, interest rates and the exchange-rate system were realigned to reflect market values more correctly, incentives were provided for export activities, and the inducement of foreign loans and direct investments was encouraged.

The most important incentives provided to encourage exports included exemption of import duties for intermediate goods, parts and components to be used for producing export products, reduction of corporate taxes for exporters (abolished in 1973), and preferential financing for export activities (abolished in 1982). These incentives were available to all export activities regardless of industry.

Korea's exports grew from $55 million in 1962 to $1,624 million in 1972, registering a 40 percent annual growth rate (see Table 6.19). This advance was partly the result of these policy changes, but mainly due to appropriate utilization of the nation's abundant and relatively well-educated labor force by Korea's innovative entrepreneurs and the political leadership's firm commitment to eco-

Table 6.19
The Changing Composition of Korea's Exports

	Primary Goods	Manufactured Goods	Total	Value ($ Mil)
1962	73.0	27.0	100.0	54.8
1972	12.3	87.7	100.0	1,624.1
1979	11.0	89.0	100.0	15,055.5
1988	6.6	93.4	100.0	60,696.4

Source: Economic Planning Board, *Korean Economic Indicators*, 1990.

nomic development. At the same time, manufactured goods, which accounted for only 27 percent of total exports in 1962, came to account for 88 percent of total exports in 1972. The industrial policies followed by the government during this period were basically neutral with respect to particular industries. Incentives in general favored export-oriented industries, but, based on growing domestic demand and protection of the domestic market, import substitution was also accomplished in such key raw material-supplying industries as petroleum refining, fertilizers, cement, and chemical fibers. Toward the end of the period, the development of the steel and petrochemical industries, which are two basic raw material-supplying industries, was also sought.

During the whole process, the government exerted little effort to promote exports of specific items. The government set annual export goals, established the Korea Trade Promotion Corporation to provide market information to what were then mostly small Korean firms, and provided certain incentives to export activities. It seldom intervened in the allocation of resources for specific export items or industries.

Promotion of Heavy and Chemical Industries (1973–79)

In the 1970s the Korean government began to feel a need to develop the heavy machinery and chemical industries. Korea's dependence on imported machinery remained very high, the prospects of maintaining a stable supply of raw material from the international commodity market deteriorated, and the country's comparative advantage position in the international market was changing rapidly. Furthermore, the advent of the Nixon Doctrine in the United States, which emphasized greater efforts for defense on the part of individual countries and the partial withdrawal of American forces from Korea in 1971, forced the Korean government to promote the development of its own defense industries. Thus, in January 1973 the president of the republic issued an urgent call for the development of the nation's heavy and chemical industries. Accordingly, from 1973 to early 1979 protection was strengthened and incentives were expanded for the so-called strategic industries, which eventually resulted in an overadjustment of the industrial structure.

Import protection was reinforced for the strategic industries. The proportion of items that could be imported without prior government approval, or the import liberalization ratio, decreased from 61.7 percent in 1968 to 50.5 percent in 1976. For the broadly defined machinery industry, which includes most of the so-called strategic industries like industrial machinery, electronics, automobiles, shipbuilding, and metal products, the import liberalization ratio declined from 55.9 percent in 1968 to 35.4 percent in 1976.

Starting in 1974, entry restrictions were reinforced in the form of controls on foreign ownership and export requirements in the field of direct foreign investment as well. Therefore, foreign investment declined sharply in 1974 and remained stagnant until the early 1980s when the policy was reversed.

In addition to protection from foreign competition, incentives were provided to domestic producers in strategic industries in the form of preferential financing and tax exemptions or reductions. Long-term loans by public finance institutions like the Korea Development Bank were directed heavily toward these industries, and even the allocation of commercial lending was strongly influenced by the government in the direction of providing maximum financing for these strategic industries.

Moreover, the National Investment Fund (NIF) was established in 1974 to expand the funds available to strategic industries. These funds were provided to businesses in the strategic industries at preferential interest rates until the late 1970s. The NIF provided low-cost financing for purchases of domestic machinery, construction of domestic heavy machinery plants, and purchases of domestically produced ships and provided additional funds for exports on deferred payment.

Domestic tax incentives were also provided for the naphtha cracking, iron and steel, nonferrous metal refining, machinery, chemical fertilizers, shipbuilding, electronics, aviation, defense, and power generation industries. Firms that made investments in those industries were allowed their choice of one of the following tax incentives: (1) exemption from corporate taxes for the first three years after the establishment of the plant and a 50 percent reduction of corporate taxes for the following two years; (2) tax credits of 8 to 10 percent of the investment amount; or (3) accelerated depreciation of up to 100 percent of the normal depreciation allowances.

Thus, from 1973 to 1979 the government was deeply involved in the allocation of resources to promote the development of specific industries. Helped partly by such strong government promotion and partly by the inevitable maturing of Korea's industrial structure, the heavy and chemical industries grew rapidly during this period. The contribution of heavy and chemical products in total exports also increased from 21.3 percent in 1972 to 38.4 percent in 1979.

Stabilization Programs and Structural Adjustment
(1980 to the Present)

As the 1980s began, the Korean economy faced severe structural difficulties. The massive investment in the heavy machinery and chemical industries was completed just at the outset of the global and domestic economic downturn, leaving many plants with severe overcapacity problems. The international competitiveness of Korean export products also began to weaken, as a result of the abnormally high growth of domestic wages during the late 1970s, the overvaluation of the domestic currency, and the underinvestment for developing technology and training skilled personnel by both the government and private sector.

Faced with these extremely adverse internal and external conditions, the Korean government began a critical reexamination of its role in the nation's overall economic development. The painful experience of having encouraged the overinvestment in heavy and chemical industries led economic planners to reevaluate the government's ability to choose the promising industries for promotion. The prolonged import protection for many Korean industries and the restrictions on direct foreign investment in many industries were also pointed out as major factors that had inhibited investment by Korean firms in technology and personnel development by providing a guaranteed domestic market. This self-examination by government planners led to a series of comprehensive institutional reforms to promote a greater role for the market mechanism and to reduce government intervention. The exchange rate was substantially devalued in early 1980 in order to compensate for the artificial overvaluation that had occurred; since then it has floated in line with fluctuations in the values of the currencies of Korea's major trading partners. To introduce more foreign competition into the economy, liberalization of imports and direct foreign investment was carried out; and to promote more efficient allocation of resources, preferences for specific industries have been reduced, competition-limiting activities have been banned, and financial reform has been carried out. In response to investment inefficiency and the emergence of declining industries for which direct government intervention was held responsible, the promotion of strategic industries with preferential credit and tax treatment gave way to a more indirect and functional support of industries.

In order to further streamline the industrial incentive system and to deal with industrial rationalization more efficiently, the Industrial Development Law (IDL) was enacted in July 1986. The IDL replaced seven individual industry-promotion laws and defined the role of the government mainly as a "troubleshooter." In two areas where "market failure" occurs, the government is supposed to intervene for the sake of industrial rationalization. One such area comprises industrial sectors whose international competitiveness is vital to the economy but is not expected when left to the market. In this case, the government encourages specialization through indirect incentives designed to promote technological advancement. The other area is declining industries on whose behalf the government may intervene in the phasing-out process. With the completion of the five-year liberalization program for 1984–88, the import liberalization ratio was raised to over 95 percent from 80 percent in 1983. About three-quarters of the remaining items under restriction are primary products, food, and beverages. Together with reduced quantitative import restrictions, the average nominal tariff rate was gradually lowered from 24 percent in 1983 to 18 percent in 1988 and to 13 percent at present. Thus far, import liberalization has not produced any major industrial dislocations. However, Korean firms will begin to be seriously affected as the liberalization of the least competitive products coincides with the appreciation of the won and large wage hikes.

In the early 1980s restrictions on direct foreign investment were relaxed substantially in recognition of its important role in promoting competition and transferring advanced technology. The revisions of the Foreign Capital Inducement Act in 1984 comprised switching to a negative list system, establishing an automatic approval system, and abolishing restrictions on the repatriation of capital and the foreign ownership ratio, to which foreign investment reacted very favorably.

Financial liberalization efforts started with the lifting of restrictions on bank management and the divestment of government equity shares in all five nationwide city banks to transfer the ownership to private hands. Furthermore, entry barriers into the financial market were lowered, and the financial services provided by different intermediaries were diversified and streamlined.

Significant progress has also been made in interest rate and credit management. By June 1982 most policy loans were no longer extended at preferential interest rates, and in early 1984 flexibility in interest rate management was introduced, allowing financial intermediaries to determine their own lending rates within a given range.

Further financial liberalization has been hindered by the legacy of the government's heavy intervention in private resource allocation during the 1970s. The government would not let troubled firms go bankrupt for fear of enormous financial losses to the banking sector and the ensuing social and economic repercussions. Government actions included helping the banking institutions by permitting attractive new services while tightening controls on nonbank interest rates, providing subsidized central bank credit, as well as exempting the capital gains tax on collateral supplied by the troubled firms. In other words, the cost of imprudent government intervention has been paid by consumers and taxpayers and has resulted in continued financial repression.

NOTES

1. The Korean tax system comprises both central government and local government taxes. In 1988 local taxes amounted to only 11.3 percent of the nation's total tax revenue, or 72.8 percent of local government financial requirements. The shortage is covered by central government subsidies. These subsidies are subject to political negotiations between

the central and local governments. Hereafter, this chapter looks only into the fiscal aspects of the central government.

2. A significant tax reform that will be in effect from 1991 is under preparation. It targets alleviating the tax burden of low-income workers, reducing tax brackets, and increasing taxes on the property and elusive capital gains of the rich.

3. In the case of the United States, individual income taxes accounted for about 47 percent of federal tax revenues in 1988.

4. The deputy prime minister is a super minister who coordinates all economic ministries and monitors overall economic policies.

5. For example, the permissible range for the value added tax rate is 8 to 13 percent, although the actual rate was set at 10 percent in 1977 and has remained unchanged since then.

6. In Taiwan, M1b, which is the sum of currency in circulation and demand and passbook savings deposits, was chosen as the intermediate target of monetary policy. The Monetary Authority of Singapore, on the other hand, has been focusing on the exchange rate as an appropriate indicator.

7. By comparison, the ratios for Japan and the United States in 1988 were 15.8 percent and 16.0 percent, respectively.

8. In Korea, the rate of adjustment was too fast; the surplus/GNP ratio declined to 2.4 percent in 1989 from 8.2 percent in the previous year. In 1990 a turnaround to a deficit is expected.

9. The term "ambitious" was used because the measures were introduced in the years when the country was most seriously suffering from the deficit problem.

REFERENCES

Asian Development Bank (1990). *Asian Development Outlook 1990*. Manila: Asian Development Bank.

Balassa, B., and Williamson, J. (1987). *Adjusting to Success: Balance of Payments Policy in the East Asian NICs*. Washington, D.C.: Institute for International Economics.

Bank of Korea (1983). *Financial System in Korea*. Seoul: Bank of Korea.

Cole, D., and Park, Y. C. (1983). *Financial Development in Korea: 1945–1978*. Cambridge, Mass.: Harvard University Press.

Cooper, R. N. (1990). *Fiscal Policy in Korea, 1973–1988*. Mimeo. Seoul: Korea Development Institute.

Hong, W. (1979). *Trade Distortion and Employment Growth in Korea*. Seoul: KDI Press.

Jwa, S. H. (1988). *Korea's Exchange Rate Policy: System, Effect, and Issues*. KDI Working Paper No. 8802.

Kapur, B. K. (1985). "A Theoretical Model of Singapore-Type Financial and Foreign Exchange Systems." *The Singapore Economic Review* 30, no. 2: 91–102.

Kim, J. S. (1990). *Regulation Policy in Korea*. Mimeo. Seoul: Korea Development Institute.

Kim, M. J., and Ro, S. T. (1989). "Korean International Macroeconomic Policy." In T. O. Bayard and S. G. Young (eds.), *Economic Relations between the United States and Korea: Conflict or Cooperation?* Washington, D.C.: Institute for International Economics.

Kim, W. S., and Yun, K. Y. (1988). "Fiscal Policy and Development in Korea." *World Development* 16, no. 1: 65–83.

Kuo, S.W.Y. (1983). *Taiwan: Economy in Transition*. Boulder, Colo.: Westview Press.

Lee, K. U. (1989). "Competition and Deregulation Policy in Korea." A seminar paper presented at *KDI/UNDP Joint Seminar on Private Sector Initiatives*, September 20–22, Seoul, Korea.

Ro, S. T. (1985). "Monetary Control and the Choice of an Intermediate Target." *Journal of Financial Studies* 1, no. 1: 1–24. (Summary in English.)

Sun, C. (1989). "Recycling Trade Surpluses: Policy Options for Taipei, China." *Asian Development Review* 7, no. 2: 48–67.

Yah, L. C., and Associates (1988). *Policy Options for the Singapore Economy*. Singapore: McGraw-Hill.

Young, S. G. (1989). "Korean Trade Policy: Implications for Korea–US Cooperation." In T. O. Bayard and S. G. Young (eds.), *Economic Relations between the United States and Korea: Conflict or Cooperation?* Washington, D.C.: Institute for International Economics.

7

NATIONAL ECONOMIC POLICIES IN LATIN AMERICA

Vittorio Corbo

INTRODUCTION

This chapter focuses on economic policies in Latin America in historical perspective.[1] First, it reviews policies in the period up to World War II, a time when the economic policies in most Latin American countries were still guided by the classical theory of international trade. That pattern was disrupted by the Great Depression, a period during which Latin America responded to the economic upheaval by pursuing a strategy of import substitution. Growth was now to be led by import-substitution industrialization.

By the end of World War II, most Latin American countries had accumulated substantial foreign reserves, while it seemed certain there would be a resurgence in world trade. The logical next step was to reduce the anti-export bias resulting from the trade policies that had been implemented in the previous fifteen years as a response to the crisis of the 1930s. Instead, Latin America pursued and even intensified the import-substitution strategy, influenced in large part by the recommendations of the Economic Commission for Latin America (ECLA). In this chapter we call this strategy of import-substitution industrialization Structuralism I. When the increasing cost of this approach, especially for the medium-sized and small countries of the region, could no longer be ignored, and the times seemed to call for a lessening of import substitution, most countries simply switched to another version of the same strategy—regional integration—ideally to be complemented by foreign aid. This second phase of import-substitution industrialization, which here we call Structuralism II, is also reviewed in this chapter, followed by an examination of the first attempts to reduce the anti-export bias of economic policies.

Our discussion then shifts to the eventual response of the Southern Cone countries to the continued economic difficulties that dogged their import-substitution strategies. Unfortunately, their positive experience with some of their liberalization reforms was overcome by an ill-fated stabilization program and, in Chile and Uruguay, by the severe external shocks of the 1970s. The final section of this chapter reviews the major policy shift of the 1980s and presents the main conclusions.

THE PERIOD BEFORE WORLD WAR II

Up to the Great Depression, the economic policies of most countries in Latin America were largely shaped by classical trade theory, and those countries were still very open to international trade. Although some countries raised their average tariff levels in the 1920s, they did so in a moderate way and mainly for fiscal reasons. Furthermore, most of them returned to the gold standard after World War I, and their macro adjustment was thus closely related to balance-of-payments adjustments (Furtado, 1976).

Critics of the prevailing free trade orthodoxy did, however, point to signs of growing protectionism in the most advanced countries (the United States and the European nations), but they did not have much influence in policy. At the country level, Argentina continued with export-led growth based on extensive agriculture which in part involved bringing new land into production (Diaz-Alejandro, 1970; O'Connell, 1986). At the same time in Argentina, discussion of the convenience of pursuing protectionist policies had already gotten underway in the second half of the 1920s, as access to export markets became more restricted.

As to Chile, it had benefited during the war from very favorable external markets, whereas its import channels had been interrupted. While its export levels remained constant, imports fell to almost half. As a result of this temporary natural protection, there had been a substantial expansion in manufacturing output (Munoz, 1968; Palma, 1984). Although at the end of the decade of the teens, nitrates, Chile's main export product at the time, collapsed, they did recover in the second half of the 1920s. The final collapse of the nitrates industry was a result of the Great Depression and the development of cheaper fertilizers.

Nevertheless, during this period, Chile raised its tariffs first in 1916 and then again in 1928. The 1928 revision further gave the president the right to increase tariffs on individual products up to 35 percent, a power that would be used extensively during the late 1930s (Ellsworth, 1945). Chile also borrowed heavily in the second half of the 1920s to finance some ambitious public investment projects. As a result of the large expansion in expenditures, it had to contend with important real appreciation of the currency in the 1926–29 period, with negative effects on the profitability of tradeable activities.

Brazil's economic evolution was still tied to the coffee cycle. Nevertheless, it had taken some import-substitution measures during the previous fifty years and had intensified these measures during World War I. By 1920 import substitution was of importance in the consumer goods sector, especially with respect to textiles. In the middle of the 1920s, however, when the real exchange rate appreciated as a result of good coffee prices and conservative monetary policies, the import-competing sectors lost some of their dynamism (Furtado, 1963).

Mexico was a special case, in that it was in the process of restructuring following ten years of revolution that had started in 1911. Its most dynamic sectors were mining and agriculture. Given that the United States was its main market, the Mexican economy followed the economic cycles of its neighbor very closely. Mexico also differed from the rest of Latin America in that the country generally discouraged direct foreign investment, except where it involved new manufacturing technology. Only a little industrialization took place in this period in light industry, and it was more the result of high income growth in agriculture and mining and of internal integration than of increased protection (Cardenas, 1984; Diaz-Alejandro, 1982).

Colombia achieved export-led growth at a later date. After a long period of stagnation following the civil war at the end of the nineteenth century, the country experienced an important expansion of exports in the first quarter of the twentieth century. This export boom was associated with the introduction of coffee into the economy and the good performance of minerals and banana exports. For the period 1925–28, important public works—financed by heavy external borrowing and good export performance—resulted in substantial growth. During this period, protection was moderate and was imposed with some selectivity; tariffs were used mainly for fiscal purposes. Manufacturing output had already expanded at the beginning of this century, partly as a result of the natural protection provided by the interruption of import channels during World War I (Ocampo, 1984).

The picture we get from the above review is that the economic policies of most Latin American countries in the 1914–29 period were very much guided by the classical theory of international trade. At this time, economic ideas were to be found in political writings or general essays on Latin America (Hirschman, 1961). However, some import substitution did develop—both naturally, as part of the normal development process following income growth and, more artificially, when the flow of imports was interrupted during World War I. Nevertheless, in general, trade policies were fairly neutral between incentives for the local and foreign market. International trade faced few restrictions, mainly in the form of low tariffs and export taxes on primary products. Also at that time, tax revenues came primarily from the foreign trade sector, and government expenditures were oriented toward the development of physical infrastructure. Macro-policies were governed mostly by the rules of the gold standard, and there was relative price stability. Capital inflows became important in the second half of the 1920s but fell substantially in 1929. Until that time, balance-of-payments crises were the exception.

The Great Depression sent many unfavorable shocks through Latin America's economies. First, as the international commodity markets collapsed, export prices fell more than import prices, and the terms of trade in individual countries dropped between 21 percent and 45 percent (CEPAL, 1976). Second, the capital inflows that had become important up to 1928 had almost disappeared by 1929. Third, the collapse in export prices substantially increased the real burden of external debt.

A fourth factor was rising protectionism in the key industrialized countries, which made the prospects for world trade very discouraging. Protectionist pressures in this period resulted in the Smoot-Hawley Tariff of 1930 in the United States, the British Abnormal Importation Act of 1931, and the Ottawa Commonwealth Preferences of 1932.

In light of these large external shocks and the lack of foreign financing, the Latin American economies were forced to adjust.[2] In modern terminology, there were, in principle, three adjustment policies or policy combinations available to them. The first, a gold standard policy, involved engineering a monetary contraction and, via domestic deflation, reducing the level of imports and increasing exports. The second policy was to alter the exchange rate so as to accelerate the switching and to avoid waiting for the domestic deflation. The third was to encourage selective switching through import restrictions, combined with exchange controls and expansionary demand policies. The dark prospects for foreign trade had an important effect on the final adjustment option selected.

The first course was judged politically infeasible for countries with a high proportion of their population in the urban sector and with well-organized labor unions.

Given the pessimistic view of future world trade, the second option was also disregarded. During and following the Depression, most industrialized countries were closing their doors to international trade, a situation that significantly reduced the market for Latin American exports. Furthermore, because most imports of developing nations did not have close domestic substitutes, their short-term import price elasticities were very low. Within this framework, a real devaluation was not favored as the main instrument for restoring an external balance.

Thus, most Latin American countries ended up following the third option— a mix of discriminatory switching and aggregate demand policies. To implement it, they abandoned the gold standard, imposed exchange controls and discriminatory trade restrictions (such as quotas, tariffs, and multiple exchange-rate systems) on imports of consumer goods, and adopted countercyclical fiscal and monetary policies.[3] This set of policies has been called the model of domestically oriented growth. Import-competing manufacturing activities were given an advantage not only through protective trade policies, but also through tax and credit incentives. Specifically, the dynamic growth element, instead of being the export sector as it was up to the eve of the Great Depression, was private and public investment in import-competing industries.

Although most Latin American countries ended up pursuing the third option, they did so not as a conscious policy choice, but as the end result of their implementation of ad hoc policy measures designed to accelerate adjustment to the severe external shocks they were facing. Indeed, those countries that broke away from the gold standard while they followed active public expenditure policies (in particular Argentina, Brazil, Chile, Colombia, and Mexico) still pursued a fiscal policy aimed at achieving a balanced budget. This approach did not keep them from running small deficits, however. Even in Brazil, whose coffee price support system that dated from 1906 resulted in a large increase in expenditures, the fiscal implications of these measures were only moderately expansionary (Cardoso, 1979; Fishlow, 1972; Furtado, 1963; Silber, 1977). In Argentina, Raul Prebisch, then the director of research at the central bank, recommended fiscal discipline to avoid an outburst of inflation. With respect to the appropriateness of the use of orthodox fiscal policies, Prebisch (1986, p. 134) notes:

I do not think it was mistaken, given the need to stop inflation and check the fiscal deficit before they become uncontrollable. What did this orthodox economic policy, for which I was totally responsible, consist of? In the first place, it took the form of a considerable fall in public expenditure, including a 10 percent cut in public sector wages; these were brutal measures that allowed for a drastic reduction. In the second place, it meant an increase in taxation; in this area we decided to seek new paths by introducing an income tax.

In Colombia, the Lopez government introduced a major stabilization program in 1934, and a fiscal surplus was achieved in 1935.

Thus, in most Latin American countries in the pre–World War II period, fiscal policy was still relatively conservative. Except in Argentina, however, monetary policy was more active. As shown in Table 7.1, growth in the real money supply in Brazil, Chile, and Colombia was higher than in the United States, in spite of a sharp drop in international reserves. Thus, those countries more than compensated for the drop in reserves with expansion in domestic credit.

On the relative price side, three main factors were at work: (1) the world Depression, with the resultant collapse in the prices of primary commodities; (2) widespread exchange controls and devaluations following the devaluation of the pound in September 1931; and (3) the multiple exchange-rate system and an increase in the levels and dispersion of nominal tariffs, with effective rates of protection many times the nominal rates and increasingly a function of the stage of fabrication. By grouping output into three categories—importables, exportables, and nontradeables—the relative prices of importables and nontradeables in terms of exportables increased. Within importables, the sharpest increases were for consumer durables.

Real exchange rates, exclusive of the tariff and nontariff effects for importables in terms of nontradeables, are presented in Table 7.2. The table shows that large real devaluations took place in most of the large countries during the 1930s. If the effects of the tariffs and other constraints on trade (such as multiple exchange rates and import quotas) are added to these rates, the increased incentives to import substitution are seen to be even sharper. Indeed, the evidence shows that

Table 7.1
Real Money Supplies, Latin America and the United States, 1928–39

Year	Argentina	Brazil	Colombia	Chile	U.S.
			(1931=100)		
1928	99.6	76.4	111.9	n.a.	105.9
1929	97.4	78.5	91.2	n.a	104.4
1930	96.5	85.6	91.3	n.a.	104.4
1931	100.0	100.0	100.0	100.0	100.0
1932	110.5	106.1	143.2	126.2	100.6
1933	96.6	104.1	172.6	120.9	93.6
1934	109.8	113.3	147.7	139.0	99.7
1935	103.2	118.6	145.3	154.4	116.2
1936	104.5	128.2	164.9	164.2	124.9
1937	108.1	122.5	166.9	154.7	120.7
1938	106.7	147.3	164.1	159.7	127.7
1939	108.3	151.2	162.2	172.8	142.2

Sources: The data for nominal money supplies and price indexes, except for Chile, are taken from
Tables 1.9 and 1.6, respectively, in Diaz-Alejandro (1983). The Chilean price level data come
from Table 5 (which refers to the cost of living index in Santiago) in Ellsworth (1945), p. 165.
The data for nominal money stock in Chile refer to the end of the year stock figures obtained
from Table 11 of Deaver (1970), p. 60 found in Meiselman (1970).

protection became redundant in Chile (Ellsworth, 1945), Argentina (Diaz-
Alejandro, 1970), and Brazil (Reynolds, 1985). The nontradeable sector expanded not only as a response to improvement in its relative price, but also
because government services and public investment in infrastructure (an important nontradeable) grew. Not surprisingly, there was substantial government
intervention in this decade, not only in economic management but also in important infrastructural projects.

With respect to overall economic performance, Latin America did quite well
in the 1931–40 period in comparison with the most advanced countries. The
average annual rate of GDP growth for the decade was 4.8 percent in Chile, 4.2
percent in Colombia, 3.6 percent in Brazil, 2.5 percent in Argentina, and 2.4
percent in Mexico, with the countries that followed the more expansionary
monetary and fiscal policies growing at the highest rates (Corbo, 1988). For the

Table 7.2
Real Exchange Rates, Latin America, 1929–39

Year	Argentina	Brazil	Colombia	Chile
		(1929=100)		
1929	1.00	1.00	1.00	1.00
1930	1.09	1.19	1.22	0.97
1931	1.41	1.84	1.34	0.89
1932	1.61	1.61	1.46	3.00
1933	1.15	1.45	1.65	2.35
1934	1.50	1.68	1.68	1.84
1935	1.41	1.87	1.71	1.74
1936	1.32	1.89	1.64	1.79
1937	1.23	1.63	1.65	1.59
1938	1.30	1.73	1.48	1.49
1939	1.43	1.83	1.37	1.45

Sources: The data for the nominal exchange rates and price level indexes, except for Chile, are taken from Tables 1.5 and 1.6, respectively, in Diaz-Alejandro (1983). The Chilean price level data come from Table 5 (which refers to the cost of living index in Santiago) in Ellsworth (1945), p. 165. The data for the nominal exchange rates are obtained from de la Cuadra and Cortes (1984).

Note: The real exchange rates are calculated in 1931 constant prices and converted into indexes with 1929 = 1.00 as follows:

$$\text{Real exchange rate} = \frac{\text{Nominal exchange rate} \times \text{U.S. price index}}{\text{Price index of each country}}$$

same period, the average annual rate of growth was 2.7 percent in the United States, −1.2 percent in France, 3.4 percent in Great Britain, and 4.1 percent in Japan (Maddison, 1982). In all Latin American countries for which we have comparable information, manufacturing was the leading sector, followed by construction and services and finally by the primary sector. Initially, the discrimination against exportable activities, mostly agriculture and mining, did not create larger efficiency-loss costs, as the expanding area of activity was labor-intensive light manufacturing where the cost disadvantage vis-à-vis imported goods was not significant. Besides, most of the export markets were highly protected and/or in major recession.

The creation of a domestic industry geared to the production of previously imported nondurable consumer goods and some raw material inputs obviously decreased imports of these goods. However, at the same time, imports of other raw materials and capital goods required for those same industries increased. To relieve the pressure on the external accounts, "nonessential" imports were restricted; this move accelerated the process of import substitution and its costs. Finally, World War II created both a boom in the prices of mineral exports and a natural suspension in the flow of imports from industrial countries. These conditions also stimulated demand in the import-competing sector.

LATIN AMERICA IN 1945–60: STRUCTURALISM I

As the postwar period opened, most Latin American nations found themselves with substantial foreign reserves in their central banks (although there were convertibility problems with the pound sterling). Despite conflicting signals about the future evolution of world trade, the Marshall Plan and the creation of international institutions, geared to avoid the trade wars of the previous twenty years, provided positive indications of an expansion in world trade. It seemed that the stage was set for a reduction in the discrimination against exportables that had evolved over the previous fifteen years.

However, an important initial condition had been built up during the previous decade. New industrialist and labor groups in the emerging manufacturing sectors strongly lobbied for the enactment of tariff protection to replace temporary natural protection; differentiated tariffs and multiple exchange rates were important elements in the arsenal of import-substitution policies deployed in the 1945–60 period. As it is a common pattern in the early stages of import substitution, manufacturing output initially achieved substantial growth, but it started to decline when the "easy" import-substitution phase was completed. One common result of these policies was slow growth in total exports and in manufacturing exports in particular: exports practically stagnated between the early postwar years and the beginning of the 1960s. This was especially the case for the Southern Cone countries (Argentina, Chile, and Uruguay), where protection was higher, and to a lesser degree for Brazil and Colombia.

Some exceptions to these policies were observed during this period. Thus, by the early 1950s Mexico and Peru realigned their exchange rates and lifted import-repressing policies so as to increase incentives to foreign trade (Diaz-Alejandro, 1983). Peru, the most important exception, continued an export-led growth process until 1960, when ECLA's ideas began to be influential (Noguès, 1985).

At this time, a debate emerged over what long-term development strategy Latin America should follow. Initially, the debate was at the country level. On the one side were the producers of exportables (agriculture and mining) and the traders of imported goods, who argued for reducing the bias of the trade regime against them. They were supported at the time by the mainstream economists of the region, who also favored a more balanced trade regime. On the other side were the leaders of the manufacturing associations, the new industrialists and organized labor in the new manufacturing industries, all of whom advocated keeping and even intensifying protectionism. Clear manifestations of this debate appeared in Argentina, Brazil, Chile, and Colombia.

In 1948 ECLA, the special Economic Commission for Latin America (then still temporary), was set up in the United Nations. It soon entered the debate. Consisting of a group of economists under the leadership of Prebisch, ECLA proposed a development strategy for Latin America that differed from the early recommendations of most economists that trade be liberalized. ECLA's was the first school of thought about regional economic development to emerge in Latin America (Hirschman, 1961). An Article by Prebisch (1950) that summarized the thinking of this group proved very influential with a large number of Latin American economists, including C. Furtado in Brazil, J. Noyola in Mexico, and O. Sunkel in Chile (all of whom became part of the staff of ECLA when it became permanent in early 1951). Prebisch (1950) presented what today is called the structural critique of the export-led growth model of the pre-1930 period. A central argument in Prebisch's thesis was that the main determinant of the rate of growth of per capita GDP was technical progress, a thesis few economists questioned.

Presbisch also asserted that the international terms of trade of primary exports from peripheral countries had a secular tendency to deteriorate vis-à-vis their imported manufactured goods. He therefore concluded that countries needed to industrialize if they were to keep the fruits of technical progress. A second component of Prebisch's thesis was that import-substitution manufacturing produced dynamic externalities.

With respect to the secular deterioration in the terms of trade, Lipsey (1963), Kravis and Lipsey (1981), and Michaely (1985) have since concluded that there is no evidence of this trend. As to the dynamic externalitics of import-competing manufacturing, again the evidence shows that export-oriented manufacturing and agriculture can create as many dynamic externalities as can import-competing manufacturing (Krueger, 1978; Little, Scitovsky and Scott, 1970).

Prebisch recommended that the state promote industrialization through protection and investment in the infrastructure to support import-competing manufacturing. Prebisch's ideas had the most impact in Chile, the country that had called for the creation of ECLA and had become its home. Furthermore, ECLA economists taught at the then prestigious Universidad de Chile and gave lectures all across Latin America. They were also very influential in Brazil, where Prebisch was invited to lecture by local manufacturing interest groups in the late 1940s. In Argentina, in contrast, the Perón government was quite hostile to Prebisch from the beginning (Diaz-Alejandro, 1983; Furtado, 1985; Prebisch, 1986), and thus ECLA's ideas were not easily disseminated. At the same time, it should be noted that under Perón's first administration, from 1945 to 1954, import-substitution industrialization with a heavy bias against agriculture was pushed further than anywhere else as a result of price controls and export taxes imposed to help urban workers, Perón's main source of political support. We could safely say that import substitution resulted from the side effect of the control and expansionary policies rather than from a deliberate development strategy.[4] Here we see his dynamic "externality" argument for industrialization in action.

Receptivity to policies of import-substitution industrialization was intimately linked to political developments in the region. Popular movements and populist governments came to power in Chile, Brazil, and Argentina in the late 1930s and the 1940s. Political developments in these countries had a common theme of removing power from conservative agrarian oligarchies and vesting it increasingly in mass movements of urban workers. These latter groups made important alliances with the new industrialists against export-oriented landowners and foreign-owned mining companies. As a part of this scenario, programs of import-substitution industrialization built up strong institutional and political support.

By the early 1940s, Keynesian demand management policies were becoming fashionable in Latin American academic circles and in ECLA and soon started to influence government policies (Pinto, 1960; Prebisch, 1947). Demand management provided analytical respectability for the expansionary demand policies starting in the late 1940s.

The expansionary demand policies and rapid use of the foreign reserves accumulated during World War II combined with increasingly restrictive trade regimes to produce accelerated inflation, balance-of-payments difficulties, and slow export growth in the early 1950s. By that time, ECLA was developing another argument for import-substitution industrialization. It was based on a foreign trade gap that could be reduced only by decreasing import requirements through further import substitution.[5] Prebisch (1959a) postulated that the relation between the rate of growth of imports and the rate of growth of output (a total income elasticity concept) was substantially higher than the ratio of the rate of growth of exports to the rate of growth output. Therefore, without further access to external financing, the only way to increase output growth without a balance-of-payments crisis was to reduce the income elasticity of imports through further import-substitution industrialization. It was not considered that, given the industrialization of the previous thirty years, manufacturing exports, not to mention primary exports, could respond to price incentives.

These policies not only failed to halt the steady growth of imports; they also led to the stagnation of exports and a series of other undesirable effects (Balassa and associates, 1971; Bhagwati, 1978; Krueger, 1978; Little, Scitovsky, and Scott, 1970). First, an inefficient, ever-growing bureaucracy emerged to enforce the often contradictory regulations enacted to support an overvalued currency.

Second, although the creation of a domestic industrial sector geared to the production of previously imported consumption goods led to a decline in imports of these goods, it simultaneously raised imports of the raw materials and capital goods required to produce consumption goods. Thus, dependence on importing increased. The availability of raw materials and capital goods became fundamental to the smooth functioning of the economy. If the supplies of foreign inputs were interrupted, not only would consumption levels fall as before, but unemployment and underutilization of the industrial capacity would result as well.

Third, there was a lack of a competition within the industrial sector. The small size of the market either precluded the existence of many efficient firms or very few firms were present, and they did not compete among themselves. This was a more acute problem in the smaller countries of the region (Chile and Uruguay).

Fourth, resources were socially misallocated, as indicated by the substantial dispersion in the computed domestic resource cost of the different import-competing industries (Bergman, 1970, Berlinsky and Schydlowski, 1982; Taylor and Bacha, 1973). This outcome was attributable mainly to the protectionist policies that closed the door on external competition and to the whole range of government intervention built up to promote industrialization.

Finally, in many cases, subsidized imports of capital goods (stemming mainly from the fact that they attracted the lowest rate in a multiple exchange-rate system) led to factor price distortions that penalized employment.[6]

The proponents of the import-substitution model probably did not clearly envisage the protective regimes that finally emerged. Indeed, their recommendations were designed to achieve a degree of industrialization as a precondition for future growth based on manufacturing exports. Over time, however, as the typically small and scattered industrial sector could not compete internationally, protection usually increased (rather than decreasing, as had initially been envisaged by the proponents of this strategy). Political economy and rent-seeking considerations sustained these policies. In this connection, it is illuminating to make a comparison with the South Korean model where the governments also intervened to promote industrialization. In Korea, however, while import restrictions (tariffs and nontariff barriers) were used as major protective devices, the government simultaneously also provided important export incentives to compensate for the bias of the import regime. Indeed, one of the most careful studies of the system of incentives in Korea has concluded that it was equally attractive for a Korean producer to produce for sheltered local markets and for world markets (Westphal, 1978). This was hardly the case in Latin America. Even in Brazil, despite the export promotion strategy of the 1960s, there was still an important anti-export bias in the trade regime (Carvalho and Haddad, 1981).

THE CRISIS OF IMPORT-SUBSTITUTION INDUSTRIALIZATION: STRUCTURALISM II

In the late 1950s and early 1960s an important group of Latin American countries (Argentina, Chile, Colombia, Uruguay, Bolivia, and Brazil) were facing recurrent balance-of-payments crises and periodic outbursts of inflation. As a consequence, some of these countries entered into International Monetary Fund (IMF) agreements to stabilize their economies. Most of the time, the IMF-type recommendations called for control of aggregate expenditures and exchange-rate unification and adjustment. Not surprisingly, these recommendations were in direct conflict with the policies being followed.

A structuralist view of inflation was developed in response to the stabilization prescriptions of the IMF (Baer, 1967; Noyola, 1965; Pinto, 1960; Seers, 1962; and Sunkel, 1958). (For an evaluation of the monetarist and structuralist views of inflation, see Corbo, 1974, Chapter 5.) This new view proved very influential in delaying the implementation of the policies required to reduce inflation. The structuralist focus on supply response diverted attention from important ways of cutting inflation, such as achieving a permanent reduction in the public sector deficit and eliminating the monetization of government deficits (Harberger, 1964). These types of policies were at odds with structuralism.

The main constraint on growth, however, was seen by the structuralists to be the scarcity of foreign exchange. Their view was that to deal with the foreign exchange constraint, Latin American countries needed to plan their economic development and to increase the size of their markets through economic integration. As planning was new to most Latin American governments, the need arose to develop an institutional capacity for preparing plans. A new United Nations Institute, ILPES (Instituto Latino-Americano de Planificacion Economica y Social), was created in the early 1960s to assist Latin American countries in preparing their development plans. The first director of ILPES was Raul Prebisch—which indicated the importance attached to planning in the early 1960s.

The programming exercises taken with the help of ILPES in many countries in Latin America followed quite closely the guidelines already laid down in CEPAL (Commission Economica para America Latina) (1955). They consisted of simple, static input-output models. The strongest incentive for preparing plans came about with the establishment of the Alliance for Progress in 1961; it required that countries prepare a plan as a precondition for aid.

By this time, ECLA was becoming increasingly concerned about the inefficiencies arising from import substitution at the country level and therefore recommended that Latin American countries needed to move on to a second stage of import substitution (Hirschman, 1961, pp. 18–19). Prebisch (1959a and 1959b) concluded that further import substitution would have to take place at a regional level.

Thus, in the 1960s ECLA started to promote regional economic integration. In 1959 Prebisch wrote:

Trade between Latin American countries forms only 10 percent of their total foreign trade, and industrial exports are relatively very small by contrast with countries such as Italy, Japan, and others with similar income level. All this has resulted in the splitting of the industrialization process into as many watertight compartments as there are countries, without the advantages of specialization and the economies of scale. (1959a, pp. 267–68)

This result was only to be expected, given a strategy that encouraged import-substituting industrialization and discriminated against actual and potential export activities, many of the latter in labor-intensive manufacturing. However, instead of concluding that the system of protection should be rationalized to reduce its anti-export bias, as Korea and Europe did in the 1960s, Prebisch recommended that

the response to this should be the enlargement of national markets through the gradual establishment of a common market. . . . Without the common market, there will be a continued tendency by each country to try to produce everything—say, from automobiles to machinery—under the sheltering wing of very high protection. (1959a, p. 268)

With the intellectual leadership of ECLA and the support of the United States, the Latin American Free Trade Association (LAFTA) was created in 1961. However, reduction of the trade barriers within the region was to be negotiated commodity by commodity, and the industrialists in the highly protected manufacturing sectors were to play a central role as members of the country negotiating teams. Not surprisingly, it proved very difficult to reach agreement on tariff reductions, except in the case of a small number of commodities whose production within the region was minimal.

Parallel with this development, Professor Hollis Chenery and his associates in the United States were formalizing the ECLA-type foreign exchange constraint on growth first in a Harrod-Domar framework (Chenery and Bruno, 1962; Chenery and Strout, 1966) and later in a more neoclassical framework that allowed for substitution in production (Chenery and Raduchel, 1971). In Chenery's type of framework, growth is limited ex ante by the larger of two gaps, one being the difference between investment and saving, and the second being the trade gap—the difference between imports of goods and services (including financial services) and total exports. These models were used mostly to articulate the potential contribution of foreign aid to growth in a foreign exchange constraint (trade-gap-binding) economy.

That latter solution was given a boost by the Alliance for Progress and the creation of the Inter-American Development Bank. However, it soon became apparent that the foreign aid being provided would not be sufficient to finance a resumption of growth. As such, regional economic integration became the central strategy.

Findlay (1971) pointed out that the binding gap (usually the foreign exchange one) must be the result of imperfections in the relevant markets or the nature of the assumptions built into the model. In particular, he questioned the assumption that trade flows do not respond to relative prices between tradeable and nontradeable goods. More importantly, the shadow prices of foreign resources implied by two-gap models are absurdly high.

In 1969, with the LAFTA initiative going nowhere, a subset of middle-sized LAFTA members formally approved an Andean Common Market Pact, an initiative that had actually first been launched in August 1966. In designing its rules of operations, members of the Andean Pact took into account many of the lessons learned from the LAFTA initiative. Tariffs and nontariff barriers were to be fully eliminated among member countries by the end of 1980; Chile and Colombia had advocated an even faster decline. Instead of proceeding commodity by commodity, tariffs were to be reduced each year by 10 percent of the minimum ad valorem tariff then existing in Colombia, Chile, and Peru, which in no case was to exceed 100 percent. Thus, reduction of the tariffs was going to be automatic. The less developed members (Ecuador and Bolivia) were given more favorable terms.

Parallel with the general rule of automatic reductions, the Andean Pact called for allocating new manufacturing activities to individual countries to avoid duplication and to reap benefits from economies of scale. The result would be import substitution at a regional level. The countries were also to negotiate a common external tariff.

If the alternative to regional integration were continued import substitution at a country level, the Andean Pact was a definite improvement in that it allowed countries to carry out intra-industry specialization and to create trade. However, to increase the benefits of this integration, a mildly protective common external tariff had to be implemented. This goal was never achieved, a failure that undermined the allocation of specific branches of manufacturing. That process involved a very tricky calculation of the costs and benefits for individual countries, and without agreement on a future common external tariff, it was very difficult (if not impossible) to allocate activities among member countries rationally. As to the main thrust of the sectoral agreements, it was continued import substitution but on a regional level. This shift by itself could have reduced the economic cost of import substitution, in comparison with the alternative option of developing these industries at a country level. Here again, however, unless the common external tariff were moderated, the welfare cost of this further import substitution could have been substantial.

The politics of import substitution at a regional level proved much more difficult than that within a country, and the Andean Pact lost its dynamism in the second half of the 1970s. The final blow came when Chile, which had played a central role in the creation of the Pact, withdrew from it after failing to obtain agreement on its proposals for sharply reducing the common external tariff and for lifting the Pact's restrictions on direct foreign investment.

In the meantime, new developments were taking place on the analytic front, especially in the area of applied commercial policy. The concept of effective protection, which had been in the process of development since at least the early 1950s, became widely known to professional economists through Corden's seminal paper (1966). His work was particularly important in terms of producing a framework for evaluating the effects of the tariff structures on value added, as well as the economic effects of different types of distortions.[7] In addition, the difference between promotion and protection was made explicit. These developments in applied commercial policy were used to evaluate the trade regimes of developing countries.

The studies (an important set of them is summarized in Balassa and associates, 1971; Bhagwati, 1978; Krueger, 1978; and Little, Scitovsky and Scott, 1970) highlighted the large economic costs associated with the import-substitution strategy and the strong anti-export bias that arose out of these policies. The costs were inversely related to the size of the economy and directly related to the intensity of import substitution. To make matters worse, according to work by Krueger et al. (1981) and Krueger (1983), in general the strategy of import substitution also hindered the growth of employment.

As such, it is ironic that as early as 1950, Viner (1953), in a series of lectures delivered in Rio de Janeiro, had rejected most of the arguments for protecting import-competing industry and recommended eliminating the discrimination against exports and improving the operations of the price system. (See Furtado, 1985, for an evaluation of ECLA's reception of Viner's talk.) Nor was Viner's the only challenge in the region to ECLA's ideas. They were questioned both by some academics and by other economists in the public and private sectors.

One of the early critics was Roberto Campos (1961), who questioned the emphasis in favor of industry and against agriculture, the confidence shown in the theory that by substituting public initiative for private initiative, new resources would be created, and the assumption that inflation could be used to increase capital formation in a sustainable way. In particular, Campos stated that economic incentives are one of the main factors accounting for Latin America's economic performance. Nevertheless, it was ECLA's thoughts on the role of the state in providing protectionism that reigned supreme up to the early 1960s. With inflation a major problem in the region, rationalization of the protection system did not seem as pressing as stabilization.

Still, in the context of the stabilization programs, overvalued exchange rates were adjusted and the multiple exchange-rate system was eliminated or improved as ways to reduce part of the anti-export bias. However, as public sector deficits were not reduced, the overvalued exchange rate returned fairly quickly, and the anti-export bias remained. There were, however, a few more substantial departures from excessive import-substitution policy, stimulated in part by the exposure of a new generation of economists to alternative schools of economic thought. In the late 1950s, and especially in the 1960s, the number of Latin Americans pursuing graduate studies in economics abroad, both in the United States and Europe, increased substantially. On returning to their countries, most of these newly trained economists contributed a marked improvement in the level of economic debate. In particular, they called into question stabilization policies, trade policies, and the selection of public investment projects (Diz, 1966; Ffrench-Davis, 1971; Universidad de Chile, 1963).

For example, in 1964 Chile decided to establish a stable real exchange rate through the introduction of a crawling-peg system, followed by some rationalization of the trade regime. Chile still retained a substantial bias against exports, however, and the first major break from import-substitution policies was actually initiated by Brazil that same year, some fifteen years after Viner questioned this type of policy. This and subsequent policy initiatives in the direction of greater liberalization are discussed in the next section.

THE LIBERALIZATION ATTEMPTS OF THE 1960s

As noted, while the rest of Latin America was still struggling to deepen import substitution, Brazil undertook a set of reforms designed to improve the functioning of its markets and the profitability of export activities. The measures included (1) a more realistic real exchange rate and the elimination of most export taxes; (2) introduction of subsidized credit and tax incentives for export activities; (3) reduction of the public sector deficit and control of inflation; (4) development of a capital market; and (5) downward adjustment of real wages. At the beginning of the Alessandri government (1958), and again during the Frei government (1964–70), Chile put in place a stabilization program that also included liberalization measures. Some of these new ideas were later incorporated into economic policies implemented elsewhere in the region; this was partly true during the lifetime of the Ongania government (1966–71) in Argentina and the government in Colombia in 1967.

After three years of adjustment without growth, Brazil's economic performance in this period was remarkable. GDP at constant prices grew at an average yearly rate of 11 percent between 1968 and 1973, and by 7.7 percent between 1973 and 1977. The value of exports rose by 23.1 percent a year on average between 1968 and 1977. By way of comparison, during the latter period the value of world exports grew at an average annual rate of 19.1 percent.

In Chile the stabilization attempt of the Alessandri administration could not be sustained as the aggregate demand and exchange-rate policy mix resulted in a real appreciation that could not be sustained. Chile again attempted to introduce some liberalization and stabilization measures during the Frei government (1964–70). The Chicago-trained economists who were running the central bank at the time announced that inflation (which was then running at an annual rate of close to 40 percent) could not be reduced abruptly without substantial unemployment. They devised a system to adjust the value of the nominal exchange rate in accordance with the evolution of domestic inflation, international inflation, and the terms of trade. The main contribution of this policy, which was subsequently adopted by many other countries, was to learn to live with 30 percent per year inflation, to avoid periodic stop-go macroeconomic crises, and to reduce the uncertainty facing potential exporters. On the trade side, the anti-export bias of the tariff structure was reduced with the introduction of a drawback system and later on with a reduction in tariffs, when the copper boom had produced an accumulation of foreign reserves that was having unwanted monetary consequences. Attempts to make a more substantial cut in tariffs had, however, faced strong opposition from an alliance of workers and entrepreneurs in the highly protected sectors.

Chile was soon followed by Colombia, which in 1967 also moved to reduce the bias against exports and to establish a more predictable and realistic real exchange policy. Export incentives were introduced to compensate for the anti-export bias of tariffs, and the average tariff level was reduced. The exchange rate was adjusted through the use of a crawling-peg formula. The value of Colombia's exports grew at an annual rate of 2.7 percent between 1961 and 1967, and at an annual rate of 19.1 percent between 1968 and 1977.

The favorable export performance of the late 1960s and 1970s allowed Colombia to avoid the periodical balance-of-payments crises of the previous fifteen years. Indeed, it has been argued that the macroeconomic gains from liberalization were more important than the static resource allocation gains (Diaz-Alejandro, 1976).

Thus, a number of economic experiments were carried out in Latin America in the late 1960s (and early 1970s). Meanwhile, countries in the subcontinent had not performed as well during the 1960s as other countries at a similar level of development. Average annual growth during the decade was 5.0 percent in Latin America, while the upper-middle-income countries (a group that included most of the large nations in Latin America) grew at 6.4 percent. In the area of inflation, Latin America did even worse.

The early 1970s witnessed an acceleration of inflation in most of the regions as well as chronic balance-of-payments problems. At that time, a very strong reaction against the extreme distortions that had been accumulating during the previous forty years emerged in the Southern Cone of Latin America. Some have called this liberalization effort a monetarist experiment, while others have called it neoliberalism. As with all reform programs, it had a little of everything.

LATIN AMERICAN POLICIES OF THE 1970s

Disenchantment with import-substitution policies and government intervention was deeper in those countries that were suffering from extreme macroeconomic problems and widespread microeconomic distortions. The countries where these sentiments were more pronounced were in the Southern Cone of Latin America. When military governments took over there in the 1970s, they implemented, to different degrees, important economic reforms that aimed not only at controlling inflation, but also at changing the overall development model, with a reduction of the role of the state and a greater integration with the world economy. Along with the earlier policy recommendations of the ECLA school, these reforms have had the strongest effect on the design of economic policies in Latin America. A group of Chicago-trained economists played a key role in the Chilean reforms and a somewhat smaller one in the other two countries.

The reforms started around 1974 in Uruguay and Chile, and in 1976 in Argentina. At that time, all three countries were in severe macroeconomic disequilibrium, with acute foreign exchange shortages and severe fiscal deficit-induced inflation. Hence, the reform packages entailed short-term stabilization policies, as well as long-term policies aimed at progressively removing government intervention in the product and factor markets (Corbo and de Melo, 1987).

The first task facing the new economic teams in each country was to control galloping inflation. The teams also diagnosed excessive government intervention as a fundamental cause of inefficient resource allocation and low growth. In their view, they had to deregulate the commodity and factor markets, including reducing the barriers to free trade and capital flows. Such measures would benefit resource allocation, eliminate recurrent bottlenecks, and lead to higher growth.

Chile went the furthest in its economic liberalization. Uruguay was in the middle, and Argentina moved the least.

Reform Measures

In the first phase, the countries based their anti-inflationary policies on major reductions in fiscal deficits and monetary growth. (The fiscal deficits were substantial long before the collapse of the civilian governments.) Chile eliminated its substantial chronic fiscal deficit by drastic across-the-board expenditure cuts (15 percent in 1975), together with a later tax reform. Uruguay reduced its fiscal deficit with the introduction of a value added tax (VAT). However, the total deficit after reaching a balanced budget in 1979–81 increased to 10 percent of output in 1982. Argentina never really controlled its fiscal deficit. These "orthodox" measures were recognized to be contractionary, but it was thought that the potential benefits would easily outweigh the temporary costs of recession.

Expenditure-reducing policies were, in themselves, viewed as insufficient to correct the internal and external balance. Hence, stabilization policies in each country also included major attempts to switch expenditures. Switching policies were implemented concurrently with policies designed to change relative prices among importables and between importables and exportables. In Chile, switching, accompanied by within-tradeables price adjustment, was achieved through a large real devaluation and a reduction of the barriers to imports. In Argentina, this same process was accomplished with a combination of real devaluation, reduction of taxes on exports, and some reduction of import barriers. In Uruguay, the switching included a combination of real devaluation, reduction of barriers to imports, and subsidies for nontraditional exports. To avoid a repetition of the external crises, these initial adjustments in each country were complemented by a passive, crawling-peg, exchange-rate regime aimed at maintaining purchasing power parity adjusted by changes in the terms of trade.

These initial policies successfully eliminated the balance-of-payments crises. However, although the rate of inflation came down considerably in each country, it remained disturbingly high several years after the contractionary policies had been implemented. This was so even when a country had achieved a fiscal surplus in 1987 (Corbo, 1990). The persistence of inflation motivated a major shift in stabilization tactics toward the use of the exchange rate as the main stabilization device. Expectations about devaluation were recognized as important in determining the dynamics of inflation, and it was assumed that exchange-rate targets—preannounced up to six months in advance and with forward devaluations at a decreasing rate—would break inflationary expectations. In practice, the rate of devaluation, set according to a preannounced schedule known as the *tablita*, was less than the existing difference between domestic and world inflation. This policy corresponded to an "active" crawling peg.

Important reforms took place on the microeconomic front. With different timing and intensity, all three countries removed price controls, liberalized interest rates, decentralized government intermediation, and partly deregulated the labor markets. All three countries also relaxed the restrictions on international trade and liberalized capital inflows. However, with the exception of domestic financial market deregulation, which proceeded rapidly in all cases, the sequencing of the reforms differed in each country. Uruguay removed all controls on capital flows and many commodity price controls early on, but progressed more slowly on the liberalization of foreign trade. Chile, to the contrary, went the furthest in eliminating domestic price controls and the endemic fiscal budget deficit and in reducing trade barriers, but it kept the controls on short-term capital flows for a long time and maintained important labor market regulations. On the other hand, Argentina also eliminated price controls and removed most restrictions on short-term capital flows and quantitative import restrictions (with some important exceptions) before it implemented some ad hoc tariff reductions.

Rapid deregulation of the domestic financial markets, a common feature of the reforms in the three countries, was important because of the many years of nonprice allocation of credit and highly negative real interest rates. All three countries substantially deregulated the domestic capital markets in two ways. First, they progressively eliminated the ceilings in interest rates. Second, they reduced the restrictions on financial intermediaries. Argentina went from 100 percent reserve requirements and directed credit programs to a decentralized fractional reserve system. The Chilean government first loosened its control of the financial system by allowing nonbank intermediaries to operate without interest rate controls. Then, in the next several years, it removed the interest ceilings on commercial banks and returned publicly held commercial banks to the private sector. In Uruguay, dollar deposits were legalized early on, and direct credit programs were dismantled. Later, in 1977, the controls on entry to the banking system were lifted.

Each country also tried to open its economy to international capital flows, but the speed and extent of this action varied. Uruguay legalized movements of private capital as early as 1974 and reached full convertibility by early 1977. Argentina eliminated most controls on capital movements in 1979. Chile progressively deregulated medium-term capital flows, eliminating the global limits on borrowing in 1979 and the restrictions on monthly inflows in April 1980. Restrictions on short-term capital inflows were not dismantled until late 1981, however.

In all three countries, there was relatively minor liberalization of the labor markets. These markets continued to be controlled through penalties or prohibitions on labor dismissals, legislated wages, and/or wage indexation. However, the weakening of trade union power amounted to de facto deregulation in the early stages of the reforms.

The Results

In the early stages, when the markets were being liberalized and inflation was being reduced through a macroeconomic policy mix that was trying to keep an "appropriate" real exchange rate and a sustainable current-account deficit, the three countries did quite well. Most of their problems started when major macro imbalances developed in the post–1978 period, as they were implementing a second stabilization attempt. In Argentina, the preannounced decreasing rate of devaluation was incompatible with the financial reforms and the irreducible fiscal deficit. As a consequence, significant capital inflows followed to finance the government deficit. In turn, the capital inflows fueled a large peso appreciation that became unsustainable. When real domestic interest rates sharply increased in anticipation of a major devaluation, the stage was set for a deep recession and the collapse of the heavily leveraged financial sector. In Chile, 100-percent-plus backward wage indexation was incompatible with a preannounced decreasing rate of devaluation and resulted in a peso appreciation that the country was unable to reverse without a crisis.

Furthermore, the availability of easy external financing at a time when it was very profitable to borrow abroad sustained the real appreciation of the peso for a long period, a situation that hurt the exportable activities, which had started to make inroads in the external markets, and the import-competing sectors, which had just completed a quite successful adjustment to the commercial policy reforms (Corbo and Sanchez, 1985). In addition, the abrupt reduction in inflation, together with some contractionary monetary policies, resulted in 1981 in a large increase in real interest rates that created substantial hardship, especially for firms in tradeable activities. Uruguay was somewhat in the middle. By historical standards it did quite well up to 1979, when it suffered from external shocks originating in Argentina, and then in early 1981, when a fiscal deficit emerged that was incompatible with the exchange-rate policy. The ensuing real appreciation discouraged the new export activities and, to a lesser extent, the still highly protected import-competing activities.[8]

LIBERALIZATION ATTEMPTS OF THE 1980s

The 1980s saw a major change in policies all over Latin America.[9] With the sudden crisis precipitated by the disappearance of voluntary private capital flows,

Latin American countries initiated a deep reexamination of their economic policies. Although each country followed its own set of policies, important common elements arose: (1) a reassessment of the role of the public sector in production and distribution with a view toward increasing the private sector's participation in these activities; (2) increasing awareness of the need to reduce public sector deficits as a permanent basis to control inflation and to reduce current-account deficits; (3) a recognition that the expansion of exports through a reduction of the anti-export bias of the trade regime should be the core of the new development strategy; and (4) a recognition of the need to introduce structural reforms in the labor market, financial markets, and domestic trade to increase the supply response to the other reforms.

These types of reforms were implemented in Mexico starting in 1983 but increasingly so in 1985, in Uruguay starting in 1984, in Venezuela in 1989, and in Costa Rica in 1985. Beginning in 1984, Chile concentrated on creating a stable macroeconomic situation as a way of providing a framework for export-led growth. Although Brazil and Argentina are still struggling to control inflation, Peru and Nicaragua postponed the adjustment and have experienced the largest deterioration in social welfare.

In the implementation of these reforms, the most difficult one has been the reforms of the public sector and of labor and domestic markets. Reforms of the public sector have faced strong opposition from rent seekers that have traditionally benefited from a larger public sector—suppliers of the public sector and the trade unions. (Argentina and Brazil are good examples here.) Major progress has been achieved in controlling inflation in Bolivia, Costa Rica, Chile, and Mexico and in opening the economy in Mexico, Costa Rica, Bolivia, and Venezuela. However, achieving a sustainable reduction in the public sector deficit and controlling inflation have been very difficult in most of the region. As governments have used most of their political capital in pursuing stabilization policies, the other fundamental structural transformations (i.e., trade reform, public sector reforms, and labor and domestic competition reforms) have been postponed. Not surprisingly, then, the growth performance in the region has been very poor. However, the debt overhang that accumulated in the period of easy spending of the late 1970s most likely has played a negative role in promoting exports.

To sustain adjustment and to restore growth, most Latin American countries need not only to reduce distortions but also to create the conditions for an eventual increase in investment. The eventual recovery of investment requires a stable and predictable macroeconomic situation where long-term commitments can be made. On the other hand, higher saving to finance the higher investment requires a major fiscal effort (Corbo and Schmidt-Hebbel, 1990).

In the early 1980s Latin America recognized its incapacity to finance its current-account deficits. The region also recognized the need for major policy reforms to enable it to achieve a sustainable current-account deficit reduction while creating the conditions for sustainable growth. Key among these reforms has been a comprehensive program of structural adjustment that concurrently addresses stabilization, efficiency, and growth objectives. The structural reform being undertaken has two principal components. One involves restoring the macroeconomic balance, with the emphasis on bringing the level of demand and its composition (tradeables relative to nontradeables) into line with the level of output and the level of external financing that can be mobilized on a recurring basis. In addition, the high rates of inflation and the external deficit must be reduced, objectives that usually require a credible and sustainable reduction in the public sector deficit. The other component aims at increasing efficiency and restoring growth, with the focus on creating more appropriate incentives, removing the constraints on factor mobility, and increasing saving and investment.

It has become increasingly clear to most countries that the two components of structural reform are mutually reinforcing. In most cases, neither can succeed independently. Nevertheless, in countries facing severe macroeconomic imbalances (Mexico, 1987; Chile, 1982–83; Argentina and Brazil, most of the 1980s), structural reforms to increase efficiency and restore growth are unlikely to succeed because the supply response to changing incentives would be severely curtailed. For these countries, there is increasing awareness that adjustment programs should focus early on structural reforms that contribute directly to restoring and maintaining the macroeconomic balance.

NOTES

1. This chapter draws largely on Corbo (1988).

2. For the policies followed by the most important Latin American countries in the 1930s, see also Maddison (1985).

3. By the end of 1933, all Latin American countries except Argentina stopped full service of their external debt. Argentina continued meeting its obligation only because most of its debt was held by Great Britain, which also happened to be its largest export market. But an emerging confrontation was developing over the increasingly restricted access of Argentinian exports to Great Britain.

4. The Libertarian Revolution of 1955 called on Prebisch to advise on Argentina's economic policies. He recommended stabilization of the economy and development of the basic metal industry, which he believed should serve as the engine of growth.

5. This argument was derived from a comparison of the relations over time in individual Latin American countries between import and output growth, on the one hand, and export and output growth, on the other. The rationale for the first type of calculation, after accounting for relative prices, is clear. However, the relationship between exports and domestic output growth could hold only in countries where exports were residual after satisfying the domestic market. The case hardly applied to most Latin American countries.

6. For another evaluation of the structuralist-ECLA type of policies, see Fishlow (1985).

7. Interestingly, Macarios (1964), then the director of research at ECLA, had already used effective protection concepts to evaluate industrialization in Latin America critically.

8. Another problem common to all three countries was the expansion of risk-taking by the financial system. The lack of appropriate supervision and evaluation of portfolio

quality on the one hand, and the de facto deposit insurance on the other, resulted in extremely risky loan portfolios and very high real interest rates.

9. For an assessment of the consensus on policy reforms, see Williamson (1990).

REFERENCES

Baer, W. 1967. "The Inflation Controversy in Latin America: A Survey." *Latin America Research Review* 2 no. 2.

Balassa, B., and Associates. 1971. *The Structure of Protection in Developing Countries*. Baltimore: Johns Hopkins University Press.

Bergman, J. 1970. *Brazil: Industrialization and Trade Policies*. London: Oxford University Press.

Berlinski, J., and Schydlowski, D. M. 1982. "Incentive Policies and Economic Development: Argentina." In B. Balassa and Associates, *Development Strategies in Semi-industrial Economies*. Baltimore: Johns Hopkins University Press.

Bhagwati, J. 1978. *Anatomy and Consequences of Trade Control Regimes*. New York: National Bureau of Economic Research.

Campos, R. 1961. "Two Views on Inflation in Latin America." In A. O. Hirschman (ed.), *Latin American Issues: Essays and Comments*. New York: Twentieth Century Fund.

Cardenas, E. 1984. "The Great Depression and Industrialization: The Case of Mexico." In R. Thorp (ed.), *Latin America in the 1930s*. New York: St. Martin's Press.

Cardoso, E. A. 1979. "Inflation, Growth and the Real Exchange Rate: Essays on Economic History in Brazil." Ph.D. dissertation, Massachusetts Institute of Technology, Cambridge, Mass.

Carvalho, J. L., and Haddad, C. 1981. "Foreign Trade Strategies and Employment in Brazil." In A. O. Krueger et al. (eds.), *Trade and Employment in Developing Countries*. Vol. 1, *Individual Studies*. Chicago: University of Chicago Press.

CEPAL. 1955. *Introduccion a la Tecnica de la Programacion* [Introduction to programming techniques]. Mexico City: United Nations.

CEPAL. 1976. *America Latina: Relacion de Precios del Intercambio* [Latin America: terms of trade]. Santiago, Chile: ECLA.

Chenery, H., and Bruno, M. 1962. "Development Alternatives in an Open Economy: The Case of Israel." *Economic Journal* (March).

Chenery, H., and Raduchel, W. 1971. "Substitution in Planning Models." In H. Chenery (ed.), *Studies in Development Planning*. Cambridge, Mass.: Harvard University Press.

Chenery, H., and Strout, A. 1966. "Foreign Assistance and Economic Development." *American Economic Reviews* (September).

Corbo, V. 1974. *Inflation in Developing Countries. An Econometric Study of the Chilean Inflation*. Amsterdam: North-Holland.

Corbo, V. 1988. "Problems, Development Theory, and Strategies of Latin America." In G. Ranis and T. P. Schultz (eds.), *The State of Development Economics: Progress and Perspectives*. London: Basil Blackwell.

Corbo, V. 1990. "Public Finance, Trade and Development: The Chilean Experience." In V. Tanzi (ed.), *Fiscal Policy in Open Developing Economies*. Washington, D.C.: International Monetary Fund.

Corbo, V., and de Melo, J. 1987. "Lessons from the Southern Cone Policy Reforms." In *World Bank Research Observer* 2, no. 2.

Corbo, V., and Schmidt-Hebbel, K. 1990. "Public Policies and Saving in Developing Countries." Mimeo. Washington, D.C.: World Bank.

Corden, M. W. 1966. "The Structure of a Tariff System and the Effective Protective Rate." *Journal of Political Economy* (August).

Deaver, J. 1970. "The Chilean Inflation and the Demand for Money." In D. Meiselman (ed.), *Varieties of Monetary Experiences*. Chicago: University of Chicago Press.

de la Cuadra, S., and Cortes, H. 1984. *Recesiones Economicas, Crisis Cambiarias y Ciclos Inflacionarios: Chile 1936–1982* [Economic recessions, exchange-rate crisis and inflation cycles]. Santiago, Chile: Instituto de Economie, Pontificie Universidad Catolica.

Diaz-Alejandro, C. F. 1970. *Essays on the Economic History of the Argentine Republic*. New Haven, Conn.: Yale University Press.

Diaz-Alejandro, C. F. 1976. *Foreign Trade Regimes and Economic Development*. New York: Columbia University Press.

Diaz-Alejandro, C. F. 1982. "Latin America in Depression, 1929–39." In M. Gersovitz, C. F. Diaz-Alejandro, G. Ranis, and M. F. Rosenzweig (eds.), *The Theory and Experience of Economic Development*. London: Allen and Unwin.

Diaz-Alejandro, C. F. 1983. "Stories of the 1930s for the 1980s." In P. Aspe-Armella, R. Dornbusch, and M. Obstfeld (eds.), *Financial Policies and the World Capital Market: The Problem of Latin American Countries*. Chicago: University of Chicago Press.

Diz, A. C. 1966. "Money and Prices in Argentina, 1935–62." Ph.D. dissertation, Chicago, University of Chicago.

Ellsworth, P. T. 1945. *Chile: An Economy in Transition*. New York: Macmillan.

Ffrench-Davis, R. 1971. "Economic Policies and Stabilization Programs, Chile 1952–69." Ph.D. dissertation, University of Chicago.

Findlay, R. 1971. "The Foreign Exchange Gap and Growth in Development Economies." In J. Bhagwati et al. (eds.), *Trade, Balance of Payments and Growth*. Amsterdam: North-Holland.

Fishlow, A. 1972. "Origins and Consequences of Import Substitution in Brazil." In L. de Marco (ed.), *International Economics and Development*. New York: Academic Press.

Fishlow, A. 1985. "The State of Latin American Economics." In Inter-American Development Bank, *1985 Report*. Washington, D.C.

Furtado, C. 1963. *The Economic Growth of Brazil*. Berkeley: University of California Press.

Furtado, C. 1976. *Economic Development of Latin America*, Cambridge: Cambridge University Press.

Furtado, C. 1985. *A Fantasia Organizada* [An organized fantasy]. Rio de Janeiro, Brazil: Editore Paz et Terra S/A.

Harberger, A. 1964. "Some Notes on Inflation." In W. Baer and I. Kerstenetzky (eds.), *Inflation and Growth in Latin America*. New Haven, Conn.: Yale University Press.

Hirschman, A. O. 1961. "Ideologies of Economic Development in Latin America." In A. O. Hirschman (ed.), *Latin American Issues: Essays and Comments*. New York: Twentieth Century Fund.

Kravis, I. B., and Lipsey, R. E. 1981. "Prices and Terms of Trade for Developed-

Country Exports of Manufactured Goods.'' NBER, Working Paper No. 744. Cambridge, Mass.: NBER.

Krueger, A. O. 1978. *Foreign Trade Regimes and Economic Development: Liberalization Attempts and Consequences*. Cambridge, Mass.: Ballinger Press for NBER.

Krueger, A. O. 1983. *Trade and Employment in Developing Countries*. Vol. 3, *Synthesis and Conclusions*. Chicago: University of Chicago Press for NBER.

Krueger, A. O., et al. 1981. *Trade and Employment in Developing Countries*. Vol. 1, *Individual Studies*. Chicago: University of Chicago Press for NBER.

Lipsey, R. E. 1963. *Price and Quantity Trends in the Foreign Trade of the United States*. Princeton, N.J.: Princeton University Press.

Little, I., Scitovsky, T., and Scott, M. 1970. *Industry and Trade in Some Developing Countries: A Comparative Study*. New York: Oxford University Press.

Macarios, S. 1964. ''Protectionism and Industrialization in Latin America.'' *Economic Bulletin for Latin America*, 9 (March).

Maddison, A. 1982. *Phases of Capitalist Development*. Oxford: Oxford University Press.

Maddison, A. 1985. *Growth, Crisis and Interdependence 1929–38 and 1973–83*. Paris: OECD.

Meiselman, David. 1970. *Varieties of Monetary Experience*. Chicago: University of Chicago Press.

Michaely, M. 1985. *Trade, Income Levels, and Dependence*. Amsterdam: North-Holland.

Munoz, O. 1968. *Crecimiento Industrial de Chile, 1914–1965* [Industrial growth in Chile, 1914–1965]. Santiago: Universidad de Chile, Instituto de Economia y Planificacion.

Nogues, J. 1985. ''A Historical Perspective of Peru's Trade Liberalization Policies of the 80s.'' Mimeo.

Noyola, J. 1965. ''El Desarrollo Economico y la Inflacion en Mexico y Otros Paises Latinoamericanos'' [Economic development and inflation in Mexico and other Latin American countries]. *Investigaciones Economicas* 16(4), Mexico.

Ocampo. J. A. 1984. ''The Colombian Economy in the 1930s.'' In R. Thorp (ed.), *Latin America in the 1930s*. New York: St. Martin's Press.

O'Connell, A. 1986. ''Free Trade in One (Primary Producing) Country: The Case of Argentina in the 1920s.'' In G. di Tella and D. C. Platt (eds.), *The Political Economy of Argentina, 1880–1946*. New York: St. Martin's Press.

Palma, G. 1984. ''From an Export-Led to an Import-Substituting Economy: Chile 1914–39.'' In R. Thorp (ed.), *Latin America in the 1930s*, New York: St. Martin's Press.

Pinto, A. 1960. *Ni Estabilidad ni Desarrollo: La Politica del Fondo Monetario Internacional* [Neither stability nor development: The policy of the IMF]. Santiago: Editorial Universitaria.

Prebisch, R. 1947. *Introduccion a Keynes* [Introduction to Keynes]. Buenos Aires: Fondo de Cultura Economica.

Prebisch, R. 1950. ''The Economic Development of Latin America and Its Principal Problems.'' New York: United Nations.

Prebisch, R. 1959a. ''Commercial Policy in the Underdeveloped Countries.'' *American Economic Review* (May).

Prebisch, R. 1959b. *El Mercado Comun Latinamericano* [The Latin-American Common Market]. New York: United Nations.

Prebisch, R. 1986. ''Argentine Economic Policies Since the 1930s: Recollections.'' In

G. di Tella and D. C. Platt (eds.), *The Political Economy of Argentina 1880–1946*. New York: St. Martin's Press.

Reynolds, L. G. 1985. *Economic Growth in the Third World, 1850–1980*. New Haven, Conn.: Yale University Press.

Seers, D. 1962. "A Theory of Inflation and Growth Based on Latin American Experience." *Oxford Economic Papers* (June).

Silber, S. 1977. "Analise da Politica Economica e do Compartmento de Economia Brasileira Durante o Periodo 1929–1939" [Analysis of the economic policies and the performance of the Brazilian economy during 1929–1939]. In F. R. Versiani and J.R.M. de Barros (eds.), Sao Paulo: Savarca S.A.

Sunkel, O. 1958. "La Inflacion Chilena: Un enfoque heterodoxo" [The Chilean inflation: An heterodox approach]. *El Trimestre Economico* (October-December).

Taylor, L., and Bacha, E. 1973. "Growth and Trade Distortions in Chile." In R. S. Eckaus and P. N. Rosenstein-Rodan (eds.), *Analysis of Development Problems*. Amsterdam: North-Holland.

Universidad de Chile. 1963. *La Economia Chilena en el Periodo 1950–1963*. Santiago: Instituto de Economia.

Viner, J. 1953. *International Trade and Economic Development*. Oxford: Clarendon Press.

Westphal. L. 1978. "The Republic of Korea Experience with Export-Led Industrial Development." *World Development* 6.

Williamson, J. 1990. *Latin American Adjustment: How Much Has Happened?* Washington, D.C.: Institute for International Economics.

8

NATIONAL ECONOMIC POLICIES IN INDIA

Deena Khatkhate

India's tryst with economic development since the 1950s is an illuminating essay, not only in economics, but also in sociology, history, and, above all, politics. At the time of emancipation from the prolonged British rule in 1947, India had several advantages: a well-oiled administrative apparatus, a large and elite educated class, an enlightened political leadership honed through a long-drawn political struggle to achieve independence, and the firm commitment of the leadership as well as the general intelligentsia to the basic tenets of democracy as the foundation of its polity and a certain vision of an egalitarian society with a modern economic structure. The country has remained a home for all kinds of ideologies—from communism at one end and the Western type of conservative private enterprise philosophy at the other, with other heterogeneous persuasions thrown in between. For all these diversities in political philosophy, the commitment to democracy and pluralism has been firm and abiding so that even the communists had to propagate their doctrine through democratic practice.

A framework of Indian economic policies evolved out of this medley of different political beliefs and, as such, lacked clarity both in regard to what was set out as their goals and how they should be accomplished. The Congress party, which was the first to obtain power and to sustain it over almost the entire period since independence, aimed at a mixed economy with the public and private sectors comingling. This approach could supposedly assure economic development rapid enough for raising the standard of living and an equitable distribution of income. But this mixed economy involved a grab bag of policy measures that gravitated neither toward a market economy nor a total command economy. The resulting fuzziness in economic policy formulation and implementation served the purpose well for a while, with a virtual national consensus on major economic issues. However, as the economy progressed with some initial good results, the policy framework remained structured as at the beginning, irrespective of the emerging changes in the economy. In fact, the commitment to the objectives was mistaken for the measures to achieve them. In the process, the means, not quite in tune with the changing economic situation, generated vested interests all around, which in turn impaired economic efficiency with a consequent waste of resources.

Even though the Congress party's rule was interrupted twice, first in 1977 and again in 1989, the instruments of management of economic power were perpetuated. These instruments consisted of industrial licensing to determine the composition of industries and to attain self-sufficiency; foreign exchange and trade controls to prevent a drain on foreign exchange reserves and to allocate the residual to the domestic sector according to a certain priority ordering; and the directed credit programs through the financial system to promote the high-priority social sectors. Whenever a change in that structure of policies was mooted, as in 1964–66, 1981–84, and since 1985 under Rajiv Gandhi's regime, the shift in policies gathered some momentum but was assailed on the ground that it would destroy self-sufficiency, the progress of import substitution, and the public sector and hurt the vulnerable sections of the Indian society. As a result, the economic liberalization policies lost steam. Although they did not change direction, their momentum slowed down considerably to accommodate some old vintage populist elements, despite the fact that the earlier policies had neither attenuated income inequality nor brought about an acceleration of economic growth, nor contributed to national self-sufficiency. In order to resolve the riddles of economic power management in India, it is necessary to probe into the political economy of Indian economic development, as Bardhan (1984) has argued; the anatomy of a rent-seeking society, which spawns inefficient policies as Bhagwati (1987 and 1988) and Bhagwati and Srinivasan (1975) have underscored; and the political process in India, which strongly makes for an interventionist tenor of policies (Khatkhate, 1977).

The rest of this chapter deals with the political element in the formulation of Indian economic policy. This discussion will help us perceive fiscal, monetary, and industrial and trade policies as having a common denominator and in their wider context. Also discussed in this chapter are the industrial policy and trade regime and fiscal and monetary policies.

THE POLITICAL ELEMENT IN INDIAN ECONOMIC POLICYMAKING

India was probably the first developing country to embark on economic development in the post–World War II period as a deliberate policy. It evolved planning models suited to its economic landscape and environment and for a while was held as an example for other developing countries. Yet India's secular growth rate has been modest at best, and disappointing at worst, when seen in relation to the growth rate in some of the other developing countries. The rate

Table 8.1
Growth Rate of Gross Domestic Product in the Indian Economy,
1950/51–1988/89 (percent per annum)

	1951-52 to 1960-61	1961-62 to 1970-71	1971-72 to 1980-81	1981-82 to 1988-89
Growth Rate of GDP	3.94	3.74	3.75	5.6
Agriculture, including mining, forestry, etc.	3.16	2.58	1.9	4.35
Manufacturing	6.28	5.58	4.01	6.91
Transport and trade	5.36	4.45	4.77	6.23
Banking, insurance	2.97	3.43	4.14	6.48
Public administration and defense	3.65	5.30	3.98	6.40

Source: Government of India, *Economic Survey, 1989–90.*

of growth in gross domestic product was around 3.5 percent (a "Hindu" rate of growth as one leading Indian economist described it) during 1950–51 and 1983–84, and only in 1985 did it pick up to around 5.0 percent, which is still less than that achieved by developing countries such as Korea, Taiwan, Brazil, Mexico, Malaysia, Yugoslavia, and Thailand (see Table 8.1). In per capita terms, their rate of growth over the last two decades has been at least twice that of India and, in some cases, even four or five times (*World Bank*, 1989). As far as income distribution is concerned (Table 8.2), India's performance may not have been worse than that of some of these countries, but certainly it was not better than that of Taiwan, Korea, or Yugoslavia (Bardhan, 1984; *World Bank*, 1989). Considering that India set a specific goal of poverty alleviation through its planning process and devised a policy framework with that goal in view, this achievement should be deemed a distinct failure (Patel, 1987).

Various explanations have been offered for India's slow growth rate, economic inefficiency, perpetuation of poverty, and inequitable income distribution. These explanations go beyond purely economic factors. Three explanations have gained wide currency, being closely related to the Indian economic and political reality. They suggest that economic policy will change only marginally, whichever government comes to power, unless there is a more thorough overhaul of the political power structure and process. The first of these suggestions is advocated by the liberal economists who stress economic efficiency as the main criterion to judge the performance of the economy (Bhagwati, 1987, 1988; Bhagwati and Desai, 1970; Bhagwati and Srinivasan, 1975). At the beginning of its planning process India introduced a series of instruments, such as industrial licensing, for the purpose of investment allocation which was thought to be sensible on economic grounds. As time went on, however, these promotional measures were transformed into a straightjacket of regulations and restrictive practices that hampered production efficiency and stifled competition. These, however, were merely the first impact results; they bred proliferating rent-seeking activities. The initial controls were the product of ideas and ideology, but they later created

Table 8.2
Income Distribution and ICP Estimates of GDP for India and Some Selected Developing Countries

	ICP Estimates GDP per capita, 1985 (US=100)	Year	Percentage share of household income by percentile groups of households					
			Lowest 20%	Second quintile	Third quintile	Fourth quintile	Highest quintile	Highest 10%
India	4.7	1975-76	7.0	9.2	13.9	20.5	49.4	33.6
South Korea	24.3	1976	5.7	11.2	15.4	22.4	45.3	27.5
Brazil	--	1972	2.0	5.0	9.4	17.0	66.6	50.6
Mexico	--	1977	2.9	7.0	12.0	20.4	57.7	40.6
Yugoslavia	29.2	1978	6.6	12.1	18.7	23.9	38.7	22.9
Malaysia	--	1973	3.5	7.7	12.4	20.3	56.1	39.8
Thailand	17.0	1975-76	5.6	9.6	13.9	21.1	49.8	34.1

Source: World Bank, *World Development Report*, 1989.

Note: ICP refers to the U.N. International Comparison Program.

the interests that stalled a shift in strategy even when the ideas and ideology changed. In the words of its foremost exponent,

the Indian regime of controls spawned its own interests. The entire society it yielded, with entrepreneurs enjoying squatter's rights, created a business class that wanted liberalization in the sense of less hassle, not genuine competition. The bureaucrats, however idealistic at the outset, could not but have noticed that this regime gave them the enormous power that the ability to confer rents generates. The politics of corruption also followed as politicians became addicted to the use of licensing to generate illegal funds for election and then for themselves. The iron triangle of business, bureaucrats and politicians was born around the regime that economists and like-minded ideologues had unwittingly espoused. (Bhagwati, 1988)[1]

Thus, the "iron triangle" of the businessmen, bureaucrats, and politicians, and the intellectuals of the older vintage, eventually arrested the progress of liberalization whenever it showed promise of succeeding. Bhagwati's thesis embodying a linkage between ideology and interests constraining a turn in ideology has much wider power to explain the slow growth of the Indian economy, covering both the public and private sectors. There has been a variation on this theme, which adds one other variable of arbitrary power of the state (Patel, 1987). The regime of subsidies and control cements an alliance between government and vested interests which exercises arbitrary power to stymie economic efficiency, responsiveness to competition, and the ability to survive in the world markets.

Somewhat with the same intent, but with a different and wider perspective, Bardhan (1984) focuses on the political constraints on the efficiency of the public sector and agricultural and industrial investments. He traces these constraints to the existence of a proprietary coalition of the industrial-capitalist class: white-collar bureaucrats and rich farmers, all of whom belong to the top two percentile of the population. There are continuing conflicts among these proprietary classes—conflicts between urban industrial and professional classes and rural classes of rich farmers; between the professional class in the public sector and the other proprietary classes in industry and trade; and so on. The consequences of these conflicts are seen in the deceleration of public investment and the rise in the capital–output ratio in the economy, which largely accounted for the slowdown of economic growth in India. The resources raised and mobilized are frittered away through the competing demands of these various classes, entailing uncontrollable expansion of the government's nonproductive current expenditure.

In the name of social welfare the proprietary groups have created a semiautonomous government that protects the administrative power of a literati bureaucracy power group, the business class that is insulated from foreign and domestic competition and most easily manipulates its way through the maze of regulatory controls, and the rich farmers who benefit from massive agricultural subsidies. This configuration of power derives its legitimacy from the populist rhetoric of national self-reliance, the role of the benign state in providing distributive justice, and the need for protection from the greed and rapacity of the unbridled private sector. In such a conjuncture of circumstances the policies evolved only eventuate in economic waste on a larger scale, a loss-making public sector, a decline in saving, and even the atrophy of the private sector which has learned to survive through patronage of the state rather than by its own efficiency.

A common thread runs through the political economy model of economic policy envisaged by Bhagwati–Srinivasan and Patel, on the one hand, and Bardhan, on the other: that is, the arbitrariness of power wielded by the political authorities in India. It is true that ideas and ideology led to the emergence of interests, which in turn prevented a desired shift in economic policy and strategy. It is also a valid proposition that the constant sparring of the proprietary groups with the conflicting objectives has paved the way for a semiautonomous state with concentration of power with its emasculating effect on executive management. But this model does not make clear why the state became autonomous, why the proprietary classes could use the state machinery with impunity for their parochial interests, and why the ideology and ideas hostile to the macroeconomic efficiency emerged in the first place.

It is in this context that the third approach, which emphasizes the role of the political system in economic decision making, seems to acquire greater significance and relevance. The paralysis of economic policy formulation and execution has its genesis in the inner working of the political system which operates in such a manner that, at one extreme, economic policy has punishment as its basis, but without any sanction for enforcing it, and at the other, incentive as its basis without any built-in mechanism to reward for success (Khatkhate, 1977).[2] The omnipresent physical and price controls and the licensing procedures that are supposed to regulate economic activity are motivated by the desire to punish a defaulting individual. In fact, their impact is so soft that the very section which the whole paraphernalia is devised to control escapes their network. In several instances those who should not be granted industrial licenses are enriched by them (Hazari, 1967); high income-earning classes that are supposed to pay high tax rates end up evading most, if not all, of their tax liabilities, and so on. The announcement of penalties is more often than not in the nature of a quietus to hold in check the restiveness of the electorate.

It is this nature of the economic policy, based simultaneously on punishment and incentive, but without any sanctions for enforcing penalty or a system for offering reward, which largely explains the frequent gyrations in economic policy since independence. When the politicians need the support of the people, they are readily inclined to proclaim a turn to the left in economic policy. This is generally on the eve of the election when the votes of the poor are solicited. But once the politicians are firmly entrenched in power, the payoff of leftism in policy posture slowly begins to dwindle. Anxiety to perpetuate themselves in power seizes them, and the search is on for funds to meet the expenses of the next election. The time is ripe then for a swing to the right in policy stance, which lasts until the coffers of the political party in power are filled. Inherently, therefore, economic policy in India moves cyclically—reminiscent of Michael Kalecki's famous political cycle: sometimes to the left but not enough to be called leftist, and sometimes to the right but not enough to be called rightist.

The reason for these opportunistic turns in economic policy lies in the concentration of political power at the center. The situation can be changed only with a radical transformation of the political process, which can ensure a diffusion of political power among state units or even lower down the ladder among the district units. Until then, the interventionist and idiosyncratic elements in economic policy with the accent on subsidies, licensing, and price controls, which encourage rent-seeking, unproductive and efficiency-debilitating activities will remain as strong as ever. Nonetheless, marginal adjustments in policies will take place from time to time in response to the situational emergencies.

INDUSTRIAL POLICY AND THE TRADE REGIME

The Industrial Policy Framework

The nature of India's industrial policy and trade regime, and the manner in which they were implemented over the years, were the direct offshoot of the choice of planning as an instrument to achieve rapid economic growth and egalitarian income distribution. Since the autonomous market forces were considered to be incapable of achieving optimal results, it was assumed that a state should take a leading role as an economic agent. As a consequence, a comprehensive regulatory apparatus emerged with its wings spreading to all sectors of the economy.

The government's policy was predicated on three basic premises. First, the economy should pull itself up by its own shoestrings, which meant in practice that it should operate almost as a closed economy, producing as many products domestically as possible and assigning a marginal role to foreign trade. The second was that the public sector should occupy the commanding heights in the economy. The economic rationale underlying this premise emanated from the Mahalanobis model, which envisaged two sectors. A leading sector consisted of basic goods like steel and machinery, and the other was a consumer goods sector that played a complementary role. Since the allocation of resources between these two sectors is not likely to be determined by autonomous forces, the government had to step in. The third premise was the understandable concern in a poverty-afflicted and overpopulated country like India that the growth should benefit the most disadvantaged classes of society, in terms of more employment opportunities and more equal income distribution.

The basic needs, which gained wide currency during the 1970s in the debate on development problems of the Third World countries, constituted the main fulcrum of the Indian planning experiment. (For a balanced presentation of Indian planning see Sundrum, 1987.) The implications of this concern for policies were clear. If the public sector was to promote heavy industry, the private sector should be denied entry into that field. If employment-generating and quick-yielding small-scale industries were to be encouraged, it could be possible only if the large industries in the private sector were prevented from encroaching on the areas reserved for the public sector. If the egalitarian goals were to be attained, it was imperative that luxury goods not be produced domestically or imported from abroad. Thus, the negative aspects with emphasis on "don'ts" rather than on "dos" received greater prominence in fashioning the industrial policy as well as the trade design. Initially, their objectives were confined to steering investment allocation where it would yield maximum benefits. Once the regulatory machinery was set in motion, however, it developed a life of its own, with constricting influence on growth in industrial production, efficiency, and trade promotion, creating vested interests in the process.

Since the government had assigned high priority to the allocation of resources between the public and private sectors, and had also predetermined the pattern of private sector investment, the instruments devised to ensure the outcome naturally had a wide domain. These were industrial licensing, foreign investment licensing, price controls, and regulation of monopolies. All these instruments except the last originated with the Industrial Development and Regulation Act 1951, although their character and coverage changed over time.

Industrial licensing was directed toward creating capacity in existing lines of manufacturing and in new areas consistent with the plan priorities. Initially, small-scale industries with fixed capital below Rs 50 million were exempted from licensing; over the years, however, this limit was raised following the rise in the general price level. Although the intention of licensing was laudable, the way it worked in practice placed obstacles to the smooth functioning of the manufacturing sector. For one thing, potential investors were discouraged from entering the field. For another, recognizing the bias of the licensing policy against existing capacity, the firms preferred to apply for new products rather than expand and specialize in the existing lines, thereby effecting overdiversification or industrial fragmentation. The issue of a letter of intent was only the first step in a series under the licensing procedure. The licensee had to go from pillar to post to provide proof that he had taken other steps to complete the preliminaries for building up the capacity or setting up a new plant before the initial letter of intent was converted into an industrial license. This process often went through a bureaucratic rigmarole involving various ministries of the government of India and other concerned agencies. By the time a license was translated into concrete action, a considerable amount of time had passed, and, in many cases, the investor either lost interest and withdrew or held the license without actually using it to start production. Finally, the most damaging result of the licensing process was the hoarding of licenses for approved projects by influential producers, solely with a view to preventing their competitors from entering the field.

In recent years, particularly since 1985, there has been considerable relaxation. Some categories of manufacturers were completely delicensed, and industrial licensing was made more flexible than before by allowing additional capacity under provisions for "automatic growth," "unlimited growth," "regulation of capacity," "modernization," "re-endorsement of capacity" and "raising the minimum economic scale of production." However, liberalization in regard to the licensing of industries has remained half-hearted with uncertainty hanging over its possible future reversal.

Whenever the industrial licensing mechanism failed to accomplish what it was designed to do, other regulatory measures emerged from its womb. One of the major measures was the Monopoly and Restrictive Trade Practice Act (MRTP), which was designed to control the size of firms. The Industrial Licensing Policy Enquiry Committee, set up to evaluate the effectiveness of the licensing policy, concluded in 1969 that the prevailing licensing framework did not succeed in regulating the growth of industrial output in the right direction. It in fact facilitated concentration of economic power and an increasing resort to monopolistic practices by a large number of leading industrial houses. The MRTP Act was passed to prevent this outcome by restraining the expansion of large industrial firms with gross assets exceeding Rs 200 million in interlinked undertakings, or of "dominant" undertakings with assets over Rs 10 million, the definition of dominance being a share in the market exceeding 33 percent until 1982 which was subsequently reduced to 25 percent. Since 1985, however, the asset limit to be exempt from the application of MRTP was raised to Rs 1 billion. As a result, the large firms had to overcome more obstacles than other industrial firms to raise the production capacity or to introduce new products. In particular, the clearance provision applied in their case was dilatory to an extent that the approval rate of industrial licensing applications was roughly half that of other industrial firms. Paradoxically enough, the MRTP-induced restrictions on large firm entry and/or expansion accentuated the prevailing market concentration and excessive profits as the threat to the existing dominant firms from new competitors was substantially reduced.

In order both to increase employment through less capital-intensive methods of production and to promote new entrepreneurship, the industrial policy favored the small-scale industrial sector through product reservation apart from various other concessions like exemption from licensing, and labor legislation, discriminatory tax treatment, and credit subsidy. Until 1977–78 sixty-six products were exclusively reserved for the small-scale industries; the number has been raised to eight hundred since then. This policy passed through many vicissitudes— sometimes dereservation of some existing production. Currently, the small-scale industrial firms exclusively manufacture about 860 products.

Foreign Investment Control and Licensing of Foreign Technology

The newly independent India, emerging from prolonged foreign rule, suffered from a phobia about the entry of foreign capital. Added to these reservations were the foreign exchange scarcity and the desire to promote domestic enterprise and indigenous technology suited to its resource endowment. First, India opted for the purchase of foreign technology and minority foreign participation in equity during the 1960s. Royalty rates and fees were prescribed, and the conditions for Indianization of management and the proportion of equity participation were laid down. The most restrictive policy was introduced through enactment of the Foreign Exchange Regulation Act in 1973, under which maximum equity participation by foreign investors was limited to 40 percent, except in export-oriented and high-technology industries; royalty rates were lowered. In terms of the impact on industrial growth, however, these restrictions were not comparable to the industrial licensing, first because foreign investment, both in stock and flow terms, had been modest in view of India's limited industrial growth, and second because the domestic industrial policy's bias against competition and high profits hardly excited foreign firms (Desai, 1984a, 1988).

Price Controls

The government has maintained price controls on commodities varying from essential goods of consumption like sugar and drugs to intermediate goods and even capital goods. There are currently about sixty-five individual goods or groups of commodities. Prices are usually set on a cost-plus basis, derived from technical relationships and the norms for reasonable rate of return on capital employed. The coverage of commodities is altered from time to time, depending on which prices need to be raised or lowered. This mode of determining prices is not uniform and varies from industry to industry. As a result, there are anomalous situations such as uniform pricing for all plants for a given product (e.g., steel) regardless of the cost conditions in each, or different prices for different plants for the same product depending on the obsolescence of the plant (e.g., fertilizers), or different prices for the same product from a given plant (e.g., levy and nonlevy cement). In a number of cases in the past, the prices of products manufactured by public enterprises were raised only to wipe out their losses and/or increase their profits. It was not recognized that the policy of jacking up prices of intermediate goods helped raise resources for financing public sector investment only in the short term, while creating a resource crunch in the medium and long run when higher intermediate goods prices augmented inflationary pressures.

The chaotic, counterproductive price control regime has been continued, despite a severe indictment of these regimes by various official committees. The government did, however, recognize the complexity and irrationality of price controls when its policy documents in 1986 recommended abolishing plant-specific, cost-plus retention pricing. Yet it persisted with the core of the administered price control system while making marginal adjustments to mollify the system's critics.

Foreign Trade and Exchange Control Regime

From the beginning the foreign trade regime and the associated exchange controls were designed to complement the domestic industrial policy. As such, they were motivated by the same set of considerations (such as self-reliance) as dominated the industrial policy. This meant in practice the protection of domestic industry, old and new, from foreign competition. This objective was achieved by licensing imports, imposition of high tariff rates on imported goods, other quantitative restrictions, and stringent foreign exchange controls including an overvalued exchange-rate policy.

The basic rationale for import substitution is provided by the "infant industry" argument that, in the presence of market failure, prevailing prices cannot provide an appropriate signal for the decision to invest. It is therefore necessary to shelter new industries from competition for the period of time required for them to attain maturity. In fact, the industries set up as a result of import-substitution strategy remained perpetually infant without manifesting any sign of attaining healthy adulthood. In practice, the control instruments used to achieve import substitution proved to be counterproductive. Imports were permitted based on the simple rule that the products were not domestically available—the so-called indigenous nonavailability—or that they were certified by the government as "essential." As Bhagwati and Srinivasan (1975) have forcefully argued, "every item of indigenous production, no matter how much its cost of production exceeded the landed c.i.f. price, was automatically shielded from competition through imports, indeed the onus being put on the buyer to show conclusively that he could not procure the item from indigenous producers (p. 27)." Though the criterion for imports was supposed to be clear-cut and unambiguous, the way it was applied made the import licensing a sheer monstrosity.

For the purpose of imports, goods in India are classified into three categories: consumption goods, raw materials, and components and capital goods. The first category was completely banned when the "Established Importers" classification was abolished in 1977. The importers classified as "Actual Users" are the manufacturers of goods who can import certain items of raw materials and capital goods under open general license (OGL). But even here, the "fairness of share" principle is used, which implies that imports are allocated pro rata to actual importers with reference to capacity installed or employment or shares defined by past import allocations, or some other arbitrary criteria. Even when imports are placed on the OGL list, it is not much of a concession inasmuch as tariff rates, which at times run as high as 200 to 300 percent, make it impossible to import any goods. High-cost domestic industry produces capital goods or inter-mediate goods at prohibitive prices, impeding export growth. Until 1966 the exchange rate was overvalued. Although its adverse impact was somewhat offset by various import entitlement schemes under which the exporters could make up the losses on exports through profits on sales of imported raw materials, the export competitiveness was not transparent because of the complexity of the export incentive schemes. The 1966 devaluation and a sustained improvement in the real exchange rates during the 1970s (and again since the late 1980s) improved the prospects for exports.

Behind this bias against exports are the beliefs that terms of trade of countries like India would continue to deteriorate, that there is low price elasticity of demand for Indian exports, that the protectionist policies of the industrial countries would hamper trade, and, finally, that the inward-looking industrialization strategy would quicken the pace of economic growth. However, these assumptions were not borne out either by India's own experience in the late 1980s, when its exports showed buoyancy under favorable conditions, or by the experience of other developing countries like Korea. As Bhagwati (1987) pointed out, "other countries which began with a much smaller industrial base are not only *exporting* more manufacturers than India but they are also catching up with India in the absolute size of their manufacturing sector. The share of Korea's manufacturing sector, for example, was less than 25 percent of India's in 1970 (measured as valued added). By 1981, it was already up to 60 percent (p. 11)."[3]

Foreign exchange controls, though alternating between relaxation and tightening over the last forty years, retained their restrictive character almost intact. It is primarily the government, particularly its Finance Ministry, which controls the strings by formulating a foreign exchange budget every six months. After preempting foreign exchange for use by what the government considers priority sectors, which include largely government and some key private sector segments, the rest is allocated by the administrative decisions consistent with the import and export policies as described earlier.

It was not as if the government did not realize the counterproductive nature of this kind of trade regime. Several government committees time and again underscored how the trade regime had impaired the efficiency and productivity of Indian industry. However, their recommendations did not get translated into concrete action, or if they did, the resulting policy was a patchwork, with some liberalization within an overall framework of a regulated trade policy. A number of policy initiatives were taken after 1984. Attempts were made to relax import controls by extending the scope of OGL lists and by taking a more benign view of import controls. The level and scope of export incentives were increased; domestic licensing and other controls on some selected manufacturing industries were relaxed to make them internationally competitive. The exchange-rate policy, too, for the first time, was flexibly administered, allowing steady depreciation of the real exchange rate through continuously downward adjustment in the nominal exchange rate. With all these adjustments in trade and exchange-rate policies, the trade regime did not become neutral between imports and exports, which is a precondition for India to reap the benefits of specialization of production.

Consequences of Industrial Policy and Trade Regime

In the 1950s, when development economics was in its infancy, it was believed that if a country could achieve a rate of saving and investment at roughly 20 to

25 percent, it could enter a self-sustaining stage of development. The implicit assumption behind this belief was that the acceleration in saving and investment rates would transmit itself into the rate of growth of the economy. If this were the only criterion for judging the progress of countries, India would have been in that happy state long ago. The average saving rate in the 1970s was 19.5 percent of GDP, a sharp rise from the 6 to 7 percent savings rate in the 1950s. It further increased to 22.0 percent during the 1980s.[4] The investment ratio was a little higher at an average of 19.7 percent during the 1970s and 24.6 percent during the 1980s, bolstered by foreign resources inflow (Table 8.3). Furthermore, financial assets as a ratio of GDP considered to be an indicator of efficiency of saving increased from 26 percent in 1981 to 45.4 percent in 1988–89, a level not reached even by a spectacular growth-achieving country like Korea (Table 8.4). Thus, in terms of saving–investment ratio, India's performance was impressive by any standard, considering the high population pressure and the low income base from which it started in the 1950s. However, the high saving–investment performance was not reflected in India's growth rate. "If we break the period into 1951 to 1965 (coinciding roughly with the Nehru and pre-wheat revolution era) and 1968 to 1984 (omitting the two severe drought years of 1965–66 and 1966–67), the trend growth rate is 3.88 percent in the former period and 3.75 percent in the latter, there being no statistically significant difference between the two rates" (Bhagwati, 1987, p. 16). The average growth rate decadewise—3.59 percent in the 1950s, 3.13 percent in the 1960s, 3.62 percent in the 1970s, and 3.72 percent in the 1980s—generally conformed to this pattern (Table 8.1). A low rate of income growth against the background of a high investment rate raised the marginal capital–output ratios in the Indian economy. Thus, the capital–output ratio rose from 2.87 in the early 1950s to 4.58 in the early 1960s and to 5.40 in the 1970s, but there was a slight reversal in the 1980s to 4.45 (Table 8.5). The only logical inference that can be drawn is that investment in the Indian economy was inefficiently managed.

The question, however, is whether the low productivity of investment could be the only inference possible, or whether alternative explanations could throw light on the increasing capital–output ratio. Two of these alternative explanations may be singled out as they have gained respectability among some economists who have pinned their faith on the prevailing industrial policy framework and trade regime. First, a technological revolution in the agricultural sector—what is known as the Green Revolution—led to the increase in capital intensity of production techniques in agriculture because more fertilizer than land was used for raising production (Chakravarty, 1987, p. 56). Second, the increasing trend in capital–output ratios is not peculiar to India because similar trends were discerned in several other industrial and nonindustrial countries. The first of these arguments has some truth, but it does not necessarily explain why the capital–output ratio in the aggregate should rise. Bhagwati has convincingly argued that the use of more fertilizer than land need not and should not raise capital intensity in agriculture, as there is some such thing as the diminishing return to investment in land. Furthermore, as Ahluwalia (1985) has proved through a comprehensive

Table 8.3
Gross Domestic Saving and Investment in India, 1951/52–1988/89 (as percent of GDP at current prices)

Year	Total Gross Investment	Total Gross Saving	Household Sector Saving	Corporate Sector Saving	Government Saving
1951–52	11.9	10.1	6.2	1.3	2.5
1952–53	7.9	8.2	6.1	0.6	1.5
1953–54	8.5	8.7	6.7	0.8	1.2
1954–55	10.6	10.5	7.8	1.1	1.5
1955–56	14.3	13.9	11.0	1.3	1.7
1956–57	16.0	13.1	10.0	1.2	1.9
1957–58	14.6	10.9	8.0	0.9	1.9
1958–59	12.7	10.0	7.5	1.0	1.6
1959–60	13.5	11.9	9.1	1.2	1.6
1960–61	15.7	12.7	8.4	1.7	2.6
1961–62	14.2	12.2	7.5	1.8	2.9
1962–63	15.8	13.4	8.5	1.8	3.1
1963–64	15.4	13.3	8.1	1.8	3.3
1964–65	15.1	12.7	7.8	1.5	3.3
1965–66	16.8	14.5	9.9	1.5	3.1
1966–67	18.4	15.3	11.6	1.4	2.3
1967–68	15.4	13.0	9.9	1.2	1.9
1968–69	13.9	12.8	9.3	1.2	2.3
1969–70	15.6	15.0	11.1	1.3	2.6
1970–71	16.6	15.7	11.3	1.5	2.9
1971–72	17.3	16.2	11.8	1.6	2.8
1972–73	15.9	15.4	11.2	1.5	2.6
1973–74	19.1	18.4	13.8	1.7	2.9
1974–75	18.3	17.4	11.8	2.0	3.7
1975–76	18.8	19.0	13.4	1.3	4.2
1976–77	19.7	21.2	15.0	1.4	4.9
1977–78	19.5	21.1	15.3	1.4	4.3
1978–79	23.3	23.2	17.0	1.5	4.6
1979–80	22.1	21.6	15.2	2.1	4.3
1980–81	22.7	21.2	16.1	1.7	3.4
1981–82	22.6	21.0	14.9	1.6	4.6
1982–83	20.8	19.4	13.4	1.6	4.4
1983–84	20.8	19.5	14.7	1.5	3.3
1984–85	20.1	18.7	14.1	1.7	2.8
1985–86	22.8	20.4	15.2	2.1	3.2
1986–87	21.7	19.5	15.1	1.7	2.7
1987–88	21.7	19.6	15.9	1.7	2.1
1988–89	23.9	21.0	17.5	1.8	1.6

Source: Government of India, *Economic Survey, 1989–90.*

analysis of Indian industry, a higher capital–output ratio prevails across the board in almost all industries in India. The second argument is a non sequitur. The capital–output ratio could increase in different countries for different reasons, such as the external shocks or macroeconomic imbalances. But neither of these has been present in India. Table 8.6 shows that the size of firms generally increased over time.

Since the industrial policy and trade regime have directly affected the industrial sector, its performance should reflect whether the policy regime was helpful or

Table 8.4

Composition of Household Sector's Saving and Financial Assets, India, 1980/81–1988/89 (in percent of GDP at current market prices)

	1980-81	1981-82	1982-83	1983-84	1984-85	1985-86	1986-87	1987-88	1988-89
Household Sector Saving	16.1	14.9	13.4	15.2	14.9	15.9	17.4	17.4	17.0
a) Net Financial Assets	6.3	6.0	7.1	6.6	7.7	7.2	8.4	8.2	7.8
b) Physical Assets	9.8	8.9	6.3	8.6	7.2	8.7	9.0	9.2	9.2

	1965	1980	1987
Financial Assets/GDP Ratio [a]	25.7	36.2	45.4

Sources: Reserve Bank of India, *Report of Currency and Finance, 1988–89, vol. 2, Statistical Statements*; and World Bank, *World Development Report*, 1989.

[a] Outstanding financial assets of non-bank public defined as bank and non-bank deposits, shares, and bonds.

Table 8.5
Incremental Capital–Output Ratios in the Indian Economy, 1951/52–1985/86

	Aggregate Capital/Output Ratios
1951/52 - 1955/56	2.87
1956/57 - 1960/61	4.05
1961/62 - 1965/66	4.58
1966/67 - 1968/69	5.05
1969/70 - 1973/74	5.86
1974/75 - 1978/79	4.28
1980/81 - 1983/84	4.45
1984/85 - 1985/86	5.31

	Sectoral Capital/Output Ratios		
	Agriculture	Mining	Manufacturing
1951/52 - 1959/60	2.18	2.59	4.47
1960/61 - 1969/70	3.23	5.62	6.49
1970/71 - 1979/80	4.22	14.56	8.20
1980/81 - 1983/84	3.17	9.98	4.36
1984/85 -	7.9		

Source: S. Chakravarty, *Development Planning: The Indian Experience*, 1987; and *National Account Statistics*, CSO, New Delhi.

Table 8.6
Manufacturing Output and Value Added by Firm Size (in percent)

Firm Size (number of workers)	Output		Value Added	
	1975/76	1982/83	1975/76	1982/83
0-49	14.1	12.7	8.2	7.7
50-99	7.3	7.1	5.0	4.9
100-199	8.2	15.0	6.8	6.3
200-499	15.3	13.0	12.5	12.7
500-999	13.7	15.5	15.4	14.0
1000-1999	16.6	12.7	18.5	14.7
2000-4999	13.4	16.3	16.7	14.8
5000 and above	11.4		16.9	24.9

Source: *Annual Survey of Industries*, 1975–76 and 1982–83.

harmful. Table 8.7 shows that the major industrial policy goal of diversification of industry was undoubtedly achieved. Thus, the proportions of basic and capital goods, both metal-based and chemical-based, all increased since the 1960s. Similarly, import substitution in respect of iron and steel, petroleum, fertilizers,

Table 8.7
Structure of Industrial Production (in percent)

	1960	1970	1980	1984
Use-based	100.0	100.0	100.0	100.0
Basic industries	26.8	32.3	35.3	40.4
Capital goods	12.9	15.7	17.6	16.6
Intermediate goods	24.3	20.9	19.6	17.8
Consumer goods	36.0	31.0	28.0	25.6
Input-based	100.0	100.0	100.0	100.0
Agro-based	47.3	33.7	28.0	24.5
Metal-based	17.1	21.9	23.6	22.2
Chemical-based	9.6	12.9	15.3	16.3
Multiple input sources	26.0	31.5	33.1	37.0

Source: Report of Currency and Finance, *Reserve of India Classification of Index of Industrial Production*, vol. 2, Statistical Statements, Reserve Bank of India, Bombay.

and newsprint, progressed a great deal between 1960 and 1980. But whether or not it has been an efficient industrialization is debatable. Here again, the evidence furnished by the Ahluwalia study (1985, p. 32) is very illuminating. After carefully sifting the statistical base, she concludes that "industrial deceleration was concentrated in heavy industries, i.e., basic goods and capital goods, while the industrial production data revealed deceleration across the board. Since the phenomenon of slowdown in growth for a substantial part of the industrial sector is associated with the evidence of slow growth for most of the remaining industrial sector, the overall picture that emerges is that of industrial stagnation."

The sluggish industrial growth, as in the case of rising trends in the aggregate capital–output ratio, has been attributed to (1) the weak linkages between agriculture and industry; (2) the skewed income distribution, reducing demand for industrial production; and (3) declining public investment in infrastructural facilities. Ahluwalia (1985) refutes all three explanations, even on the assumption of a close economy model. As for the weakness of linkages between agriculture and industry, the study shows that there was no wage goods constraint; the agricultural raw material constraint only marginally affected industry, and that, too, for only a part of it. That industry did not realize its potential even at a lower level of agricultural growth. With regard to the unequal income distribution affecting demand for industrial goods, the evidence on income distribution such as exists with all its limitations does not unambiguously show that it has worsened. Even if it has, it could not have accounted for the industrial stagnation that was concentrated in capital goods industries and not in the consumer goods industries.

The third factor, the slowdown in public investment, was also inadequate to explain industrial stagnation. Public investment did indeed slow down, but there is no reason why it should affect the whole industrial sector: it should impact only on those industries for which the demand emanated mainly from public investment. Furthermore, as long as the overall investment rate was high and rising, industrial sectors as a whole should have thrived rather than stagnated. Even more importantly, if the public investment had slowed down, it was not because the government, obsessed as it was with the public sector growth, was for some strange reason reluctant to do so. The main constraint on public investment, as shown in Table 8.10, arose because of a decline in public savings, which in turn was due mainly to the widespread epidemic of loss-making public enterprises. Thus, the slackness in public investment occurred primarily for the same reason that the stagnation in the private industrial sector occurred.

A simple and commonsensical explanation for the slowness of industrial growth lies in "the cumulative impact of the growing inefficiencies in factor use over time" (Ahluwalia, 1985, p. 146; Shroff, 1988). This phenomenon is not of recent origin, however; it has persisted since the 1950s. Bhagwati and Srinivasan (1975) have presented extensive documentation in support of the fact that the estimated rate of technical change in Indian industry was abysmally low, indeed negligible. The lack of technical upgrading and the inefficient factor use are reflected in the spread of sickness among Indian private sector industry. As of 1988, there were twenty-two thousand such industrial units. Such units are defined as those that incur losses in the previous year, are expected to incur losses in the current and the following year, have a debt–equity ratio of less than 1:1, and have existed for at least seven years. The number of these units rose by 70 percent between 1983 and 1988. The gravity of this phenomenon could be surmised from the fact that as much as 20 percent of total bank credit was purveyed to the sick units, implying that the industrial disease had also spread to the financial system, jeopardizing its viability (Reserve Bank of India, 1989).

A cherished goal of industrial and other regulatory policies was the promotion of the small-scale industry by reserving the production of certain specified commodities. Table 8.6 shows that the policy has not succeeded, as the share of small enterprises employing fewer than one hundred workers has declined over the years. More significantly, the emphasis on small-scale production has militated against an increase in the scale of production with all its advantages. Restriction on the size of firms, the encouragement of small-industry entry in industries with significant scale diseconomies, and the limited size of domestic markets protected by high trade barriers induced small-scale industries not to graduate to an unprotected category. If they grew to medium and large size, they would attract labor laws and high taxation. A rationale for preferring small-scale industry was that they would have low capital–output and capital–labor ratios. But this was not borne out by the evidence. As Sandesara (1969) has pointed out, there is "a lack of positive association between size and capital intensity as well as a positive association between size and output–capital ratio" (quoted in Ahluwalia, 1985, p. 161). The net impact of the promotional policies of the small-scale industry has been a staggering number of sick units—204,259 as at the end of 1987 (Reserve Bank of India, 1989).

When domestic industry operates wastefully, it denies the economy the opportunity to derive gains from trade. Several studies (Bhagwati and Srinivasan, 1975; Panchamukhi, 1978; and Wolf, 1982) have demonstrated that the domestic resource cost of earning a unit of foreign exchange for different kinds of exports has been extremely high, accounting for a relatively weak performance by India. The detrimental impact of industrial and trade policies was reinforced by the policy of an overvalued exchange rate. Thus, the effective exchange rate for exports was persistently lower than that for imports, except during the period 1985 to date, when it was decided to adjust the normal exchange rate in a downward direction to achieve a depreciated effective exchange rate for exports. The Committee of the Government of India (the Tandon Committee) threw a searching light on this bias: a trade regime in which there is significant reliance upon tariffs and licensing affords substantial effective protection to domestic production in import-competing lines, while exports receive no comparable protection. In fact, since this type of protection raises the general cost-structure of industry, exports actually suffer from negative protection. This import bias in policy is in contrast to a neutral regime in which both export-oriented production and import-substituting production face the same degree of effective protection (Shroff, 1988 a and 1988 b).

Several attempts have been made to exonerate the trade regime, the industrial policy, and the exchange-rate policy by downplaying their adverse impact on India's exports (e.g., Bagchi, 1990, Chakravarty, 1987, Nayyar, 1988). Two main arguments have been proposed to justify the present industrial trade and payments regime. First, government intervention in India is not a unique phenomenon, and successful exporting countries like Korea also maintain strong interventionist policy. If the existing Indian trade regime has not succeeded in export generation on a desired scale, its implementation should be mproved rather than throwing the baby of trade regime away with the bath water (Chakravarty, 1987; Nayyar 1986). Second, India's exports have suffered more because they face rather sticky markets; the global inelasticity of demand or the trend rate of growth of demand is low, or the protectionism is rampant in the industrial countries and there are many other low-cost competitors, often pressed by mounting debt-service charges, to export the same or similar products (Bagchi, 1990). It is therefore suggested that for better export-import balance, a combination of judiciously deployed export subsidies, import tariffs, quota restrictions should be adopted (Bagchi, 1990). In short, India should adopt more of the same policies as in the past whose contribution to trade was negative.

The first argument is a red herring. Those who favor neutral trade strategies have not denigrated state intervention per se. The trade regime with government intervention can be nondiscriminatory against exports and even helpful. As Bhagwati (1988) has argued, the government intervention can be of great value and almost certainly has been so, in making the natural incentive trade strategy work successfully when the Government can bend in some cases toward ultra-export promotion and generate enough confidence in investors to undertake costly investment and programs in order to take advantage of a shift in such a trade policy. Thus, the failure of the Indian industrial and trade policy is due not so much to its interventionist content as to its bias against exports.

The other contention that India's exports were impeded by protectionist measures in the industrial countries and the low income elasticity of demand for the type of goods produced by India is simply not borne out by the empirical evidence. Tables 8.8 and 8.9 present statistics on exports from India and two groups of Asian countries—outward-oriented countries and moderately outward-oriented countries for selected years. It will be seen that the rate of growth of India's exports is one of the lowest and that India's share in the world market for merchandise exports as well as manufactured exports has fallen sharply over the years. If we assume that the income elasticity of demand for production from the developing countries is low, there is no reason why India's share in world exports should have been declining while the share of other developing countries exporting similar products was rising. It is true that the tariff and nontariff discrimination against imports from developing countries by the industrial countries posed serious barriers, but these barriers were against all the developing countries. And yet, the East Asian and Pacific countries with different but efficient trade regimes have exported more to the industrial markets. The share of developing countries as a whole in three industrial countries—the United States, Japan, and the EEC in 1984—was 28.5 percent, 27.8 percent, and 11.4 percent, respectively. The corresponding percentages for seven East Asian and Pacific countries (Korea, Taiwan, Singapore, Hong Kong, Indonesia, Thailand, and Malaysia) were 17.6 percent 20.0 percent, and 3.6 percent (Bhattacharya and Linn, 1988). This means that the share of the East Asian and Pacific countries accounted for a little less than two-thirds of the total developing countries' exports of manufactures to the United States, which is a little short of three-fourths to Japan and about one-fourth to the EEC. Obviously, countries like India lagged far behind in exporting to the markets where its competitors succeeded remarkably despite trade barriers. This certainly is no tribute to India's trade and payments regime.

That the old trade regime was obstructive of India's exports has been convincingly shown in a recent study by Virmani (1990). The government of India has liberalized trade policy in an important, though half-hearted, fashion since 1985. In the 1980s this shift was instrumental in narrowing the trade gap defined as the difference between exports and commercial imports (i.e., total imports minus government priority imports including defense), the latter magnitude being sensitive to prices as well as liberalization measures. Import liberalization, depreciation of the effective exchange rate, and an array of export incentives have for the first time reduced the discriminatory character of the trade regime, which

Table 8.8A
Merchandise Exports as Percentage of World Exports

	1970	1975	1980	1985	1988
INDIA	0.70	0.53	0.44	0.53	0.50
COUNTRIES WITH OUTWARD-ORIENTATION					
KOREA	0.29	0.61	0.92	1.68	2.27
TAIWAN	0.49	0.64	1.04	1.71	2.26
SINGAPORE	0.54	0.65	1.02	1.27	1.47
HONG KONG	0.87	0.73	1.04	1.68	2.36
COUNTRIES WITH MODERATE OUTWARD-ORIENTATION					
THAILAND	0.25	0.26	0.34	0.40	0.59
INDONESIA	0.36	0.86	1.15	1.04	0.73
MALAYSIA	0.58	0.46	0.68	0.87	0.79
PHILLIPINES	0.37	0.27	0.31	0.26	0.26

Memorandum Item: In Millions of US Dollars

WORLD EXPORTS	289700	829500	1897600	1800200	2679600

Table 8.8B
Textile Exports as Percentage of World Textile Exports

	1970	1975	1980	1985	1988
INDIA	3.98	2.42	2.23	2.18	
COUNTRIES WITH OUTWARD-ORIENTATION					
KOREA	0.73	2.63	4.29	5.33	
TAIWAN	1.70	2.63	3.46	5.26	12.52
SINGAPORE	0.47	0.53	0.72	0.75	1.89
HONG KONG	1.82	1.75	1.78	2.11	5.46
COUNTRIES WITH MODERATE OUTWARD-ORIENTATION					
THAILAND	0.07	0.32	0.64	0.88	
INDONESIA	0.02	0.01	0.09	0.51	
MALAYSIA	0.05	0.14	0.31	0.36	
PHILLIPINES	0.05	0.09	0.15	0.08	0.19

Memorandum Item: In Millions of US Dollars

TOTAL	11574	24688	51199	47304	36293

Table 8.8C

Manufacture Exports as Percentage of World Manufacture Exports

	1970	1975	1980	1985	1988
INDIA	0.60	0.42	0.49	0.55	0.77[a]
COUNTRIES WITH OUTWARD-ORIENTATION					
KOREA	0.36	0.88	1.48	2.49	3.09[a]
TAIWAN	0.62	0.91	1.64	2.49	4.95
SINGAPORE	0.27	0.49	0.98	1.20	2.60
HONG KONG	1.33	1.19	1.71	2.50	2.40
COUNTRIES WITH MODERATE OUTWARD-ORIENTATION					
THAILAND	0.04	0.08	0.18	0.25	0.38[a]
INDONESIA	0.01	0.02	0.05	0.22	0.43[a]
MALAYSIA	0.07	0.15	0.23	0.38	0.63[a]
PHILLIPINES	0.05	0.08	0.20	0.24	0.39
Memorandum Item: In Millions of US Dollars					
TOTAL	175948	472765	1062798	1112088	1121619

Sources: For Tables 8.8A, B, and C, World Bank, *World Tables*; and International Monetary Fund, *International Financial Statistics*.

[a] Estimate for 1987.

bolstered Indian exports in dollar terms to the average of 13 to 14 percent, a rate rarely achieved in the past. Virmani's conclusion (1990) is unambiguous: there is a sharply improving trend over the rest of the eighties. Some commentators have implied that the deterioration in the trade deficit in 1985–86 was due to import liberalization-related policy reform. This is incorrect as the ratio of commercial imports to GDP in 1985–86 was virtually identical to that in 1984–85. If, with some marginal adjustments in trade and industrial policies, India could achieve such an improved export growth, and that too at a time when the economy was bedeviled by severe fiscal and other macroeconomic imbalances, how much more could it have progressed if the suffocating framework of industrial and trade policy was completely dismantled, giving a free rein to competitive forces?

INDIA'S MULTIDIMENSIONAL FISCAL POLICY

Although India's fiscal policy is motivated primarily by the need to mobilize resources, several facets of it bear on social equity, maintenance of economic stability, and allocation of resources according to a predetermined scheme of

Table 8.9A
Merchandise Exports, Total (in millions of U.S. dollars)

	1970	1975	1980	1985	1988
INDIA	461	597	1141	1033	
COUNTRIES WITH OUTWARD-ORIENTATION					
KOREA	85	649	2197	2523	
TAIWAN	197	650	1771	2490	4545
SINGAPORE	54	130	367	353	686
HONG KONG	211	433	909	998	1980
COUNTRIES WITH MODERATE OUTWARD-ORIENTATION					
THAILAND	8	80	330	416	
INDONESIA	2	2	46	239	
MALAYSIA	6	34	161	170	
PHILLIPINES	5	22	74	39	69

World Exports: In Millions of US Dollars

	1970	1975	1980	1985	1988
TOTAL	289700	829500	1897600	1800200	2679600
MANUFACTURES	175948	472765	1062798	1112088	1121619
TEXTILES	11574	24688	51199	47304	36293

Table 8.9B
Merchandise Exports, Textiles (in millions of U.S. Dollars)

	1970	1975	1980	1985	1988
INDIA	2026	4365	8332	9465	13313
COUNTRIES WITH OUTWARD-ORIENTATION					
KOREA	835	5081	17483	30283	60697
TAIWAN	1428	5302	19786	30696	60582
SINGAPORE	1554	5377	19376	22815	39506
HONG KONG	2514	6019	19703	30185	63163
COUNTRIES WITH MODERATE OUTWARD-ORIENTATION					
THAILAND	710	2195	6505	7121	15830
INDONESIA	1055	7130	21909	18711	19465
MALAYSIA	1687	3847	12939	15632	21110
PHILLIPINES	1060	2218	5788	4629	7032

World Exports: In Millions of US Dollars

	1970	1975	1980	1985	1988
TOTAL	289700	829500	1897600	1800200	2679600
MANUFACTURES	175948	472765	1062798	1112088	1121619
TEXTILES	11574	24688	51199	47304	36293

Table 8.9C

Merchandise Exports, Manufacture (in millions of U.S. dollars)

	1970	1975	1980	1985	1988
INDIA	0.60	0.42	0.49	0.55	0.77[a]
COUNTRIES WITH OUTWARD-ORIENTATION					
KOREA	0.36	0.88	1.48	2.49	3.09[a]
TAIWAN	0.62	0.91	1.64	2.49	4.95
SINGAPORE	0.27	0.49	0.98	1.20	2.60
HONG KONG	1.33	1.19	1.71	2.50	2.40
COUNTRIES WITH MODERATE OUTWARD-ORIENTATION					
THAILAND	0.04	0.08	0.18	0.25	0.38[a]
INDONESIA	0.01	0.02	0.05	0.22	0.43[a]
MALAYSIA	0.07	0.15	0.23	0.38	0.63[a]
PHILLIPINES	0.05	0.08	0.20	0.24	0.39

Memorandum Item: In Millions of US Dollars

TOTAL	175948	472765	1062798	1112088	1121619

Sources: For Tables 8.9A, B, and C, World Bank, *World Tables*, 1988–89; and International Monetary Fund, *International Financial Statistics*.

[a] Estimate for 1987.

economic priorities. This policy framework originated with the First Five-Year Plan and developed in new directions as the planning process became complex and pervasive. Under Indian conditions it has a longer reach and a different connotation than in other countries, if only because the fiscal policy is a principal instrument to augment public saving, influence private saving both in its magnitude and disposition, finance public investment, and determine the pattern of income distribution. This tall order of demands, as well as the lack of consistency among them, severely tested the role of fiscal policy over the years. As a result, it did not succeed to the extent expected, in achieving its objectives. A seemingly bold attempt was made in 1985 to revamp the fiscal policy, but the themes of a "New Fiscal Policy" petered out soon after 1987.

Table 8.10 displays the developments in public sector operations between 1981 and 1989. With regard first to the resource mobilization aspect, fiscal policy can be evaluated with reference to the tax effort, public saving, and private saving—the last because India's fiscal policy heavily influences the disposable income of the private sector consisting of households and corporate and incorporate enterprises. Clearly, fiscal policy has well succeeded in raising tax revenue, which now constitutes around 22.0 percent of GDP. Considering that this ratio was under 7.0 percent in 1950–51 and 19.6 percent in 1984–85, it was

Table 8.10

Government Current Receipts and Expenditures (as percent of GDP at market prices)

	1970-71	1975-76	1980-81	1984-85	1988-89
Current Receipts	13.7	16.8	18.5	19.6	21.7
Tax Revenue	12.3	15.5	16.8	17.3	16.7
Non-tax Revenue	1.4	1.3	1.7	2.3	5.0
Current Expenditures	12.3	14.0	15.9	20.0	26.3
Defense	3.1	3.5	3.2	3.5	2.8
Interest payments	0.5	0.7	1.2	2.5	3.7
Subsidies	0.8	1.5	2.2	3.3	4.4
Other	7.9	8.3	9.3	10.7	15.4
Revenue accounts Surplus (+)/deficit (-)	+1.4	+2.8	+2.6	+0.4	-4.6

Sources: Government of India, *Issues of National Accounts Statistics*; and Central Statistical Organization, Government of India, *Economic Survey, 1989–90*.

Table 8.11
Elasticity and Buoyancy of India's Tax System

	Elasticity[a]		Buoyancy[b]	
	1966-67 to 1983-84	1970-71 to 1983-84	1966-67 to 1983-84	1970-71 to 1983-84
Corporation Tax	1.0621	1.0841	1.1662	1.1931
Income Tax	0.8827	0.7967	0.9306	0.7983
Union Excise	1.0542	1.1749	1.4190	1.5086
Sales Tax	1.3140	1.3020	1.4241	1.4144
State Excises	1.1292	1.1044	1.3389	1.2994
Stamps and Registration	0.8869	0.9111	1.0253	1.0629
Land Revenue	0.2909	0.2746	0.4714	0.4977
Tax Revenue (center)	0.8857	0.8891	1.2071	1.1699
Tax Revenue (states)	1.1192	1.1077	1.2869	1.2838
Total Tax Revenue	0.9608	0.9598	1.2329	1.2071

Source: National Institute of Public Finance and Policy, New Delhi (as reproduced in Acharya, 1988).

[a] Elasticity considers other variables such as changes in tax rates.

[b] Buoyancy is the change in the tax revenues/changes in GNP.

quite an achievement for the government. This strong intertemporal performance is also borne out by the buoyancy over the years in almost all major taxes (Table 8.11). But an increase in resources does not in itself offer proof of the efficiency of resource mobilization. If the strong tax effort is accompanied by a rise in current government expenditures, it is not likely that sufficient public saving will be generated to support a rising investment expenditure in the public sector.

Public sector saving was around 2.9 percent of GDP at market prices in 1970–71. It reached 4.9 percent in 1976–77, a peak level, and then started declining. In 1988–89 it stood at 1.6 percent, a level reached in 1955–56 (Table 8.3). The falling trend in public saving, though disturbing by itself, would demonstrate how the planning process, which was predicated on growing public sector saving, became increasingly unrealistic. For instance, in all the five-year plans, the resources projected to sustain the ballooning size of total investment, particularly the public sector component of it, were constantly underrealized. Yet the planners persisted with these optimistic projections. The target of public saving in the Seventh Five-Year Plan was fixed at 6.0 percent of GDP, even when the actual performance of public saving during the earlier plan periods held little promise of reversing the earlier declining trend. The foremost cause of the decline in public saving was the burgeoning expansion of current government expenditure even when the tax revenue receipts recorded an impressive performance.

Perhaps the very success in resource utilization through taxation proved to be a built-in accelerator for the expansion of current expenditure which not only threw out of gear the planning process, but also tended to aggravate the financial crisis of the governments both at the center and the state levels. Thus, the government's current expenditure as a ratio of GDP rose from 12.3 percent in 1970–71 to almost 26.3 percent in 1988–89, while the tax revenue proportion to GDP increased from 13.7 percent to 21.7 percent in the same period (Table 8.10). The declining government saving, however, was offset by the corresponding increase in the saving of the public sector enterprises whose ratio to GDP almost doubled from 1.7 percent in 1970–71 to 3.5 percent in 1987–88. Although this compensating expansion in public enterprise saving was stabilizing, it was not an unqualified tribute to the surplus-generating capacity of these units because "each year public investment augments, by substantial amounts, the capital stock employed by PSEs (Public Sector Enterprises)" (Acharya, 1988).

There were several reasons for the dismal public saving performance. First, the government's current expenditure increased mainly because of the increasing interest rate burden and the subsidies mainly to agriculture. Although India's defense expenditure has been large in relation to GDP, this proportion has hardly increased since 1970–71 (Table 8.10). The real squeeze came because of the sharp rise in net interest payments and subsidies whose respective proportions to GDP increased from 0.5 percent and 0.8 percent to 3.7 percent and 4.4 percent between 1970–71 and 1988–89. The upsurge in interest payments came because the government growingly resorted to the public debt to finance not only the public sector investment, but also the current account deficit. Normally, by itself this should not have posed any serious problem for the fiscal authorities, if the public sector enterprises had yielded sufficient rate of return. This leads to the second reason why the public saving has fallen over the years.

A full picture of the financial performance of the PSEs belonging both to the central government and the state governments since 1980–81 is presented in Table 8.12. The number of PSEs belonging to the central government increased from 163 to 222 between 1980–81 and 1988–89; capital employed in the form of equity increased from Rs 182 billion to Rs 675 billion; net profits before tax as a ratio of capital employed rose from 0.0001 percent to 6.0 percent; and net profit after tax, which could be taken as a real measure of profitability of enterprises, increased from 1.1 percent to 4.4 percent. Even this rate of profit does not accurately reflect the efficiency of the central government's enterprises. Of the 222 PSEs, only about a half dozen petroleum sector enterprises contributed to the bulk of these profits—Rs 256.4 billion of the total of Rs 291.1 billion in 1988–89 (Economic Survey, 1990). This meant that the other two hundred odd nonpetroleum enterprises yielded the meager sum of Rs 41.7 billion, or less than 1.0 percent of capital employed. In earlier years, the nonpetroleum enterprises, far from earning profits, incurred heavy losses. The profits of PSEs would have been even less than what these had been, or the losses would have been larger than what they were, if the administered prices of the output of these enterprises, particularly petroleum-related units, steel, and fertilizers, were not raised during the last three or more years. The performance of the state-level PSEs has been

Table 8.12A
Financial Position of the Central Government's Public Enterprises

	Units	1980-81	1983-84	1988-89
No. of Public Enterprises	number	163	201	222
Capital employed	Rs billion	182	298	675
Gross profit before interest and tax	Rs billion	14.2	35.6	85.4
Net Profit before tax	Rs billion	0.19	14.8	43.7
4 as percent of 2	--	1.09	4.9	6.5

Table 8.12B
Profit and Loss of the Commercial Enterprises of State Governments (in million rupees)

Public Enterprises	1985-86	1987-88	1988-89
Forestry	4980	5430	4410
Power projects	-750	-1160	-770
Road and Water Services	-260	-1100	-1090
Dairy Development	-990	-430	-480
Industries	-140	-200	-470
Mines and Minerals	410	270	420
Irrigation Projects	-8710	-13440	-16860
Profit of Profit-Making Enterprises	5370	5700	4840
Losses of Loss-Making Enterprises	-10850	-16360	-19690

Source: For Tables 8.12A and B, Government of India, *Economic Survey, 1989–90*.

even worse (Table 8.12B). Between 1985–86 and 1988–89, net losses increased from Rs 54.7 billion to 148 billion. Barring forest-related enterprises and mines and minerals, all the rest incurred heavy losses.

The existence of PSEs has created large distortions in the macroeconomic situation in India. Judging by the financial performance of the central government's PSEs, we observe that their gross profit before tax, including interest, constituted roughly 12 percent of capital employed. If we assume that interest paid was around 10 percent, we can conclude that they have earned hardly 2 percent on their capital. This has two implications. First, if the capital used in PSEs had been put elsewhere in the private sector, it would certainly have yielded a much higher return, which meant that capital was most wastefully employed. (See also Minhas, 1987, for a more penetrating analysis of the public finance issues and their implications for macroeconomic policies.) Second, if the rate of return on the capital had been at least 10 percent, the government of India could have reduced its revenue account deficit in 1989 by one-third, or by about 5 percent of GDP, thereby reducing the need to resort to the banking system for inflationary financing of its deficit. It could also have enabled the government to curtail the size of public debt, which ensnared the Indian economy into an internal debt trap.[5]

Impact on Private Saving

The fiscal policy impact on public sector saving is not likely to be assessed properly until its effects on private saving are considered simultaneously. By offering a variety of tax incentives, Indian fiscal policy has influenced the dispensable income of the household sector, the corporate sector, and the nonincorporated enterprises. Indian tax policy has been harnessed over the years to induce (through allowing interest paid on them to be deducted from the taxable income) the household and other parts of the private sector to hold their savings in instruments like life insurance, provident funds, an array of small saving schemes like the National Saving Certificates. Interest income from bank deposits, dividends from certain company shares, units of the government-owned Unit-Trust of India (UTI), and debentures of the Industrial Development Bank of India (IDBI) and some other central government agencies are exempted, with certain limits, varying from investment to investment. Some of these investments enjoy tax preferences to a point that the resulting return to investors is excessively high. For example, a 10 percent per annum tax-free public enterprise bond could yield as much as 20 percent per annum to an investor in the 50 percent tax bracket; the tax-adjusted return on National Savings Certificates could be as high as 32.8 percent per annum for a taxpayer able to get the maximum out of available deductions and exemptions. In addition, the investments in equities of newly created industrial enterprises have enjoyed corporate tax and wealth tax concessions. Although it can be argued that only the liberal tax incentives permitted the private sector saving to have risen so high, thereby compensating to some extent for the fall in the public sector saving, these tax refunds, perhaps unwittingly, created serious distortions in the interest rate structure. As noted earlier, the tax-free return was as high as 50 to 60 percent on certain instruments. This sum was not only out of alignment with what was warranted in the Indian conditions, but was also instrumental in diverting savings to the public sector, which used it to finance the most unproductive enterprises. Raising the resources and mobilizing them is only one dimension; their efficient use is another and a far more important dimension which, in the ultimate analysis, determines the economy's rate of growth and indirectly lessens income disparities.

Despite India's faltering performance in efficiently managing both public and private sector investment and the dissipation of mobilized resources, some economists have argued that if one takes care of investment, saving will take care of itself. This is a typical but now generally discarded Keynesian recipe for the developing countries. According to this view, if there is excess capacity in Indian industry as is currently the case, the government, instead of liberalizing imports, should undertake large investment programs in the public sector. Since there is an adequate food surplus and excess capacity in the public capital goods sector, a larger public investment financed by a draft on private saving which would otherwise have been expended on inessential private investment (Rakshit, 1988) would increase demand for these goods. However, there is clearly a fallacy in this reasoning. The public sector has been operating so inefficiently in terms of resources that it has been continuously seeking private saving. However, the return on the public sector investment has been significantly lower than the interest rate paid on borrowed funds. This has widened the budgetary deficit, thereby dissipating both public and private saving. Thus, the Keynesian remedy of investment leading to more saving generation is no more than a mirage in Indian conditions.

Resource Mobilization, Government Expenditure, and the Emergence of an Underground Economy

An underground economy, or what has come to be known as a black economy in India, escapes the impact of government economic and regulatory policies. It has been booming over the last forty years, but its growth has accelerated in the last two decades. Although several policies such as industrial licensing, subsidies, and price controls are all instrumental in propelling its growth, the ill-designed, complex, and convoluted tax policies and the rapid expansion of public expenditures have been the major factors. A recent comprehensive study on India's black economy has concluded that "we side with those who believe that high effective rates of taxation are a major contributing factor to tax evasion and black income generation in India. Improved tax compliances can result from significant and sustained reduction in the effective burden of those who are liable to tax" (Acharya and Associates, 1986, p. 232). Until the 1970s, direct tax rates were exceptionally high; the same was true of indirect taxes. The one major consequence of a hike in tax rates in general was to create a favorable environment for widespread tax evasion, which largely contributed to a sharp decline in Indian tax elasticity (Acharya and Associates, 1986). Apart from the rates, certain other features of the Indian tax structure made it easy for the individual manager and producers to pursue a rent-seeking activity. Thus, the tax structure and statutes had become so complex and discretionary that they could not easily be understood either by the taxpayers or by those who were placed in charge of interpreting and administering them. Thus, high rates combined with ineffective administration compounded the problem of tax evasion and generated the black economy.

The complexity of the tax policy and its implementation were not the only causes of the black economy. Leakages of different kinds from public expenditures were increasing by leaps and bounds, as well documented by Acharya (1988, p. 287).

As in the case of taxes, the potential and scope for leakages vary across different kinds of public expenditure programs. What this means in practice is that efficiency of public expenditure can be quite different across different sectors even if the anticipated return were more or less uniform. For example, it has been suggested that important public sector investment decisions are sometimes biased in favor of the new "greenfield plants" and against consolidation and expansion of existing units because the former offers much more scope for illicit cuts and commissions on larger foreign contracts—not suprisingly the concern for quality and accountability in the public expenditures decline. The predictable consequence of all these factors is a decline in the efficiency of public projects and programs.

On the whole, India's fiscal policy, conceived and articulated within an overall interventionist framework of economic policy, failed in its main goals of mobilizing resources, achieving a dynamic and efficient public sector, and permitting social equity. On the surface mobilization was impressive, but its potential could have been reached if the fiscal policy had been endowed with simplicity and appropriate incentives. It allowed too many leakages through excessively generous tax incentives to the household sector, and in the end it distorted the interest rate structure. The spending of mobilized resources was counterproductive, first because much of the expenditures seeped into the underground economy where the allocation actually undertaken was far from the government's ex ante expectations. As the black economy, spurred by the fiscal policy, among other factors, spread, even the social equity that was so greatly lauded as the lodestar of India's economic policy faded away. Since the high-income earners are more prone to evade income, the income distribution has become more skewed with the emergence of a black economy to the disadvantage of India's poor classes.

Since 1985, a bold attempt has been made to rationalize the fiscal policy by divesting it of its long-standing ad hoc character which placed it on a predictable long-term path. To this end, systematic efforts were made to simplify the tax structure and tax laws. The direct tax rates were reduced for individuals as well as for corporations, with a reasonable assurance that future changes in rates would be minimal in the medium term and predictable. It was indicated that reliance would be placed as far as possible on nondiscretionary fiscal and monetary measures than on physical controls. A framework was provided in the government's paper "On Long-Term Fiscal Policy" (Government of India, 1985), which itself was somewhat of an innovation. Although all their initiatives were in the right direction, they failed to acquire a momentum later as the Indian government became embroiled in political troubles. Indeed, it is inconceivable that the fiscal policy, which was the most potent among the available policy instruments, could have changed so radically, as long as the political economy of the Indian state or its ideological configuration remained as entrenched as it had during most of the period since Indian independence.

MONETARY POLICY—A COMMAND APPROACH

Indian monetary policy, as it has come to be designed and implemented, has differed considerably from the normal concept of monetary policy in economic literature, which is identified with the regulation of cost and the availability of credit. Its identity as an independent tool was erased once India embarked on planned economic development in 1952. It has been operated as an adjunct of an overall economic policy which throughout remained strongly interventionist. In actual practice it has come to be only the penumbra of a fiscal policy, with a much greater accent on direct methods of control. Of course, occasional departures from this mold of monetary policy have occurred as in 1986 and thereafter when attempts were made to shed some of the features smacking of direct controls. Nonetheless, its basic tenor remained. Indeed, such attempts at change only threw in bold relief the ingrained difficulties involved in measured modification of its structure without having to liberalize the whole system.

Indian monetary policy is always required to reconcile multiple objectives that are often mutually conflicting. The dilemma facing the monetary authorities arose from the tasks set for it by the country's First Five-Year Plan, which argued that the direction of investment should not be guided solely by profit considerations. At the same time the plan added a rider that "the relationship between costs and return even in the public sector has to be judged, at least as a final approximation in terms of market prices" (First Five-Year Plan, Government of India, 1952, p. 36). It reinforced this criterion by laying particular emphasis on the structure of prices, such that the resultant allocation of resources would remain consistent with the targets defined in the plans. The objectives derived from the plans were as follows:

1. Saving of the community should be mobilized, and its financial component should be steadily enlarged.
2. The saving so mobilized should be allocated to the sectors in accordance with national economic goals as set out in the country's five-year plans.
3. The resource needs of the major entrepreneurs in the economy, that is, the public sector, should be met as a priority.
4. The price stability should be maintained. (For details, see Report of the Committee to Review the Working of the Monetary System [RCRWM], Reserve Bank of India, 1985.)

Little thought was given to the mutual inconsistency of these objectives. The Reserve Bank of India has admirably achieved the first of these objectives—mobilization of saving—through a variety of measures. The saving so mobilized is also sought to be rechanneled to the priority sectors, including the government sector. But whether or not the allocation remains efficient is considered to be of secondary importance. The instruments of monetary policies devised for this purpose were selective controls, or what is commonly known in other countries as directed credit programs, to regulate credit flows to the priority sectors. Liquid assets and cash reserve ratios were employed to channel credit to the public sector enterprises and the government. Nonetheless, the emphasis on priority sectors continued without any regard to whether these sectors were efficient or whether the public sector, occupying the commanding heights in the economy, yielded even the minimum rate of return. In the end, the consequences were far from what were expected. The banks were saddled with bad portfolios, and the public sector losses constantly fueled an ever-expanding fiscal deficit, financed by the banking system. Thus, the price stability was frequently threatened, though it was never allowed to go out of total control. In pursuing the conflicting goals, the Reserve Bank could not avoid a "mismatch between its responsibility to supervise and control the functioning of the monetary system on the one hand, and its authority to do so on the other" (RCRWM, 1985).

It is ineluctable that the monetary policy should lose its identity and tend to become indistinguishable from a fiscal policy because of the way the monetary policy is formulated in India. First, a demand for money is estimated in the usual way. Then the supply of money is estimated on certain assumptions, based partly on the historical experience and partly on expectations about the movement of future economic events such as output and tolerable price level. The magnitude of the quantity of money so projected is considered to be noninflationary. Working backward and allowing for changes in net foreign assets, we arrive at domestic bank credit. From this estimated bank credit, the share of the public sector in the form of investment in government securities—long and short term—is preempted and the residual is left for the private sector. This is monetary programming based on a simple quantity theory approach to monetary policy. When it is married to the physical plan, however, all manner of difficulties begin to arise in implementing monetary policy, as often happened in the Indian case.

The monetary authorities have designed an array of policy instruments to regulate credit flows in the planned direction. Although this effort implied close consultations between the Planning Commission, Finance Ministry, and the Reserve Bank, it in fact led to a monolithic decision-making process in regard to the monetary policy formulation and its implementation. As such, it could not have been different in nature, impact, and scope from the government's fiscal policy. Thus, the direct rather than indirect methods of control have acquired primacy in Indian monetary management.

Control of Reserve Money

On a macro level, the target of monetary policy in India has been the control of reserve money mainly because of the relative stability of the money multiplier over a medium term, whether it is related to a narrow or to a broad money concept. The currency–deposit ratio, which is the main constituent of the money multiplier, has changed but slowly as the banking habit formation has itself been a slow process. The other constituent—the excess bank reserves–deposit ratio—is relatively unimportant because the size of the excess reserves, through convention and tradition, has remained small and is rarely found to fluctuate. Change in reserve requirements, a third element in the formation of the money multiplier and a policy variable, has a significant impact on the money multiplier. Empirically, it has been found that the money multiplier has not varied much, particularly over the medium and long term except when reserve requirements are changed (Table 8.13) (Rangarajan and Singh, 1984; RCEWN, 1985; Singh, Shetty, Venkatachalam, 1982). The reserve money is regarded as critically affecting the domestic price situation.

It is one thing to focus on reserve money as a target and another to be able to regulate it in a desired direction. It is interesting to see how the reserve money has moved over the years. Table 8.13 shows that the most important factor affecting reserve money is the net RBI claims on the government which is identical with the concept of deficit financing adopted in India. The Reserve Bank's extension of credit to the government accounts for as much as 85 percent of reserve money variation. As a result, the Reserve Bank's other credit operations involving banks have been rendered marginal to the functioning of the monetary policy. Thus, the variation in reserve money is largely a fiscal phenomenon in India. Here the critical question is which of the instruments of monetary policy could be effective in regulating reserve money changes. The Cash Reserve Ratio (CRR) is used most frequently to neutralize the impact of reserve money changes on credit operations of banks. This ratio is maintained at a very high level, entailing a heavy tax on the banking system, which limits changes in it beyond a limit. Refinancing facilities, even when all combined together, are not large enough to make a dent in reserve money variations, thus, the open market operations are left as the only potent instrument.

It is a misnomer to describe the Reserve Bank's purchase and sale of government securities as open market operations, as will be clear from a forthright statement in the official document:

Open-market operations are conducted by a central bank mainly with a view to directly or indirectly affect the reserves of banks and thereby the extent of monetary expansion and in the process to create and maintain a desired pattern of yields on government securities and generally to help the Government raise resources from the capital market. Thus this policy instrument has two aspects viz the monetary aspect and the fiscal policy aspect. For the conduct of open market operations as a monetary instrument, the market for government securities should be well organized, broad-based and deep, so that the central bank is in a position to sell/buy securities to the extent it considers desirable. A prerequisite for the emergence of such markets is that the rate of interest offered on government securities is competitive. Since these conditions are not met by the Indian Capital Market, open market operations are of minor importance as a monetary instrument though they serve as an *adjunct of fiscal policy in India to some extent*. (RCRWM, 1985, pp. 262–63 [Emphasis added]).

Thus, the exigencies of planned finance for public sector development rather than monetary policy considerations dictate changes in the reserve money.

The targeted ''safe level'' of deficit financing, based on the monetary framework referred to earlier, almost always deviated from what transpired in the end. This result was inevitable because of the very approach adopted in regard to financing public investment under the five-year plans. In the plan documents, a

Table 8.13

Factors Affecting Reserve Money, India, 1981/82–1985/86 (in billions of rupees at end of period)

	1981/82	1983/84	1985-86	1987-88	1988-89
Reserve money	204.6	288.2	378.6	533.0	622.4
Factors affecting reserve money					
Net RBI claims on Government	196.7	266.3	389.0	527.9	600.2
Claims on National Bank for Agricultural and Rural Development	- -	12.0	22.9	39.3	63.2
Net RBI claims on commercial sector	19.1	23.8	30.7	38.1	49.5
Net foreign assets of RBI	26.2	16.2	33.4	52.7	59.0
Net nonmonetary liabilities of RBI	-61.2	-51.1	-97.4	-125.0	-149.5
Money Multiplier					
M3/Reserve Money	3.579	2.958	3.108	2.587	3.140
M2/Reserve Money	1.264	1.134	0.991	0.801	0.949

Source: Reserve Bank of India, *Report on Currency and Finance, 1988–89.*

certain pattern of financing public sector outlay is laid down. The projections are made for the balance of current revenue at preplan rates of taxation, additional taxation, surpluses from the public sector enterprises, market and nonmarket borrowings, and term loans from the financial system, treating the residual as "deficit financing." Admittedly, a shortfall in any other estimated magnitudes almost automatically leads to the corresponding enlargement of the so-called safe level of deficit financing. Throughout the planning period the experience has been that the surpluses of public enterprises as well as the saving on current account are grossly exaggerated. The only success achieved has been in respect to additional taxation, which not only met the targets but also surpassed them most of the time. It is therefore not surprising that deficit financing has often remained elusive—so often that the whole monetary policy formulation has become an exercise in futility.

If the monetary authorities' control over monetary expansion is weakened by the prior claims of the public sector, it can be reinforced by the compensatory adjustment in the money multiplier or by diverting even more credit to the government at the cost of the private sector. The first is done by using the cash reserve ratio. Before 1984 it was at a relatively low level of about 7 to 8 percent on an average, but presently it is pitched as high as 15 percent. The tax impact of this high ratio on the banking system is assuaged to some extent by paying 10.5 percent interest on cash reserves beyond the first 3.0 percent. While the adjustment in cash ratio moderates monetary expansion via the reduction in the money multiplier, it affords the government even greater scope to borrow from the Reserve Bank with its expansionary impact on reserve money, which is sought to be prevented in the first place.

The banking system can also control credit creation by making a change in the liquid asset ratio, under which banks and other credit institutions are required to hold a part of their deposits in the form of government bonds, other government-approved securities, and Treasury bills. This ratio was relatively low during the 1970s, but currently it is as high as 38 percent. However, the statutory liquid assets ratio is not meant to be an instrument to regulate the monetary base so much as a device to allocate more funds from the banking system to public investment. As the report on the monetary system unequivocally stated, the objectives to be achieved by the measure (i.e., the statutory liquid assets ratio) are (a) to create or support a market for government securities in economies which do not have a diversified capital market; and (b) to allocate resources to government for augmenting the resources of the public sector (RCRWM, 1985).

These objectives have the following consequence: the banks earn less on these assets than they could have earned on credit to the private sector. It is estimated that the average return on these investments, constituting as much as 38 percent of bank deposits, works out to about 8.0 percent in 1986, which is less than the average return on bank deposits (10 percent). The government could not have raised this rate to the same level of deposit rate without further worsening its budgetary position. Thus, the statutory liquid assets ratio is not intended to be a monetary policy instrument to control either availability or cost of credit; rather, it is employed purely to divert the private sector's saving to the public sector.

Selective Credit Policy

The monetary authorities also employ selective credit controls to ensure that bank credit flows to certain sectors of the economy considered to be priority sectors, such as agriculture and small-scale industry. The technique employed relies on setting margins, quantum in terms of proportion of total credit and the interest rate subsidy. The proportion of such credit has varied over the years, depending on the public policy objectives of the government; it is currently around 40 percent of total credit. These credits are admittedly very costly operations. First, they involve a heavy interest rate subsidy, estimated to be about 6.6 percent of the banks' earnings. Second, another type of subsidy is implicit in the nonrecovery of credit, following compromises in lending procedures; credit default has been a more dominant feature of loans by the small-scale industry (Economic Survey, 1989–90). The accumulation of bad and doubtful debts, estimated to be roughly 25 to 30 percent of deposits, has wiped out the entire capital base of several banks.

Interest Rate Policy

India has not relied on market mechanisms to bring about a desired change in the structure of interest rates. Interest rates have been administered ever since the independent central bank was set up. The Reserve Bank, through the periodical issue of directives, often fixes the minimum and maximum deposit and lending rates and maintains the return on government loans at a level consistent with those on banks' assets and liabilities. This is not difficult because the market for government loans is a captive market. The government gives banks, term lending institutions, provident funds, and insurance companies (which are by and large state-owned) detailed instructions about how they should invest their funds. These regulations have overwhelmingly favored government bonds even when the return on them has not been competitive.

Until the 1980s interest rates were negative, but during the last few years the administered system has yielded generally positive real interest rates (Table 8.14). More strikingly, the rates on government securities, which used to be too low in nominal terms and negative in real terms, have moved up to a positive level. As a result, financial assets as a ratio to GDP have increased impressively, even compared to some of the newly industrializing countries like Korea. This indicates that positive real interest rates could be achieved even under the administered system and need not have to be left to the market forces as advocated by the neo-financial liberalists (Cho and Khatkhate, 1988).

Since 1988–89 system-administered interest rates have experienced significant

Table 8.14
Selected Interest Rates, Price, and Nominal Exchange Rate Changes in India (end period: percent per annum)

	1970-71	1984-85	1986-87	1987-88
Bank Rate	5.0-6.0	10.0	10.0	10.0
Export Refinancing Rate	--	10.0	9.0	9.0
Rate on Commercial Bank Deposits				
1 to 3 years	6.0-6.5	8.0-9.0	8.50-9.0	9.0-10.0
over 5 years	7.25	11.0	11.0	--
Commercial Bank loan rate				
General (ceiling)	--	18.0	17.5	16.5
Exports (minimum)	--	12.0	9.6	9.5
Treasury Bill rate (3 month)	3.0-3.5	4.6	4.6	4.6
Treasury Bill rate (6 month)	--	--	10.0	10.25
Government Bonds Maximum Yield	--	10.5	11.5	--
National Saving Certificate	--	12.0	11.0	11.0
Call Money Rate	6.38	9.95	10.0	--
Debenture Ceiling Rate	8.0	13.5	13.5	12.5
Prime Lending Rate of				
Term Lending Institution				
IDBI	8.5	14.0	14.0	14.0
ICICI	8.5	14.0	14.0	14.0
IFCI	9.0	14.0	14.0	14.0
Wholesale Price Changes	--	7.6	5.3	10.6
Consumer Price Changes	--	5.0	7.5	9.8
Nominal Exchange Rate Changes				
(rupee/SDR)				
(- for depreciation and				
+ for appreciation)	--	-8.2	-15.7	-11.1

Source: Reserve Bank of India, *Report on Currency and Finance, 1988–89.*

changes. While the earlier approach to bank deposit-rate determination was continued, the Reserve Bank switched to stipulation of a floor rate for bank lending. Thus, beginning in 1988 banks were allowed to lend at any rate above 16 percent—a floor rate that replaced a ceiling rate of 16.5 percent prevailing earlier. This was followed by setting a floor rate of 15 percent for term loans and 16 percent for housing loans. More measures of far-reaching implications were introduced in 1989, when ceilings on money market rates were removed, ostensibly to make them flexible and transparent. At the same time, ceilings of 10.5 to 11.5 percent on interbank term money and 12.5 percent on rediscounting of commercial and on interbank participation without risk were also removed, and two new instruments—certificates of deposit and commercial paper—were permitted to be issued at a rate to be determined freely by the market forces (Economic Survey, 1990). These developments signified that, as far as the interest rate policy was concerned, the Indian monetary authorities had made bold moves toward financial liberalization.

The mobilization of savings through interest rate and other organizational policies could only be a first step toward rationalizing monetary and financial policy in a country like India, contrary to what the advocates of financial liberalization believe (McKinnon, 1973, 1988; Shaw, 1973). Mobilization of savings does not in itself ensure that resources so garnered will be efficiently allocated. More importantly, a positive interest rate-induced resource mobilization tends to create problems for a fiscal policy, unless that policy is substantially recast in a different mold.

We can understand this point more clearly in regard to what is being currently contemplated in India about reforming open market operations to make them a more effective instrument of monetary control. The RCRWM has recommended raising interest rates on the public debt in order to make them competitive with those prevailing elsewhere in the economy. This suggestion is based on the assumption that a competitive return would widen and deepen the market for government bonds. The Committee, however, as well as those who looked at open market operations in isolation from the fiscal policy, did not see that the consequent rise in market-determined interest rates on government debt could not be sustained. Interest payments that figure prominently in the current account of the government budget constitute almost 40 percent of current expenditures. This burden would further increase with the rise in interest rates, as well as the expansion of the size of the public debt, which amounted to over Rs 600 billion in 1989. The interest rate on public debt higher than that prevailing could have been supported only if the return on public investment had been higher than the rate of interest. However, as mentioned earlier, public enterprises are earning much less than the amount of interest paid. As long as this is the case, the market-determined interest rate on public debt will only lead to further erosion of government saving. The government therefore has to jettison many of the loss-making public enterprises or enhance their efficiency through cost-cutting measures, or simply go on borrowing to meet the interest rate obligations. A move in a new direction is possible only if the authorities are prepared to make a radical departure from the prevailing design of monetary, fiscal, and trade and industrial policies.

DIVINING THE FUTURE

Indian economic policy, which has often been buffeted over the years on ideological considerations, can best be characterized as "unlearning by learning." Since the very beginning, in the 1950s, the basis of the economic policy and its instruments were influenced by the strong perception that there was a pervasive market failure in the Indian system and that salvation lay in frequent and decisive government intervention. The effectiveness of this interventionist approach was judged in terms of its "first-impact effects." If the industrial licensing was issued to determine output pattern, import quantity, and its composition, it was believed that the final outcome would conform to the ex ante intentions; if foreign exchange was allocated according to a scale of priorities, these priority sectors were assumed to have received the intended allocation; if the bank credit was selectively channeled to what were designated as essential sectors like agriculture and small-scale industries, it was concluded that the earmarked sectors were the real beneficiaries.

As it turned out, the ex ante effects of the remedies directed toward eliminating market failures were vastly different from the final impact results. Industrial production was diversified, but it remained high cost and low quality, unable to withstand competition. Small-scale industries, however, proliferated and consumed both more capital and labor, belying the expectations that they would be employment-generating and self-sustaining outfits. The financial system was saddled with huge loans to agriculture and small-scale industry, a large part of which could not be recovered. Instead, the public enterprises, which were heralded as the instruments of resource mobilization and income distribution, drained away the resources mobilized by the government through massive tax efforts. However, such was the mesmerizing appeal of intervention that it took decades before the targeted groups could realize its pernicious consequences and utter futility. In the meantime, parasitic middlemen mushroomed all over to hijack the gains flowing from the interventionist policies. It went unnoticed for a long time that the market failure which the government was attempting to eliminate through intervention could lead to another type of failure—government failure, in addition to the existing one. The combined effects of these twin failures could have a far more damaging impact on India's growth and income distribution.

The question is why such a democratic polity and its highly modernized political and intellectual leadership did not learn from the decades-long frustrating experience of the interventionist policies. One plausible explanation could be that the mind-set of the Indian leadership, as well as the intellectuals, has absorbed an amalgam of idioms of Marx, Gandhi, and Adam Smith, which blurred the clarity of substance and implications of public policy. If for some reason the intervention is diluted and the liberalization process is strengthened, a guilt complex often seizes the leadership as if it has betrayed its long-cherished ideology. Then there is a reversion to the atavistic economic policies. Not that the importance of competition and efficiency was not recognized. But there were quick retreats from these deviations, on the slightest sign of a protest supposedly on behalf of the low income classes. The conflicting pulls of the ideological paradigms on the Indian intellectuals are reflected in the manifestoes of the political parties from the right, center, and left. Despite the superficial diversity in political coloration, a strong uniformity is often found in regard to the basics of the economic policy. Those who advocate liberalization and those who favor interventionist policies agree more or less that the state should not abdicate its responsibility in economic management. If there is a difference between these two ideological camps, it is only about the degree of intervention. Although the parties rationalize their advocacy of state intervention in the name of the poor and the downtrodden, the real reason lies in the enormous power they would wield and the patronage they would dispense if the state remained strongly interventionist.

Bardhan (1984) has rightly attributed the state's overpowering presence as an autonomous agent in India to the dominance of the proprietary classes. While this explains why the state acts the way it does, it does not tell us why in a functioning democracy as in India the state should emerge as an autocratic and a corrupt apparatus. Despite the rhetoric, there has been little distributive justice over the years; self-reliance may have been extolled, but it is nowhere in sight. The landless laborer is multiplying, and so is unemployment among the urban classes. Yet the behemoth of the omniscient state still acquires more power and commands followers. Under Indian democracy where the electorate has often sent the corrupt and the incompetent packing home, a respect for a munificent state has not wavered.

What India needs is not economic and political reform as such; it requires a different mind-set through an intellectual revolution that can help reevaluate democratic precepts and practices. With all its multifarious failures, the state still commands awe and obeisance, perhaps because under the present political institutions all power is concentrated at the center. There are no rival centers independent of the state patronage where the issues of public policy can be debated dispassionately. This, together with the fact that the intelligentsia are themselves a part of the ruling classes perhaps by proxy as Rudra has pointed out (1989), makes an intellectual revolution all the more difficult. Perhaps if the locus of power is split to diffuse power among multiple centers, there might be greater pluralism in economic policymaking. Until then, the present "left-right" march of Indian economic policy will continue without any watershed reform.

NOTES

The author thanks Chris Cochran for valuable editorial and statistical assistance in preparing this chapter.

1. Many of the unsavory consequences of planning and government intervention were anticipated by Latin Professor B. R. Shenoy in his minute of dissent in the report of the panel of economists submitted to the Indian Planning Commission in 1956 on the eve of the formulation of the Second Five-Year Plan based on the Mahalanobis model.

2. For analysis somewhat along this line, but with a greater focus on leadership, see Minhas (1988).

3. Myron Weiner (1986) has also shown that if India had achieved the GDP growth rate Korea attained for the period 1960–80, its per capita growth could have increased by two and a half times.

4. Even allowing for the skepticism about overestimation of saving, the saving rates achieved in India are admittedly impressive (see Rakshit, 1982; Report of the Working Group, 1982).

5. Even those like Professor Chakravarty (1987), who believes strongly in the commanding height philosophy of public sector enterprises, concedes that there is a deep and pervasive "fiscal crisis" in India's public economy, but the solution offered is "resource mobilization on a national scale." However, nowhere is it specified how to mobilize resources when the public enterprises that swallow the mobilized resources either incur losses or yield much less than what is sunk into them. We do not have to enter the "terrain of fiscal sociology" to resolve this question. All that is required is the old-fashioned virtue of fiscal rectitude.

REFERENCES

Ahluwalia, Isher Judge. *Industrial Growth in India: Stagnation Since the Mid-sixties*. New Delhi: Oxford University Press, 1985.
———. "Industrial Policy and Industrial Performance in India." In R. Lucas and G. Papanek (eds.), *The Indian Economy: Recent Development and Future Prospects*. Special Studies on South and Southeast Asia. Boulder, Colo.: Westview, 1988.
Acharya, Shankar. "India's Fiscal Policy." In R. Lucas and G. Papanek (eds.), *The Indian Economy: Recent Development and Future Prospects*. Special Studies on South and Southeast Asia. Boulder, Colo.: Westview, 1988.
Acharya and Associates. *Aspects of the Black Economy in India*. New Delhi: National Institution of Public Finance and Policy, 1986.
Bagchi, A. K. "An Economic Policy for New Government." *Economic and Political Weekly*, February 10, 1990.
Bardhan, Pranab. *The Political Economy of Development in India*. Oxford: Basil Blackwell, 1984.
Bhagwati, Jagdish N. *Indian Economic Performance and Policy Design*. Sir Purshotam Thakundas Memorial Lecture, Bombay, 1987.
———. "Poverty and Public Policy." *World Development* (May 1988).
———, and Padma Desai. *India: Planning for Industrialization*. OECD Development Center. London: Oxford University Press, 1970.
———, and T. N. Srinivasan. *Foreign Trade Regimes and Economic Development: India*. NBER. New York: Columbia University Press, 1975.
Bhattacharya, B. B., and Srabani Guha. "Internal Public Debt of the Government of India: Growth and Composition." *Economic and Political Weekly*, April 14, 1990.

Bhattacharya, A., and Johannes Linn. *Trade and Industrial Policies in the Developing Countries of East Asia*. World Bank Discussion Papers 27 (1988).

Chakravarty, Sukhamoy. *Development Planning: The Indian Experience*. London: Oxford University Press, 1987.

———. "On the Question of Home Market and Prospects for Indian Growth." *Economic and Political Weekly*, Special Number, 1979.

Cho, Yoon-Je, and Deena Khatkhate. *Lessons of Financial Liberalization in Asia: A Comparative Study*. World Bank Discussion Papers 50 (1988).

Committee on Export Strategy. *Report on Export Strategy*. Ministry of Finance, Government of India, 1982.

Dandekar, V. M. "Indian Economy Since Independence." *Economic and Political Weekly*, January 2, 1988.

Desai, Ashok. "Market Structure and Technology." Paper presented at the Conference on Technology Transfer and Investment, European Community—India, Berlin, 1984a.

———. "Technology Imports and Indian Industrialization." Paper presented at the Conference on Technology Transfer and Investment, European Community—India, Berlin, 1984b.

———. Technology Acquisitions and Application: Interpretations of the Indian Experience." In R. Lucas and G. Papanek (eds.), *The Indian Economy: Recent Development and Future Prospects*. Special Studies on South and Southeast Asia. Boulder, Colo.: Westview, 1988.

Dhar, P. N. "The Political Economy of Development in India." *Indian Economic Review* 22, (1987).

Echeverri-Gent, J. "Economic Reform in India: A Long and Winding Road." In R. Feinberg, J. Echeverri-Gent, and F. Miller, (eds.), *Economic Reform in Three Giants. U.S.–Third World Policy Prospectives*, No. 14. Washington, D.C.: Overseas Development Council, 1990.

Economic Advisory Council. *The Current Economic Situation and Priority Areas for Action*. Government of India, 1989.

Economic Survey, 1988–89, 1989–90. Ministry of Finance, Government of India.

First Five-Year Plan. Government of India Planning Commission, 1952.

Hazari, R. K. *Industrial Planning and Licensing Policy*. Planning Commission, Government of India, 1967.

Khatkhate, Deena. "Restructuring of the Political Process: Agenda for the New Government." *Economic and Political Weekly*, July 2, 1977.

———. "Trade Policies and Business Opportunities in Southern Asia." Paper submitted at the Congress on The World Economy: Challenges and Business Opportunities, Vienna Institute for Comparative Economic Studies, Vienna, 1990.

Kohli, Atul. "The Politics of Economic Liberalization in India." *World Development* (April 1988).

Long-term Fiscal Policy. Government of India, Ministry of Finance, New Delhi, 1985.

McKinnon, Ronald I. *Development: A Reassessment of Interest Rate Policies in Asia and Latin America*. International Center for Economic Growth, 1988.

———. *Money and Capital in Economic Development*. Washington, D.C.: The Brookings Institution, 1973.

Minhas, B. S. *Leadership, Public Policy and Socio-Economic Change*. Mimeo. New Delhi: Indian Statistical Institute, 1988.

————. "The Planning Process and the Annual Budgets: Some Reflections on Recent India Experience." *India Economic Review* 22, no. 2 (1987).

National Institute of Public Finance and Policy. "Income and Price Elasticities of Central and State Taxes." Unpublished, 1984.

Nayyar, Deepak. "India's Export Performance 1970–1985: Underlying Factors and Constraints." In R. Lucas and G. Papanek (eds.), *The Indian Economy: Recent Development and Future Prospects*. Special Studies on South and Southeast Asia. Boulder, Colo.: Westview, 1988.

Panchamukhi, V. R. *Trade Policies of India: A Quantitative Analysis*. New Delhi: Concept Publishing, 1978.

Patel, I. G. *Economic Policy at the Crossroads*. IDBI Silver Jubilee Commemoration Lecture, 1990.

————. "On Taking India into the Twenty-First Century (New Economic Policy in India)." *Modern Asian Studies* 21, no. 2 (1987).

Patnaik, P. "An Explanatory Hypothesis on the Indian Industrial Stagnation." In A. K. Bagchi and N. Bannerjee (eds.), *Change and Choice in Indian Industry*. Calcutta: Baghi, 1981.

Rakshit, M. K. "Income, Saving and Capital Formation in India: A Step Toward a Solution of the Savings-Investment Puzzle." *Economic and Political Weekly*, Annual Number (1982).

————. "Uses and Abuses of Instruments for Rescuing Mobilization: The Indian Experience." In R. Lucas and G. Papanek (eds.), *The Indian Economy: Recent Development and Future Prospects*. Special Studies on South and Southeast Asia. Boulder, Colo.: Westview, 1988.

Rangarajan, C., and A. Singh. "Reserve Money: Concepts and Policy Implications for India." Reserve Bank of India Occasional Paper, June 1984.

Report of the Committee to Review the Working of the Monetary System (RCRWM). Bombay: Reserve Bank of India, 1985.

Report of the Working Group on Savings, Capital Formation and Saving in India. Bombay, 1982.

Reserve Bank of India. *Annual Report, 1988–89*.

————. *Report on Currency and Finance, 1987–88 and 1988–89*. Vols. 1 & 2.

Rudra, Ashok. "Emergence of the Intelligentsia as a Ruling Class in India." *The Economic and Political Weekly*, January 21, 1989.

Sandessara, J. C. *Size and Capital Intensity in Indian Industry*. Bombay, 1969.

Seventh Five-Year Plan. Government of India Planning Commission, 1985.

Shaw, Edward S. *Financing Deepening in Economic Development*. New York: Oxford University Press, 1973.

Shroff, Manu. *Current Issues of Economic Policy*. Y. B. Chavan Memorial Lecture, Indian Institute of Public Administration, Maharastra Branch, Bombay, 1988a.

————. "Learning by Learning: India's Development Experience." *Economic Times*, January 11, 1988b.

Singh, A., S. L. Shetty, and T. R. Venkatachalam. *Monetary Policy in India: Issues and Evidence*. Supplement to Reserve Bank of India, Occasional Papers 3, no. 2 (June 1982).

Sundrum, R. M. *Growth and Income Distribution in India: Policy and Performance Since Independence*. New Delhi: Sage Publications, PVT Ltd., 1987.

Virmani, Arvind. "Rising BOP Deficit: Liberalization, Culprit or Scapegoat?" *Economic Times*, January 7, 1990.

Weiner, Myron. "The Political Economy of Industrial Growth in India." *World Politics* 38, no. 4 (July 1986).

Wolf, M. *India's Exports*. New York: Oxford University Press, 1982.

World Bank. *World Development Reports*. Washington, D.C., 1982–89.

9

NATIONAL ECONOMIC POLICIES IN AFRICA: EGYPT, KENYA, AND NIGERIA AS CASE STUDIES

Adebayo Adedeji

INTRODUCTION

At independence, most African countries shared one fundamental characteristic: economic backwardness. This backwardness was manifested in the low volume of output of goods and services, as measured by the gross domestic product (GDP); primary-activity-dominated production structures; low level of manufacturing activities; low level of social services; lack of basic infrastructural facilities; and, above all, excessive external dependence. It was, therefore, not surprising that independent African countries embarked on a planned approach to economic development with the hope of engineering a high rate of growth and socioeconomic transformation as well as an equitable distribution of income. National economic planning and management thus became crucial to the economic policies of these countries. Indeed, donor countries, led by the U.S. government, made this a major condition for aid and went as far as providing technical assistance to economic planners to help them develop short- and medium-term plans.

The three countries under consideration in this chapter, Egypt, Kenya, and Nigeria, share not only the usual characteristics of underdevelopment, but also the cherished objectives of fast development and transformation, the desire to improve the people's standards of living, and the quest to realize economic independence as a guarantee of political sovereignty. Second, they present different approaches to national economic management, ranging from strong public sector dominance in economic activities, to a mixed economy with the government exercising substantial control over the operations of the private sector, to a more liberal free enterprise economy. A review of national economic policies in these countries could therefore throw some light on the objectives of national economic policies in Africa and their relative effectiveness.

This chapter briefly discusses the framework within which national economic policies have been and are being pursued in various African countries. It contains a comparative analysis of national economic policies as well as performance evaluation of such policies in the three African economies before 1960 and in the 1960s and 1970s on the one hand (the prestructural adjustment programs era) and the 1980s and 1990s (the regime of structural adjustment programs) on the other. The chapter also reflects on policy directions for the future in the light of *African Alternative Framework to Structural Adjustment Programmes for Socio-Economic Recovery and Transformation (AAF-SAP)*.[1]

ECONOMIC POLICY FRAMEWORK

Economic policy is normally formulated to achieve desired general and specific economic and/or social goals, such as employment creation, relative price stability, equity in income distribution, balance-of-payments equilibrium, and economic growth and transformation. These goals represent the ultimate targets of policy and require an appropriate policy mix in their realization. The art of policy formulation necessarily involves a choice of policy approach and instruments. This will be shaped by the prevailing economic environment and its associated physical, human, and technological constraints. The physical setting provides the resource endowments and their quality. The human dimension, on the other hand, gives the sociocultural setup and behavioral and human resource capability. Similarly, the technological portfolio gives the nature and vintage of the accumulated capital stock, the know-how in society, and the techniques and different ways of utilizing resources to produce goods and services that satisfy wants. To the extent that these factors vary from one set of countries to the other, the complexion and content of economic policy also vary.

The stage of development is also an important argument in policy formulation. In the developed countries, economic infrastructure is already well developed, and the performance of the economy in any one year is usually marginally influenced by further extensions and improvements of the infrastructure. Under the circumstances, the main focus of economic policy will be the maintenance of balance-of-payments equilibrium, full employment, stable prices, and the increase in consumption (as the capacity is already there). In a developing country setting, on the other hand, greater attention should naturally be focused on development and the associated socioeconomic transformation. Here, the short-term policy concerns cannot be divorced from long-term development objectives and perspectives. Given this situation, the choice of approach and its constituent policy instruments are critically dependent on the policy environment, both domestic and external, on the one hand, and the uncertainty of the relationships between the instrumental variables and the ultimate target variables, and the uncertainty regarding the effect of nonpolicy influences and the intermediate and ultimate policy variables, on the other.

With respect to external factors, it is perhaps not an overstatement to say that, with developing countries, the policy decision-making process and hence the charting of the development strategies are often at the mercy of international commodity pricing, external markets for agricultural products and raw materials, sources of technology, suppliers of heavy capital goods, as well as other providers of foreign exchange and development assistance. Hence, the deterioration of the international economic environment, particularly during the 1980s, further complicated the task of economic policy, essentially through the foreign exchange squeeze that arose from the collapse in commodity prices, debt overhang, and stagnating resource flows. Since the early 1980s policy options have been constrained by the linkage of assistance with the adoption of International Monetary Fund (IMF)/World Bank-type stabilization and adjustment programs in defiance of the objective structural, physical policy reforms, and in negation of their national development objectives. Yet, in the final analysis, the relevance and efficacy of the economic policies adopted should be assessed in relation to the stated goals, particularly those impinging on the realization of the long-term development objectives of the societies under consideration and the suitability of the policy instruments used to achieve them.

While policy approaches have varied among the countries, there has been consistent adherence to state-led development, with emphasis on industrialization and institution building. The rationale for active government involvement in the economy is based on the recognized structural deficiencies in these economies, such as imperfections in the product and factor markets that may result in the failure of market forces to attain efficient allocation of resources; a weak institutional framework; a lack or dearth of private domestic capital and entrepreneurship; and the possibility of divergence between marginal net social benefit and marginal net private benefit arising from dynamic externalities consequent upon private economic pursuits. Thus, the special significance of the state in overcoming the economic strictures of developing countries is associated with the urgent need to speed up their socioeconomic progress.

ECONOMIC POLICY PACKAGES PRIOR TO THE STRUCTURAL ADJUSTMENT PROGRAM ERA

The SAP period in Egypt covers mostly the period of Nasserism, lasting from the 1952 Revolution to the 1970s, which can also be further subdivided into three subperiods. The initial phase, lasting roughly from 1952 to 1956, saw a limited role for the public sector, but through the land reform measures and the undertaking of social policies directed toward bolstering the people's morale and standard of living, it set the tone and direction of subsequent policy stances. The second phase, roughly from 1957 to 1960, was characterized by widescale nationalization of foreign-owned enterprises and national banks, progressive industrialization, and the consolidation of state control over the economy. Subsequently, capital formation came rapidly into the hands of the state. The third phase, extending from 1961 to 1973, could rightly be described as the era of central planning, expansion of the public sector, heavy industrialization, and progressive implementation of broad-based social welfare policy devised to govern income distribution, and the guarantee of a minimum subsistance level to the people. This policy was initially supported by price controls and later by a system of subsidies. For Kenya, the pre-reform period spans the period from independence in 1963 to the end of the 1970s, while in Nigeria, it went from independence in 1960 to about 1982, and covers both the pre-oil boom and the oil boom periods, and terminates at the beginning of the collapse in oil prices.

Major Development Concerns

In its first National Development Plan covering the period 1962–68, Nigeria aspired to initiate a development process designed to harness the utility of its abundant natural resources and its large population to achieve a level of development that would raise the living standards of all the people.[2] Egypt, following the 1952 Revolution, adopted policies designed to improve the well-being of the ordinary people. Growth and equity in distribution of income were the principal aims of the Revolution. On achieving independence in 1963, Kenya set out to formulate a blueprint for the socioeconomic development of the nation, which was outlined in the paper entitled ''Sessional Paper No. 10 of 1985 on African Socialism.'' All three countries thus resolved to initiate a development course that accords priority to growth, equitable distribution of income, and other broad-based socioeconomic development goals. To date, each country has had nearly three decades of national economic management with the full involvement of and, more often than not, under the surveillance of Bretton Woods institutions, notably the IMF and the World Bank and donor countries.

Although strategies have changed profoundly, the basic socioeconomic objectives of the Egyptian society have remained largely the same since the 1952 Revolution. The two central objectives relentlessly pursued by the various Egyptian governments since the Revolution relate essentially to the realization of higher growth and transformation of the economy, and a progressively fairer income and wealth distribution in the society. This was primarily a reaction to the onerous conditions that prevailed in the rural areas, the social stratification, and the need to exercise economic independence. In terms of strategy, three major approaches were employed to help achieve these objectives, namely: (1) central planning; (2) land reform; and, (3) welfare policies, pursued largely through universal and free education and health facilities, labor legislation, and subsidies. The economic management machinery has been reoriented and increasingly geared toward the implementation and overview of these policies. This has necessitated a greater and a more dominant role for the state and the public sector, exercised through increased public sector investment and the regulation of the economy. During the period under review, the country passed from a mixed economy with a limited role for the government to widespread planning, emphasizing industrialization and public sector control, back to a mixed economy strategy with increased emphasis on free market principles. Also during this period, under the influence of both domestic and external factors, concern gradually shifted, from questions of long-term socioeconomic transformation and pan-Arab activities to the adoption of strategies emphasizing internal economic consolidation and the maintenance of domestic social stability.

The main objectives of Kenya's development policy have been political equality; social justice; human dignity, including freedom of conscience and freedom from want, disease, and exploitation; equal opportunities; and high and growing per capita income that is equitably distributed. Kenya's development strategy advocates a rural-urban balance approach whose thrust is diversification of economic activities in the rural areas and in the peri-urban centers that are to be developed for servicing the rural areas. The strategy also favors the development of small-scale farming and industrial, commercial, and service sector development.

The immediate concern of economic policies in post-independent Nigeria was to lay the foundation for the development of the economy. The specific development concerns are best exemplified by the objectives of the four development plans (1962–68; 1970–74; 1975–80; and 1981–85) that the country has prepared and executed to date. Common to these development plans are the objectives of accelerated economic growth and development, price stability and external balance, indigenization of economic activities, and social justice. Thus, the First National Development Plan (1962–68) asserts that the "basic objective of planning in Nigeria is not merely to accelerate the rate of economic growth and the rate at which the level of living of the people can be raised, it is also to give her an increasing measure of control over her destiny." Among the strategies adopted in pursuit of these objectives have been public sector dominance in economic activities, industrialization through input substitution, and more local control of economic activities through the indigenization policy.

Of course, in Nigeria, as well as in other countries, the fundamental objectives of economic policies remain essentially the same. However, the emphasis on individual objectives varies in time and space in accordance with the prevailing economic situation and philosophy within the economy, as well as changes in the external environment. For instance, in Nigeria, the emphasis on growth as a precondition to meaningful distribution of the fruits of development, generally relegated the issue of distributive equity to the background, just as the resurgence of external disequilibrium shifted emphasis to the maintenance of both internal and external balance in the 1980s.

In pursuit of the stated objectives of development policies, the three African countries have adopted a variety of economic policies and measures to which attention will be given next.

Policy Measures

Fiscal Policy

Fiscal policy involves governmental determination of the level and structure of taxes and expenditures and the manner of financing a budgetary surplus or deficit in order to achieve various macroeconomic goals.

As indicated above, the major decisions of the military in Egypt after the 1952 Revolution had to do with agrarian/land reform; a larger measure of state intervention in the economy culminating in comprehensive national planning and subsequent nationalization; and welfare concerns. It is in the pursuit of these programs that we can piece together the various economic policies of Egypt's government. For one thing, it has been asserted that a major flaw in the pursuit of Egypt's broad developmental objectives through the central planning process during this period has been the absence of explicit macroeconomic policies that would enable the government to elicit the desired responses.[3]

In the area of fiscal policy, Egypt adopted a number of measures to realize its developmental objectives. The land reform program was seen as a means of directing private capital from the land market to industry. It also contained an ingenious fiscal arrangement whereby compensation to the dispossessed landlords in the form of nonnegotiable bonds with 3 percent annual interest and redeemable in thirty years was to be financed by contributions from the beneficiaries of the requisitioned land who were required to pay in equal installments over thirty years the compensation plus 15 percent in charges as well as an annual interest rate of 3 percent.[4]

In addition, the beneficiaries of the requisitioned land were required to join cooperative societies, which the government then used for disguised fiscal purposes. Members of the cooperatives subscribed the capital, and hence the cooperatives were an avenue for mobilizing resources from members. The cooperatives were the sole suppliers of agricultural inputs—fertilizers, seeds, and chemical inputs. Farmers were also compelled to sell their products through them. In their capacities as suppliers of farm inputs and marketers of the final product, the cooperatives became an instrument for the appropriation of agricultural surplus by selling the inputs at a premium to the farmers and by paying less than the market price for the products.

In pursuit of the objective of social welfare, the fiscal tools employed included subsidization of essential commodities and housing, expansion of free public education, increased provision of health and other social services, and offer of employment to many by the public sector. The government also adopted a progressive tax structure. For instance, the 1952 income tax law exempted people with an annual income of not more than LE 150 from tax obligations and incorporated progressive tax rates ranging from 2 to 9 percent. The 1952 law was subsequently replaced by Law 199 of 1960 which raised the exemption level to LE 250 and made the tax rate more progressive, with the range of tax rates extended from 2 to 22 percent. It is, however, widely believed that the progressive income tax structure did not do much to redress the inequality in the distribution of income, as there was large-scale tax evasion. Moreover, whatever gains in terms of distributive equity might have been realized from a progressive income tax structure were negated by heavy reliance on the taxation of goods and services as a source of government revenue. For instance, taxes on goods and services, which are generally regressive, contributed 67.4 percent and 69.2 percent of the total tax revenue in 1952 and 1971, respectively. Thus, substantial elements of inequality persisted in the Egyptian tax structure during the 1952–72 period.[5]

The policy of using the public sector as the main engine of growth, coupled with the social welfare objective, resulted in very rapid expansion of government expenditure and created serious financing problems during the period.

Fiscal policy in the early independence period in Nigeria was aimed at the increased provision of funds to finance development by mobilizing domestic resources and attracting capital from overseas. The increased provision of social amenities and the protection of home industries from foreign competition were additional objectives of fiscal policy during this period. However, economic policies making for expansion, such as accelerated government-deficit financing, the surge of capital goods import occasioned by the needs of development, and the expansion of bank credit to the private sector, aggravated the demand and balance-of-payments pressures on the economy. Hence, additional concerns of fiscal policy toward the end of the 1960s included balance-of-payments deficits and threatening inflationary pressures on the economy.

The main fiscal instruments included changes in taxation rates, government expenditure, and public debt. For instance, the generation of budget surplus was approached from both the expenditure and revenue sides of the budget, first by pruning recurrent government expenditures, and, second, by increasing the rates of existing taxation. Fiscal measures to encourage and assist industrial development were provided by way of tax relief to pioneer industries and relief from import duties. To protect domestic industries from foreign competition and to arrest the balance-of-payment deficits, import taxes were raised.

The objectives of fiscal policy in the 1970s were not radically different from those of the earlier period. However, the emergence of oil as a major source of revenue during the period obviated the need to rely on fiscal policy as a major instrument of raising public revenues. Rather, fiscal policy during the period reflected some soft-pedaling with respect to some of the stringent measures introduced during the preceding period, especially during the civil war years (1967–70). These included the liberalization of import duties on goods considered essential to postwar reconstruction; and a general reduction of the surcharge on imports in order to reduce the cost of living and of duties on imported raw materials and in excise duties. In general, fiscal policy for most of the 1970s was designed to induce an increase in the volume of goods and services available to the economy, not necessarily through increased mobilization of domestic resources but through massive importation of both finished goods and intermediate inputs—an exercise made possible by the stupendous increase in oil revenue.

A remarkable feature of fiscal policy in Nigeria, especially during the 1970s, was the phenomenal rise in public spending which reflected, in part, a determined effort to broaden the scope of the public sector in the economy, and, in part, the abundant resources which the oil sector placed at the disposal of government. For instance, the federal government's revenue increased tenfold from N1,169 million in 1971 to N11,979 million in 1981, while government expenditure increased sixteenfold from N639 million in 1971 to N10,774 million in 1981. During this period, too, oil revenue, as a proportion of federally collected revenue, rose from 43 percent in 1971 to 83.6 percent in 1980. An even more astonishing feature of government spending in the 1970s was the government's ingenuity in matching the rapidly increasing oil revenue with even greater increases in spending, thus resulting in wider fiscal deficits. For instance, the government's overall deficit increased ninefold from N305 million in 1970 to N2,745 million in 1980.

The phenomenal increase in government spending in the 1970s was in part attributable to the growth of public enterprises. Statutory corporations and state-owned companies were seen as tools of public intervention in the development process. Thus, their primary objective was to stimulate and accelerate national economic development under conditions of capital security and structural defects in private sector organizations. Other basic considerations relating to the reliance on public enterprises arise from the danger of leaving vital sectors of the national economy to the whims of the private sector, often under the direct and remote control of foreign large-scale industrial combines. Hence, public enterprises were considered crucial to the quest for true national economic independence and self-reliance, just as the indigenization policy was aimed at putting the control of the economy in the hands of Nigerians.

Monetary Policy

Monetary policy involves measures designed to regulate and control the volume, cost, availability, and direction of money and credit in order to achieve some specified macroeconomic objectives. The monetary authorities of Egypt, Kenya, and Nigeria have designed policies and invoked monetary and financial regulations to promote growth. Setting the levels of money supply and interest rates, and determining the allocation of credit to the private and public sectors and the direction of credit have been the main monetary instruments used. Departing from the orthodox approaches of free market, system-determined allocation of financial resources with interest rates playing a decisive role, these countries have striven to regulate the creation and allocation of credit in order to promote the growth of the priority sectors of the economy.

In Egypt, an increase in the volume of rural credit was among the most important complementary measures in the land reform program. An agricultural credit bank was authorized to borrow money from the central bank and, later,

Table 9.1
Money Supply, Kenya, 1966–87

As at end of	Currency outside Bank plus Private demand deposits	Other deposits	Total
1966	59,181	31,091	90,272
1967	63,762	36,341	100,103
1968	70,509	43,189	113,698
1968	80,740	50,051	130,791
1970	94,680	66,237	160,916
1971	102,027	73,242	175,269
1972	121,026	78,783	199,809
1973	147,683	100,015	247,698
1974	160,244	106,943	267,186
1975	226,996	113,711	340,707
1976	283,715	139,018	422,733
1977	421,368	199,287	620,655
1978	465,057	240,833	705,890
1979	531,847	287,964	819,811
1980	494,977	315,424	810,401

Source: Kenya Central Bureau of Statistics; *Economic Surveys (1967–81)*.

to issue bonds to finance its operations. Hence, agricultural credit increased rapidly—from £E16 million in 1952 to £E81 million in 1969–70. This credit was made available to the cooperatives for distribution among the members. The interest rates on the loan, though variable, remained low during the period. The interest rates on the cooperative loans were abolished in 1962 but were later reestablished when it became apparent that interest-free loans led to an inefficient allocation of scarce resources and discouraged savings, and could not be justified on equity grounds when extended to medium and large landlords. In addition, an industrial development bank was established to finance industrial projects. With nationalization, the government became the owner of some important commercial banks, specialized credit institutions, and insurance companies.

The basic principle that has guided the management of money supply by Kenyan authorities has been the maintenance of levels of money supply that adequately service economic activities. In the period 1964–71, money supply expansion averaged 15 percent per annum in current prices, slightly higher than the growth of GDP during the period. Between 1966 and 1971 the money supply rose from KL.90.3 million to KL.175.3 million (Table 9.1). In the period December 1971 to April 1973 the annual increase in money supply rose at the average of 19 percent per annum.

The recession of 1974 prompted the formulation of measures designed to reduce the money supply, especially in the second half of 1974. The measures enforced by the central bank to reduce the expansion of the money supply, and thus control the inflation that rose rapidly in the 1973–75 period, included the following:

1. Restriction of expansion of commercial bank credit to the private and public sectors
2. Extension of the 15 percent liquidity ratio provision to cover both commercial banks and nonbank financial institutions
3. Local borrowing by foreign-controlled companies being restricted to 20 percent of their investment in Kenya

These measures helped reduce the money supply increase in 1974, but in 1975 there was a resurgence in its growth arising not only from the improved economic environment, but also from the increase in loans and advances by commercial banks, increased holdings of government securities, and an increase in commercial bank holdings of investment securities. Between the end of 1974 and the end of 1975 the liquidity ratio of commercial banks declined from 27 to 19 percent.

From the very beginning, policy was accorded due recognition in the management of the Nigerian economy, and the central role of mobilizing domestic resources for development was assigned to the Central Bank of Nigeria (CBN). Hence, the primary objective of monetary policy in the early period (1960s) was to provide cheap money to finance government capital expenditure and investment in the private sector. Monetary policy during this period was also directed at containing pressures of consumption expenditures on the balance of payments and generally preventing an uncontrolled weakening of the external reserve position to a dangerous position.

The generation of cheap money to finance capital projects and private investment resulted in a great expansion of demand, the consequences of which were pressures on the external balance and the domestic price level. Moreover, in the 1970s there was excess liquidity with the banking system as a result of reduced government borrowing following an increase in revenue inflow from oil. In spite of this excess liquidity, some key sectors of the economy were desperately in need of credit. Hence, monetary policy was used as an instrument to correct the maladjustment in the monetary sector. Quantitative restrictions and direction of credit were thus introduced. Interest rates on deposits and lending rates were to be kept in line with the general policy of generating optimal savings and investment with minimum inflation, while credit guidelines took the form of putting ceilings on credit to broad sectors of the economy as well as the direction of credit to specified sectors of the economy.

In terms of specific monetary instruments, the tools that the CBN applied at various times can be categorized as quantitative, cost, and directional tools.[6] The quantitative tools include reserve requirements, liquidity ratios, cash reserve requirements, and special deposits; the cost tools are the rediscount rates and

Table 9.2
Sectoral Allocation of Commercial Bank Credit in Nigeria, 1970–79

								(Percentages)
	1973		1975		1977		1979	
Sectors	P	A	P	A	P	A	P	A
Preferred Sectors								
Production	45.0	38.2	48.0	44.2	48.0	53.2	53.0	59.3
General Commerce	32.0	34.4	32.0	30.4	30.0	23.8	24.0	19.2
Services	11.0	8.2	10.0	7.5	10.0	9.3	11.0	8.2
Less Preferred								
Others	12.0	19.2	10.2	17.9	12.0	13.7	12.0	13.2

Sources: Central Bank of Nigeria, *Annual Report and Statement of Accounts*, various issues; and *Economic and Financial Review*, various issues.

Note: P = prescribed ratio; A = actual ratio.

other interest rates; and the directional tools are credit guidelines/direct control of credit.

In spite of their use by the CBN, changes in the quantitative and cost tools were very infrequent before the 1980s. For instance, the reserve requirement remained at 25 percent throughout the 1970s and up to 1987. The CBN minimum discount rate ranged between 4.5 and 5.0 percent between 1970 and 1979, while the savings rate minimally increased from 3.0 percent in 1970–74, to 4.0 percent from 1975 to 1978 and 5.0 percent in 1979. The first class lending rate ranged from 7 to 7.5 percent between 1970 and 1979.

That leaves direct control of credit as the major monetary tool in use prior to the adjustment process of the 1980s. Between 1970 and 1972 the policy took the form of credit ceilings that were set for the broad sectors of the economy. In 1972 it was broadened to include new guidelines, which indicated the proportions of total credit to be made available to the various economic sectors. The CBN prescribed sectoral and subsectoral allocations of credit in such a way that available bank loans and advances were allocated to the borrowing sectors and subsectors in accordance with the desired objectives of policy. For the purpose of such sectoral and subsectoral allocations of credit, the sectors and subsectors were categorized into preferred sectors (Production, General Commerce, and Services) and less preferred sectors (others). The sectoral distribution of commercial bank credit between 1973 and 1979 is shown in Table 9.2. In addition to limits on the rate of expansion of total credit in the economy, there were also specified ratios for credit allocation to the private and public sectors. The posture of credit ease and cheap money policy, coupled with movements in government expenditure, inevitably resulted in rapid expansion in the money stock. Thus, between 1970 and 1980 the money supply (M1), which is currency in circulation plus demand deposits with commercial banks, increased nearly tenfold from N370.4 million to N3,589.5 million, while total money, that is, M1 plus quasi-money (savings and time deposits with commercial banks), increased fifteenfold from N956.9 million to N14,397.4 million.

External Trade and Foreign Exchange Policies

Egypt, Kenya, and Nigeria share a common feature of export dependence in the sense that external trade has a large impact on the performance of their economies. The large share of exports and imports in their GDPs expose them to considerable external shocks, especially with their monocultural export dependence. Hence, depressed export prices of their principal exports, such as oil and cotton for Egypt, oil for Nigeria, and coffee and tea for Kenya, have considerable adverse effects on the foreign exchange earnings and balance of payments of these countries. On the one hand, the commodity export prices of these countries have faced declining trends. On the other hand, prices of industrial goods that comprise the bulk of their imports maintain a rising trend. These countervailing forces have resulted in sustained deterioration in terms of trade, which has aggravated the imbalances in the external accounts of the three countries.

For instance, petroleum assumed such increasing importance in the export sector in Nigeria that, by 1980, 96.1 percent of total export earnings was from crude oil. The implication is that the level of export earnings and balance-of-payments position was determined largely by events in the international oil market. It is, therefore, not surprising that the tumbling of oil prices from around U.S. $35 per barrel in the early 1980s to about U.S. $18 per barrel by the mid-1980s precipitated a depression unparalleled in the nation's history. In Egypt, where the industrial program required heavy doses of imports of capital goods and intermediate inputs, the failure of export performance to keep pace with imports created serious financial bottlenecks. In addition, Egypt's engagement in bilateral trade arrangements, especially with the Eastern Bloc often involving countertrade deals, aggravated the problem of access to hard currency to pay for other essential imports.

The major concern of foreign exchange policy prior to the reform programs in these countries was how to minimize the drain on foreign exchange in the face of threatening crises in the balance of payments. In the absence of inflow of foreign assistance at the anticipated levels, the primary objective of exchange-rate policies was to conserve foreign exchange or moderate its outflow. For instance, in the face of its deteriorating balance-of-payments position in the late 1970s and early 1980s, Nigeria had to resort to the use of import licenses in allocating scarce foreign exchange. Although there was some devaluation in Egypt in the 1960s and in Kenya and Nigeria in the 1970s, the major tinkering with the exchange rates was to come with the structural adjustment and reforms of the later periods.

Industrial Policy

Africa is the least industrialized region of the world. In 1960 Africa accounted for 4 percent of world industrial output, which, through the last two decades, declined to 1 percent in 1987, even though the sector was given priority in Africa's development plans. The sector has been accorded priority through the realization that it produces goods that satisfy a major part of the needs of the people and thus holds potential for growth in the region. For several decades Egypt, Kenya, and Nigeria have endeavored to accelerate the industrialization process. Domestic industries have been provided protection from external competition through quantitative restrictions of imports and import duty levied on imports. Industrialization in Africa has focused on the substitution of local production for imported manufactures. Industrial protection through tariff protection and quantitative restrictions has been justified by infant industry arguments.

Africa's lack of progress in industrialization is an outcome of many factors, including fragmented economies with too small markets to provide economies of scale, inadequate numbers of skilled personnel, capital scarcity, and lack of technological know-how. These factors apply to Egypt, Kenya, and Nigeria as well. In Egypt, industrialization has been promoted by the public sector which still plays a large role in basic industries—iron and steel and petroleum industries. Whereas in Kenya and Nigeria the private sector accounts for the larger share of manufacturing value added, in Egypt the private sector is confined to small enterprises. In Kenya and Nigeria the predominant part of manufacturing value added is derived from consumer goods industries, principally textiles, food, and beverages. The petrochemical sector has, however, developed rapidly in Nigeria from the mid-1970s and now accounts for a substantial share of manufacturing value added. A major weakness of the African industrial development strategy arises from excessive reliance on external sources for capital equipment, semi-processed inputs such as component parts in assembly enterprises, and raw materials.

Egypt aimed at the diversification of its economic structure through industrialization. Hence, the economic system was transformed from free private enterprise with moderate government intervention into a new situation in which the states involvement in the economy through planning and the operation of a large public sector became significant. Between 1952 and 1972 the policy orientation of the Egyptian government focused on nationalization. This policy resulted in the increase in the share of the public sector in the production sector. Basic industrial enterprises and the petrochemical industries were publicly owned. Thus, the share of public resources in total investment increased significantly during this period. Investment resources were generated from a strong petroleum sector with a large exportable surplus, rapidly growing worker remittances, long-term foreign capital inflows, and revenue from the Suez Canal.

The Nigerian government's objective at independence was to encourage industrialization via import substitution. Hence, a number of incentives were showered on that sector. The import-substitution strategy in Nigeria, however, turned out to be a ruse, as it bore little or no relation to domestic availability of raw materials and other imports. It was a strategy, par excellence, of substituting the import of finished goods with the import of raw materials, machinery, spare parts, and completely-knocked-down (CKD) parts for final touch assembling in Nigeria, an excise that added more to the import bill but very little to domestic value added. Thus, even though the value of manufacturing in absolute terms rose more than twelvefold and the manufacturing index rose from 100 to 432 between 1972 and 1982, the share of manufacturing in the GDP fluctuated between 4.5 percent and 11.4 percent during the period.

Overview of Performance

As indicated in Table 9.3, the 1980s opened with the economies of Egypt, Kenya, and Nigeria worse off than they had been in the earlier period. Manifestations of false starts made by these three African countries are found in the structural weaknesses of their economies thirty years after independence. These include excessive dependence on external trade and on a limited range of commodities for export earnings. By the beginning of the 1980s, the three economies faced acute balance-of-payments problems and continued to rely on external resources for their development funding, a situation that created serious debt problems for them. The general price level was going up, and unemployment, especially among the youth, the majority of whom were educated up to the secondary school level, was high and rising. Income differentials were widening, and public services including basic needs services such as health and education were compromised in terms of volume and quality.

Egypt achieved modest rates of growth of GDP before the reform programs of the 1970s. For instance, the annual average compound rate of growth of real GDP was between 4 and 5 percent in the 1950s and 1960s.[7] There was also some evidence that the lopsided distribution of income before the Revolution was somehow mitigated during this period, thanks to such policies as better distribution of such public goods as education, health, and other social services, rent controls, subsidies, and expansion of employment in the public sector. However, it did not appear that the diversification of the economy vigorously pursued during this era succeeded in lessening Egypt's dependence on exports of primary products and long-term foreign capital inflows, and hence its vulnerability to external events. In spite of the agrarian reforms, the share of agriculture in the total GDP declined from 22.8 percent in the 1950s to 15.0 percent in the 1960s, and Egypt continued to depend on highly subsidized food imports to feed its population. It would, therefore, appear that Egypt's economic growth during this period was not accompanied by an ability to generate and sustain growth from within.

The performance of the Kenyan economy has varied over the past twenty-five years. The period 1964–72, following achievement of independence, was char-

Table 9.3
Growth Rates of Selected Socioeconomic Indicators, Egypt, Kenya, and Nigeria, 1975–88, Selected Years

	1975-80	1980-85	1985-88
Egypt			
GDP	8.3	6.8	4.5
Per Capita GDP	6.1	4.5	2.4
Agricultural Production	1.5	3.7	2.9
Manufacturing Production	6.8	8.2	7.2
Total Consumption	5.5	15.2	4.5
Gross Domestic Investment	11.3	4.4	3.5
Import Volume	15.8	6.5	0.0
Export Volume	21.1	6.4	-0.8
Kenya			
GDP	5.0	3.6	4.5
Per Capita GDP	1.9	-1.1	2.8
Agricultural Production	3.4	2.3	4.2
Manufacturing Production	7.1	4.2	5.6
Total Consumption	5.1	3.0	5.1
Gross Domestic Investment	6.9	-2.5	9.9
Import Volume	2.5	-7.9	12.6
Export Volume	2.1	-1.0	4.8
Nigeria			
GDP	9.3	-1.8	0.0
Per Capita GDP	5.2	-9.3	-3.8
Agricultural Production	1.9	1.8	1.9
Manufacturing Production	13.8	1.5	2.4
Total Consumption	8.2	1.1	-0.7
Gross Domestic Investment	10.4	-13.3	-5.0
Import Volume	-0.5	4.5	-29.1
Export Volume	2.4	-0.3	-4.3

Source: UN–ECA data files.

acterized by a favorable domestic and international economic environment. In the domestic economy, the agricultural and industrial sectors expanded rapidly. The stable commodity prices in the international market were favorable. However, subsequent to the first oil shock in 1973, the Kenyan economy faced large imbalances in its external accounts, and the economy was characterized by a recession that led to a fall in GDP growth from 6.8 percent in the 1964–72 period to 1.2 percent in 1974–75. There was, however, a recovery in the period 1976–79 when GDP registered an average growth rate of 6.3 percent. Growth in the 1980s has been low, resulting in an annual decline of per capita income of −1.0 percent.

With respect to Nigeria, it is perhaps fair to say that, even after nearly thirty years after its launching, the laudable aspirations of the First National Development Plan (1962–68) are yet to be fulfilled. The plan projected that "within a reasonable period of time, Nigeria should be in a position to generate from its diversified economy sufficient income and savings of its own to finance a steady rate of growth without any dependence on external source of capital and manpower." As indicated earlier, the Nigerian economy was more dependent on external sources by the end of the 1970s than ever before. By then, national expenditures and production had become highly linked with imports. By 1980 imports had reached a level equivalent to one-quarter of the GDP, that is, double the ratio that prevailed in the early 1970s. Nigeria had progressively become a major importer of food, and the structure of policy incentives, as noted earlier, had encouraged manufacturing production based on imported inputs. The federal government deficits had increased from N304.4 million in 1970 to N3,498.9 million in 1978. Nigeria's total outstanding foreign debt, which amounted to N489 million in 1970, had reached the N2.00 billion mark by 1980. The rate of inflation had risen from 2.8 percent in 1972 to about 16.6 percent in 1978.

The assertion of the Third Plan (1975–80) turned out to be a mirage. The Plan had stated that "in the relatively short time that the economy will enjoy a surplus of investible resources, it is intended that maximum effort will be made to create economic and social infrastructure necessary for self-sustaining growth in the longer run." Rather, the fortuitous combination of luck and nature's bounty enabled Nigeria to pursue the growth objective with little or no attempt to redress the basic structural weaknesses of the economy. The Third Plan also promised that "since oil is a wasting asset, the development strategy of the government is to utilize the resources from oil to develop the productive capacity of the economy and thus permanently improve the standard of living of the people." But it would appear that, although some Nigerians were diligently keeping vigil for the "national cake" to be full-blown, others had dug an underground tunnel under the oven and were continuously slicing an ever increasing chunk of the cake. Hence, whatever modest growth in GDP Nigeria might have achieved prior to the 1980s could, at best, be described as growth without development.

MAJOR CONCERNS OF ECONOMIC POLICY UNDER STRUCTURAL ADJUSTMENT PROGRAMS

The deteriorating economic conditions forced the three African countries to adopt reform programs. The reform phase in Egypt runs roughly from 1974 up to the present, although its "tango" with the IMF dates back to the 1960s when Egypt started asking for the Fund's Standby Arrangements (SBA). For Kenya and Nigeria, the worsening economic situation reached crisis proportions in the 1980s. Although Kenya had been benefiting from the IMF Extended Fund Facility

Table 9.4
Government Budget Deficit/Surplus, Egypt, Kenya, and Nigeria, 1982–88

Year GDP	Kenya		Egypt		Nigeria	
	K. Shs. millions	Per cent of GDP	E.L millions	Per cent of GDP	Naira millions	Per cent of GDP
1982	-4,462	6.30	-3,554	17.00	-6,104	10.10
1983	-1,597	2.10	-2,364	9.50	-5,070	8.00
1984	-2,710	3.10	-3,258	11.40	-2,900	4.10
1985	-3,775	3.80	-3,439	10.10	-1,999	2.50
1986	-5,586	4.80	-4,655	12.20	-2,774	3.50
1987	-9,841	7.50	-2,613	5.90	-9,702	8.80
1988	-5,526	3.60	-4,716	-	-8,585	6.30

Source: International Monetary Fund, *International Financial Statistics*, November 1989.

(EFF) and SBA as far back as 1975 and 1978, respectively, it was in 1980 that it benefited from the World Bank Structural Adjustment Loan (SAL). Thus, all three countries, in varying degrees, have been going through IMF/World Bank-sponsored reforms/adjustment programs.

A typical IMF/World Bank-sponsored Structural Adjustment Program (SAP) normally involves the use of fiscal, monetary, and exchange-rate policies to achieve the desired objectives, principal among which is the maintenance of internal and external balances. The predominant concern of fiscal policy under the SAP is the maintenance of fiscal balance. Maintenance of fiscal balance or reduction of fiscal deficits implies either drastic reductions in government expenditure or increases in government revenue, of which the revenue increases are more difficult to treat. As indicated above, the governments of Egypt, Kenya, and Nigeria have pursued policies that have resulted in the expansion of the public sector, principally to provide essential administrative, social, and economic infrastructures and services. The public expenditure share in GDP has consequently risen in all three economies, but that has also meant widening fiscal deficits as shown in Table 9.4.

In the area of monetary policy, the major areas of concern in the adjustment process have been putting a lid on the expansion of the money supply and on the magnitude of credit extended to government by the banking system, encouragement of domestic savings, and deregulation of interest rates. Growth in the money supply in the three economies is presented in Table 9.5. The annual average rate of growth in Egypt was about 13.7 percent for the period 1982–88 and 10.9 percent and 14.3 percent for Kenya and Nigeria, respectively, during the same period. The share of total domestic credit going to the central government is presented in Table 9.6. On the average, the central government in Egypt received about 46.6 percent of total domestic credit between 1982 and 1988, while the ratios were 36.2 percent and 54.1 percent for Kenya and Nigeria, respectively, over the same period.

Table 9.5
The Money Supply, Egypt, Kenya, and Nigeria, 1982–88

Country Year	1982	1983	1984	1985	1986	1987	1988
Egypt (E.£. mi)	9,552	10,933	12,443	14,696	15,973	18,241	20,579
Kenya(K.Shs.mi)	10,635	11,473	13,095	12,923	17,522	18,917	19,160
Nigeria (Naira mi)	10,049	11,283	12,204	13,227	12,663	14,906	21,446

Source: International Monetary Fund, *International Financial Statistics*, November 1989.

Perhaps the most novel aspect as well as the most controversial aspect of the monetary policy measures that accompany the adjustment programs is the deregulation of interest rates. The deregulation of interest is anchored on the principle of letting market forces determine the allocation of resources in the economy. The advocates of interest rate deregulation argue that interest rates have remained very low (with the real interest rate being negative most of the time) and that this discourages savings. Freeing interest rates from control will enable resources to flow to the most worthy causes as determined by the lenders (bankers) and the borrowers (investors). With respect to the first point, empirical evidence on the influence of interest rate on savings is inconclusive, with the majority of studies pointing to its ineffectiveness as a determinant of savings. However, there is a general belief that higher interest rates might influence the form in which savings are held, with a bias toward financial savings. On market-determined lending rates, the critical issue relates to the possible divergence between market-determined priorities vis-à-vis what one might call the developmental objectives of the society. It has also been argued that very high interest rates tend to encourage speculative and trading activities to the detriment of productive investment.

Table 9.7 shows the movements in predominant interest rates in Egypt, Kenya, and Nigeria in the 1980s. In most cases, the changes in the deposit and lending rates were gradual and minimal except in Nigeria after August 1987.

Conventional adjustment programs normally assign a principal role to exchange-rate adjustments as a means of achieving a balance in external accounts and establishing an equilibrium in domestic supply and demand. The achievement of these objectives is expected to be an outcome of changes in prices that have a depressing effect on the domestic consumption of imported goods, arising from the increased cost in the domestic currency of the imported goods. In addition, devaluation increases receipts in domestic currency per unit of exports, thus providing an incentive for the expansion of production of export outputs. Its price elasticity effect on increasing demand for exports is supposed to have the same effect. Devaluation is also expected to promote the shifting of resources from nontraded goods toward the sector-producing tradeable goods. The shift is expected to correct the imbalance both in the BOP current account and in the aggregate supply and demand of goods and services. It should be emphasized,

Table 9.6
Distribution of Credit Between the Central Government and the Private Sector, Egypt, Kenya, and Nigeria, 1982–88

	1982	1983	1984	1985	1986	1987	1988
Egypt (E.£. mi)							
Domestic Credit	22,008	26,104	31,553	37,674	44,747	52,476	63,052
Claims on Central Govt.	11,390	12,441	14,733	17,053	19,484	23,464	29,186
Claims on Private Sector	5,549	6,876	8,284	10,145	12,888	17,330	11,867
Per cent of Central Govt.	51.8	47.7	46.7	45.3	43.5	44.7	46.3
Per cent of Private SEctor	25.2	26.3	26.3	26.9	28.8	33.0	18.8
Kenya (K.Shs. mi)							
Domestic Credit	26,058	25,944	28,626	32,173	41,025	49,139	52,529
Claims on Central Govt.	10,703	8,710	9,569	10,363	15,552	19,912	18,375
Claims on Private Sector	14,357	15,380	16,944	19,491	22,684	24,154	28,064
Per cent of Central Govt.	41.1	33.5	33.4	32.2	37.9	40.5	35.0
Per cent of Private Sector	55.1	59.3	59.2	60.6	55.3	49.2	53.4
Nigeria (Naira mi)							
Domestic Credit	21,900	27,590	30,423	31,900	36,409	40,209	50,680
Claims on Central Govt.	10,528	15,465	17,823	18,297	18,827	21,157	27,488
Claims on Private Sector	11,372	10,567	11,071	11,823	12,822	16,690	17,918
Per cent of Central Govt.	48.1	56.1	58.6	57.4	51.7	52.6	54.2
Per cent of Private Sector	51.9	38.3	36.4	37.1	35.2	41.5	35.4

Source: International Monetary Fund, *International Financial Statistics*, various issues.

however, that the ability of devaluation to achieve these desirable effects is contingent on the prevalence of certain preconditions in the economy.

First, it is essential that production factors in the economy be mobile to facilitate the shift of resources to export goods and tradeable goods production. An analysis of the situation in many developing economies points to the difficulty in shifting resources from nontradeables to tradeables, especially capital stock and the largely unskilled labor. Moreover, where the major commodity exports

Table 9.7
Trends in Predominant Interest Rates in Egypt, Kenya, and Nigeria, 1980–88
(percent per annum)

Country	Year	1980	1981	1982	1983	1984	1985	1986	1987	1988
Egypt										
(CR)[1]		12.00	13.00	13.00	13.00	13.00	13.00	13.00	13.00	
(DR)[2]	n.a.	n.a.	11.00	11.00	11.00	11.00	11.00	11.00	11.00	
(LR)[3]	n.a.	n.a.	15.00	15.00	15.00	15.00	15.00	16.00	17.00	
Kenya										
(CR)		8.00	12.50	15.00	15.00	12.50	12.50	12.50	12.50	16.00
(DR)		5.80	8.90	12.20	13.30	11.80	11.30	11.30	10.30	10.30
(LR)		10.60	12.40	14.50	15.80	14.40	14.00	14.00	14.00	15.00
Nigeria										
(CR)		6.00	6.00	8.00	8.00	10.00	10.00	10.00	15.00	12.75
(DR)		5.30	5.70	7.60	7.40	8.30	9.10	9.50	11.00*	*
(LR)		8.40	8.90	9.50	10.00	10.20	9.40	10.50	15.00**	

Source: International Monetary Fund, *International Financial Statistics*, various issues.

[1] CR = discount rate.

[2] DR = deposit rate.

[3] LR = lending rate.

n.a. = not available.

* Negotiable as from August 1987. By December 1988 the deposit rates varied between 11.50 percent and 15.00 percent, while the lending rates ranged from 14.00 percent to 21.50 percent.

are perennial agricultural crops that have a long gestation period from initial planting to harvesting, devaluation may induce farmers to plant more coffee and tea in Kenya and more palm oil and cocoa in Nigeria. The results of this incentive are not known, however, for some four to five years. Hence, supply elasticities are factors to reckon with in appraising the potential effects of devaluation on production.

Second, the shifting of resources as a result of devaluation is supposed to be toward production activities in which the devaluing country has a comparative advantage. Given trade liberalization that is also a component of the adjustment package, this points to primary production for most developing countries. Given the increasing protectionist tendencies in the markets of the major commodity-importing countries, and increasing substitution of primary products with synthetic materials, the result of any supply response to short-term illusory price increases will be commodity glut, worsening terms of trade, and reduction in export earnings in the long run.

Table 9.8
Exchange Rate, Egypt, Kenya, and Nigeria, 1982–88

Year	1982	1983	1984	1985	1986	1987	1988
Country							
Egypt							
Principal Rate	1.2950	1.3645	1.4574	1.3006	1.1679	1.0070	1.0616
Kenya							
(Shs per US$)							
Market Rate	12.725	13.796	15.781	16.284	16.042	16.515	18.599
Nigeria							
(Naira per US$)							
Market Rate	0.6702	0.7486	0.8083	0.9996	3.3167	4.1408	5.3533

Source: International Monetary Fund, *International Financial Statistics*, various issues.

Finally, the effect of devaluation on reducing imports depends on the price elasticity of demand for such imports. Where the demand is inelastic, as is the case with many imported consumer goods, the effect of devaluation in discouraging imports appears to be very minimal. Yet a typical adjustment package would frown against the use of more direct and effective nontariff tools such as quotas and prohibitions to curtail imports. In addition, where domestic manufacturing depends heavily on the import of raw materials, spare parts, and capital goods, devaluation invariably produces two results: underutilization of installed capacity and inflation. The reduced ability to import the necessary inputs results in excess capacity, with attendant fall in output and loss of jobs. The increase in input prices as a result of devaluation leads to cost-push inflation. For instance, the marked depreciation of the Nigerian naira led to increases in the cost of industrial production and the prices of manufactured goods, while industrial capacity utilization fell from an average of 40.7 percent to 31.0 percent in 1989.

Trends in exchange rates in Egypt, Kenya, and Nigeria are shown in Table 9.8. The table shows that Egypt has been more successful in resisting pressures to devalue than Kenya and Nigeria, with the Nigerian case being worse than that of Kenya.

The period of reform in Egypt witnessed the shift toward economic liberalization, greater private sector activity, and higher levels of domestic resources and foreign assistance. This supported enhanced public and capital formation, particularly in infrastructure and industry, and higher levels of imports, particularly for consumption. The main argument offered in favor of the new policy orientation was the need to attract foreign capital and technology and to utilize the country's abundant trained personnel. A number of financial incentives were given, tax exemptions were offered, and the levies for the repatriation of profits were eased. Managers in the public sector were also given more leeway in running their corporations. As a reflection of the new drive, the investment ratio rose to over 30 percent, while the rate of GDP growth climbed to about 8 percent by 1980. Although own reserves increased—from exports, the Suez Canal, tourism, and remittances from nationals working abroad—the level of external assistance started to stagnate and the servicing of the external debt emerged as a major development constraint. The rise in the international prices of subsidized imported food items also put increasing pressure on the government budget and the balance of payments. Direct subsidies rose from LE113 million in 1973 to LE680 in 1978 to LE2.54 billion in 1984–85.

With the intensification of economic problems, particularly during the 1980s, Egypt's government opted for a consolidated reform program with two central objectives: the continued transformation of the economy along more liberal lines and the maintenance of its welfare policy. In this effort the government was faced with the sensitive issues of removing the subsidies and the challenges of improving the competetiveness of industry and convincing its creditors of its policy stances to attract more inflow of resources and secure reasonable terms of managing its huge external debt. The government now found itself at loggerheads with the IMF. The IMF started putting pressure on Egypt as early as 1973 to eliminate the subsidies, streamline the public sector, remove the price controls, and devalue and unify the exchange rate of the Egyptian pound. In 1977 the government decided to eliminate most of the subsidies on basic consumer goods. Following this decision, riots broke out in Cairo, and the stability of Sadat's regime was placed in serious jeopardy. Realizing the limits of action, the government has since opted for gradualism. Indeed, in the Egyptian case, the issue of subsidies is central to economic policy because of the role they play in determining the distribution of income, relative price, and the performance of the inflationary process, its impact on the government budget and its repercussions on the country's balance of payments. Yet, the maintenance of this system along with price controls is a necessary condition for fulfilling the objective of guaranteeing a minimum subsistence level to the population.

A corollary policy instrument is the exchange-rate policy. Egypt maintains a multiple exchange-rate system. Although the country has continuously devalued its currency, it still retains this system. This has also been an important issue of disagreement with the IMF, which argued in favor of devaluation to enhance exports and to unify the price of the currency. The Egyptians contended that problems relating to the expansion of their exports could be traced back to limited-supply capacity and that devaluation, in the absence of substantial efforts to enhance this capacity, would only lead to increased inflation which could further complicate the subsidy issue.

Another area of policy that drew continuous criticism was the interest rate policy. The IMF called for an inflation-adjusted interest rate, claiming that prevailing interest rates were too low to attract savings. The Egyptians, on the other hand, contended that unwarranted high interest rates would depress investments, the rate of which was already falling. The disagreement with the IMF on these issues has repeatedly led that institution to refuse to back Egypt's reform programs and is responsible for the consequent lack of progress on rescheduling its external debt.

The IMF's credit and the Bank's SAP lending to Kenya included policy packages that featured exchange-rate adjustments, government expenditure and revenue ceilings, and budget deficit targets; limits on the expansion of the money supply; targets for public and private sector shares of total domestic credit; and interest rate liberalization. With the ratio of Kenya's budget to the GDP rising from 22 to 38 percent in the period 1964–81, the stabilization and adjustment programs aim at achieving a balance between government expenditure and revenue. Here attempts have been made to reduce the fiscal deficits to one digit level. Another area of fiscal policy during the adjustment process is the reform of the tax system aimed at increased equity and greater growth elasticity in revenue generation. To this end, tax reforms have shifted emphasis from indirect to direct taxation. Reforms have also been advocated for reduction of excessive centralization of government financial management.

The balance-of-payments problems confronting Kenya's economy prompted several adjustments in the country's exchange rate. In 1982 and 1983 the Kenyan shilling, which was pegged to the SDR (Special Drawing Rights), was devalued twice at the rates of 15 percent and 7.5 percent. Thereafter, a flexible exchange rate was established. Although the devaluation of the shilling averted distortions in factor prices in the economy, it has contributed to the inflationary creep in the economy. Apparently, the increase in import prices accounted for much of the internal price increases as wages for labor and prices for other production inputs either declined or stagnated in real terms.

The worsening oil market situation beginning in 1982 triggered a recession in the Nigerian economy that has persisted. The government was compelled to put together a package of austerity measures under the Economic Stabilization Act 1982. By the mid-1980s the severe problem of the economy remained very much unabated, forcing the government to opt for SAP.

The main objective of SAP in Nigeria included the restructuring and diversification of the productive base of the economy; achieving fiscal and balance-of-payment balances; reducing the dominance of the public sector in the economy; and intensifying the growth potential of the private sector. As in Kenya, the key elements and policies of SAP in Nigeria include the deregulation of the economy from administrative controls (especially with respect to exchange rates, interest rates, and prices); trade and payments liberalization; and rationalization of public expenditures and public enterprises (including privatization).

The maintenance of fiscal balance in Nigeria emphasizes adjustments in public expenditures as needed to reflect the revenue constraints, with the aim of containing the budgetary deficits to within 3 percent of GDP. The main thrust of the expenditure reallocation policy includes maintenance of restraints on the public wage bill, reduction in nonstatutory transfers to economic and quasi-economic parastatals, and the elimination of all transfers to fully commercially oriented parastatals (implying subsidy removal). In the area of policy, the revenue aspect of direct taxes (especially company tax) and customs tariffs seems to have been deemphasized under SAP in favor of using direct taxes as an incentive measure to the private sector and customs tariffs as a means of protecting local industries. Rather more emphasis is being placed on the less equitable (more regressive) consumption taxes as a means of generating additional revenue— hence the removal of all sorts of subsidies.

With the deregulation of interest rates in 1987, deposit rates, which stood at 11 percent at the beginning of 1987, varied between 11.5 percent and 18.5 percent in the first half of 1989, while lending rates, which averaged 15 percent at the beginning of 1987, varied between 14.0 percent and 24.0 percent in the first half of 1989. The naira tumbled from naira 0.9996 per U.S. $1.00 in 1985 to naira 7.6 per U.S. $1.00 by the end of 1989.

The preceding analysis indicates that the orthodox adjustment programs have not provided the impulse they were supposed to possess for alleviating the adjusting countries' economic ills and moving them to the path of recovery as indicated in Table 9.9.[8] Although the orthodox adjustment programs aim at restoring growth, generally through the achievement of fiscal and external balances and the free play of market forces, these objectives cannot be achieved without addressing the fundamental structural bottlenecks of the economies in question, among which are weak production structures, external dependence, neglect of the informal sector, and other related issues. Thus, the *African Alternative Framework to Structural Adjustment Programmes for Socio-Economic Recovery and Transformation* asserts, for instance, that

the ultimate objectives of alleviating mass poverty and raising the living standard of African people will only be attainable if pursued in tandem with the objective of establishing self-sustained development. This encompasses three interlocking subgoals, namely: (i) maintenance of sustained economic growth; (ii) transformation of the African economies; and (iii) maintenance of a sustainable resource base.[9]

Unfortunately, the conventional adjustment programs do not address the last two subgoals.

The aspects of the policy package under the Fund and the Bank-sponsored stabilization and adjustment programs that have come under fire include credit policy, interest rate deregulation, foreign exchange policy, trade liberalization, privatization, across-the-board reduction in budget deficits, and reliance on market forces.[10]

As indicated earlier, conventional stabilization and adjustment programs implemented in the African countries in the last decade have incorporated the policy of restraining the growth of outlays in various sectors of the economy. Social services, especially education and health, have been the hardest hit. These services, however, are the ones that have direct effects on the public welfare. Reduction of outlays on health compromises improvement in the health service. For education, reduced outlays have impacts that are inimical to the future productivity of the national workforce.

Expenditure restraints have not been limited to social services. The stabili-

Table 9.9
Intercountry Comparison of Selected Economic Indicators, 1973–87

	Egypt		Kenya		Nigeria	
	1973–80	1980–87	1977–80	1973–80	1973–80	1980–87
GDP (annual growth rate)			4.2	3.8	3.4	-1.7
Per Capita GDP (annual growth rate)			1.3	-0.9	1.2	-4.8
Total consumption (annual growth rate)						
Gross Domestic Investment (annual growth rate)			4.4	-2.3	6.6	-14.8
Export volume (annual growth rate)			-0.1	-0.6	-1.0	-5.1
Import volume (annual growth rate)			3.5	-3.0	21.2	-14.0
	1980	**1987**	**1980**	**1987**	**1980**	**1987**
Terms of Trade (1980 – 100)			100	80	100	54
Total External Debt (US$m)			3,507	5,950	8,854	29,778
Long-term Debt as Ratio of GNP			39	64	5	111
Debt Service as Ratio of GNP			5.5	7.6	0.8	3.9
Current Account balance (before official transfers in US$m)			-1,006	-639	5,299	-380
Gross International Reserves (US$m)			539	294	10,640	1,498

Sources: World Bank, *World Development Report* (various issues) and *Sub-Saharan Africa: From Crisis to Sustainable Growth*, 1989.

zation and adjustment policies of the past decade, which have aimed at constraining government expenditure, have also had adverse effects on capital accumulation and thus have compromised long-term developments. The share of the public sector in capital formation in the three economies is substantial. Reduced growth of public expenditure has resulted in lower rates of growth of capital formation. Moreover, although there might be conventional wisdom in cutting one's coat according to one's cloth, there is nothing intuitively appealing about balanced budgets, especially from the growth point of view.

A worrisome aspect of the financing aspect of the orthodox adjustment programs is the prominence given to new loan facilities and debt rescheduling, resulting in the compounding of the debt burden in one case and the postponement of the evil day in the other.

The credit policy used in orthodox structural adjustment programs, more often than not, leads to output contraction and acceleration of inflationary pressures and, while it might succeed in improving the current account position, to a reduction in investment. Generalized devaluation results in socially unsupportable increases in prices of critical goods and services; raises the domestic costs of imported inputs and undermines capacity utilization; triggers general inflation; and diverts scarce foreign exchange for speculative activities. Unsustainably high real interest rates shift the economy toward speculative and trading activities by becoming a disincentive to productive investment, just as import liberalization leads to greater and more entrenched external dependence, and jeopardizes national priorities such as food self-sufficiency and local sources of materials.

POLICY CONCERNS AND DIRECTIONS FOR THE FUTURE: ADJUSTMENT FOR SOCIOECONOMIC TRANSFORMATION

The preceding analysis shows that neither the development strategies and economic policies adopted in the earlier period nor the policies incorporated in the reform and adjustment programs of the 1980s produced the desired effects on African economic development in terms of its long-term development objectives. Given Africa's long-term objectives of establishing a self-sustaining process of economic growth and development, and a human-centered development, there is need for some reorientation in economic policies directed toward achieving these objectives in the future.

In the area of fiscal policy, the restraint on public spending has to be applied selectively if adverse effects on long-term development are to be averted. In situations where the public sector is a major contributor to domestic capital formation, a decline in the volume of resources directed to gross capital formation would have adverse effects on capital accumulation in the economy. Moreover, expenditures in the area of human investment (education and health, for instance) should not be reduced to such a level that it becomes ruinous of the long-term objective of a human-centered development. The priorities accorded to education and health by many African countries at independence were not misplaced and are no less valid today and in the future than they were in the past. Hence, improving the human resources capacity must be accorded the priority that it deserves in future policies.

It has also been pointed out that it is unwise to achieve fiscal balance at the expense of constraining productive capacity, and thereby sacrificing the future for the present. Perhaps the problem is not with deficit financing per se but with the uses to which it is put.

Our reservations concerning restraint on public spending do not apply to policies aimed at minimizing nonproductive expenditures such as military spending. The examples of the superpowers tend to indicate that the sky is the limit to defense spending. Since there might be some disagreement as to the upper limit of defense spending, it might be easier to start off with setting minimum standards of health, education, shelter, and food to which every citizen ought to be entitled. After all, no citizen would want to be so adequately protected against external aggression only to die of internal starvation.

Although the importance of external resources in Africa's recovery and transformation is recognized, the prominence given to external finance in the orthodox adjustment programs does not augur well for the future development of African economies. It not only reinforces the dependence syndrome and exacerbates the debt burden, but it also militates against greater and more efficient mobilization of domestic resources. Hence, future policies should be directed toward greater domestic resource mobilization through improvement in the financial structure and greater mobilization of the people.

Finally, there is a need for a better debt management strategy that would limit debt–service ratios to levels consistent with sustaining and accelerating growth and development by freeing resources for productivity activities. A situation in which an average 60 percent of recurrent expenditures and 40 percent of total government expenditures are devoted to debt services, as was the case in Nigeria during 1987–89, is certainly inimical to long-term growth prospects.

In the area of monetary policy there is a need to use selective interest rates in such a way that interest rates on loans for speculative activities will be greater than the rates on loans for productive activities. The controversy surrounding the influence of interest rates, particularly real interest rates, on savings notwithstanding, *AAF–SAP* has suggested that the choices of the different rates should be such as to ensure that the weighted average of the two borrowing rates (i.e., on speculative loans and loans for real production) would result in a real positive rate applicable for savings. The differential interest rate policy should be complemented by credit guidelines that channel resources to the priority areas such as the domestic food subsector and small-scale indigenous enterprises. Hence, development-determined priorities as against market-determined priorities should provide a guide to the allocation of scarce resources in the economy.

Given the failure of generalized devaluation or currency depreciation to achieve its intended objectives and its rather adverse effects on African economies, a case can be made for a managed exchange-rate regime as against market-determined rates. In such a regime a de facto multiple exchange-rate system would be used in order to favor the input of goods considered essential to the economy (such as capital goods, essential agricultural inputs, and drugs) and to discriminate against the import of nonessentials, for which foreign exchange can be bought at market-determined rates.

Finally, given their economic conditions, trade liberalization is not in the best interest of developing economies. For instance, import liberalization leads to greater external dependence; jeopardizes national priorities such as food self-sufficiency; and threatens the survival of infant industries. Hence, future trade policy should be in the direction of using a combination of tariff and tax measures to change the consumption pattern, protect local industries, and encourage the domestic sourcing of industrial raw materials.

NOTES

1. UN-ECA, *African Alternative Framework to Structural Adjustment Programmes for Socio-Economic Recovery and Transformation (AAF–SAP)* (Addis Ababa, 1989).

2. Federal Republic of Nigeria, *First National Development Plan 1962–68* (Lagos: Ministry of Information, 1962).

3. Robert Mabro, *The Egyptian Economy 1952–72* (Oxford: Clarendon Press, 1974), p. 120.

4. There were, of course, subsequent modifications to this policy. For instance, in 1958 the interest on compensation was reduced to 1.5 percent and the redemption period extended to forty years, while all interest payments were discontinued and bonds became irredeemable by 1964.

5. M. Abdel-Fadil, *The Political Economy of Nasserism* (Cambridge: Cambridge University Press, 1980).

6. G. O., Nwankwo, *The Nigerian Financial System* (London: Macmillan Press, 1980), p. 30.

7. Mabro, *The Egyptian Economy*, p. 166.

8. World Bank, *Africa's Adjustment and Growth in 1980*, and UN-ECA, *Statistics and Policy: ECA Preliminary Observations on the World Bank Report: Africa's Adjustment and Growth in the 1980s*, Addis Ababa, 1986.

9. UN-ECA, *African Alternative Framework to Structural Adjustment Programmes for Socio-Economic Recovery and Transformation (AAF–SAP)*, 1989.

10. Ibid., pp. 18–20, 37–38.

REFERENCES

Abdel-Fadil, M. *The Political Economy of Nasserism*. Cambridge: Cambridge University Press, 1980.

Al-Hakim, Tawfig. *The Return of Consciousness*. London: Macmillan Press, 1985.

Aliboni, Roberto, et al. *Egypt's Economic Potential*. London: Croom Helm, 1984.

Commander, Simon. *The State and Agricultural Development in Egypt since 1973*. London and Atlantic Highlands, N.J.: Overseas Development Institute, Ithaca Press, 1987.

The Economist Intelligence Unit. *Country Profile Egypt 1988–89*. London: September 1988.

The Economist Intelligence Unit. *Egypt, Country Report No. 21989*. London: 1989.

The Economist Intelligence Unit. *Nigeria, Country Profile 1989–90*. London: Business International.

The Economist Intelligence Unit. *Nigeria, Country Report No. 21989*, London: Business International, April 14, 1989.

Mabro, R. *The Egyptian Economy 1952–72*. Oxford: Clarendon Press, 1974.

McDermott, Antony. *Egypt from Nasser to Mubarak: A Flawed Revolution*. New York: Croom Helm, 1988.

Nwankwo, G. O. *The Nigerian Financial System*. London: Macmillan Press, 1980.

Radwan, Samir. *Capital Formation in Egyptian Industry and Agriculture 1882–1967*. Oxford: St. Antony's Middle East Monographs No. 2, London: Ithaca Press, 1974.

UN-ECA. *African Alternative Framework to Structural Adjustment Programmes for Socio-Economic Recovery and Transformation (AAF-SAP)*. 1989.

UN-ECA. *Statistics and Policy: ECA Preliminary Observations on the World Bank Report: Africa's Adjustment and Growth in the 1980s*. 1989.

World Bank. *Arab Republic of Egypt: Current Economic Situation and Growth Prospects*. Washington, D.C.: October 5, 1981.

World Bank. *Arab Republic of Egypt: Domestic Resource Mobilization and Growth Prospects for the 1980s*. Washington, D.C.

World Bank. *Egypt Review of the Finances of the Decentralized Public Sector*. Vol. 1. Washington, D.C.: March 1987.

World Bank. *Nigeria Macro-Economic Policies for Structural Change*. Washington, D.C.: August 15, 1983.

World Bank. *Sub-Saharan Africa: From Crisis to Sustainable Growth: A Long-term Perspective Study*. Washington, D.C.: November 1989.

PART IV

NATIONAL ECONOMIC POLICIES
IN EASTERN EUROPE AND CHINA

10

NATIONAL ECONOMIC POLICIES IN THE SOVIET UNION

Jozef M. van Brabant

INTRODUCTION

Since Mikhail S. Gorbachev's ascent to the General Secretaryship of the Communist party of the Soviet Union in March 1985, Soviet society at large has undergone spectacular change. Transformations in economic life constitute only one, so far comparatively minor, facet of this unprecedented mutation in a centrally planned economy (CPE), which was started in early 1986 and given a major impetus in mid-1987. Significant economic change has already been registered, and much more is the object of prospective macro- and microeconomic policies. *Perestroika* has been bold, inordinately difficult, contradictory, unique, and full of pitfalls—a complexity that is unlikely to abate soon.

In this chapter we focus on the problems of the transition from a well-entrenched traditional CPE, such as the Soviet Union's, to a more market-oriented economic environment. At the inception of the drift toward *perestroika*, which involves changing both the traditional economic model and development strategy almost from the ground up, the leadership was not fully aware of the almost insuperable obstacles that such an initiative would pose. This is not so surprising. Key decision makers of CPEs have repeatedly underestimated both the depth of the root problems that reforms are to cure and the required time and cost to do so. It is only by clarifying the transition phase itself, wherefrom this gradual mutation derives its principal traits, and in which direction it may be heading, that the woes of Soviet and related reforms can be properly assessed.

This chapter introduces the salient features of the traditional Soviet economic model and its associated development strategy; outlines the central goals and components of the Gorbachevian reforms; discusses the legacies of the traditional economic model and development strategy of CPEs for the transition phase; and sketches the obstacles yet to be squarely faced. The chapter concludes with a synoptic overview of what macroeconomic policy in the USSR is likely to look like in the years ahead.

MODEL AND STRATEGY OF THE TRADITIONAL CPE

The model and strategy of the traditional CPE are best discussed with reference to the more abstract, prototype CPE because it offers an opportunity for systematic analysis.

The First Strategy of Socialist Economic Development. A growth strategy is a complex of measures that ensure resource allocation with a view to attaining long-term development objectives. Following the immediate postwar period of economic reconstruction and consolidation of Communist party rule, the quintessential socialist development strategy adopted by the CPE was centered on industrialization in breadth of mostly backward, agrarian economies. This objective was to be implemented by manipulating key policy instruments, by transforming the economic institutions in place, and by prescribing some behavioral rules that together made up the model.

Socialist development processes, anchored to the pursuit of forced industrialization in breadth, played a crucial role during the first decades of the CPE's evolution. This concern was so overwhelming that decision making about the overall allocation of resources was almost exclusively geared by the priority role of industry in the elaboration of a more or less autarkic economic complex. Autarky here is not synonymous with complete severance of all foreign contacts, although at one time a narrowly defined type of economic self-sufficiency was certainly immanent in the socialist concept of how best to allocate resources. The pivotal focus of economic policy is the creation of a diversified industrial economy that can function relatively independently of disturbances propagated from abroad.

Not only the strategy but also the model ultimately derives from the metaeconomics of Marxist-Leninist precepts—the so-called economic laws—of the historical path to socialist development (Brabant, 1980, pp. 63–69). This body of ideological beliefs is used as inspiration or ex post rationalization, and the paramount strategic objective is centrally steered, balanced growth paced by extensive industrialization, with the purpose of completing the material-technical foundations of socialist society as rapidly as feasible. That is to say, the CPE's initial development strategy aims, among other objectives, at full employment, rapid socioeconomic growth, extensive industrialization as the foundation for steady economic development, and a substantial degree of domestic policy autonomy. Policymakers in CPEs assign a pronounced priority role to selected industrial branches for which they mobilize material and human resources almost regardless of true scarcity gauges. At least, most of the current "surplus value," that is, the excess of normal revenues over fixed and variable costs, is appropriated not for present consumption but to finance the expansion of selected production sectors at the expense of agriculture and services in particular. As evinced during the early industrialization stages, the populace's levels of living could even decline for a few years. Furthermore, these decisions are carried out through central planning and its particular institutions and instruments.

THE TRADITIONAL ECONOMIC MODEL

A growth strategy must be buttressed by an appropriate economic model or combination of institutions, micro- and macroeconomic policies, behavioral rules, and policy instruments that help to foster industrialization. Behavioral prescriptions are by definition normative, and they are sanctioned as such. The CPE model is dominated by a hierarchical system of planning and management. The decision-making authority is vested at the center of national power to ensure a close and particular interdependence between political and economic functions.

When first introduced, the economic model consisted of (1) central planning in physical detail of nearly all economic decisions and restrictive regulation of the decision-making role of economic agents; (2) nearly exhaustive nationalization of capital, natural resources, and, in most cases, land; (3) collectivization of agriculture in combination with state agricultural enterprises; (4) strict regulation of labor allocation; (5) pronounced disregard of indirect coordination instruments and associated policies and institutions for steering resource allocation; (6) managerial autonomy highly circumscribed by central planning and by the controls exerted by the local party and, in most countries, trade union interest groups as well; (7) the channeling of most economic decisions through a complex administrative hierarchy, which tends to handle matters rather bureaucratically; (8) in spite of central regulation and administration, a minimum of personal initiative in order to implement plan instructions at all levels of production and consumption; and (9) rather rigid separation of the domestic economy from foreign economic influences. Some of these characteristics need to be clarified briefly.

Comprehensive Central Planning

As the core of the traditional model, planning means selecting development targets and allocating resources to fulfill those aims as well as possible. In the traditional CPE, the planning instruments and objectives are determined by a select circle of party members, especially the Politburo, on behalf of the Communist party as society's vanguard. Resources are essentially allocated by central fiat—not necessarily by one central administration. The plan endeavors to formulate instructions so that they leave no alternative to their execution. The objective is to ensure a close linkage between political and economic functions. For that reason, the plan assigns producers mandatory targets on inputs, outputs, pricing, wages, capital allocation, and other aspects of what would normally be within the compass of entrepreneurial behavior. In other words, questions concerning what is to be produced, how production is to be organized, what inputs are to be used, and so on are, in principle, settled by the norms specified in the plan, not by the foresight, risk-taking, and creative ability of an entrepreneurial elite; their initiative and leadership, if present, are not to impinge on the priority of physical yardsticks.

Needless to say, the real world of production and consumption differs substantially from this paradigm. For one, conscious human activity cannot be reduced to the simple act of pulling a lever. Some scope for decision making needs to be reserved for agents because the planning center cannot possibly steer the economy in detail. Even if this omniscience is not already fictitious at the outset of socialist planning, the appropriate functioning of an increasingly complex economy on the basis of coordinated directives and regulators demands that modifications be introduced. In fact, as a rule its compelling logic emerges very early on in the functioning of the traditional CPE, if only to come to grips with various levels of uncertainty in economic decisions. This uncertainty arises from the existing or rapidly growing complexity of steering an economy. It also emanates from planning being intrinsically a stochastic process, if only because some sectors, including international trade and agriculture, depend on events that are largely beyond the scope of the information at the disposal of central planners and, moreover, beyond their control. Such uncertainty has to be mitigated either through more flexible planning or by ad hoc solutions formulated by microeconomic agents. Because the lower tiers of the planning hierarchy normally harbor preferences that differ from those of the central policymakers, only by fluke do their decisions coincide with the center's. The plan must, therefore, eventually be supplemented with proper criteria for guiding the choices of economic agents.

Efficiency Indicators in Resource Allocation

Technical rules on static economic efficiency are rather primitive and passive. The theory of planning has generally crystallized around quantity calculations, as distinct from value planning. Ideological precepts and historical circumstances may have contributed to considering the dynamic results of economic expansion far more important than static efficiency. From the beginning of socialist economic organization, it has been accepted as axiomatic that socialism implies the effective control of the economy by society in pursuit of its objectives by appropriate policy instruments and associated institutions. The latter revolve around the planned steering of economic life by the state. Without this being necessarily well articulated, the accepted premise of central planning has been that the tools of indirect regulation are not dependable; hence, resource allocation must proceed largely through other, at times concealed, signals.

Indirect Coordination Instruments and Institutions

Market-type instruments and institutions under central planning are rather primitive and passive. Socialist price policies provide a case in point of the subordination of value criteria to physical targets. The center traditionally calculates industrial wholesale prices on the basis of average sectoral costs without making due allowance for capital and land scarcities. Hence there is a severe downward bias in prices with a high resource content (Petrakov, 1986, 1987). Furthermore, the true cost of imports and the real opportunities for exports are poorly reflected in administrative prices. Agricultural procurement prices are set differently depending on the organization of agriculture, the government's specific goals with respect to its agricultural procurement prices, and the planning center's influence over free peasant markets. Consumer prices are, as a rule, divorced from wholesale prices by a complex network of subsidies and taxes that in part reflect government preferences.[1] In addition to these major dichotomies, prices are generally held unchanged for long periods of time for rather eclectic reasons (Brabant, 1987b, pp. 34–62), but also to facilitate plan implementation and to guide consumer behavior. Note that each price regime is steered rather separately through particular institutional and policy choices. The disparity is maintained because the price regimes are modified according to criteria deemed suitable to reach social objectives or to enhance plan formulation, implementation, and control. Because prices are averaged for the branch, there are always firms that lose and others that make a nominal profit. This calls for the continual redistribution of value added in each sector.

The deliberate choice to underplay value planning encompassed nearly all familiar market-type instruments and institutions. In fact, the organization of the economy and macropolicy are simply to enhance the realization of priority goals expressed mostly in physical terms. Other instruments were not to interfere with the plan's execution, although they did to some extent.

The CPE's fiscal policy is almost exclusively concerned with indirect taxation (that is, turnover taxes) to ensure some equilibrium between demand and supply of consumer goods. Incomes in sectors other than agriculture, services, and handicrafts are essentially limited to wages and bonuses, with little variation among workers or correlation with effective productivity levels. In cooperative agriculture, incomes depend on nominal profits derived from assigned output and sales at administratively set procurement prices. Additional revenues are obtained through sales on free peasant markets and the initially highly confined second economy. Both are regulated indirectly by the center, including through moral suasion and voluntary restraints on the part of agents.

Based overwhelmingly on the real bills' doctrine, which posits that credit should reflect real flows, in which sense it becomes "productive" and hence conducive to monetary equilibrium, monetary policy has, at best, been passive. Accordingly, in most CPEs loans are extended for well-specified purposes, granted for fixed periods of time, secured by real assets, repayable, and centrally regulated or even administered on a planned basis. At the macroeconomic level, this model operates with a monobanking system. Money plays a passive role, particularly in the production sphere, where it simply facilitates the allocation of resources previously earmarked in physical terms in the plan. Financial assets for households are generally limited to cash, lottery tickets, savings deposits, and occasionally government or enterprise bonds. The assets of firms are as a rule limited to bank deposits. Fiscal policies are subordinated to the general aims of the plan and social precepts on income differentiation, profits, and price regulations. Most enterprise profits and losses are ventilated through the central budget. Managerial and worker incentives seek to overfulfill quantitative production targets, on which bonuses are predicated.

Credit policy is geared toward facilitating interfirm transactions. Capital investments, usually financed through the budget, which for this purpose collects virtually all enterprise profits, are undertaken with minimal regard for macroeconomic efficiency, and no scarcity levies are applied. Credit institutions are expected simply to finance the investment targets chosen by the center, regardless of how these decisions are formulated. A more active monetary policy to equate consumer revenues plus net changes in private savings with the value of consumer goods earmarked for distribution during the plan period is sporadically instituted to counter dangerous open or repressed inflation.

Foreign Trade and Payments Regime

The foreign trade and payments regime is passive in the selection and implementation of the development strategy. An integral element of the CPE model is the more or less complete disjunction of the domestic economy from external influences, especially in the microeconomic sphere, by means of special instruments and institutions. Interaction with other economies is compressed to the minimum that is still compatible with the overall development goals centered on rapid industrialization. For economies that cannot be autarkic because of size or resource endowment, severing domestic decision making from world market criteria has had several important drawbacks.

The institutions and mechanisms for conducting trade were selected as a direct consequence of the failure to adopt a comprehensive, internally consistent regional economic policy in the late 1940s (Brabant, 1989a, pp. 25ff.) in the context of the Council for Mutual Economic Assistance (CMEA). By reducing the interaction with other economies to the minimum still compatible with rapid industrialization, each CPE sought to isolate itself from the world economy, including other CPEs, in search of protection against foreign events. A state monopoly of foreign trade (MFT) and payments was expressly instituted to neutralize all influences from abroad, whether positive or disruptive, including with respect to other CPEs, and thus to further domestic policy autonomy.

External economic relations do not form a coherent component of the CPE.

Organizationally, there is virtually complete disjunction of the domestic economy from activities abroad. This is accomplished by "nationalization" of the foreign trade and exchange systems (Grote, 1981; Konstantinov, 1984). While the Ministry of Foreign Trade is in principle in charge of the MFT, it usually delegates the authority to trade to a few foreign trade organizations (FTOs) organized by broad economic sectors, trade direction, and possibly currency of settlement. These organizations purchase domestic products for export and sell imports at domestically prevailing prices. The differences between *fiat* domestic and foreign prices expressed in domestic currency are offset through the so-called price-equalization account, which is a component of the central government budget.

Trade decisions in the CPE usually result from a combination of economic and other factors. Trade serves chiefly as a means of fulfilling the overall development goals. The planning of the level and composition of trade is intermeshed with the overall system of material balances. The problem of whether to import or to produce domestically is usually resolved by considering the domestic availability of inputs and the necessity to pay for imports. In any case, the central planner exhibits only marginal interest in reaping the benefits of export-led growth or in minimizing the real cost of the preferred import substitution. Planning the geographical distribution of earmarked trade is largely a function of the home economy's need for noncompeting imports and their availability in alternative markets, export commitments, and consciously planned relative surpluses and shortages in the material balances to comply with commitments in bilateral trade and payments agreements (BTPAs). Comparisons of prevailing prices as basic inputs into trade decision making are rarely undertaken as the price-equalization mechanism siphons off (covers) apparent trade profits (losses). Such differences are inconsequential for subsequent allocation policies. This near-irrelevance of prices also applies, of course, to the official or commercial exchange rate.

Trade is by definition a sector that eludes the complete control of one planning center and that can hardly be managed in quantitative terms only. To gain greater stability in domestic economic activity, the CPEs also aim at forecasting trade flows as accurately as possible. But not all activities and fluctuations abroad are predictable. Born out of the postwar economic, political, and strategic constellation of forces, detailed ex ante BTPAs at relatively stable, if artificial, prices[2] suited administrative planning. It also facilitated the implementation of the political aspirations of some CPEs whose realization would have been chancier in a multilateral environment.

The insulation of domestic processes from direct interaction with agents abroad in the real sphere is accomplished by letting FTOs keep apart home and foreign economic agents. Indirect influences are also minimized. Actual trade events can impact on the domestic economy, but usually not through price pressures because domestic prices are set autonomously by administrative fiat; nominal gains and losses from trade are simply absorbed by fiscal means. There are macroeconomic impacts, however. A disturbance from planned import cost and export return, if accommodated, affects the disposable budget, and ultimately consumer income, as well as the foreign exchange situation (see Brabant, 1987a, pp. 110ff.; Lawson, 1988; Wolf, 1988). Planners attempt to neutralize the impact of this disturbance by sterilizing trade results that deviate from planned magnitudes. Alternatively, they offset trade gains or losses by varying other budgetary outlays, or they postpone adjustment until the next plan schedules a replenishment of foreign exchange reserves or servicing of foreign debt. This potential indirect influence does not play an overriding role in decision making, however, because the bulk of trade is in any case regulated through comprehensive BTPAs with rather autonomous prices.

As a crucial implication of this trade model, macroeconomic decision makers are unaware of the real economic cost of their import-substitution policies. From the planner's point of view, this does not matter much as long as autarky reigns supreme. Although a state may successfully cripple the price mechanism on a national scale, if it allows external processes to actively supplement domestic availabilities, even if only for informational purposes, it is not quite clear how the inherently uncontrollable foreign opportunities can be dovetailed with the rigidly centralized internal economic relations.

There is, of course, a microeconomic equivalent to the lack of interest in trade results per se by central decision makers: Economic agents remain ignorant of the true scarcity cost of world market availabilities and requirements. This assumes particular importance once the potential for extracting the surplus from the traditional sector nears exhaustion and policy options in the CPEs come to parallel those typical of market economies (MEs). In particular, the CPEs stand to benefit from improved allocatory efficiency and from reduced imbalances.

THE OBJECTIVES OF SOVIET ECONOMIC REFORMS

As experience has demonstrated, the centralized economic model was suitable for carrying out a consistent, rapid, and radical transformation of a relatively backward economy, such as Russia, into an industrial society by overcoming various bottlenecks to steady growth. These included an unstable global economic environment, initially domestic strife over sociopolitical organization, inexperienced management, a labor force unaccustomed to the industrial production mode, a burdensome agrarian overpopulation, and others. But such a centralized model is less suited to ensure steady growth in a moderately to highly diversified industrial economy that can no longer extract the desired output increment chiefly from the addition of primary production factors to the production process. This sets the stage for reform.

In its most general connotation, an economic reform is a process aimed at enhancing the way in which resources are allocated, with the goal of satisfying present and future, private as well as social, needs better than before the reform. As such, its features may range from the philosophy of development policies to economic institutions and technical guidelines for economic behavior. These wide-ranging issues, touching on social, political, humanitarian, economic, literary, ideological, and other aspects of society, to a larger or smaller extent, are inextricably intermeshed with economic reforms. Because they cannot possibly be discussed adequately in one brief chapter, here we will emphasize the technical economic aspects of reform. Even in that area, reforms have affected so many aspects of the economy and society that it would not even be possible to list all of them in the space available here. My aim is more modest: in addition to touching on the core objectives of the reform, this chapter briefly describes the most important aspects of reforms in enterprise behavior, wholesale trade, pricing, foreign trade, wage and related benefits, and the financial sector.

Overall Reform Objectives

Variants of the traditional model were tried out in the USSR from the late 1950s until the early 1980s. These include the territorial restructuring of planning and administration introduced in 1957, the managerial decentralization attempted in 1965, and the several experiments to modify the central model launched in the 1970s and early 1980s. As distinct from reforms in Eastern Europe, two features must be pointed out. First, decentralization of management in the USSR remained by and large confined to the administrative streamlining of planning and microeconomic decision making. Even so, policymakers never progressed very far beyond the initial reform stage and thus preserved virtually all elements of the traditional CPE. Second, a major reconsideration of the role of foreign trade in bolstering growth intensification never occurred in the Soviet Union.

In 1987, however, a major new thrust in reshaping Soviet economic policy was launched in line with the call made at the twenty-seventh Party Congress in early 1986 to undertake "radical reform aimed at constructing a new economic mechanism." The reform announcements made since then have been a logical evolution of the reform intentions enunciated since mid-1985, which were themselves based on the managerial experiments of the early 1980s to endow firms with greater responsibility for their own performance. Indeed, policymakers have made it clear that, in spite of recent setbacks, the measures enacted since the June 1987 Plenum of the Central Committee, which envisage mainly the assimilation of new micro- and macroeconomic management methods throughout the economy, constitute only the opening phase of a much broader-based societal reform, whose nature and scope are without precedent. This is also setting an overall sociopolitical environment that is more congenial and, indeed, conducive to launching new economic policies and renewing institutions and policy instruments, even if only on an experimental basis. Of the measures introduced or discussed so far, the position of individual and cooperative firms, foreign economic ties, income distribution, the banking sector, agricultural reform, and property relations have been elaborated the most thoroughly. Other areas are to be tackled soon; some are already in an advanced draft. We cannot do full justice to them here.

Perhaps the most outstanding feature of the perceived need for basic change in the economy is that Soviet policymakers now rule out the earlier piecemeal approaches to reform and openly advocate comprehensive changes that will reverberate throughout society. The present reform strategy reaches well beyond such traditional remedies as shifts in investment policies, partial streamlining of organizational links, and pressuring unprofitable firms to change by administrative means. The new arrangements for the economy at large include reducing the number of centrally set targets; providing firms with considerable latitude in determining employment, wages, prices, and investment; linking managerial incentives to fulfillment of delivery contracts; and requiring firms to finance a greater share of their current and capital outlays from their own revenues. These measures mandate organs of state control to concentrate on strategy and rates and proportions of development, to abstain from interfering in the day-to-day affairs of economic units at lower levels of the planning hierarchy, and to foster the transition from an excessively centralized system of management to one actively encouraging self-management. At the same time, these measures are aimed at eventually demarcating unambiguously the functions of party organs, local government, and socioeconomic organizations in economic decision making. In the end, their success is predicated on fundamentally changing the working style of all sociopolitical and economic organs. Some of the measures are intended as levers to accelerate this attitudinal transformation.

Economic reform is considered to be the key factor in gearing the system of planning and management toward laying the foundations for sustainable per capita growth from gains in factor productivity. It is conceived as a sequence of gradual transformations of economic sectors rather than as an abrupt switch to a completely new, internally consistent, economic mechanism. The reform measures enacted thus far are the first steps in that direction. Continued progress must be ensured through detailed legislation on various aspects of implementing the reform and rounding off its legal interpretation and administrative application.

Another critical feature of the measures adopted in June 1987 is the modification in the philosophy of social ownership and how social property can be rationally allocated. Earlier views advocated that only the state could fully represent the preferences emanating from the social ownership of the means of production, including those appropriated in the microeconomic sphere. With reform, strong support has emerged for the view that the firm, as such, represents the interests of public ownership. The firm is expected to utilize the means of production assigned to it for the benefit of society as a whole under the guidance of an appropriate economic mechanism. Furthermore, whereas previously the state arrogated to itself the right to be the sole owner of the means of production, under some conditions firms can now be owned privately or cooperatively. Provided they are supported by appropriate and simultaneous adjustments in planning procedures and management practices, the practical ramifications of this doctrinal shift can be far-reaching.

Key Sectoral Issues

At the core of the reform provisions stands the creation of an economic environment conducive to self-financing and self-management of firms. To this end, each firm is authorized to adopt annual and five-year plans based on contractual obligations and government orders, and to procure the necessary inputs primarily through wholesale trade. Compulsory state orders are to claim only a fraction of the unit's productive capacity so that direct relations among firms— genuine wholesale trade—can be fostered and detailed planning will not be perpetuated under a different guise. This proper share is to be attained over some transition period.

Firms are expected to bear full responsibility for their overall performance and how they discharge their obligations.[3] Financing of enterprise investments from the central budget is to be restricted to major projects only because bankruptcy and an effective capital market are lacking. Exceptions are for comparatively minor projects in the private and cooperative sectors. Their success is directly determined by the degree of access to inputs and capital goods—hence the importance of wholesale trade. However, even usage of state investments, unlike the case in the traditional planning system, is to be regulated through long-term, stable parameters for payments for fixed assets and natural resources, which complement the norms on labor and profit taxes.

Soviet policymakers emphasize that interfirm competition should be encouraged so as to cater to demand and ease the effects of the monopolistic position of producers in a sellers' market. In addition, firms must move to self-management with the help of Workers' Councils, which elect their own managers. Firms must have considerable leeway in selecting inputs, outputs, and business partners. Fulfillment of contractual obligations is to be the main performance indicator, but the scope for price flexibility under the new potential for competition remains confined by design. For the time being, as long as the sellers' market persists, the state quality-certification agency acts as a surrogate of competition. In the future, however, contractual freedom among state units should stimulate competition.

As a direct counterpart of the emphasis on enterprise autonomy, centralized macroeconomic control should motivate individual agents through appropriate economic levers to optimize the benefits to society as a whole. In addition to streamlined central planning, these levers include financial and credit relations, prices and exchange rates, material and technical supplies, and foreign exchange controls. The central planning agency is entrusted with the elaboration of the concept and the guidelines for the economic and social development of the USSR for the next fifteen years, the five-year plan being the principal instrument of economic control. But the main operative components of the plan should be indicative targets rather than compulsory quotas: long-term stable economic "norms," which are essentially standard ratios between indicators of performance and the distribution of revenue among the central budget, the ministry, and the firm itself according to performance indicators; government orders for the most important products; and quotas for centralized investments and centrally distributed supplies.

The centrally set distribution parameters should prevent the firm from channeling an excessive share of profits into wages and encouraging decision makers to explore new avenues for improving performance. To that end, they should be predictable. Norms are therefore to remain stable in the medium run, perhaps within the context of the five-year plan. The selection of performance indicators and of norms with a view to rewarding improvement as fully as feasible is critical to the thrust of the reform and to steering a steady course toward a fully reconstructed economic mechanism. Organizational innovations include granting firms the right to establish joint production facilities on a cooperative basis or through complete merger. Industrial ministries are to be relieved of executive control over producers. They are to be transformed into centers for the coordination of research and development, the promotion of steady gains in the quality of output and quality control, technological policymaking, and related tasks.

Third, the gradual introduction of genuine wholesale trade in the means of production, including trade in capital goods, to substitute for major components of the present administrative distribution of resources is another salient feature of the reform. Only a comparatively small share of fuel and energy resources, raw materials, and high-technology products are slated to be centrally allocated. Government requests or state orders channeled through the state supply system were initially to be the only exception to the gradual dismantling of the orthodox material-technical supply system in favor of direct interfirm relations. Even they, however, were intended to result from genuine economic bargaining between the center and economic agents, rather than being imposed hierarchically on microeconomic units.

Fourth, directly related to the autonomy of firms and the sustainability of wholesale trade are the soundness of price signals and the availability of bank credit. Because prevailing prices do not reflect scarcities and the mainstream views on price reform continue to stress average sectoral costs plus some profit margin, the role of the price mechanism in the efficient allocation of resources will in effect remain subdued for some time. A major change can occur only if central policymakers decide to proceed with comprehensive price reform and to infuse much greater flexibility into the price system than appears to be envisaged at this stage.

Yet, some commitments were made to shift price determination away from the traditional average cost-plus basis. Increasingly, first for selected products and gradually for a growing number of them, prices are to be contractually determined by supply and demand. Some modest changes have already been made in the system of price markups and discounts for many products to encourage firms to improve product quality, expand their output mix, and introduce new products. The highest placed policymakers have left no doubt that a radical reform of pricing must eventually become an integral part of restructuring. This was initially envisaged to involve a coordinated revision of wholesale, procurement, and retail prices. Industrial and agricultural procurement prices need to reflect scarcity tradeoffs and to provide appropriate guidance for managerial decisions on input–output mixes, including interregional and intertemporal ones, and for the proper assessment of factor productivity. Similarly, retail prices must become a lever for streamlining distribution and balancing consumer markets. An important objective in reforming wholesale prices in particular is to bridge the gap between prices of manufacturing and extractive industries without raising the overall price level. Procurement prices for agricultural products and prices for construction services should increasingly result from stable contractual negotiations. In that respect, macroeconomic policies regarding the overall price level and shifts in relative prices should become an important component of five-year plans with a view to reflecting more fully the tasks and conditions of the national economy. The consumer's role in determining prices is to rise sharply, and price-setting procedures are to be simplified by drastically curtailing the share of centrally determined prices.

Policymakers are hoping to contain the upward pressure on prices by increasing domestic competition, eliminating shortages, and curtailing all forms of monopolistic pressure. Regulations governing contract price negotiations are to be worked out as well. Because retained profits are intended to become the major source of investment financing, firms are expected to become more interested in active price negotiations.

Fifth, the reform seeks to coordinate improvements in the price system with changes in the fiscal and monetary spheres. With regard to fiscal changes, the priorities of gearing monetary circulation to the turnover of material resources, reducing gratuitous disbursements of financial funds for investment purposes, and transferring budgetary receipts on a normative basis are stressed. Budgetary financing of investments is to be restricted to a narrow range of high-priority, goal-specific programs of national importance and is to be kept separate from loans issued by special banks on the basis of the economic viability of the loan request. Money circulation is to be entrusted to the central bank, whereas commercial functions need to be increasingly discharged by specialized banks.

In this connection, policymakers are keen to consolidate the purchasing power of the ruble at home and to create the conditions necessary to utilize it in foreign transactions. Given the dichotomy between domestic and external pricing systems, ruble convertibility is potentially a critical objective of change, a beacon for policymakers rather than a short-term policy goal. Convertibility of the ruble would require substantial institutional and policy transformations, in addition to those currently set in train (Brabant, 1989c).

The reorganization of banking institutions involves giving them complete financial accountability and creating for them adequate incentives to improve the return on loans, making the financial performance of firms a basic criterion for loan disbursements, and preventing intraministerial redistribution of circulating capital, depreciation funds, and profits among subordinate firms. The first practical step in this direction was set in July 1987 with the establishment of six specialized banks. Since then many more have been created primarily in the cooperative sector but also in cooperation with foreign banks.[4] A major impetus was provided by the ineffectiveness of the reorganization of banking introduced in 1987 and 1988 (Bogdonkevich and Zayash, 1988; Sheludko, 1988).

Sixth, provisions of the reforms call for strengthening the link between labor remuneration and productivity. This endeavor is to be fostered by the wide-scale introduction of the collective contract system (which governs the determination of wages and bonuses), by making enterprise profits the sole source of the social consumption fund, and by lifting all restrictions on combining jobs. The wage reform, finalized in January 1988, in essence grants firms nearly full rights and imposes on them corresponding obligations, in setting payment scales according to merit and productivity within the provisions of the total wage fund. The reform sets growth in labor productivity as the upper limit for the expansion of nominal wages, which itself has to be wholly financed from enterprise profits and thus can be introduced as firms earn resources.

Instead of clinging to the de facto lifetime job guarantee, the labor reform emphasizes the urgency of utilizing labor more effectively. This may require temporary layoffs, whose adverse implications need to be mitigated by providing, in effect, unemployment compensation. This is being introduced in conjunction with the creation of a network of job placement centers entrusted with relocating and retraining workers. These centers themselves are to be self-financing from placement commissions. Labor mobility is to be encouraged to staff private and cooperative enterprises under the provisions of the draft law of March 1988. This legislation may be enacted in anticipation of what, in a decade or so, may amount to a massive redeployment of 15 to 17 million workers.

Fostering labor productivity through wage and related incentives places higher demands on the process of diversification of assets available to households and especially the supply of consumer goods with a high income elasticity. To meet these demands, the provisions adopted also establish a framework for changing the composition of output. An urgent task is to balance supply and demand in retail markets. Recently enacted provisions on private and cooperative ventures, which have been described as ''market medics'' (*Pravda*, March 10, 1988, p. 3), are aimed especially at improving the supply of consumer goods and alleviating price pressures.

Seventh, although reform has emerged more slowly in agriculture than in industry, provisions are now in place that permit farms to sell a larger share of production at decontrolled prices and to market products more flexibly. Many arrangements already introduced in the industrial sector, such as normative planning, self-financing, and the use of contracts, are to be extended to farms too. Emphasis on local decision making, within the context of the contract brigades or similar farm production units, is evident. Such units are allocated land and livestock on a long-term contractual basis. Remuneration is based on output.

These important features of the rural reform provide the basis for the functional decentralization of decision making in agriculture, which may lead to a breakthrough in the level and composition of farm output. Because of the disappointing results (in part because independence eludes farm managers and infringements of their rights are widespread), agricultural reform is not at all straightforward. In the meantime, further changes have been enacted in terms of long-term leasing of land and making such rights transferable. The rural sector is increasingly encouraged to foster small-scale private or cooperative firms, including in manufacturing activities and services, to mobilize available resources, to facilitate the redeployment of labor, to enhance the allocation of capital in rural segments of the economy, and indeed to improve consumer supplies.

Finally, a core focus of the reform architects was the potential contribution of foreign economic relations to renewing the Soviet economy. The law on foreign economic activity introduced in 1986 essentially has three components: (1) decentralization of foreign economic decisions in favor of selected firms, trade organizations, and republican offices; (2) the enabling law on joint ventures; and (3) changes in the macroeconomic administration of Soviet foreign trade, including in the Ministry of Foreign Trade, which was ultimately abolished, and the administration of foreign exchange controls. A logical component of the law, though not detailed there, was facilitating direct enterprise relations.

Equally important is looking at the instruments put in place to facilitate these direct trading transactions. Rather than keep separating domestic from foreign prices and allocating foreign exchange by central fiat, the foreign trade law ushered in three important changes in that regime. For one, firms would now be entitled to negotiate prices directly. Second, their profitability would be codetermined through the use of "currency coefficients" or different de facto exchange rates.[5] Finally, they would be entitled to currency retention quotas that would be at their disposal to finance imports and possibly to sell in the domestic market at a different rate from the official exchange rate, with a minimum of interference from the supervisory ministry.

The foreign trade reforms are expected ultimately to affect trade with all partners. The most visible effects are likely to be in Council for Mutual Economic Assistance (CMEA) relations, about which Soviet dissatisfaction has been pronounced for many years. These feelings have been further sharpened by the Soviet drive to reform the CMEA institutions, redraw integration policies, and generally improve the environment for synergetic reforms throughout the CMEA. Progress is being made as a result of a sequence of high-level meetings since November 1986 (Brabant, 1989a) on several different fronts. These include the organizational structure of CMEA; policies with respect to development assistance to the non-European members of CMEA—Cuba, Mongolia, and Vietnam (Brabant, 1989b); the formulation of a new integration strategy for the period 1991–2005 to come to grips with the severe internal and domestic economic constraints faced by virtually all of Eastern Europe in the early 1980s, to enhance effective production specialization, and to lay the groundwork for the eventual establishment of a socialist common market; the redesign of planning, monetary, and financial cooperation mechanisms in light of ongoing and desirable reform processes in key CPEs; and the invigoration of the economics of interfirm relations and the pivotal need to invest such relations with economic guidance rules and institutional instruments to facilitate management. Although many elements of these debates sound familiar from past reform attempts that miscarried, there is now cause for cautious optimism (Brabant, 1989a).

Soviet reforms are likely to have major repercussions on trade and financial relations with MEs. Given Soviet intentions to raise exports of manufactures markedly over the next decade or so, new markets will need to be explored. The developing countries (DEs) might constitute profitable outlets, particularly for products embodying medium-level technology, provided a commercial *quid pro quo* can be struck as a result of gearing the Soviet economy more to its comparative advantage. There is ample room to phase out labor-intensive processes and redirect such demand to imports. Soviet policymakers have already indicated that there is ample room for all DEs to capitalize on Soviet markets, and that access will be facilitated.

In relations between the Soviet economy and other MEs, Soviet reforms are likely to have a number of distinct impacts. The joint-venture provisions are probably better suited to these relations than to those with DEs or even with other CPEs, especially if effective decentralization of commercial decision making takes hold. Policymakers are bent on reducing the relative importance of raw materials in their exports and on promoting manufactures. Capturing such markets is predicated on considerable "investment" in retooling, marketing, setting up servicing infrastructure, and the like, which may have to be financed mainly through borrowing from global financial centers.

To realize those trade and external finance goals, the Soviet Union may also have to explore the possibilities of establishing relations with the existing international trading, financial, and monetary systems in spite of long-standing misgivings. It seems to be bent on pursuing the first, in the context of GATT, with considerable vigor (Brabant, 1991).

LEGACIES AFFECTING REFORM IMPLEMENTATION

So far, the economic reform has had a much smaller impact on economic performance than Soviet policymakers had anticipated, and there have been marked deviations from the reform precepts. Weaknesses have been of two kinds. Perhaps most conspicuous are the inconsistency, incoherence, and contradictory nature of various reform measures. Even more critical is that by necessity reforms have to be superimposed on the model in place and hence have to grapple willy-nilly with the legacies of the centralized system.[6] In spite of the protracted experience of CPE reform, Soviet policymakers have vastly underestimated the crucial role of the starting conditions, hoping perhaps that sheer hortatory proclamations would suffice to instill a new spirit in economic agents. Among the many weaknesses, we will touch on only four here:

Regarding the microeconomic sphere, provisions on enterprise self-financing are well ahead of effective economic reorganization and price reform. As a result, profits necessarily reflect the lack of competition, administratively fixed prices, and the prevailing structure of fixed assets that firms themselves are unable to improve on in the medium run for lack of funds. Even those accounting profits are subject to confusing rules on how and by whom profit distribution is determined. Emerging price flexibility, who can monitor it, and what criteria will govern the creation and distribution of credit are incompletely resolved critical issues in formulating enterprise policies.

The results of the experiment in self-financing to date indicate the pervasiveness of the legacies of the traditional approach to management, as exemplified by the overwhelming weight still attached to volume indicators, particularly gross output. Although volume of sales and tradeable output is increasingly used as a performance indicator instead of gross output, ministries still consider the output increment over the level achieved in the previous year—the so-called ratchet principle—to be the central criterion of success. Attempts to exert administrative pressure to coax agents into fulfilling unbalanced and unrealistic plans continue to encourage shortages, disrupting smooth operations. The intention to have firms and central bodies negotiate over contracts has failed because of the inertia of traditional administrative practice. This has enabled central bodies to resort to compulsory assignments, including those on the mix and volume of output,[7] through administrative pressure, even without the ministries ensuring the requisite resources. The share of state orders in total enterprise output (hence, central control over output) has remained very high.[8] Control indicators, which were to replace mandatory quotas and norms for different aspects of enterprise performance previously imposed by the center, continue to be imposed by the ministerial bureaucracy in part because the bureaucracy is held responsible for ensuring planned output volume. Because plan fulfillment is perceived as the ministries' foremost political task, it gives them powerful leverage over subordinate economic agents.[9] Attempts to curb inefficient production have been largely ineffectual as firms lack flexibility. To mitigate this problem, the long-term leasing of firms by employees from state agencies has been promoted since late 1988 and has been reported to have increased productivity and efficiency. The state seeks to expand the experiment as well as to pursue the formal bankruptcy of unprofitable firms (Rysina, 1988, p. 5).

Because of the vagueness of legal details, definitions, and interpretations of reform regulations, in particular on norms and state orders, the impact of the reform measures has been seriously blunted and implementation of many measures has been slowed down.[10] In the same vein, norms lack uniformity and fluctuate too much, which puts additional pressure on firms already working efficiently and yields windfall gains to those with concealed reserves. The administrative sequestering of retained depreciation funds occurs, as do arbitrary changes in output quotas, supply allocations, and surcharges for extra quality and export production. All this undermines investment capabilities and financial stability of de jure self-financing firms. The profit tax is as yet not governed by economic considerations, and managers continue to expect ministries to muster emergency financial aid in case of a liquidity crisis.

Similarly, the shape and scope of the emerging wholesale trade in the means of production are as yet unclear. Efforts to stimulate it are being thwarted by persistent shortages and imbalances that encourage hoarding. In spite of attempts to combine a more balanced central plan with microeconomic autonomy and adequate incentives to husband scarce inputs, the scale of the state supply system cannot be compressed noticeably in the short run. Confusion about transforming the material-supply system into genuine wholesale trade, aggravated by imbalances between financial and material resources, seriously impairs the practical impact of these reform provisions.

The gradual approach to reform and the phasing in of the transition regime during a protracted period of time may also exacerbate the contradiction between short- and long-term development goals. An abrupt switch to a new economic mechanism away from target output increments is too risky. However, in the long term, gradualism may seriously weaken the impact of reform measures and undermine their effect on economic efficiency. In this connection, it is important to ensure internal coherence through proper coordination of the different components of the reforming economic mechanism. Microeconomic autonomy is a function not only of the financial resources at the disposal of a firm, but also of gaining access to inputs and the ability to negotiate over input and output prices. These in turn depend on the flexibility of the distribution system. Results to date have not been particularly encouraging. However, as a result of pressures on inefficient firms and the creation of greater autonomy through leasing and share financing,[11] the volume of genuine wholesale trade has increased markedly since mid-1988, in part because firms could exchange surplus goods and those produced above planned output.

Another important element of flexibility has been through the creation of cooperatives, whose number grew from 3,700 in July 1987 to nearly 50,000 at year-end 1988 and has continued to expand since. Although total employment in this sector is still less than 1 percent of the labor force (*Ekonomicheskaya gazeta*, 1988: 52, p. 4), the potential for rapid growth is present. The liberalization of the legal and fiscal regulations of the sector in 1988, including the formation of their own banks (*Izvestiya*, August 26, 1988, p. 1), has had a salutary impact.

Arguably the core of the reform concerns pricing. Key here is the adjustment in relative prices in line with at least prevailing domestic economic scarcities. This adjustment may exert an upward push on the price level, given the sheer differential weight of the commodity classes whose relative prices need to be revised. This inflationary impact in terms of statistical indicators is much less worrisome than the one caused by a genuine drift in absolute prices on account of inherited and prevailing imbalances. In particular, the inherited monetary overhang exerts upward price pressure in a reforming CPE. In addition, the monopolistic nature of the economic structure and the unfamiliarity with market operations, if authorities are indeed encouraging the emergence of real competitive markets, are likely to push prices up. Instead of reflecting underlying economic scarcities, these adjustments represent rents that accrue because of highly fragmented Soviet markets.

Third, it is regrettable that Soviet reformers have waited so long to come to terms with the monetary overhang and the continuing fiscal imbalance. However uneasy this may render decision making, it is a technical matter that economic experts should have addressed head on. Unfortunately, Gorbachev has not been getting the kind of technical economic advice that would have enabled him to assess for himself the real options at his disposal, even without encroaching on the ideology of socialist property. On the contrary, some of his advisers have been dead wrong on critical issues, including the disastrous fiscal consequences, wanton capital destruction, and consumer frustrations over the anti-alcohol campaign. But there are other instances.

Potentially the most serious issue in keeping the reform on track stems from the conflict between the goals of reconstruction (*perestroika*) and growth acceleration (*uskorenie*), which was taken as the key twin slogans at the outset of the reform. High growth targets have usually meant "taut" planning. Full resource utilization normally generates tensions and shortages that could call for dysfunctional intervention by the central authorities. This, in turn, could legitimize bargaining for temporary exemptions (such as subsidies, tax treatment, additional allocations, and permission to hoard resources) from the reform measures. The ambition to step up growth has therefore had to be sharply reduced by emphasizing the quality of growth so as to accommodate steady reform of the economic mechanism, but this has not worked out well.

Perhaps the gravest shortcoming of Soviet reforms is that most policymakers and often their economic advisers have shown only the barest understanding of the intricate functioning of economies once the basic strategy of central planning is abandoned by fiat. In particular, they have not been very imaginative—or successful for that matter—in formulating what they would like to see emerge from the transition phase, in assessing the realism of these policy goals, and indeed in designing the transition phase with a view to minimizing its adverse impacts. Especially marked has been the scant attention paid to the need to formulate a coherent macroeconomic policy of the reforming and reformed CPE. Yet, such is absolutely required to underpin the reform with the proper institutions for monetary and fiscal policy, and indeed to widen the scope of indirect economic policy instruments and, where needed, to innovate such instruments and their necessary institutional supports. This is all the more startling as reforms simultaneously require massive structural adjustment, economic stabilization, and current macroeconomic policy for a more market-oriented type of decision making. Separating the compatability of the basics of socialism—not necessarily of societal control—with technical instruments and institutions of market-oriented economies from areas that may give rise to serious sociopolitical and ideological conflicts is pivotal to designing more effective reform policies and minimizing their adjustment costs.

Fourth, the most impressive change envisaged in the foreign trading system was the dissolution of one essential aspect of the MFT, namely, the devolution of the operational activities resorting under the MFT to firms, republican ministries, and related organizations. This was odd, to say the least, since this decentralization applied only to selected manufacturing sectors, and hence a comparatively small component of trade. The newly gained independence of lower level organs was highly circumscribed because of inflexible BTPAs with CPEs, and the bulk of exports to MEs comprises goods excluded from the decentralization drive. Similarly, on the import side a good part consists of foodstuffs, and, as far as manufactures are concerned, decentralized units in any case had to generate their own foreign exchange to import.

The foreign trade reform has also suffered from the fact that it was drawn up without thorough preparation of home firms or foreign partners, including CMEA members, and without a comprehensive assessment of how it could fit into the planning framework. Domestic firms unaccustomed to competing for markets have been bewildered about the best way to take advantage of their newly acquired latitude. Furthermore, the financial and related infrastructure for direct trade relations was inadequate. Weak energy export earnings and rising prices for manufactures procured in MEs did not help either. Even considerable borrowing did not suffice to permit policymakers to foster the modernization of engineering sectors that had been so vigorously encouraged in the 1986–90 plan. Finally, as regards infusing the CMEA with new life and thus finding support for modernization and domestic reforms throughout the group, disappointment has been pervasive (see Brabant, 1989a). Results can only be expected slowly.

The tepid response in foreign trade prompted the authorities to change course. In October 1988 the Politburo called for a radical expansion of foreign trade and a gradual move toward ruble convertibility. These new reforms were set forth in a decree in early December 1988 which, as of April 1, 1989, permits all firms regardless of ownership to engage in trade on their own account. New commercial policy regulations are to be worked out, and a law on foreign trade will be prepared. The decree also calls for the proper fiscal regulation of foreign exchange earnings, the introduction of a uniform exchange rate by phasing out the thousands of currency coefficients, and currency auctions under the auspices of the state bank. Moreover, the joint-venture law has been further relaxed in the sense that foreign majority ownership is now allowed, with more flexible rules on labor. In mid-1989 about 250 joint-venture agreements were signed, but the bulk had not yet commenced operations on a meaningful scale.

DESIRABLE DIRECTIONS OF ECONOMIC REFORMS

To come to grips with the fundamental determinants of the long-term decline in the pace of growth and chronic domestic and external imbalances, technological innovation and modernization are required. Transferring producers expeditiously to a system of full-cost accounting and motivating top management to maintain stable growth are the most important issues on the policy agenda for the next several years. By 1990 reforms of finances, wholesale prices (retail prices having been indefinitely postponed), banking, and the replacement of the material-supply system by wholesale trade are slated to be completed. That is, the main task ahead is to improve the economic mechanism, making it more consistent and transparent to strengthen managerial autonomy, the legal basis for public scrutiny of economic activity, and the reform of pricing and banks, while at the same time eliminating contradictions of the CPE in transition.

The Costs of the Transition Phase

The years ahead will be characterized by painful adjustments, difficult choices, and at times tumultuous socioeconomic and political debates whose intensity is unlikely to abate during the early 1990s. As outlined, measures to provide for an orderly transition to the new economic mechanism are as yet incompletely defined. Nonetheless, they need to be at the center of reform efforts in the years to come if only to compress the adjustment burden to the inevitable minimum through proper policy design and unwavering commitment. Unambiguous and tangible results of the ambitious economic reform are not likely to become transparent until well into the 1990s, when the interrelated problems of price, finance, and wholesale trade will have been tackled. Even that will succeed only with persistence and the political will of the leadership to remove ambiguities and outright distortions in implementing reform measures, and thus gain a solid economic footing. This commitment can materialize only if the active support of the population for economic reorganization is mustered, in spite of slow benefits and growing uncertainty as regards job security, prices, and incomes, and the resistance to reform of those whose social standing, privileges, and influence the reform may jeopardize.

Coming to Grips with Setbacks

The postwar track record on modifying CPEs is unambiguous: Reforms are rarely viewed holistically or formulated into a clear blueprint (comprehensive plan if you wish) that is implemented according to a set schedule, and they invariably face internal and external obstacles that were not at all or not fully heeded when the reform was conceptualized. Instead, a reform is essentially a process of learning even at the highest party and government levels. Hence, the prevalence in all reforms of instability, even outright vacillation, in rules and regulations; disagreement or divergent views on what is to be done and how changes should preferably be carried out; and willingness quickly to intervene through recentralization rather than tolerance for the zigzagging are necessary concomitants of any societal transformation process. In any case, there appears to be one constant: Regardless of the ambitious nature of the reform, it invariably falls short of the goals envisioned at its inception; the Soviet experiment is no exception, as may be seen from the genesis of the transition.

At the start of the current Soviet reform process, the reformers strongly focused on ensuring the swift realization of fairly straightforward administrative decentralization. Through this device, policymakers expected self-financing economic agents to be in a position to utilize more fully their local knowledge and latitude for initiative with a view to improving their microeconomic performance. Through sociopolitical coaxing (such as the anti-shirking campaign) or draconian legal measures (such as the anti-alcohol campaign) purely temporary benefits were generated. It took time for the leadership to realize that more was needed to ensure steady growth. As a result, both the depth and scope of the ambition of the reform were redrawn as outlined. However, in a situation characterized by pervasive monopoly power, allowing firms some scope for negotiating input and output prices is bound to generate large swings as firms adjust their production and marketing profile to new success criteria and take advantage of their monopoly power. This is particularly the case when local parameters of choice are not the proper ones from a social point of view, and the gap is aggravated by greed, exploitation, aberrations, loopholes in macroeconomic control, or slack in supervision.

Under the circumstances, policymakers have little choice but to tolerate the aberrations or to sit back and redesign the phasing of the reform. Soviet policymakers appear to find themselves in that position once again and are consequently confronted with many painful choices. Perhaps the most difficult choice derives from the conflict between rectifying the idiosyncratic price system, and yet ensuring equity and social stability.

Inflationary Impacts of Reform

As argued earlier, it is critical that policymakers distinguish between movements in relative and absolute prices and take prices to mean all kinds of indirect economic indicators (such as rents, interest rates, wage schedules, and exchange rates). The primary emphasis of the reform should be on changing relative prices, because those are what in the end matter in promoting a more efficient allocation of resources. However, in an environment with a pervasive monetary overhang, upward price pressures are bound to manifest themselves. Tackling the overliquidity of the economy in a transitional period presents perhaps the key technical problem of moving toward a more transparent price system.

Although policymakers have committed themselves to comprehensive price reform, it is as yet unclear which prices will be set by administrative *fiat* and which by direct agreements between producers and purchasers and on what basis these levels can proceed. From the ongoing policy discussions, the majority of wholesale prices will initially be reset on a cost-plus basis. The flareup in retail prices in late 1988 and early 1989 led to social unrest, which in turn forced the Soviet government to postpone indefinitely the retail price reform that had been envisaged for 1991. This is most regrettable. If firms are not granted some leeway over retail prices, the kind of rationalization that can be engineered on the basis of redesigned wholesale prices becomes sharply limited. Reportedly, a revision of wholesale prices is still being planned for early 1991, but it remains to be seen how the authorities will cope with the firms' inability to pass on changes in their input costs.

Pressures on absolute prices will not abate unless a variety of measures are introduced to divert the monetary overhang and gain control over current imbalances. The latter is a matter for proper current macroeconomic policy. Meeting the challenge of the inherited monetary overhang, however, is a much more difficult task that may require using some unpalatable policy measures. These measures may range from confiscating the monetary overhang to creating a diversity of financial assets for households. The first extreme is no longer a real policy option without Gorbachev losing much of his already tarnished credibility with the Soviet consumer. The second extreme touches on a number of exceedingly sensitive policy precepts, including private property, partial divestment of state and cooperative property, the setting of positive real interest rates to foster long-term savings, and the earmarking of foreign exchange for procuring goods and services to be placed on the domestic market at a realistic exchange rate, one that is slightly better than the black market rate.

None of the proposed alternatives is by itself likely to correct the built-in inflationary pressures in their entirety. However, a proper combination of policy options, of which a useful start was made in mid-1989, including extra foreign exchange earmarking, buildup of cooperative and private property, long-term government bonds at a positive real interest rate, and others might be required and might go a long way toward blotting up the monetary overhang and restoring consumer confidence in the currency. The share to be reserved for each measure is an important consideration, but it is not easily determined. Whether this will suffice to bring down inflationary pressures to an acceptable level remains to be seen, however.

Reallocating Resources and External Relations

Thinking in technical terms about CPE reform is to envisage resource reallocation, the depreciation or scrapping of certain assets, the retraining or pensioning off of labor, and the capital expenditure required to emplace new policies with their institutions and instruments to reset priorities and tradeoffs of economic agents. This is not very different from adjustment in any other economy. Yet, being fully cognizant of such capital costs has not been a high priority for top-level economists and policymakers in the Soviet Union or other CPEs for that matter.

Rather than design the reform around the above issues, policymakers and their advisers initially placed great faith in the contribution from abroad to domestic reform, including regaining a comparatively high pace of economic growth and facilitating economic restructuring through joint ventures, free trade zones, loans, and similar measures. These were not fully embedded in a coherent program of economic change, and policymakers have become only weakly cognizant of the potentially disastrous cost of forging a reformed market through such channels, particularly when trade in manufactures accounts for a small share of the overall economy. The unwarranted optimism regarding foreign relations, given the sharp dichotomies between domestic and foreign markets and the palpable disparities between CMEA and East-West markets, is even less understandable and may in part stem from a fundamental lack of appreciation of how markets operate.

The Role of Agriculture in Reform

Reforms that have encountered some measure of success, including reforms in China and Hungary, have typically started with agriculture. At first glance, this way of tackling the manifold issues of reforming a CPE may seem odd. However, in order to come to grips with existing disequilibria and to ignite the change in economic structures, quick and visible results are more easily obtained from reforming agriculture and, as China and Hungary did so successfully in terms of output and income gains, by permitting shifts in the organization and management of rural activities.

Regrettably, Soviet reformers have waited a long time to capitalize on the initiative and flexibility of the rural sector, including through the leasing of equipment and allocating resources to nonagricultural activities. Chronic shortages in agricultural production, shortcomings in bringing in harvests and ensuring reliable supplies, and in the distribution of foodstuffs to retail markets must have been known to policymakers. In addition, the problems of raising productivity and production per se in the agricultural sector and the ability to diversify into industrial activities cannot have escaped the current leadership. The most probable explanations are ideological inhibitions regarding the disintegration of agricultural cooperatives, which were after all a truly Soviet invention, and reluctance to distinguish between property and property rights, a basic conundrum of socialism since the inception of Soviet power. Inadequate understanding of the best way to operate the rural resources also contributed to the painfully slow recognition of the vital contribution of the sector to stability and reform.

The authorities have only gradually recognized that the command system has given farmers little autonomy and even fewer incentives to raise output. Because piecemeal measures proved to be ineffective, in March 1989 corrective actions were taken, allowing individual farmers and their associations, possibly small cooperatives, to take long-term leases on land and fixed assets; phasing out unprofitable cooperatives under laws on land use yet to be promulgated; and introducing self-financing and autonomy to the farm. The measures also promised that soon steps will be taken to overhaul the price and credit system and eventually to abolish food subsidies (*Pravda*, March 16, 1989, p. 1).

Macroeconomic Policy at the Crossroads

Perhaps the most striking feature of the reform process in CPEs is the rather casual way in which the problem of coordinating decisions and the institutional infrastructure and policy instruments required to do so has traditionally been treated (Brabant, 1989d). Rarely has the leadership of a reforming CPE deliberated about a coherent technical framework to replace central planning as the chief coordinating mechanism. Yet, coordination is central in devolving decision making from the higher to the lower tiers of the economic hierarchy in the expectation of thereby enhancing the efficiency of resource allocation. This entails, among other things, moving away from rather inflexible, if not necessarily rigid, central planning to an environment that is expected to correct the perceived shortcomings of implementing the "centrally planned" design. Proper policy coordination may require frequent finetuning of policies, institutions, and instruments in response to performance assessments, with a view to guiding the reform back on track. Professional and technical appraisals of inevitable disruptions and adjustment costs cannot, of course, take ascendancy over the political process. However, technically warranted advice phrased within the context of decentralized coordination should constitute one critical input into the decision making of the socialist political leadership.

In this connection, the question that arises is, what should statewide economic policy in a reformed CPE be all about? Clearly, differences between social and private preferences need to be bridged by "guiding" or "intervening" in purely privately motivated decisions; sociopolitical preferences need to be safeguarded centrally, though implemented according to reformed rules of the game; the nonmaterial sphere remains largely under central control; and infrastructural and large-scale projects need to be initiated at the top level, though certainly not in an economic vacuum. There may be wide agreement about these priorities and responsibilities. Rarely is it realized, however, that such a new constitutional arrangement has to emerge from the economic structures, institutions, and policy instruments—the economic model—in place rather than in a vacuum.

In this respect, those who are managing the transition toward a reformed setup must institute comprehensive monetary and fiscal policies to steer the behavior of individual agents. Furthermore, proper incomes and price policies are needed to enhance social priorities. In economies that wish to integrate themselves into the global economy, these macroeconomic policies must also encompass commercial policies. Instituting coherent macroeconomic policies in lieu of traditional central planning is an exceedingly complex assignment, if only because the traditional CPE has not been deeply concerned about them, given the supreme role of central planning in all economic affairs.

CONCLUSIONS

Policies in the years ahead should be constructed around three major themes. First is economic stabilization. Gaining control over monetary and fiscal affairs in a decentralizing environment is an absolute necessity. At the same time it requires that policymakers come to grips with the monetary overhang to ease legacies from the past that are choking ongoing flows. Second, the issues of reform and its transition phase need to be addressed, though they might usefully be linked to both stabilization and laying the groundwork for sustainable growth. Here price reform and genuine wholesale trade rank at the top of the agenda. Finally, formulating proper macroeconomic policies for a reformed CPE continues to be a critical task. In this connection, questions arise as to the role of monetary and fiscal policies in a society that professes to be socialist and the degree to which they need to be complemented with incomes and price policies to safeguard social priorities without exacerbating inflationary pressures.

NOTES

1. There are, of course, other prices, such as prices for handicraft and free peasant markets (see Brabant, 1987a, pp. 129–63), but the three regimes outlined will do.

2. For CMEA trade, a special transferable ruble price (TRP) mechanism was inaugurated in 1958, although some of the core principles were first applied in the postwar BTPAs between the Soviet Union and Eastern Europe (see Brabant, 1987b).

3. By the end of 1988, nineteen thousand industrial associations and enterprises, accounting for 55 percent of the industrial labor force and producing about 60 percent of industrial output, were operating on the basis of full economic accountability and self-financing (*Izvestiya*, December 9, 1988, p. 2). In the course of 1989, virtually all economic activities should function according to this regime.

4. During 1988 alone, forty-one commercial banks were created, of which twenty-four were organized cooperatively (Zakharov, 1989, p. 9). In mid-1989 there were no fewer than eighty-five commercial banks separately from at least fifty cooperative ones (*Moscow Narodny Bank Bulletin* 18 (1989), p. 20–24.

5. These are essentially purchasing power parities calculated at some point in time for highly selected groups of goods and services, possibly identified by commodity groups, trade direction, or currency of settlement, or even a combination thereof. For details, see Brabant (1987a), pp. 198–207.

6. For an interesting evaluation, see the interview with Leonid Abalkin in *Ogonek* 13 (1989): 6–7, 18–20.

7. In direct contradiction to the provision that they deal only with final products, state orders are often issued for intermediate goods and services (see Figurnov, 1988 and *Ekonomicheskaya gazeta* 3 (1989): 5).

8. Thus, in 1988 state orders on average accounted for 91.6 percent of output in machine building, 92.1 percent in metallurgy, and 97.2 percent in fuel and energy, whereas for many other branches and firms they covered 100 percent of production plans. Plans for 1989 envisaged reducing compulsory output quotas to less than 60 percent of output in most sectors but to only 25 percent in the machine-building industry (*Pravda*, December 19, 1988, p. 2), but these plans have thus far been only partially carried out.

9. Details on these issues can be found throughout the daily press. For examples, see *Izvestiya*, January 11, 1988, and *Ekonomicheskaya gazeta* 7 (1988), 14.

10. Sharp cutbacks in the ministerial bureaucracy have disrupted the vertical network

of management and demoralized the civil service, thus continuing to further impede swift decision making (*Sotsialisticheskaya industriya*, May 13, 1989, p. 2).

11. The regulations were promulgated in late 1988; see *Ekonomicheskaya gazeta* 45 (1988): 23.

REFERENCES

Bogdonkevich, S., and V. Zayash. "A nuzhny li spetsbanki?" *Ekonomicheskaya gazeta* 51 (1988): 19.

Brabant, Jozef M. van. *Socialist Economic Integration—Aspects of Contemporary Economic Problems in Eastern Europe*. New York and Cambridge: Cambridge University Press, 1980.

Brabant, Jozef M. van. *Adjustment, Structural Change, and Economic Efficiency—Aspects of Monetary Cooperation in Eastern Europe*. New York and Cambridge: Cambridge University Press, 1987a.

Brabant, Jozef M. van. *Regional Price Formation in Eastern Europe—On the Theory and Practice of Trade Pricing*. Dordrecht-Boston-Lancaster: Kluwer Academic Publishers, 1987b.

Brabant, Jozef M. van. *Economic Integration in Eastern Europe—A Reference Book*. Hemel Hempstead: Harvester Wheatsheaf, 1989a.

Brabant, Jozef M. van. "Socialist Countries and Development Assistance." In *Alternatives to Superpower Competition in the Third World—Latin America and Beyond*, edited by John Weeks. New York: New York University Press, 1989b.

Brabant, Jozef M. van. "Ruble Convertibility in the Reform Process—A Sobering Note." Paper presented at the conference on Foreign Capital and Monetizing the Soviet Economy, Middlebury, Vt., October 1–4, 1989c.

Brabant, Jozef M. van. "Economic Policy Aims and Their Implementation—Summary." In *Economic Reforms in the European Centrally Planned Economies*, New York: United Nations, published by Adeco, Geneva, for the United Nations, 1989d, pp. 219–25.

Brabant, Jozef M. van. *The Planned Economies and International Economic Organizations*. Cambridge: Cambridge University Press, forthcoming.

Brabant, Jozef M. van. "Trade Policies in the Council for Mutual Economic Assistance." In *National Trade Policies*, edited by Dominick Salvatore. Westport, Conn.: Greenwood Press, 1991.

Brabant, Jozef M. van. "Is There a Place for Socialist Integration in the 1990s?" In *CMEA in the 1990s*, edited by Vladimir Sobel. Boulder, Colo.: Westview Press, forthcoming.

Figurnov, Evsey. "Zakazyvaet tot, kto platit." *Ekonomicheskaya gazeta* 6 (1988): 5.

Grote, Gerhard. "Einige theoretische und praktische Fragen des staatlichen Monopols auf dem Gebiet der Aussenwirtschaft." *Wirtschaftswissenschaft* 2 (1981): 143–52.

Konstantinov, Yuriy A. "Valyutnaya sistema sotsialisticheskogo gosudarstva." *Finansy SSSR* 3 (1984): 28–35.

Lawson, Colin. "Exchange Rates, Tax-Subsidy Schemes, and the Revenue from Foreign Trade in a Centrally Planned Economy." *Economics of Planning* 1/2 (1988): 72–77.

Petrakov, Nikolay Ya. "Planovaya tsena v sisteme upravleniya narodnym chozyayst-vom." *Voprosy ekonomiki* 1 (1987): 44–55.

Petrakov, Nikolay Ya. "Tsena—rychag upravleniya." *Ekonomicheskaya gazeta* 16 (1986): 10.

Rysina, T. "Arenda." *Ekonomicheskaya gazeta* 48 (1988): 5.

Sheludko, I. "Bank: chto meshaet stat' partnerom." *Ekonomicheskaya gazeta* 50 (1988): 10.

Wolf, Thomas A. *Foreign Trade in the Centrally Planned Economy*. Chur, Switzerland: Harwood, 1988.

Zakharov, V. "Novye banki—zachem oni?" *Ekonomicheskaya gazeta* 2 (1989): 9.

11

NATIONAL ECONOMIC POLICIES IN POLAND

Dariusz K. Rosati

INTRODUCTION

The economic history of Poland after World War II displayed characteristic cyclical behavior. Periods of accelerated growth fueled by extensive investment programs, implemented at the cost of stagnating or declining consumption, were followed by periods of rapidly growing disequilibria and social discontent. The increasingly outspoken calls that emerged for economic and social reforms were invariably rejected by the conservative bureaucratic and party apparatus, leading eventually to popular protests and ending typically with more or less far-reaching changes in the government. New authorities, while assuming office, rushed to respond to social expectations with promises of radical reforms. Once firmly in power, however, they became increasingly reluctant to make any significant concessions. Instead, they tried to solve chronic economic problems with the use of traditional, "nonsystemic" measures, like temporarily reducing the rate of investment, squeezing resources from traditional and private sectors (agriculture, light industry, handicrafts) and diverting them to preferred sectors (heavy industry, mining and energy, manufacturing), borrowing from abroad, or simply printing more money (see Brada, Hewett, and Wolf, 1988). But no real systemic and policy adjustments were ultimately made. It is in this sense that the economic history of postwar Poland is the history of "aborted" reforms—in 1956, 1971, and 1981–82.

Each cycle ended with more violent and widespread protests, and therefore the new cycle started with more radical reform programs. Yet, the economic situation was gradually deteriorating, with inflation, shortages, and foreign balance deficits growing higher and higher. The fourth consecutive major crisis that occurred in 1988–89 not only was the most severe of all, but it also produced a long awaited political breakthrough. For the first time after World War II, a noncommunist government assumed power in Poland, embarking immediately on a radical reform program.

There are several reasons why the consecutive reform attempts in postwar Poland repeatedly failed. The most fundamental cause was probably rooted in the totalitarian political system adopted in Poland in the late 1940s under pressure from the Soviet Union. The Communist party rule of Stalinist vintage was based on highly centralized decision making and overwhelming state control over the economy. By contrast, the essential idea of economic reforms was always to make the economy decentralized, allowing for more freedom in economic activities. The two concepts were obviously incompatible, and their (partial) reconciliation was possible only for a very short time, under conditions of emergency, when social discontent was becoming dangerous for the stability of the system. That is why periodical efforts to introduce progressive reform were always quickly abandoned, yielding to old, centralized, bureaucratic, and politically dominated methods of economic regulation.

Another reason for the lack of progress was that subsequent reform programs displayed numerous conceptual and operational deficiencies and flaws, based in an inadequate theoretical background, simplistic assumptions, and naive views on how to improve or "perfect" the central planning system. Most important perhaps was the belief that the market mechanism could be consistently introduced without removing the so-called fundamentals of the socialist system, that is, the monoparty rule, the central command planning, and the state ownership of the means of production.

Moreover, the impact of the international environment on the willingness and ability of consecutive governments to implement genuine reforms should not be disregarded. The so-called Soviet factor has definitely played a crucial role in slowing down and even blocking at times the reform process in Poland as well as in other countries of Central and Eastern Europe, especially in the 1960s and 1970s. (Not surprisingly, it also played a positive role in the acceleration of political changes in the second half of the 1980s.)

All three categories of factors—political, conceptual, and international—contributed to the failure of the economic reform program undertaken in 1981–82. Their significance was different than it had been in the past, however, especially with respect to the adverse influence from the Soviet Union, which since 1983–84 has been of much less importance. Launched in the period of dramatic social struggle, the Polish economic reform quickly lost its momentum and got stuck in endless bureaucratic debates and procedures, without producing any significant results in terms of increased efficiency and competitiveness, accelerated growth, or structural change. Attempts to introduce a market-oriented system as envisaged in the reform blueprint prepared in 1981 were effectively blocked by short-term economic policy measures aimed at maintaining political controls over the economy. Furthermore, the reform project itself was based on an erroneous assumption about the practical feasibility of combining central planning and predominantly state ownership with arbitrarily selected elements of market mechanism into a sort of hybrid system called market socialism. Finally, the imposition of martial law in December 1981 under pressure from the Soviet Union and other conservative regimes in Eastern Europe created the least favorable environment for any kind of systemic change being at variance with traditional socialist principles.

THE FAILURE OF THE REFORM PROCESS, 1982–89

The Economic Reform of 1982: An Overview

At the end of the 1970s the Polish economy entered the deepest and most serious economic and social crisis in its postwar history. Faced by falling output and exports, drastic market shortages, and rising inflation, the Polish government yielded to mounting social pressures and decided to prepare in 1981 a new program of comprehensive economic reform. After several months of intensive debates, the final blueprint of the reform project was eventually approved by the Polish Sejm on September 25, 1981, and the reform was to get started in January 1982. The general idea of the project was to reduce considerably the extent of direct administrative controls over the economy, and to replace them with a variety of indirect economic measures working through the market mechanism.

The most important element of the program was unquestionably the elimination of the central command planning, accompanied by granting large formal autonomy to state enterprises. (See Law on State Enterprises of September 25, 1981, and Law on Socio-Economic Planning of February 26, 1982.) The autonomy, nicknamed "3S" after the Polish initials for independence, self-management, and self-financing, freed enterprises from compulsory planned targets, imposed by government authorities, allowed them to set their own production and sales program, and endowed them with (limited) powers to decide on the distribution of profits. Conversely, it was also assumed that state enterprises would cover all costs with sales revenues and bank credits, acquire necessary inputs through regular commercial transactions, and thus break away from the traditional administrative allocation system. This particular component of the reform package clearly followed from the Hungarian experiment of 1968.

The idea of planning was not, entirely rejected, however. On the contrary, the system of central annual and multiyear plans was to be maintained and even improved, and the program *explicitly* called for a "strengthening of strategic functions of the national planning." The so-called Central Annual Plan (CPR) and National Socioeconomic Plan (NPSG) were to be submitted by the government for the approval of the Sejm every year and every five years, respectively. While planned targets were not mandatory for enterprises, at least formally, except for some specific areas like military and state security activities or fulfillment of trade agreements with CMEA countries, a number of additional legal regulations severely limited the formal independence of enterprises. Among these regulations we should mention the large scope of administrative distribution of many production inputs and investment goods, which at that time were in short supply, and the obligation imposed on enterprises to provide government agencies with detailed information about production and investment plans. Furthermore, managers of state-owned companies continued to be dependent, formally and informally, on higher levels of government administration with respect to their personal remunerations and promotion.

Failing to make managers of state enterprises genuinely independent from administrative agencies and political parties, the reform actually made them more dependent on their own employees. One of the compromises reached between the Communist party and the Solidarity-led opposition during the political struggle in 1981 was to adopt a law giving large powers to Workers' Councils, among them the power to "hire and fire" managers. The solution, modeled this time on the Yugoslav experience with the self-management system, was meant to limit the party's powers within enterprises on the one hand, and to prevent political opposition from gaining too much control over enterprises on the other hand. This highly problematic regulation proved increasingly embarrassing— first for the communist government (and most recently also for the Mazowiecki government), as it introduced a systematic bias in enterprise policy in favor of maximizing current income and wage bills rather than profits.

The package of the new systemic solutions approved by the Sejm on February 26, 1982, also included a new Law on Prices, which introduced a general rule that prices be fixed by the market mechanism. Although administrative price setting was indeed lifted for many products, important restrictions remained imposed on the prices of primary inputs (like coal, fuel, energy, steel products, cement, metals, fertilizers, and many others), basic consumer goods and services (food, clothing, transport fares, rents), procurement prices for agricultural products paid to private farmers, and other selected goods. These prices were called administrative prices (*ceny urzędowe*), whereas free prices were called contract prices (*ceny umowne*). Prices for some other goods and services, though not directly fixed by the government, were subject to government controls and had to be set on the basis of a specific "cost-plus" formula (so-called regulated prices—*ceny regulowane*).

An important provision in the new law stipulated that prices for primary commodities would be fixed at the level corresponding to international prices (see Law No. 243 of November 30, 1981). But this principle was never implemented in practice, and until 1990 domestic commodity prices were maintained administratively below international levels.

As a result, a specific "dual" price system was introduced in the Polish economy. Contract prices were allowed to rise in response to market shortages, production cost increases, and monopolistic practices (although the government tried to keep them under controls through indirect influence). However, administrative prices were kept constant for longer periods, therefore being permanently below equilibrium levels. Relative prices were thus heavily distorted, leading both to growing shortages and to excess consumption and hoarding of primary goods and basic consumer goods.

Decisions on wages and salaries were in principle delegated to enterprises, but again, because of the strong inflationary pressures that plagued the Polish economy in the early 1980s, this right could not be implemented in practice. Monthly wage limits, coupled with progressive taxation of excess wage bills, did not leave enterprises too much freedom in their wage-setting policy.

More significant were changes introduced in the foreign sector of the economy. The so-called state monopoly of foreign trade, one of the most typical elements of the centrally planned economies, was formally dismantled, and all enterprises—public, private, or cooperatives—could apply for a license to carry out export or import operations. The license could be granted only provided specific requirements had been fulfilled, including the minimum share of exports in total output (at least 20 percent), or, alternatively, the minimum required level of annual export sales (initially, the limit was set at approximately U.S. $12.5 mln). More arbitrary was another condition, requesting a potential exporter (importer) to prove that he was endowed with "sufficient" professional and technical capabilities to enter international trade. This point (like many others) opened the way for considerable discretion in the licensing-granting procedures.

Part of the reform was the new foreign exchange-rate system and policy. Law No. 244 of November 30, 1981 determined that the exchange rate of the *złoty* against a basket of major convertible currencies would be fixed at the level ensuring a profitability of 75 to 85 percent of export sales to the so-called second payments area (convertible currency exports)—that is, at the so-called submarginal level. The same principle was adopted with respect to the transferable ruble which was used as a settlement currency unit within the "first payments area" trade (CMEA countries). Although the convertibility of the Polish currency was mentioned as an ultimate goal, no practical steps were envisaged in the program to introduce the convertibility in the foreseeable future. Perhaps the most innovative change within the foreign exchange regime was the possibility offered to exporters to retain some proportion of their export earnings in convertible currency for use on necessary imports. These export retention quotas—or ROD accounts (*rachunki odpisów dewizowych*)—varying from 2 to 3 percent to 40 to 50 percent for particular enterprises, were commonly regarded as an important incentive for export expansion. It should be stressed, however, that the allocation of a large majority of foreign exchange was still to be effected through administrative rationing procedures for many years ahead, and no specific provisions for the creation of the foreign exchange market were made within the new regime.

The reform package of 1981–82 also included several other systemic regulations of lesser importance. They included a law modifying the commercial banking system, a law on national statistics, and a statute concerning the National Bank of Poland.

The economic reform program of 1981–82 was obviously a compromise reached between two contradictory tendencies. On one hand, the traditional socialist system was vigorously defended by conservative party ideologists and government bureaucrats; on the other hand, far-reaching market-oriented changes were backed by the political opposition and many independent economists. True, included in the program were important concessions in favor of genuine decentralization and the market mechanism, like the abolition of the central command planning and the state monopoly of the foreign trade, or the establishment of a formal link between domestic and international prices. They were, however, effectively neutralized by a number of important restrictions, aimed at protecting political controls of the party and the government apparatus over the economy. The significant scope of administrative allocation of many inputs, the large powers of branch ministries, the more or less compulsory unions of enterprises, the dual price system, and many other regulations reduced the extent of possible market influence on economic activities. Furthermore, many important market institutions, such as the capital market, the foreign exchange market, the separation of the central bank from the competitive commercial banks, and the establishment of a two-tier banking system, were not even envisaged in the original reform program. Finally, ideological and political reservations blocked any attempt to transform the ownership structure of the Polish economy and did not permit the expansion of the private sector.

Implementation of Reform and Economic Policy, 1982–88

The economic situation in Poland became extremely difficult and precarious in 1981. Rapidly falling output and growing market shortages, coupled with increasing social tensions, massive strikes, and political confrontation between the communist-led government and Solidarity-led opposition, put the Polish economy at the threshold of total collapse. The martial law imposed on December 13, 1981 replaced the emerging chaos with the military rule that suspended civic freedoms and cut off the economy from Western markets. Nevertheless, the government decided to start with the reform program. The political, economic, and international environment was so unfavorable, however, that from the very beginning the implementation of necessary changes faced daunting difficulties and obstacles.

The year 1982 marks the trough of the crisis: net material product (NMP) declined by 17 percent as compared with 1980 and by 24 percent as compared with the peak in 1978, but the NMP distributed (NMP corrected by the trade balance) sunk by 20 percent and 27.5 percent, respectively. Imports went down by 22.5 percent as compared with 1978, but imports from Western countries fell by more than 50 percent, producing a tremendous supply-side shock in the production sector of the Polish economy. Recovery started in 1983, but after two years the rate of growth diminished, and stagnating tendencies began to be more and more visible. Table 11.1 provides data on the economic development of Poland in 1981–89.

It seems likely that the government mistakenly took the initial recovery in

Table 11.1
The Polish Economy, 1981–89 (main economic indicators)

Item	1981	1982	1983	1984	1985	1986	1987	1988	1989
			Preceding year = 100						
NMP^a	88.0	94.5	106.0	105.6	103.4	104.9	101.9	104.9	100.5
NMP_d	89.5	89.5	105.6	105.0	103.8	105.0	101.8	104.7	100.8
NMP_d/p.capita	88.7	88.7	104.6	104.1	103.0	104.2	101.3	104.2	100.8
CPI^b	121.2	204.5	121.4	114.8	115.0	117.5	125.3	161.3	337.9
Investment	77.7	87.9	109.4	111.4	106.0	104.5	104.1	106.1	98.0
Industrial prod.	86.8	98.5	106.6	105.6	104.1	104.4	103.4	105.3	99.4

Source: Main Statistical Office (GUS).

NMP_d = NMP distributed.

[a] Net Material Product

[b] Consumer Price Index (year-to-year basis).

1983–84 as a symptom of a longer term sustainable-growth tendency, produced by the implementation of the reform package in 1982. As a result, the readiness of the political authorities to introduce more radical systemic changes, even those originally included in the reform program, weakened significantly. However, the apparent recovery was mainly the result of restoring the elementary discipline in the economy after the period of massive strikes and political struggle in 1980–81, which simply permitted better utilization of existing production capacities. Under the shield of martial law, the government managed to increase domestic prices by more than 100 percent, thus reducing real wages by more than 30 percent in 1982, without confronting major popular protests. The improvement of the economic situation thus obtained had little to do with the new economic system and policy. It was more and more obvious that systemic changes were not accompanied by a change in economic policy. Actually, traditional methods still prevailed. That was one reason why the government's attempt in 1985 to accelerate growth through increased investment expansion failed, the only result being larger imbalances.

Stagnating tendencies in output and foreign trade intensified in 1986–87, leading to a new wave of strikes and political protests in the spring of 1988. The subsequent governments of Prime Ministers W. Jaruzelski and Z. Messner, though recognizing to some extent that political constraints were causing insufficient progress, were clearly unable to overcome these barriers and to reach a consensus over necessary policy adjustments. The economic policy over that period was dominated not by economic objectives like efficiency, optimal resource allocation, and growth, but mostly by political considerations. From today's perspective it seems clear that the fundamental objective of the government—though not *explicitly* formulated—was simply to stay in power at any price. Indeed, an ever higher price was being paid in terms of a gradual collapse of the national economy. The failure to revert the unfavorable course of events resulted in exploding inflation, market panic, and, eventually, in the dramatic political change of September 1989.

As mentioned earlier, the political resistance of conservatives as well as the numerous gaps and errors in the reform program turned out to be decisive in the ultimate breakdown of the program. Both factors best manifested themselves in the economic policy followed by the government during 1982–88. The policy measures not only remained in deep contradiction with the package of systemic changes introduced by the Sejm in 1981–82, but they also prevented the introduction of new solutions to improve the existing system.

The contradictions between the nature of the market-oriented, pro-efficiency reforms, and the general pattern of the socioeconomic policy, dominated by short-term political considerations and constrained by ideological dogmas, could have been seen in virtually all areas: price and incomes policy, fiscal policy, monetary and credit policy, and foreign exchange policy.

Contrary to the original schedule, the extent of administrative controls over prices was not being limited. Although the number of goods with "administered" prices was gradually reduced (to some 20 percent of products, mostly primary commodities, main agricultural goods, and basic foodstuffs), additional restrictions were imposed on "contract" prices, making them indirectly but effectively controlled by the government rather than by the market. The government was using a variety of limits for contract price increases, imposed the obligation on enterprises to inform the Ministry of Finance about intended increases, and had powers to veto price increases if they were regarded as "unjustified." These measures not only obviated the interaction of supply and demand forces as an objective price-making mechanism, but also opened large possibilities of bargaining with government authorities over permissible price increases. Furthermore, primary commodity prices were consistently maintained below international levels, presumably to contain the cost-price inflationary spillovers. The government coped with the chronic shortages of fuels, raw materials, byproducts, and foodstuffs—which naturally emerged as a result of low prices—neither with price adjustments nor with supply-side incentives, but rather with expanding rationing schemes.

In its attempt to fight inflation, the government introduced numerous restrictions on growth of wages and salaries. However, although high and progressive taxes were imposed on excessive wage bills (so-called PFAZ until 1987 and PPWW after 1987), the discipline of paying these taxes was low, and it was quite easy to negotiate with the Ministry of Finance to obtain relief or exemptions. The government was not able to resist pressures from big state-owned enterprises and from various "branch" lobbies to increase wages, or to provide subsidies, or at least to suspend excess wage tax collection. Furthermore, the existence of the famous Kornai's "soft" budget constraints allowed many enterprises to finance increasing personnel costs with bank credits (no Polish bank ever refused credits for wages in the 1982–88 period, no matter what the financial position of the company was), with so-called interenterprise credits (a peculiar "curb" market emerged in Poland with all enterprises financing their customers and simultaneously being financed by their suppliers!), with tax exemptions, or, finally, with direct grants from the budget. The rather frustrating result was that, except for two years (1982 and 1987), wages and salaries were increasing during the 1982–88 period at a much faster pace than prices, adding to the existing inflationary pressures.

The fiscal policy in the analyzed period was dominated by three tendencies: fiscalism, that is, excessive use of fiscal charges to reduce the liquidity of enterprises and to restore domestic balance; nonneutrality of taxes, that is, a combination of high tax rates for efficient enterprises with massive subsidies for inefficient units, thus involving a redistribution of profits on a large scale; and ample possibilities to obtain tax relief and exemptions for various reasons, through informal and nonmarket bargaining with fiscal authorities. The result was that inefficient but politically strong enterprises paid the highest wages and embarked on extensive investment programs, without paying attention to cost reductions or to restructuring of existing capacities. On the other hand, profitable enterprises could not expand their production. Moreover, the fiscal discipline was very low, and budget revenues frequently fell short of originally planned targets.

The government was finding it more and more difficult to keep budget expenditures in line with revenues. Inconsistent price and financial policies caused government subsidies to grow out of proportion. Direct subsidies to inefficient enterprises and to commodities with administered prices constituted the most important single item in the central budget, with their share increasing from 25 percent in 1983–84 to 36 percent in 1988. With their allocation left in most cases to the discretion of the powerful Planning Commission and particular ministries, the subsidies quickly became the most important source of excess monetary expansion.

Perhaps the worst situation existed in the area of the monetary and credit policy, left virtually unchanged since the early 1950s. As in other centrally planned economies, the money supply was endogenously adjusted to the needs of the so-called real sphere, that is, material production. In the 1980s the money supply accommodated itself more to immediate needs, dictated frequently by the desire to "buy" social support for the government. The elimination of the foreign trade monopoly and the introduction of foreign currency accounts for enterprises and individuals changed the role of international reserves in the money creation. Nonetheless, credit policy remained essentially the same; that is, annual credit ceilings were administratively allocated to all regional branches of the National Bank of Poland (the central bank), which was the only bank allowed to extend credits to enterprises. But these limits were not observed in practice, and if any enterprise got into financial trouble, bank credits were granted almost without restriction. Yet no minimum reserve requirement was applied for commercial banks. The budget deficit was automatically financed at the request of the government, and no interest was charged on these credits. Although the reform program called for more restrictive monetary policy, throughout the whole period under discussion interest rates on credits and deposits were negative in real terms. Not surprisingly, this led to high demand for credits and their inefficient use on one hand, and to low savings levels and increased money velocity on the other hand. No money or capital markets were foreseen within the original reform project, and the role of money was to remain passive.

The reform project established problematic rules for foreign exchange policy: for example, the concept of "submarginal rate" was both theoretically deficient and inappropriate in specific conditions of the Polish economy. (It had no connection with high foreign debt.) Although the convertibility of the Polish złoty had indeed been formulated as one of the long-term policy objectives, it remained a very elusive goal. Foreign exchange among potential importers was allocated through administrative procedures for a large proportion of import transactions—from 95 percent in 1982 to some 60 percent in 1988 for the "second payments area," and almost 100 percent for the transferable ruble area. Being as imperfect as it was, the government still did not observe the law on foreign exchange: it introduced an undervalued dollar rate at the very beginning of the reform implementation in 1982, and the official rate never reached the brackets prescribed by the law, securing a profitability of no more than 60 to 65 percent of exports. The notoriously undervalued official foreign exchange rate led to excessive imports, required special incentives for exports, and heavily distorted domestic prices.

Among the most harmful implications was the necessity to maintain an extensive price equalization system, whereby losses and profits on foreign trade transactions resulting from the undervalued exchange rate were settled by the central budget via specially designed differential tax-cum-subsidy scheme. During 1984–88 the share of central rationing in the foreign exchange allocation was reduced only marginally, from 70 to 61 percent. Under pressure from enterprises and criticized strongly by reform-minded economists, the government decided to introduce foreign currency auctions to increase the flexibility of the allocation mechanism, but amounts of currency sold at these auctions remained negligible during the entire period (from U.S. $1 mln in 1982 to 86 mln in 1988; that is, they never accounted for more than 1 percent of total import expenditures in convertible currency). Moreover, various types of auctions, addressed to different categories of customers, introduced many separate segments in the foreign exchange market and produced a large variety of dollar exchange rate, differing sometimes by as much as 600 percent. Distorted exchange rates blurred the efficiency calculus of enterprises, diverting resources away from comparative advantage areas.

Both domestic and foreign economic policies were essentially dominated by two objectives: to reduce inflation (from three-digit levels in 1982) and to stabilize the political situation in the country. That explains the reluctance to allow for a true market mechanism, as under conditions of shortage it would immediately mean a higher price inflation. Similarly, fiscal and foreign exchange-rate policies were also used mainly as anti-inflationary tools. Lack of popular support did not allow the government to pursue a more vigorous restructuring policy, involving bankruptcies of state-owned enterprises and massive unemployment. That is why the monetary policy was so relaxed. But such a policy mix could by no means produce expected results, and the government failed on both targets. In 1988 the official price inflation reached 60 percent, not to speak of repressed inflation, and the resulting political upheaval could not be delayed any longer.

Economic policy is the art of making necessary, though often difficult and politically demanding, choices and tradeoffs involving income distribution. In Poland during 1982–88 urgent decisions on these choices were generally delayed and suspended, and too many goals, sometimes contradictory, were attempted to be pursued by the government in the hope of avoiding unpopular decisions, which might further antagonize the revolted society. Trying to restore domestic market equilibrium and faced by the alternative of imposing price controls or allowing the market mechanism to set prices at equilibrium levels, the government invariably opted for the first solution, regarding direct controls as politically less dangerous in the immediate perspective. Similarly, when trying to restructure Polish industry, the government would always prefer to implement extensive administrative income redistribution schemes, rather than permit the market mechanism to eliminate inefficient state-owned companies. Admitting officially that a substantial reallocation of personnel among sectors and branches was indeed necessary, the government would nevertheless dare to allow open unemployment. Short-term political preferences and ideological principles effectively paralyzed any attempt to introduce a genuine market mechanism.

Economic policy is the art of establishing a fine balance between economic efficiency in the production sphere and social justice in the income distribution. In Poland, egalitarian tendencies, rooted in socialist doctrine, have always had the upper hand over social diversification; thus, decisions on income distribution were subordinated to political goals. Obviously, efficiency suffered, and in the long run there was less and less income to distribute. The fiscal policy, aimed at leveling off after-tax profits for all enterprises and sectors, provides an excellent example of the excessive income redistribution.

Economic policy is also the art of applying the most effective instruments to achieve planned targets. Until 1989 economic policy in Poland always tended to use excessively direct administrative measures, and it displayed consistent disregard and distrust for indirect, parametric measures. This approach led to the domination of bureaucratic allocation systems for many essential inputs, capital goods, and foreign exchange. It also led to the multiplication of numerous bureaucratic regulations, giving large powers to government agencies and replacing market rules with a large scope of administrative discretion. Short-sighted, politically oriented, and inconsistent policies blocked and neutralized those few market mechanisms that had been introduced in 1981–82. The market did not regulate prices and wages; foreign exchange rates and interest rates were strictly controlled and kept at artificially low levels; the freedom of formally independent enterprises was severely restricted by numerous administrative regulations; the factor market was virtually nonexistent; and the private sector was not allowed to expand. Under these conditions, the Polish economy was trapped in a systemic "vacuum" wherein neither central planning nor market mechanism operated.

The Failure of the "Second Stage" of the Reform and the Crisis of 1989

The urgent need to speed up the reform process was increasingly recognized not only by the large majority of the population, but eventually also by the conservative bureaucracy in the party and the government. Lack of tangible successes and the gradually deteriorating market situation undermined the self-confidence of the authorities. Moreover, the *perestroijka* campaign in the Soviet Union removed many ideological barriers obstructing the reform process and encouraged more reform-minded groups in Poland to strengthen pressure on the government. The idea of the second stage of the economic reform was launched in late 1986, initially as an extension and reformulation of already scheduled reforms. Only later was it transformed into a comprehensive critique of government policy, and it provided a framework for much more comprehensive systemic changes than originally envisaged.

Initially, the government was not politically and conceptually prepared to accept the idea of radical market reform. The inability to break away from the old standards was perhaps best demonstrated during the preparation of the five-year socioeconomic plan for 1986–90, wherein both the development objectives and the ways and means of their realization were formulated in a traditional manner, reflecting a conservative, orthodox planning philosophy. The plan, regarded as the most authoritative and prestigious statement on the Polish economic strategy, actually assumed the strengthening of central government controls over the economy and called for accelerated investment expansion in heavy industries, especially coal mining and energy production. On the international plane, the plan assumed further strengthening of trade and cooperation with the CMEA countries, in particular with the Soviet Union, and a practical freeze on economic relations with the West. The plan did not propose any increased reliance on the market mechanism in attempting to improve resource allocation and economic efficiency. The economic policy was to remain essentially based on direct administrative measures.

The plan document, eventually approved by the Sejm in November 1986, was perhaps the most striking and frustrating evidence of how strongly the central political and administrative bureaucracy resisted giving up some of its economic and political powers. It also showed up the narrowmindedness and naiveté of officially advanced concepts of the transition from the traditional planning system to market socialism.

As a result, only a few genuine innovations were introduced in 1986–87. They included the long awaited law on joint ventures, which the conservatives strongly criticized on ideological grounds. The law was finally approved with a number of restrictions on foreign capital participation, extension of foreign exchange auctions based on competitive bidding (but still for a very tiny fraction of total import expenditures—only U.S. $9.1 mln in 1987), reduction of some direct price controls, and reconstruction of the central government administration (elimination of some ministries).

As before, however, these minor changes were more than offset by further continuation of the conservative economic policy. For instance, the widely publicized reduction of the central government was neutralized by the immediate establishment of monopolistic structures in heavy industries (the so-called Wspólnota, or union of enterprises), which effectively resumed powers from old ministries. In its attempts to stabilize the ailing economy, the government increasingly resorted to administrative measures: price and wage controls, generally high and individually determined fiscal charges, and direct allocation of resources (capital, foreign exchange, essential inputs). The existing "dual" price system was going out of control, with "contract" prices constantly rising faster and faster (50 to 80 percent a year) and some administered prices remaining fixed for prolonged periods, thus producing shortages and requiring ever-growing subsidies. The repeated attempts to curb rising inflation through various price control schemes, high income taxes, or taxes charged on "excessive" wages could not have been successful, for at the same time other policy measures, such as accommodating monetary policy and ballooning budget expenditures, were of highly inflationary character.

One of the most important components of the second stage was supposed to be a massive price increase, which was intended to restore the market equilibrium at "one stroke." Using the euphemistic term *the price-income operation*, Messner's government wanted to raise the main commodity and food prices by 60 to 80 percent in order to remove major price distortions stemming from the dual price system. The radical restructuring of relative prices, coupled with a massive deflationary operation, was considered crucial for the success of the second stage of the economic reform. This time the government, trying to win a social mandate for this highly unpopular decision, resorted to an all-country referendum in November 1987, but it failed to get the required majority. Nevertheless, the government decided to introduce planned price increases, though of lower scale and accompanied by wage compensation schemes.

The operation that took place in February 1988 proved to be a real disaster: under conditions of no restraint in the monetary and fiscal policy, the price increases were immediately followed by a much larger increase in wages and salaries. If in 1987 prices and average monthly wages increased, respectively, by 25.3 percent and 21.1 percent, thereby leading to a drop of real wages by 3.5 percent, in 1988 the corresponding figures were 61.3 percent and 81.9 percent, yielding a real wage increase of 14.4 percent! State enterprises granted generous wage hikes without having sufficient financial means. But the banking system and the budget accommodated to the increased demand for credits and subsidies, as the authorities tried to avoid the political confrontation with workers employed in financially troubled companies. Moreover, as the increases were announced well in advance (again, for political reasons the government did not want to take people by surprise), the speculative purchases of many products intensified, producing chaos and panic in the market. Thus, the "price-income operation" only produced much higher inflation and growing shortages, but on the political plane, it ignited a new wave of strikes that erupted in the first half of 1988. Coming under heavy critique from all groups of the society, Messner's government was eventually forced to resign in October 1988.

Rakowski's government, fully aware of the nearly catastrophic economic situation, promptly moved to introduce some of the measures that had been previously rejected on ideological grounds. At that time inflation was already running at the annual rate of 60 percent (as compared with 25 percent in 1987), the foreign trade surplus was shrinking rapidly, and the market situation was constantly deteriorating. The government prepared a package of measures, called the consolidation plan, which included four important systemic innovations.

First, the law on entrepreneurship, approved by the Sejm in December 1988, introduced virtually unrestricted freedom of economic activities, and for the first time in the postwar history put the private sector on an equal footing with the public sector. The fundamental principle introduced by the new law—that "everything is permitted unless explicitly forbidden by law"—created new, vast opportunities for undertaking economic activities for all sectors.

Second, the government introduced large-scale auctions for foreign exchange, intending to reduce substantially the extent of administrative rationing, and providing a vehicle for achieving the convertibility of the Polish złoty within a three-year period. In 1989 more than U.S. $2 bn, that is, some 30 percent of all import expenditures in the "second payment area," were to be sold at auction at market-clearing exchange rates. The government also legalized the foreign currency market for individuals, thus eliminating the notorious "black market" and allowing private companies (exchange houses—kantory) to sell and buy foreign currencies legally.

Third, the government substantially modified the joint-venture law, making it more attractive for foreign investors and practically eliminating all existing financial constraints, except for restrictions imposed on transfer of profits.

Fourth, the government established a two-tier banking system, creating nine new commercial banks in January 1989 and breaking the monopoly of the National Bank of Poland in providing financial services to economic sectors.

Unfortunately, these and some other systemic reforms (like granting exit passports to all Polish citizens) did not produce the expected breakthrough, and for good reasons. First, they were undertaken too late in the sense that Polish society, deeply disappointed by the overall outcome of the forty-year communist rule and not trusting the new government, already demanded much more fundamental political change. Rakowski's reforms were in most cases correct and heading in the right direction, but they should have been effected in 1982–84; in 1989 they were definitely not sufficient. Second, as under previous governments, the economic policy was very short-sighted, politically biased, and hence inefficient. Not only the 1989 budget was planned with a built-in high deficit to be financed through money creation, but also the government quickly lost control over budget expenditures and was not in a position to secure the proper timing of tax collection. Under high inflation (an annual rate of 80 percent in the first half of 1989), the budget always displays a strong tendency toward deficit because of the so-called Tanzi effect. (Taxes are collected on a half-yearly basis, which reduces the real value of revenues, whereas expenses are made more or less on a continuous basis.) This is exactly what happened in Poland in the first half of 1989, when the budget deficit grew almost twice as high as all budget revenues. Lack of autonomy of the central bank (NBP) permitted unrestricted financing of this deficit through noninterest borrowing, giving rise to an explosive money creation.

Two examples may be given to illustrate the domination of political goals in the economic policy in this period. First, right after assuming office, Rakowski's government substantially raised the agricultural procurement prices in November 1988, making the increase retroactive to July, in the futile hope of gaining more political support from farmers. Second, growing weaker and weaker, the government under pressure from Solidarity, agreed at the Round Table negotiations to institutionalize the price-wage spiral in the form of the wage indexation scheme, relating wage increases to the cost of living index with the coefficient of 0.8. Both moves immediately added fuel to the inflationary process (see Frydman, Wellisz, and Kołodko, 1990).

Another highly controversial decision on freeing agricultural procurement prices in August 1989, though in principle unavoidable, was made, however, without proper preparation in terms of the necessary demonopolization of supply and distribution systems. As a result, retail food prices increased by 80 percent in August only, with very little increase on the supply side. Since food accounts for some 50 percent of household expenditures, the Consumer Price Index rose by 39.5 percent in one month. This was accompanied by the increase in nominal wages by more than 100 percent connected with the activation of the indexation scheme in August. With accommodating monetary policy, the Polish economy entered the hyperinflation stage. Consumer prices rose at the rate of 35 to 50 percent a month during August–November 1989, output and exports rapidly fell. But then, the political transformation was already underway.

An overview of the economic policy in the 1982–89 period clearly demonstrates that it was not only very inefficient in restoring domestic and external balance, but it was also inconsistent with the nature of the systemic reforms that

were being (half-heartedly) implemented. While the reforms were aimed at establishing an efficient market economy (albeit within a modified planning system
with a relatively high degree of government interventionism), the former policy
was mostly serving the political objective of retaining maximum control over
the economy. As a result, pro-market reforms, even if formally introduced by
parliamentary legislation, remained in practice "on paper" and could not have
been activated. This fundamental inconsistency between the reform and the
policy, of course, had its origins in the overall political setup. The people did
not trust the party-supported government, and more radical, drastic measures to
stop inflation and eliminate shortages would probably have provoked large-scale
social protests. Apparently what was still feasible and not excessively costly in
terms of anti-inflationary policies in 1982–84 became politically unfeasible and
economically too demanding in 1986–88. The communist authorities in Poland
were eventually trapped into a specific cul-de-sac type of situation. Although
they were formally and verbally committed to proceed with market reforms, they
were not ideologically, politically, and conceptually prepared to face the unavoidable reduction of their powers. Lack of popular support and mounting
pressures from the political opposition further diminished the government's readiness and willingness to "gamble" with the genuine reform process. The resulting
"paralysis" of the reform was the main reason for the lack of progress in
overcoming the Polish crisis. The only solution that appeared to be more and
more obvious was a fundamental political change, which would lead to establishing a new government, backed by mainstream social and political groups.
This is precisely what happened in the third quarter of 1989.

THE NEW ECONOMIC PROGRAM OF 1990:
STABILIZATION AND INSTITUTIONAL
TRANSFORMATION

The Preparatory Stage (September-December 1989)

The Solidarity-backed government of Prime Minister T. Mazowiecki assumed
office on September 16, 1989, and immediately started to prepare a program of
radical economic and social reforms. The program proposals were formulated
in close collaboration with the International Monetary Fund, as the financial
support from the IMF in the form of the standby arrangement was to be one of
the most important pillars of the program. While working on the final draft to
be implemented in January 1990, the government introduced a set of emergency
measures designed to arrest the deterioration of the economy and to lay the
foundations for the comprehensive adjustment program in 1990. The immediate
measures included:

• Taxes of 100 to 200 percent on wage increases exceeding 80 percent of the monthly
  rise of the cost of living index, in order to curb wage inflation.

- Accelerated tax payments and cuts in budget expenditures, mostly subsidies, which helped to reduce the prospective budget deficit from 10 to 7 percent of GDP
- The lifting of many price controls, aimed at preparing the ground for the major price liberalization in January 1990
- Intensified credit restraint, intended to curb excessive money creation, being the second major source of inflation (next to the budget deficit)
- Accelerated depreciation of the official exchange rate to narrow the spread between the official rate and the rates in the parallel market, and to establish the foundations for the introduction of the unified rate early in 1990

Despite these measures, the economy remained very weak and shaky. The monthly inflation rate increased from 35 percent in September to 54 percent in October, before easing to some 20 percent in November-December 1989 in response to anti-inflationary measures. The Convertible currency trade surplus was vanishing quickly (from U.S. $920 million in 1988 to U.S. $126 million in 1989), because of the emergency imports of consumer goods and the diversion of export supplies to the domestic market. Industrial output was declining, and food shortages were intensifying as farmers hoarded their products in anticipation of further inflation. On the positive side was the people's unprecedented readiness to accept harsh and radical measures and to support the new government in overcoming the crisis. The enthusiastic popular support and the international assistance package provided initial key foundations for implementing the stabilization program in January 1990.

The Stabilization Program

The program of economic reform that started January 1, 1990, consisted of two main parts: (1) the stabilization package, aimed primarily at reducing the inflation rate to about 1 percent a month in the second half of the year and restoring the fundamental equilibrium in the domestic market, and (2) the institutional change that seeks to transform the formerly centrally planned economy into a Western-type market economy.

The stabilization package was prepared by the team of Polish economists led by Deputy Prime Minister L. Balcerowiczin in close collaboration with the international experts (mostly IMF staffers and consultants). It reflects the standard IMF approach to stabilization policies, based essentially on monetary and fiscal restraint (see IMF, 1987). The package included five main policy measures that focused primarily on drastic reduction of domestic demand:

1. Fiscal policy: almost complete elimination of the huge budget deficit, which reached 7 percent of GDP in 1989, mostly through deep cuts in government expenditures, like food and energy subsidies, military and internal security expenses, as well as expanding budget revenues through elimination of various tax exemption schemes, increase of sales tax rates (from the average 10 percent in 1989 to more uniform 20 percent), and

strengthening of the fiscal discipline of tax collection. Cuts in subsidies were of particular importance, and the share of subsidies in government expenditures was to decline from 36 percent in 1989 to some 10 percent in 1990.

2. Monetary policy: drastic restrictions imposed on credit creation and the money supply by raising interest rates to positive real levels, eliminating automatic financing of budget expenditures through noninterest-bearing central bank credits and introducing bank-specific credit ceilings, also for the government sector.

3. Foreign exchange-rate policy: two parallel policy measures applied by the government, including the sharp devaluation of the Polish złoty (the official rate increased from 5,400 zł/dollar on December 22, 1989, to 6,500 zł/dollar on December 28, and to 9,500 zł/dollar on January 1, 1990, that is, by more than 75 percent within ten days only), and the introduction of the so-called internal convertibility of the Polish currency. The moves were intended to balance the supply and demand for foreign exchange, remove administrative restrictions in foreign exchange allocation, and unify a segmented foreign exchange market.

4. Tax-based income policy: a very restrictive incomes policy introduced with prohibitive taxes (of 200 to 500 percent) imposed on any increase of wage bills, exceeding predetermined indexation coefficients linked to the current inflation rate. Wage bills in all enterprises (of public and private sector alike, with the only exception being joint-venture companies) were allowed to rise by only 0.3 of the inflation rate in January, 0.2 of the inflation rate in February-April, and 0.6 of the inflation rate in May-June, thus implying a sharp and continuous drop in real wages. Enterprises exceeding these limits by less than 2 percent were punished with an excess-wage tax of 200 percent paid out of net profits, and 500 percent, if the wages grew more than 2 percent above the limit. The limits on wages together with the new exchange rate provided two nominal ''anchors'' for the stabilization program.

5. Price policy: price liberalization including a sharp increase in coal and energy prices by 400 to 600 percent, and removing most of the remaining price controls on January 1, 1990. By the end of the month, no more than 10 percent of prices were still subject to some administrative control, compared with 50 percent in 1989. A massive increase in energy prices was a particularly painful operation, as it contributed largely to the jump in the monthly inflation rate from 18.4 percent in December 1989 to 78.6 percent in January. But it was necessary to cut subsidies and to eliminate the major market distortion in the form of the notorious undervaluation of energy and coal. (In December 1989 the domestic price of coal was only 10 percent of the corresponding international price.) Although the price liberalization should essentially be regarded as an institutional reform, it had a strong stabilization impact, because, together with the wage freeze, it contributed to the rapid elimination of excess liquidity, helping to restore the fundamental market equilibrium.

The stabilization program was immediately supported by three categories of external financial assistance. First, the IMF provided a standby credit of SDR 545 million (U.S. $730 million) for balance-of-payments purposes until the end of March 1991; the Polish government drew a first portion of U.S. $200 million at the end of December 1989, but no further disbursements had been made by August 1990. Second, the OECD countries (the so-called G–24 group) provided a stabilization fund of U.S. $1 billion, deposited with the Federal Reserve Bank of New York, to support the switch to internal convertibility of the Polish złoty. No drawings from this fund have been necessary thus far. Third, the EEC countries offered humanitarian and food assistance, supplying Poland with meat, grain, butter, edible oil, and medicines totaling U.S. $220 million in 1989 and 1990.

Poland also obtained access to World Bank credits for food-processing, energy-saving, and export-oriented projects. It also concluded a number of agreements with Western countries on bilateral financial assistance for training in management, marketing, and banking services, private investment protection, and credit guarantees.

Economists and journalists alike have rightly termed the stabilization program a "crash" or "big-bang" program (see IMF, 1990). It may be argued that its extreme, drastic measures could have been applied only under unique Polish political conditions, where popular enthusiasm in the wake of the abolition of the communist rule after forty years made such harsh measures politically and socially feasible. It seems unlikely, however, that the Polish experience will be successfully emulated in other countries where the political environment is not so favorable.

The Institutional Change

The strategic objective of the new government is to establish an open market economy in Poland, relying on a strong private sector and guided by the profit motive. With this objective in mind, the government started with three broad initiatives: foreign sector liberalization; large-scale privatization of the state sector of the economy; and the introduction of market economy institutions and mechanisms.

First, the government largely liberalized foreign trade and foreign exchange regimes. The reform, eliminating few remaining elements of the state monopoly, permitted all economic agents virtually unrestricted access to foreign trade activities. Licenses were no longer required for foreign trade, except for transactions involving radioactive and nuclear materials, as well as weapons and arms. In addition, all quantitative restrictions were lifted in imports, and only a few remained on exports (for goods that are either in short supply in the domestic market or fall under import restrictions in other countries, like the EEC member countries, the United States, or Canada). Quantitative and other administrative restrictions were replaced by customs tariffs on the import side and limited tax-cum-subsidies measures on the export side. The new tariff introduced in January 1990 was prepared in accordance with the General Agreement on Tariffs and Trade (GATT) Harmonized System. The average tariff incidence was 12 percent but 21 percent for manufactured goods, thus pushing effective protection as high as 30 to 35 percent. Most of the tariffs were significantly reduced in April and then suspended in July until the end of the year (for 2,600 customs positions, mostly materials, intermediates, and investment goods).

The foreign trade liberalization was accompanied by a corresponding liberalization of the foreign exchange system. Administrative allocation of foreign currencies was removed, and all economic agents are now free to buy foreign exchange at the official rate according to their needs. The banking system is responsible for maintaining sufficient liquidity at the foreign exchange market in order to meet the demand. It should be noted that intervention by the central bank has thus far not been necessary to defend the foreign currency market, nor has recourse to the stabilization fund or IMF credit been needed.

The government declared that it would privatize a large number of state-owned enterprises as quickly as possible in order to establish a strong private sector in the Polish economy within the next several years. At present, the share of the private sector in industrial output is only about 8 percent. Moreover, limited amounts of capital in the hands of the Polish population and the lack of the tradition of making financial investments make the privatization process a truly formidable and long-term task. In January 1990 no comprehensive legal framework for massive privatization was yet in place; the law on privatization was eventually approved by the Sejm in July 1990, after long, highly controversial debates.

Other institutional changes to be implemented in 1990–91 included the following:

- Establishing a capital market in the form of a security exchange (scheduled at the beginning of 1991).
- Providing for the large-scale sale of state-owned nonproductive assets, like apartments, houses, real estate, hotels, and shops.
- Enhancing competition and curbing monopolistic practices by removing restrictions on setting up new companies and encouraging new entries into monopolized sectors.
- Modernizing the commercial banking system by strengthening existing and developing new commercial banks, introducing new financial instruments and techniques, and improving banking, accounting, and auditing procedures.
- Developing a labor market, with a fundamentally changed Labor Code, which allows more flexibility in labor mobility and higher discipline.
- Effecting a radical and comprehensive tax reform, aimed at introducing individual income taxes (so far absent) and a value added tax.

The ambitious task of transforming the Polish economy from the centrally planned system to a market economy within a few years is probably a much more demanding and difficult endeavor than the "big-bang" stabilization program. No country in the past has ever undertaken this kind of transformation, and so there is no precedent on which to draw. In addition, the theory of this type of transition is still to be formulated. This point should be kept in mind when we make any evaluation of the program's results after only six months.

Main Policy Dilemmas

The lack of practical experience and the largely inadequate theory on transition from plan to market have had important implications for the design and implementation of the stabilization program in Poland. As we will see, this lack was probably the main reason for the apparently excessive application of many stabilization measures, in order to ensure a sufficiently large safety margin in view of the unknown behavior pattern of the centrally planned economy. Perhaps more important in the immediate perspective was the need for the Polish government to decide on many policy dilemmas and choices, which emerged just before and during the implementation of the program.

First, the government had to decide on the speed of the adjustment process. Faced with the choice between the gradual approach, which would assume extending the implementation of the program over several years, and the "shock" treatment, the government opted for the second alternative. It introduced a package of radical measures virtually overnight, being aware that the disintegrating economy could collapse in a very short time. This approach was apparently supported by the IMF, which always prefers quick, massive adjustment over step-by-step, evolutionary changes (see Michaely, Choksi, and Papageorgiou, 1989).

Second, the government had to decide whether the macroeconomic stabilization should come first, and the institutional reform only later, or vice versa. Many economists indicate that monetary and fiscal instruments of expenditure reduction may not be effective when applied in an economy that is highly monopolized and predominantly state-owned, and lacks essential market institutions (like the capital market). The Polish government, through sharing these concerns, nevertheless decided to go ahead with both stabilization and the institutional parts of the program simultaneously, arguing that their necessary interaction was crucial for the ultimate success of the program.

Third, being confronted with a rapidly growing inflation and shortages in the domestic market on one hand, and with huge foreign debt and falling exports on the other hand, the government had to clearly establish its priorities in restoring equilibrium. In a remarkable departure from standard IMF requirements, the Polish government won the support of the international community for the policy decision to concentrate on reestablishing the domestic balance first, and only afterward to undertake efforts to improve the balance-of-payments position.

Fourth, there was great uncertainty about the optimal composition of the stabilization package and tasks assigned to particular policy instruments. The government decided to focus on demand reduction measures, assuming that excess demand and inflation were the main obstacles to stabilization, and largely neglecting the need for supply-side measures.

Fifth, the government had to decide on the optimal degree of domestic protection—or degree of openness—during the period of program implementation. While being aware of the low competitiveness of Polish industry, the government still decided to liberalize the foreign trade and foreign exchange regimes, thus opening the Polish economy to international markets. The most controversial and perhaps most impressive move was to introduce the internal convertibility of the złoty right from the start of the program.

Finally, the government had to solve an important problem involving the distribution of the social costs of transition. The fundamental questions were, what were the limits of social approval for necessary sacrifices connected with program implementation, and to what extent would the government, which rose to power supported by the Solidarity labor union, now be allowed to carry out a program involving large-scale reductions of real incomes and savings? The government decided to make economic stabilization the first priority, reducing social protection measures to a minimum and allocating losses mostly to wage and salary earners.

These and other policy dilemmas have been solved without resorting to elaborate and extensive studies. The final outcome is yet to be seen. The Polish reform, pioneering the transition from plan to market in Eastern Europe, is unquestionably an experiment of historical significance. That is why the failure of the program would not only decide the future of Poland, but would also have a tremendous impact on the course of reform in other countries (as well as in the Third World). Failure would probably diminish their readiness and support for more radical changes, and extend necessary systemic transformations over much longer periods.

EVALUATION OF THE ECONOMIC PROGRAM AFTER THE FIRST HALF OF 1990

The Financial Versus the Real Side

After only six months of program implementation we do not have sufficient grounds for making a comprehensive assessment of the program which was in effect until December 1990. However, an evaluation of on-going processes is warranted and advisable in order to check on how actual developments match planned targets and to determine what should be done in case some corrections in the original program are needed. It is not easy to conduct this "interim" evaluation, however, for Polish statistical services have not been adequately restructured to reflect the process of economic and systemic transformation. For instance, official statistics almost entirely ignore the activities of the private sector in Poland; in addition, GNP/GDP statistics are processed and published only annually and with substantial delay, which does not permit a quarterly analysis of macroeconomic activity.

When speaking about the effects of the program, it is customary to distinguish the financial sphere and the real sphere, as results in both areas are indeed entirely different. The conventional opinion, repeatedly expressed by the Polish government, is that the program has worked exceptionally well on the financial side but has produced severe recession on the real side. That is why preliminary and unofficial assessments of the program made by the IMF and the World Bank experts are sometimes ambiguous and vague. While praising the government for the determination, they are still uncertain about final results. In my opinion, there exists a strict, inverse correlation between the financial and real sides: the more impressive are achievements in eliminating excess liquidity, the higher is the probability of reducing demand below the equilibrium level, and the higher will be the stabilization costs in terms of decline of real income, output, and employment.

In the most concise form, major accomplishments on the so-called financial side can be illustrated as follows:

1. Reduction of the inflation rate from the monthly rate of 30 to 40 percent in August-December 1989 and 78.6 percent in January 1990 to 3 to 5 percent in May-July 1990

2. Practical elimination of market shortages and restoration of a fundamental financial equilibrium in the domestic market

3. Replacement of the huge budget deficit of about 7 percent of GDP in 1989 by the budget surplus of about 3 percent of GDP in the first half of 1990

4. Reduction of real wages by some 35 percent and practical elimination of the ''inflationary overhang ''

5. Stabilization of the foreign exchange market at the initially established dollar exchange rate, without drawing on international reserves or external credits.

6. Substantial increase of international reserves

Similarly, the failures on the real side can be summarized as follows: (1) A drop in real output of the so-called socialized sector by 28 to 29 percent; (2) a gradual rise of unemployment to more than seven hundred thousand people at the end of July 1991; and (3) a lack of any significant restructuring tendencies in the production sector.

It seems that speaking about financial-side successes and real-side losses is not fully legitimized, because such an approach does not take into account the mutual relationship between the two spheres. The most essential problem is that the real excessive costs are being paid precisely because financial measures have been overused and sometimes misused. What at first glance appears to be a financial success has in most cases the reverse real side, which looks far less optimistic. The available data make it clear that the stabilization program actually ''overshot,'' producing excessive financial results obtained at excessive real costs. This hypothesis will be discussed below.

The main target of the stabilization effort was, of course, the elimination of hyperinflation. Indeed, after a price jump of 78.6 percent in January (the highest monthly rise in postwar history), owing largely to official energy price increases and the freeing of many controlled prices, the inflation was gradually subdued to a monthly rate of 3.4 percent in June (equivalent to 50 percent of annual rate),

Table 11.2
Price Inflation, Wage Raises, and the Central Budget Balance in Poland

Period	Retail price index (previous month = 100)	Wages & salaries in real terms	Budget balance in bn zł (cumulative)	as percent of revenues
January	178.6	69.7	+913	11.7
February	123.9	89.8	+3784	20.1
March	104.7	113.6	+2160	8.0
April	108.1	107.8	+5417	13.5
May	105.0	83.7	+7205	13.8
June	103.4		+6828	10.8
July	103.6			

Source: Compiled from data of the National Bank of Poland.

the lowest monthly rate for more than two years. Table 11.2 provides selected data on financial stabilization in Poland.

The drop in the inflation rate is indeed remarkable, the more so because it was coupled with the elimination of "repressed" inflation, which was bound to add impulse to upward price pressures. There are two points of concern, however. First, the inflation has not disappeared altogether; the monthly rate of 3 to 4 percent still represents a high level of inflation, at least by Western standards, and may indicate that the fundamental sources of inflation have not yet been eliminated permanently. At present, this seems to be the main concern for the government, which vigorously rejects any suggestion for more significant loosening of financial restrictions on the ground that it is too risky and may fuel inflation. The government is clearly afraid that the inflation may still go easily out of control; therefore, the restrictive fiscal, monetary, and income measures cannot be lifted. This view may be challenged on the basis that underlying sources of the present inflation have not been correctly interpreted. Specifically, if structural cost-push-type causes play the major role, rather than demand-pull-type, monetary causes—which seems plausible—then the one-digit monthly inflation may be a more durable phenomenon and cannot be quickly and effectively tackled with further financial restrictions. This point will be discussed in more detail later.

Second, this (relative) price stabilization has been achieved at a much higher nominal price level than was originally expected. Let us recall that the program assumed an inflation rate of not more than 75 percent for the first quarter of 1990 (45 percent in January, 15 percent in February, and 5 percent in March), whereas for the rest of the year it would not surpass 1 to 2 percent a month, thus giving the total price increase not exceeding 100 percent (from December

1989 to December 1990). The reality was more disappointing. The first-quarter inflation was actually 132 percent, while subsequent monthly price increases indicate that the inflation in the entire year may reach some 220 percent. Therefore, cautiousness and moderation are advised in assessing the anti-inflationary efficiency of the stabilization program.

Next, the unquestionable achievement of the first phase of the program is the radical elimination of chronic shortages and market deficits. Although no precise data are readily available to assess the drop in the repressed inflation, the improvement of the market situation is clearly visible. We have plenty of anecdotal evidence that there is less queueing and that a much larger variety of goods are available. Thus, the program helped get rid of "excess liquidity," which was one of the most persistent and devastating barriers to the market mechanism. Using the familiar Kornai terminology, the Polish economy turned from a "resources-constrained" into a "demand-constrained" economy almost overnight. The major reservation that may be raised at this point is that the elimination of shortages was achieved almost entirely through massive price increases and reduction of demand, resulting in sharp decline in real consumption, with almost no reaction on the supply side.

Another largely publicized success is the dramatic change in the central budget position. The program assumed that after the first six months a budget deficit of 2 to 3 percent of GDP might emerge, to be financed through short-term borrowing from commercial banks and to be repaid essentially by the end of 1990. Instead, the budget balance has been consistently positive from the very beginning of the year, with the surplus varying around 10 to 13 percent of all revenues, that is, roughly 3 percent of GDP. While actual expenditures were made according to schedule, revenues were much higher than originally planned, mostly because of higher income tax and customs duty payments. A careful observer must ask, however, what is the justification for maintaining the substantial budget surplus in the situation, when output declined owing to the slump in effective demand, real income went down by 35 percent, unemployment was rising at the rate of one hundred thousand people per month, and political tensions were mounting dangerously.

Fourth, the incomes policy proved to be quite successful, keeping the growth of wages and salaries under control and within the limits established by the restrictive excess-wage tax scheme. As can be calculated from Table 11.2, nominal wages grew less than prices, thus leading to a substantial decline of real wages by some 35 percent over the first half of 1990. (The conventional concept of real wages under conditions of widespread shortages is, of course, highly dubious, but because we lack reliable data on the extent of shortages— or repressed inflation—it is difficult to apply alternative measures; see Lipton and Sachs, 1990). Moreover, the high inflation of January-February 1990, coupled with deep cuts in the real money supply, drastically reduced the real value of savings. Nominal money stock in the hands of individuals, including cash balances, savings accounts, and foreign currency accounts with Polish banks

(M3), rose from zł 64,435 bn on December 31, 1989, to zł 98,323 bn on June 30, 1990; that is, its real value declined by 45 percent. Therefore, both the drop in real wages and the decline of real purchasing power of individual money holdings and savings secured the success of the deflationary operation of unprecedented scale. Again we may ask whether this operation did not go beyond necessary limits, not only eliminating the excess liquidity carried over from 1989 ("inflationary overhang"), but also substantially reducing voluntary savings and lowering standards of living below levels necessary for restoring the market balance.

Fifth, the government managed to stabilize the foreign exchange market during the first phase of the program, maintaining the initially established exchange rate of 9,500 złotys per U.S. dollar. The rate may indeed have been highly overvalued at the beginning of 1990, but that was apparently a deliberate move by the government intended to maintain a stable exchange rate in anticipation of the forthcoming inflation. At midyear, however, the rate level already seemed to be just right, given the existing constraints on the money supply.

The questions that remain are whether the margin of the initial overvaluation of the dollar was not excessive, leading to a sudden drop of imports and contributing to cost-push inflation through an increase in imported input prices, and whether the extent of monetary restrictions and the resulting recession are not too high a price for defending the stable exchange rate at the predetermined level.

The foreign balance improved dramatically in the first half of 1990. The trade surplus with the convertible currency area exceeded U.S. $2 bn. Similarly, with the transferable ruble area the surplus reached TR 2.4 bn. As a result, convertible currency reserves increased (in gross terms) by almost U.S. $1.4 bn during the first six months. This is probably the most unexpected outcome, as the stabilization program actually assumed the decline of international reserves by U.S. $290 mln after the first quarter and by U.S. $165 mln after the second quarter. Again, the problem that arises concerns the social costs of this "overshooting" in terms of reduced domestic absorption (because of sharp terms of trade deterioration against nontradeables) and the economic costs of higher inflation (because of the "pass-through" effect on prices of the higher cost of imported inputs). Moreover, this substantial increase of international reserves should be, and indeed has been, sterilized through corresponding reduction of domestic credit.

As can be seen, Poland's "financial" successes are apparently not so obvious as they may look at first glance. In most cases they simply reflect the deep recession in the real sphere and therefore should not be considered independently from the behavior of real variables, like output, real income, absorption, and employment.

The process of the financial stabilization in Poland can perhaps be best illustrated by an analysis of the consolidated balance sheets of the banking system (Table 11.3). This analysis confirms earlier observations. Let us note, first, that

Table 11.3
Main Positions of the Consolidated Balance Sheets of the Polish Banking System, December 31, 1989–June 30, 1990 (in billion złotys)

Item	31 Dec. 1989	30 Jun. 1990	Change(Δ)
A. Assets.			
1. International reserves[a]	23780	36700	12920
2. Commercial credits	33476	73076	39600
3. Government debt	6496	-7570	-14066
4. Other assets	32087	33717	1630
B. Liabilities.			
1. Cash balances	9880	26040	16160
2. Saving deposits (individuals)	8629	22423	13794
3. Deposits (enterprises)	7841	30446	22605
4. Foreign currency accounts			
4.1. Individuals	45926	49850	3924
4.2. Enterprises	22683	6632	-16051
5. PKO S.A. coupons[b]	881	532	-349

Source: National Bank of Poland.

[a] Gross, converted into złotys at 9,500 zł/dollar.

[b] PKO coupons were used for purchases in convertible currency shops.

the total nominal money supply (M3—together with foreign currency accounts) increased by only 42.5 percent, which means that the large measure of money supply in real terms declined by 47 percent (because of price inflation of 169.8 percent) over the analyzed period. On the other hand, the supply of domestic currency increased by 200 percent, exceeding the inflation rate by some 30 percentage points. At the same time real income went down by some 25 to 30 percent, which means that a strong increase of the domestic money supply in real terms has occurred. The economy's absorption of these increased real domestic money balances was made possible by two factors. First, enterprises, finding themselves under a strong credit crunch, were massively converting foreign currency deposits into złotys, in order to build up domestic cash balances for transaction purposes. Thus, the restrictive monetary policy had a strong substitution effect in the portfolio composition of monetary assets of enterprises (substitution of dollars for złotys). A similar reaction has been observed in individuals' behavior: it may be noted that, while the foreign currency deposits of individuals increased only marginally by a mere 8.5 percent, their domestic currency deposits went up by 159.9 percent. The buildup of domestic currency balances (especially cash balances—by 163.6 percent) under conditions of falling output indicates a significant slowdown in the velocity of circulation. The substitution of dollars for złotys and the decline of the velocity should be regarded as one of the most impressive results of the stabilization program.

Second, the main source of the increase in the money supply was the domestic credit expansion (an increase by 118 percent), whereas the increase of international reserves (by zł 12.9 trillion) was effectively sterilized by a sharp reduction of net government borrowing (by zł 14.1 trillion). Thus, the central bank was able to neutralize inflationary pressures resulting from the high current-account surplus, which allowed the dampening of hyperinflation and the stabilization of price rises at comparatively low levels after only two months of program implementation.

Turning now to the real-side effects, we should stress that the most troubling outcome of the stabilization program is, of course, the deep recession, manifesting itself in the decline of output by roughly 30 percent, compared with the corresponding period of 1989. True, this figure should be taken *cum grano salis* for many reasons. First, it refers to the so-called sold output of the socialized sector in the material sphere; that is, it ignores private sector activities (which are expanding rapidly, increasing their share in total industrial output from 3.8 percent in 1985 to 7.4 percent in 1989). Second, it does not take into account the value of nonmaterial services. Third, it gives an excessively pessimistic picture of the actual decline in real consumption, because a growing proportion of retail trade is outside the official distribution network. All these reservations notwithstanding, it may be assumed that the drop in output has not been less than 25 percent, which is still large enough to cause deep concern. Let us recall that the program assumed an output decline for 1990 of not more than 5 percent; there is simply no chance to defend this target. Even under the most optimistic scenario, the recession for the entire 1990 year cannot go less than 15 to 20 percent in terms of reduced output, as compared with 1989.

The fall in domestic demand could not have been fully compensated by increased expansion to international markets, because of the low share of the foreign sector in the Polish economy. Exports to the convertible currencies area rose by 22.4 percent during January-June 1990, as compared with the corresponding period of 1989, which may be considered a remarkable result (by Polish historical standards). In addition, exports to a transferable ruble area rose by 13.0 percent, being deliberately discouraged by the government with the use of differential exchange rates for transferable rubles. (For instance, in exports to the Soviet Union, the government applied the official rate of 2,100 zł/ruble only for transactions included in government protocols and 1,000 zł/ruble for all other transactions.) The export performance could have been even better if the government had agreed to provide exporters with preferential short-term supplier credits. At a monthly interest rate surpassing 36 percent in January and 22 percent in February, combined with the fixed exchange rates, however, it was absolutely impossible for Polish exporters to extend their accounts receivable, even for one to three months. (In January 1990 exports were 20 percent lower than they had been in January 1989.) Thus, because of its low potential as well as supply-side constraints, the export sector has not been able to pull the economy out of recession.

What is quite surprising about the Polish recession is that the employment level decreased much less than the output. In July 1990 the unemployment rate (outside agriculture) reached 5.4 percent, which shows that enterprises have hoarded labor while reducing output. This type of reaction may be explained by the specific behavior patterns of socialized sector enterprises, which are less motivated by profit maximization than by immediate worker interests. Moreover, the low share of personnel costs in total production costs (only 16 to 18 percent in the industrial sector) makes enterprises relatively insensitive to employment variations. The perspectives are gloomier, however: by the end of 1991 unemployment may reach 1.3 to 1.5 million, that is, 10 to 11 percent of the total labor force. This is because enterprises, after having used up other reserves (like foreign exchange accounts, "interenterprise" credits, excessive stocks) and coming under more and more heavy financial pressures (assuming the government does not radically change its policy), will probably be forced to cut production costs, thus laying off more workers. Although further decline in output does not seem likely, we can certainly expect a further continuous rise in unemployment, which thus far has lagged behind the falling level of production.

Institutional Reform and Structural Change

One of the most disturbing problems that arose during the first phase of the program was the very slow pace of institutional change. Except for price and foreign trade liberalization, all other reforms have not been completed yet. The privatization process may soon take off, as the privatization law was finally approved by the Sejm in July, but the government expected the law much earlier. The law itself seems to be very imperfect and inconsistent, as it emerged as a compromise between liberal and self-management tendencies. Moreover, the privatization process will take many years. Similarly, the competition conditions are still rudimentary, as monopolistic state companies defend their market positions, and new entrants are very few and inexperienced. The traditional monopolistic structure also dominates upstream and downstream sectors of agriculture (supply of fertilizers, pesticides, agricultural machinery, and distribution channels for agricultural products). No effective institutions exist to secure smooth reallocation of capital from declining sectors to expanding and modern ones. The labor market is segmented and very inelastic because of low regional and sectoral mobility. The banking system is underdeveloped, and the quality of financial services is very low (e.g., money transfer within the country takes two to three weeks).

Lack of appropriate institutional infrastructure hampers necessary structural change. The dominant type of reaction in the economy is to reduce output and to raise prices; by contrast, only a few enterprises try to restructure their production program or to improve the production cost structure. Monopolistic position, which still is not seriously jeopardized by potential imports because of serious quality and price differentials, allows many companies to survive the period of financial squeeze at a reduced level of activity. Almost no bankruptcies took place among state-owned enterprises within the period analyzed, which indicates that no fundamental restructuring has started yet.

The rupture of synchronization between stabilization measures and institutional change poses a great danger for the program, because financial restrictions, coupled with a severe drop in standard of living, do not lead to required changes in the economic structure. The stabilization effort may therefore be largely wasted. But limits of social endurance may be dangerously close, as illustrated by new strikes (farmers, railway workers) in May and June 1990, and Polish society may not want to tolerate further sacrifices after one year of Solidarity rule.

CONCLUSIONS

After the first six months of the new program implementation, the central question is whether the stabilization measures applied were too restrictive and led the economy into the deep recession, or whether the stabilization package should not have been less restrictive if inflation was to be effectively eliminated. The government adheres to the second view, arguing that the stabilization program was designed and implemented correctly and that the creeping inflation of 3 to 4 percent per month is still too dangerous to allow a relaxation in financial policies.

While there is little disagreement over the general philosophy underlying the economic program (i.e., the general pro-market orientation and the extensive use of financial instruments for stabilization purposes), the actual composition of the stabilization package and the sequence of particular measures are open to discussion. The most important deficiency of the package is its "one-sidedness," that is, the almost total concentration of policy measures on demand reduction, with practical negligence of any strong supply-side incentives. It may be observed that the set of policy measures had strong antisupply impact. Among five main components of the stabilization package, three (monetary policy, tax policy, and wage restraint) not only affect demand, but also reduce output and supply. Therefore, it was quite clear that, in the absence of active institutional incentives, the reaction of the economy would follow the "L" curve rather than the "U" curve. That is, one can expect a deep and long recession (Rosati, 1990).

The apparent "overperformance" of the program seems to be the result of using too many different instruments aimed at only one target: reducing demand. This redundancy (which violates the Tinbergen principle on the optimal correspondence of policy objectives and policy tools) was probably caused by erroneous evaluation of the scope of excess liquidity at the end of 1989. The reasoning of the government (and the IMF alike) remained strongly influenced by the "disequilibrium syndrome" which is so typical for centrally planned economies. That is why the applied measures were so drastic and far-reaching. Yet, the excess liquidity seems to have been much smaller; not only real value of savings has been wiped out by rampant inflation, but also the nominal money supply in 1989 was much smaller than the inflation, thus leading to the almost complete elimination of domestic currency cash balances. That in turn was caused by the high velocity of money (normal for high inflation episodes) and the market panic (due to spreading shortages), which led individuals to hoard consumer goods and foreign currencies and enterprises to accumulate excessive stocks.

Stopping inflation at the end of January and securing free access to foreign exchange at the official rate reversed these tendencies, changed inflationary expectations, and encouraged individuals and enterprises to rebuild their domestic cash balances to normal levels, corresponding to their real incomes. On the other hand, the freeze on wages and high rates of taxation under conditions of uncontrolled prices reduced real incomes. The increase of demand for cash balances combined with the decline of real incomes and liquidation of excessive stocks led to an unexpectedly sharp drop in effective demand, and the result was the deep recession.

The errors and mistakes in the program design were further reinforced by some unfavorable developments during the program implementation. Weaknesses of the institutional reform, lack of structural adjustment, and the apparent misinterpretation of the causes of persisting inflationary tendencies in the second quarter of 1990 put the government on the defensive and raised serious concerns about the fate of the whole program.

RECOMMENDATIONS

The economic policy package planned for the second half of 1990 displays some indications that the government may be contemplating some minor corrections in the program. The reduction of the central bank base interest rate to 34 percent and of the discount rate to 28 percent on an annual base has been announced, together with the opening of preferential credit lines for agriculture (bearing interest 20 percent p.a.). Next, the government intends to increase budget expenditures, but still it is planned that the overall budget balance will be positive with the surplus of zł 6 trillion. The government also modified rules of excess wage taxation, increasing the indexation coefficient to 1.0 in July (but returning later to 0.6 in August-September) and slightly lowering tax rates (up to 3 percent of excess wages—100 percent, 3 to 5 percent of excess wages—200 percent, and above 5 percent the tax rate is 500 percent). Furthermore, the government suspended customs tariffs for more than 2,600 commodities until the end of 1990. Finally, an acceleration of the process of institutional changes has been declared (privatization, joint-venture law, streamlining of bankruptcies procedures, and development of the securities market).

Still, these changes do not seem to be sufficient to revitalize the economy, especially on the supply side, and more effective measures should be suggested. Essentially, they should be aimed at removing the excessive restrictiveness of the program, rather than changing its fundamentals. The measures would include:

1. Monetary policy: While still adhering to the principle of positive interest rates in real terms, the government should be more active in applying preferential credit conditions in selected sectors (mainly agriculture, exports, and private sector activities). In addition, the central bank should consider lower levels of the real interest rate, which in May 1990 was about 27 percent and in June 20 percent per annum for commercial credits.

2. Fiscal policy: The corporate income tax rates, including so-called dividends on state-owned assets, at present amount to 45 to 50 percent of taxable profits. Fiscal charges should be reduced to not more than 40 percent. On the expenditure side more spending should go into infrastructural investments, like telecommunications, financial services, institutional support for enterprises, and factor markets.

3. Incomes policy: The prohibitive wage restraint system should be replaced by a flat tax rate of 100 percent on all wages. This move should be combined with introducing serious limitations on the powers of Workers' Councils, in order to protect state-owned companies from spending an excessive proportion of revenues on wages and salaries.

4. Foreign exchange and foreign trade policies: The basic exchange rate for the dollar should not be changed as it serves as an important stabilization "anchor." However, a wide range of export promotion schemes (export credits, export guarantees, promotional support, tax exemptions, etc.) should be introduced to supplement customs tariffs suspension, in order to make trade policy more export-oriented and less protective for import substitution.

It may be argued that these proposals are too expansionary and may lead to a new inflationary spiral. The creeping inflation of 3 to 5 percent per month observed in May-July 1990 is of a cost-push character, however, and will not be significantly affected by macroeconomic policy adjustments. Neither will it be reduced to the zero level through further restrictions, nor will it be boosted by more relaxed policies (within reasonable limits, of course). The present inflation is being caused mainly by monopolistic pricing, an inflexible production structure, low elasticity of demand at its unusually reduced level (low segments of the demand curve), as well as the high sales tax and customs duties surcharges on domestic prices. The government should not try to reduce inflation to zero levels through continuous use of demand-reducing measures, as macroeconomic costs of such attempts would be too high. Besides, realistically it is not feasible. Proposed expansionary measures would allow relatively high increments of output and income, with low inflationary effects. As soon as the present depression is overcome, the government should use an expansionary fiscal policy combined with a restrictive monetary policy in order to achieve moderate growth without inflation. It should be remembered that the success of the Polish economic reform does not depend solely on internal policies; the external environment can make the transition more or less difficult. The foreign debt of U.S. $42 billion poses a special problem, which probably cannot be solved without a radical debt-relief operation.

REFERENCES

Brada, J. C., Hewett, E. T., and Wolf, T. A. "Economic Stabilization, Structural Adjustment and Economic Reform." In *Economic Adjustment and Reform in Eastern Europe and the Soviet Union*, edited by J. C. Brada, E. T. Hewett, and T. A. Wolf. Durham, N.C.: Duke University Press, 1988.

Frydman, R., Wellisz, St., and Kołodko, G. W. "Stabilization in Poland: A Progress Report." Revised version of a paper prepared for the conference on Exchange Rate Policies of Less Developed Market and Socialist Economies, Berlin, May 1990.

International Monetary Fund. "Theoretical Aspects of the Design of Fund-Supported Adjustment Programs." IMF Occasional Papers, No. 55, September 1987.

International Monetary Fund. *IMF Survey*. 19, No. 4 (February 19, 1990).

Lipton, D., and Sachs, J., *Creating a Market Economy in Eastern Europe*: *The Case of Poland*. Brookings Papers on Economic Activity, No. 1, 1990.

Michaely, M., Choksi, A., and Papageorgiou, D. "The Design of Trade Liberalization." *Finance and Development* (March 1989).

Rosati, D. K. "Teoria i polityka programów stabilizacyjnych Mirdzynarodowego Funduszu Walutowego." *Studia i Materiały*, No. 13. Warsaw: Instytut Koniunktur i Cen Handlu Zagranicznego, 1990.

12

NATIONAL ECONOMIC POLICIES IN CHINA

Zhang Yunling and Li Rongzhang

Significant changes have taken place in the Chinese economic system and in the policies adopted since the reform started in 1978. This chapter evaluates those changes and their impact by focusing on some major macroeconomic policies, specifically, fiscal, monetary, industrial, foreign trade, and environmental policies.

FISCAL POLICY

The traditional economic management model in China has two striking characteristics. The first is highly centralized economic management through central planning under which both macro- and microeconomic activities are administered by various mandatory plans. This, of course, ignores and rejects the function of the market mechanism. The second is the combination of the widespread ownership of means of production and the management of the enterprises, with state ownership dominating. The enterprises are run by the state under a highly centralized financial system through unified income and expenditure, and unified losses and profits. Under this system, all profits and even most of the depreciation funds must be submitted or remitted to the state, and all the losses of the enterprises are borne by the state. All investment funds are then supplied by the state. Thus, the state financial department is the "general manager" of both macro- and microeconomic activities. The fiscal system under this highly centralized form of planning has many fundamental disadvantages since it is impossible to solve the macroeconomic dynamic equilibrium by all-inclusive planning. Many ups and downs have been experienced in the last forty years, the most glaring difficulties being serious disequilibria and imbalances in economic structure, great waste in investment, and high inefficiency in economic management and activities.

At the same time, the unified income and expenditure structure within this fiscal system hampered the enterprises, especially their initiatives in developing and increasing profits. As a result, the enterprises lacked both internal dynamics and outside pressure to improve efficiency.

Under the old system, the function and responsibility between central and local governments were not clearly identified. Both the scope of the expenditure and the source of income were very much confused. However, the reform has introduced many changes. Following are the three major changes.

First, the financial power of the local government at various levels, as well as the functions of the state-owned enterprises, has expanded, and their decision-making powers in fiscal fields have been enlarged. As a result, the financial ability of both the local government and state enterprises has increased rapidly. The share of central government finance in total national fiscal revenues decreased from 66.1 percent in 1981 to less than 50 percent in 1988. Meanwhile, the proportion of profits turned over to the central government by the state-owned enterprises declined from 92.1 percent in 1979 to 41.3 percent in 1986. Therefore, the profits retained by enterprises accounted for 7.9 percent and 58.7 percent, respectively. (These figures include the profits used for the repayment of bank loans before tax.)

Second, the profit submission of state-owned enterprises was replaced by taxation; thus, a system of independent-accounting contribution to the state through tax and being responsible for profit and loss was established for state-owned enterprises. Before 1979 most government fiscal revenues came from state-owned enterprises, with profit submission as the major source. With the replacement of profit submission with taxation, tax revenues now account for more than 90 percent of all revenues. This is important in establishing a sound relationship between state and private enterprises, strengthening the financial responsibility of the enterprises, and encouraging their enthusiasm.

Third, financial allocation to state-owned enterprises was replaced by bank credits, which enhanced the efficiency of investment. Since 1979 bank loans have also been provided for investment in capital construction. Since 1985, almost all capital construction has been financed through bank credits. Meanwhile, a capital construction fund was set up, which is managed by state-investment corporations. Corporations, closely following the state economic development strategy and industrial policy, have full rights to use the funds, but they are responsible for increasing economic efficiency. This is considered a big step in China's capital investment financing. Furthermore, in 1980 a contract system for institutions related to culture and education, the sciences, public health, agricultural business, as well as state administrations, was introduced.

Reforms in China's fiscal system should have the following aims for the future:

1. A classified taxation system needs to be established, which makes financial sources clearly divided and secured between central and local governments. For

a long time, the division of revenues and expenditures between central and local finance has been based on the administratively subordinate position of enterprises and institutions. This system not only created blind expansion and fragmentation of domestic markets, but also hindered the rational structure of social production, optimization of distribution, and flow of national resources. The establishment of a classified tax system is aimed at overcoming those drawbacks and rectifying fiscal relations. By classifying taxes into central and local, and indicating how they are to be divided, a clear and stable structure of central and local finance can be built up, thus unifying the financial power and responsibility of businesses.

2. With regard to the fiscal relationship between the state and enterprises (mainly the state-owned), the mid- and long-term target of the reform is to establish a system that separates profit and tax in distribution and management. On the one hand, enterprises that use state property in conducting business must submit a certain proportion of their profits to the state; on the other hand, both enterprises and individuals must pay taxes as a source of government finance. However, balancing the budget must be the target of China's fiscal policy. Budget deficits have occurred in nine of the last ten years, and the accumulated deficits were as large as 67 billion yuan (RMB). This bleak financial picture is considered to be the consequence of mistakes made in economic policies. These policies are now the object of sharp criticism, and the government has begun to make serious efforts to find solutions. Balancing the budget poses many difficulties, however. First, the share of budget revenue in national income is too low, and this significantly limits the growth and ability of government finance. In the past, the share of government budget revenues usually accounted for 35 percent. Following the structural change in distribution of national income, especially the expansion of the financial power of state-owned enterprises, the share decreased rapidly, from 31.8 percent in 1979 to 19.3 percent in 1988. This sharply reduced the financial base for government macroeconomic management and control, and become an important factor in creating large budget deficits.

Many Chinese economists argue that the government should increase the proportion of financial revenues in national income in order to provide the necessary conditions for financial balance. Furthermore, the share of central finance in total fiscal revenues has also declined, from 66.1 percent in 1980 to less than 50 percent in 1988. Nevertheless, the expenditure of the central government has increased rapidly. As a result, the budget deficit of the central government has become larger and larger, and the ability of its macroeconomic adjustment has been greatly reduced. In the future, it will be necessary to make a clear division between central and local government revenues and expenditures, as well as gradually increase the share of central government revenues from less than 50 percent to 60 to 65 percent.

Second, the increasing burden of the fiscal subsidies has caused many difficulties in balancing the budget in the near future. Subsidies in government finance accounted for 31.3 percent of total revenue in 1988 (as high as 76.9 billion yuan). The subsidies are used mainly for losses of state-owned enterprises, which reached 44.6 billion yuan in 1988 and accounted for 58 percent of total subsidy expenditures; and for prices, which increased rapidly, reaching 31.7 billion yuan in 1988 and accounting for 41.2 percent of total subsidy expenditures, or 2.4 times higher than the sum of 9.4 billion yuan in 1978.

The fiscal burden of subsidies is expected to increase further. To that extent, it will become more difficult to balance the budget without solving the problem of the low efficiency of the state-owned enterprises and controlling inflation. However, the government has placed these problems on its agenda.

Third, the economy is structurally disallocated. Sluggish growth in energy raw material production, and inadequate development of communications and social infrastructure are most serious. At present, two striking problems dominate China's economic development: (1) Total social demand greatly exceeds total social supply and it is difficult to control expanding social demand in the short run; (2) the structure of the national economy is seriously disallocated. The industrial sector and infrastructures do not match the increasing demands for economic development. Not only is the growth of agriculture far behind that of industry, but there is also a misallocation within industries. For example, capacity utilization is only 67 percent because of the shortage of energy. Rail communication can only satisfy 60 to 70 percent of actual demand and, in some important lines, as little as 30 to 40 percent. The development of basic industries and social infrastructure requires larger investments, construction time is relatively long, and profits come slowly. These all add more pressure and difficulties to the target of balancing the budget.

A kind of "sloping investment policy" has now been adopted, which supports basic industries and infrastructure with tax incentives, subsidies, and differential interest rates, as well as positive readjustment and guidance so that investment funds can be used more efficiently.

MONETARY POLICY

There was almost no monetary policy in the pre-reform economy since the traditional Chinese economic system did not need a monetary policy. Under the old system, the management of social production relied mainly on mandatory planning and administrative measures, which gave more attention to the movement of material objects and downgraded the movement of capital. The tools of financial policy and monetary policy were almost totally subordinated to the needs of mandatory macro planning. In fact, the old system ignored the relationship between commodities and the money supply.

On the other hand, the egalitarian and low wage system left people with little money for savings, thus largely limiting deposits in banks and the source of capital used for credits. Indirect credits were underdeveloped, and there was no room for the direct credit means (stocks and securities). They all reduced the role and effectiveness of the monetary and financial funds available.

Before the reform, investment fund sources and the finance channel were very simple. Investment in the fixed capital of state-owned enterprises relied primarily on financial allocations, and bank credits were used only for part of the circulating capital, not for investment in fixed capital. This greatly narrowed the field of activities of bank credit and financial instruments and weakened the function of monetary policy, as well as the effectiveness of many of the tools of macroeconomic management.

For many years after 1949, the central bank and the special banks (the investment bank and the commercial bank) were under one unified management system. The different functions, such as issuing banknotes, credit supervision, adjusting interest rate, and formulating macro financial policies, were all mixed together in the formulation of monetary policy, while the utilization of monetary tools was disregarded. This system not only undermined the role of macroeconomic management, but also distorted the functions and activities of monetary policy.

Economic reforms in the last ten years have significantly enhanced the importance of monetary policy and created a possible and practical environment for it. Following the introduction of the market economy in cities and rural areas and structural changes in the distribution of national income and the source of social investment capital, the position and role of the financial mechanism and the utilization of credits in economic activities have been greatly strengthened.

Deposits in state banks were 2.23 times higher in 1987 than in 1981, reaching 657.2 billion yuan. Savings from citizens increased 4.83 times, to 206.4 billion yuan. Meanwhile, the net credits provided by state banks were 2.27 times higher, having increased from 276.5 billion yuan in 1981 to 903.2 billion yuan in 1987. At the same time, the ratio of net savings in the national income increased from 3.15 percent to 9.15 percent in 1987. Presently, bank credits account for about 67 percent of the total capital invested in the economy. This, of course, has created the general condition for better utilizing the tools of monetary policy for macroeconomic management.

Bank credits now play an increasing role and reach into almost all kinds of economic activities. Before the reform, the circulating capital of state-owned enterprises was provided mainly by state financial allocations; only a small part, such as incidental or seasonal adjusting requirements, were from bank credits. After 1983, all new circulating capital requirements came from bank loans. In fact, state financial allocations have been withdrawn from this area.

Since 1979 state banks have begun to provide loans for investment in fixed capital, primarily midterm and long-term loans for capital investment and the technological upgrading of enterprises. The net amount of those loans expanded from 5.55 billion yuan in 1980 to 128.7 billion yuan in 1987, which represented an increase of 22.2 times in eight years. In addition, bank credits have expanded from developing new products and new technologies to supporting student studies at the universities. More importantly, a central bank system and a rudimentary financial structure have been established, which provide the necessary conditions for utilizing various kinds of monetary policy instruments. The People's Bank has become independent of the national central bank since 1983. Furthermore, various kinds of financial activities have been turned over to special or authorized banks, such as the Industrial and Commercial Bank in charge of credit and financial business in cities, the Agricultural Bank in the area of rural development, and the Bank of China in foreign exchange business. The China International Trust and Investment Corporation and various leasing companies have also been established to conduct authorized business. Meanwhile, beginning in 1980, city credit cooperatives whose business focuses mainly on collective and private economic activities in cities have gradually developed. Another development that should not be overlooked is the reestablishment of the Communication Bank in 1986, whose ownership is based on shares with the state as the major owner. Its business includes both domestic RMB credits and foreign exchange. The above developments form part of China's embryonic financial system.

Following the transition from financial allocation to bank credits, the role of the interest rate has been strengthened in balancing the demand and supply of capital. Since 1985 the central bank has ceased to provide funds to special banks and has asked them to finance their operations by taking deposits. At the same time, interest rates have been classified and adjusted according to the structure of credits, with floating rates and differential rates as the effective means of managing the financial market and conducting monetary policy.

The financial market has developed rapidly through the expanding scale and role of various kinds of credit instruments. Commercial notes, securities, shares and bonds, and the like, have begun to develop to a certain extent. Insurance companies resumed operations in 1980. They now have developed more than one hundred kinds of business, with total income as high as 100 million yuan a year.

Meanwhile, more extensive relations are developing between Chinese and international financial institutions. Chinese financial institutions have entered the world financial market by selling securities and in other ways. The Bank of China has established more than four hundred overseas branches or offices and has agent relations with more than one thousand foreign banks. These are all helpful in providing a more extensive base for monetary policy.

In the meantime, many new problems have emerged which need to be solved. For current and midterm economic development, the following problems must be resolved.

1. China's monetary policy must be built on the base of stabilizing the value of the currency and the money supply. The levels of Chinese retail prices increased 23.4 percent in 1984–87 and only 18.5 percent in 1988. At the same time, the ratio of circulating money to the total retail value of commodities increased from 1:8.05 in 1978 to 1:4.4 in 1988, while the ratio between the amount of circulating money to the amount of retail commodity stocks increased from 1:4.54 in 1978 to 1:1.6 in 1988, and the ratio between the surplus of social purchases to the value of retail commodity stocks increased from 1:1.2 in 1978 to 1:0.6 in 1988. These ratios point to an increasing imbalance between money

supply and commodity supply. Therefore, the central government has decided to take steps to overcome this problem and control inflation.

2. China must tighten its monetary policy in order to constrain the rapid expansion of social demand and ensure that the total social supply matches social demand under a dynamic equilibrium.

Shortage has become one of the common features of socialist countries. One reasons why is that high economic growth is sought without consideration of realistic supply constraints. Future reforms are needed to correct this problem. Of course, it is impossible to correct the shortage problem in the short term. For example, in the process of reform, because of conflicts between the old and new system, and the desire for high growth, the gap between total demand and total supply has not been reduced; in fact, it has increased significantly. During 1979–87 the average growth rate of GNP was 9.4 percent, while the average growth rate of fixed capital investment in state-owned enterprises was 14.7 percent. In 1988 the growth rate of GNP was 11.2 percent, while investment in fixed capital increased by 18.5 percent. At the same time, social consumption expanded rapidly. The average growth rate of productivity in state-owned enterprises was 4.6 percent in 1979–87, while the average growth rate in payments to workers and staff members was 10.1 percent. In 1988 these figures were 9.3 percent, and 22.1 percent, respectively. Because of the expansion of both investment and consumption, it is more difficult to reach equilibrium between total social demand and total supply. This represents an internal unstable factor in the continuous growth of the Chinese economy. Therefore, tightening both monetary and financial policies is needed in order to effectively control social demand and to correct the disequilibrium that exists between total social demand and total supply.

An effective monetary mechanism cannot be established without a sound general economic system. Therefore, more radical reforms are required in the Chinese economy. An independent central bank system is needed in order to make and implement monetary policy. The present central bank system is tied to central government functions, which makes it subordinate to central government policies. Thus, monetary policy becomes the initial factor of disequilibrium in the process of economic development.

INDUSTRIAL POLICY

Industrial policy is an integrated part of China's macroeconomic policy and plays a very important role. Next we will analyze two major related issues: industrial management and industrial development policy.

Industrial Management

Industrial management under a centralized planning system has a unique role in state macroeconomic management. The evolution of the Chinese industrial management system can be divided into three periods: 1949–57, 1957–78, and 1979 to the present.

During 1949–57 the management system was characterized by multiforms of ownership and economic activities. The main production of state-owned enterprises was under direct state planning; other enterprises followed the market function and the guidance of state planning for the most part.

During 1957–78 the ownership structure was dominated by the state and collectives. In 1978 state-owned enterprises accounted for 80.7 percent of total industrial output, and collective enterprises accounted for 19.2 percent. Although many readjustments took place during this period, all changes were limited to the expansion or reduction of the relative powers of the central and local authorities. Enterprises were never given basic decision-making powers. Thus, the management system, by its very nature, was ossified.

In the area of distribution, the state controlled wage levels and wage increases. Thus, income had no direct relation to performance.

In financial affairs, all profits of state-owned enterprises had to be turned over to the state, all losses were subsidized by the state, and all funds required by the enterprises were supplied from the government budget. Collective enterprises were managed by the local government in the same way.

With regard to production, it was the state, rather than the enterprise, that decided the amount and kind of goods to produce, and the goods produced by the enterprises were distributed by government institutions. All materials needed were supplied according to state planning, and prices were formulated by the state at the different levels: the central government, the ministries, and the local governments.

Management of the labor force was also highly centralized. The same system applied to both state-owned enterprises and collectives, under which enterprises had no right to choose workers and workers had no right to choose their employers.

This kind of industrial management system seriously hampered the creativeness and dynamics of the enterprise; price mechanisms, competition, and technological inventions all failed to play their roles.

From 1979 to the current period, reforms were directed at correcting the maladies of the traditional economic system. The major reforms centered on changing the ownership structure of state-owned enterprises, including selling off or leasing out some small enterprises, promoting the merger of enterprises, and issuing stocks and securities; introducing the responsibility system by letting enterprises have decision-making powers so as to become independent commodity production units, and thereby increase productivity; and reducing the scope of mandatory planning and expanding market functions through the guidance plan and competition, and returning the basic functions of micromanagement to the enterprises.

Following the reforms, the efficiency of production, the consciousness of competition of the enterprises, and the promotion of competition through the market function have become important elements of Chinese industrial policy.

Industrial Development Policy

China has made great progress in industrial development. The value of industrial and agricultural output increased from 43.1 percent in 1952 to 74.7 percent in 1987. However, the modernization of China's industries, that is, establishing a modern industrial structure, still has a long way to go. The development strategy is of great importance in the country's industrial policy. From a general view, China's industrial development policy should follow the following guidelines:

Coordination of Industrial and Agricultural Development Policies. China is a large country with a population of 1.1 billion, which gives agriculture special importance. Because of slow agricultural growth, not only the food supplied to the increasing population has been affected, but also industrial development has been restricted. In the 1953–87 period the average growth rate of total industrial output was 11.5 percent, while agricultural output increased by only 3.8 percent. During the reform era, from 1979 to 1987, industrial output grew by 12 percent and agricultural by 6.5 percent. Especially during 1985–88 the imbalance between the two sectors was further reduced, with the industrial as high as 17.8 percent and the agricultural only 13.9 percent. This is not to say that the two sectors should grow at the same rate, but an equilibrium in their growth should be maintained in the longer run.

Keeping a Rational Structure Within the Industrial Sector, with special attention to balancing development between manufacturing and basic industries, as well as between commodity output and social infrastructure. Because of the serious imbalance in the industrial sector, and between manufacturing and social infrastructures, many industries suffer "congenital" or "postnatal" malformation, which represents an internal restriction to their future development. During 1979–87, the average growth rate of China's industrial sector was 12 percent, while that of coal was only 4.6 percent, oil 2.9 percent, electricity 7.6 percent, and steel 7.9 percent. Among the heavy industries, the ratio of the growth rates between raw materials and manufactures changed from 1:0.99 in 1978 to 1:1.67 in 1988. At the same time, the development of communication, telecommunications, as well as other public service industries, has lagged far behind. According to a national survey, the lost value per year caused by the shortage of electricity is more than 150 billion yuan. Industrial losses per year stemming from the lack of communications ability are close to 100 billion yuan. Owing to the shortage of materials, idle productive capacity is very significant. Therefore, it is of determinant and long-term strategic significance to readjust and improve the existing industrial structure, especially the backward conditions of energy, communication, raw materials, and the social infrastructure. The ratio of investment in the social infrastructures out of total investments is now only 2.3 percent. This is considered too low and must be raised to 10 to 15 percent in the near future, so that the basic industries can be adapted to the requirements of other industries.

Making Industrial Development the Base of Internal Expansion, with technological progress and innovation as the focal point and economic efficiency at the core.   Since 1949 the growth rate of China's industry has been high and the value of fixed capital increased over forty times, but efficiency, for example, the input-output ratio remained very low. In 1979, for instance, the growth rate of the net industrial output was 7.7 percent, the growth rate in the supply of inputs factor was 5.7 percent, and the productivity of comprehensive factors[1] was only 2 percent. It has continuously declined since 1985. It was −7.1 percent in 1986 and −5.2 percent in 1987. The profit realized from a 100-yuan input in state-owned enterprises declined from 34.6 yuan in 1957 and 24.8 yuan in 1979 to only 20.3 yuan in 1987. At the same time, the consumption of materials has been increasing; for example, energy consumption in 10,000 yuan national income was 6.6 tons of standard coal in 1953 and increased to 12.8 tons in 1986.

The technological level of China's industry is relatively low. According to a survey conducted in 1985, among the industrial equipment of large-state owned enterprises, those similar to the international level accounted for only around 13 percent (on the value base). From 1964 to 1982 the average growth rate of the technological level in the whole industrial sector was only 1.82 percent. Even in Shanghai, where the technological level is much higher than the national level, the figure was only 2.34 percent. Following the reform and the opening policy, however, the technological level of industry has increased rapidly, and quite a few industries have caught up to the international technological level of the late 1970s, or even the early 1980s. Investments in technological developments have increased, reaching 12.44 billion yuan in 1988 (double the investment in 1986–88). The investment in technological innovations now accounts for nearly one-third of total investment in fixed capital. This has promoted the regeneration of many industries.

Formulation of the future industrial development policy should be based on three strategies.

1. Priority should be given to increasing the general level of the whole industry sector through internal expansion (i.e., relying mainly on technological progress and intensive management,) rather than external expansion, (i.e., relying mainly on more inputs of capital and labor).

2. High-tech industry should play an important role in future developments. A selective development policy of high-tech industry is needed, which focuses on electronics, computers, biotechnology, and new raw materials. This development is aimed not at immediately competing with the advanced production in the world market, but at building up a base for future mass production and competitive ability.

3. The whole industrial system until the year 2000 will be one of multistructures. Technologically speaking, a target should be at least one-fifth of the industries at the international advanced level, 50 percent at the midlevel, and the rest at the level of the 1960s or 1970s.

The above industrial development policy can be realized only with a market economy that not only competes in the domestic market, but also more and more in the world market.

FOREIGN TRADE POLICY

The Foreign Trade System and Development

In 1950 China's total value of exports and imports was only U.S. $1.135 billion. By 1988 it had reached U.S. $80.49 billion, of which imports were $39.85 billion and exports $40.64 billion. Generally speaking, the growth of China's foreign trade has been high. During the 1950–87 period the annual growth rate was around 12 percent. The percentage of foreign trade in GNP has been on a remarkable rise, and by 1988 it was about 13 percent.

Before 1979, state monopoly and direct government management were prevalent. The main manifestations are as follows: (1) There was no functional division between the government and the enterprises. The central government ministry responsible for foreign trade exercised direct control through specialized national import and export corporations. (2) A comprehensive, mandatory, planned management was implemented. The mandatory plans were pervasive in all aspects, such as purchasing goods, exporting, importing, foreign exchange income and expenditure, packing, transporting, and accounting. (3) The financial affairs of foreign trade were handled solely by the state, and the state was responsible for all its income and expenditure, and profits and losses under a unified system. (4) Production enterprises provided foreign trade corporations with goods according to the prices specified in the plan. They had no direct links with the world market.

The old foreign trade system had great limits. First it was too rigid to allow rapid development and changes in the world market. Second, it had low efficiency. In fact, following the increase in exports, the losses have been growing. The system needs to be restructured, especially when China opens further to the outside world.

The Main Measures Introduced in the Reform

Since 1980 China has been moving toward reforming its international trading system, delegating power to the lower level, separating the functions of government from those of the enterprises, and making enterprises responsible for profits and losses.

Decentralizing the Managerial Power to the Lower Level.   As early as the beginning of the 1980s, China relaxed its overcentralized foreign trade system. Localities and some departments were permitted to export directly to foreign countries. Some departments even established their own export-supplied corporations or import and export companies. However, during this period, the scope of decentralization was very limited.

In September 1984, when the state council approved "the report on the reform of foreign trade," submitted by the Ministry of Foreign Economic Relations and Trade, the state's powers were further decentralized. The government endorsed the establishment of a dozen specialized import and export corporations in industries, such as nonferrous metal, metallurgy, electronics, shipbuilding, and petrochemistry. Some large-size and medium-size state-owned enterprises with better production and technical conditions were also authorized to engage in foreign trade directly. According to the statistics, in 1979 there were 132 companies conducting foreign trade, the number increased to four thousand by the first half of 1989.

Integrating Industry with Foreign Trade and Introducing the Agent System.   Industry can be combined with foreign trade in three ways: (1) foreign trade companies invest directly in production enterprises, or support export bases; (2) large- and medium-size state-owned enterprises organize into a group of export corporations; and (3) industry–trade joint management is established under the contract, including the procurement and agent system.

Under the procurement system, producers have links only with foreign trade companies. The agent system, by contract, allows the producers and clients of both sides to enjoy definite rights, responsibilities, and interests; that is, they are directly linked together. However, the reform is still in a transition stage, and the conditions are not yet ripe for replacing the procurement system with the agent system. Nonetheless it provides the direction for future reforms. In the future, the agent system will be popularized not only in the export business, but also in the import business.

Increasing Incentives for Exports.   In the past, the main incentives for exports were preferential credits and financial subsidies. The subsidies have become a heavy burden on the state budget owing to their rapid increase. Some critics view these subsidies as "unfair trade." There are two reasons for the subsidies. First, domestic prices are distorted by planned management compared with world prices; second, the RMB exchange rate is irrational. For example, the exchange rate of RMB for U.S. dollars has not changed since July 1986 when the RMB was devalued against the dollar (1 dollar = 3.71 yuan). Since then, however, inflation in China has increased, and the comprehensive cost of foreign exchange for each dollar earned from exports has been over 4 yuan for a long time. In mid–1989, in China's foreign exchange centers, the rate was 6.7 yuan per dollar. Under such circumstances, losses are unavoidable if exporting and importing are in accordance with planned domestic prices and the fixed exchange rate. The subsidies to cover these losses are, in fact, the compensation for price and exchange-rate distortions under the planned management. However, subsidies are not the ideal way to correct for the distortions and should be changed in future reforms. The newly adopted measures for the export are as follows:

1. *Introducing the System Refund of Tax on Exports.*   Like most goods sold in the domestic market, exported goods are also taxed indirectly in the process of their production, and they are taxed again when they are imported after having earned foreign currency. Such a tax takes the form of an internal product tax on the value of import and a value added tax. These two kinds of taxes should be removed if China's foreign trade companies are to meet international competition. In the late 1980s the government began to take measures to pay back the various indirect taxes.

2. *Implementing the System of Foreign Exchange Retention by Foreign Trade Companies and Enterprises.*   Foreign exchange retention is used for the purpose of importing advanced technology and equipment, or boosting exports through imports. Nevertheless, with the increase in foreign exchange at the local level and the extension of local powers on foreign trade, managerial capability is left behind. In order to control the black market of foreign exchange and provide incentives to foreign trade companies and enterprises, foreign exchange centers were established. This increases flexibility in using retained foreign exchange. In foreign exchange centers, the foreign exchange rate for RMB is higher than the official one.

Introducing the Contract Responsibility System by Being Responsible for One's Profits and Losses.   Reform of the foreign trade system was speeded up in 1988, and since then the contract responsibility system has been introduced widely. National export and import corporations can now break their administrative and financial ties with national corporations. Foreign exchange earnings are shared by the central and local governments, with the largest part turned over to the central government. However, the contracting parties retain most or all foreign exchange earnings in excess of their contracting quotas. Similarly, the local government subcontracts the quotas to the enterprises and the companies. The contract responsibility is probably a better form of organization because the enterprise is responsible for its own profits and losses, which is an inducement to improve its efficiency. Many shortcomings still remain in the contract responsibility system. One example is excessive concern with short-run profitability.

Separating the Functions of the Government from Those of the Enterprises and Defining the Division of Functions.   The foreign trade system has three main functions: administration, management, and coordination. These functions are undertaken by the government, corporations, and associations of exporters and importers, respectively. It is important to separate the functions of the government from those of the enterprises and associations. The division of functions after the reform is as follows. Foreign trade corporations conduct exclusively the export and import business. The Ministry of Foreign Economic Relations and Trade has the main task of studying, formulating, organizing, and implementing the state strategy for foreign trade and for developing state policy, regulations, and rules. The associations are responsible for coordinating the companies' and enterprises' interests, and providing the information, business advice, and personnel training, as well as developing foreign connections and cooperations.

Although China has carried out many reforms in the field of foreign trade, direct control remains the main practice in macromanagement. Indirect management, that is, through monetary policy and financial policy, has not yet been introduced. Future reforms in the foreign trade system will probably not focus on transformation from direct control to indirect control. Rather, they will concentrate on perfecting the institutional mechanism of control and management through planning, export and import controls (licenses, quotas, classifications), custom supervision and tariff adjustments, as well as the management of foreign exchange. However, without perfecting the general economic system, for example, rationalizing the price structure, exchange rates, and so on, the reforms cannot succeed.

From a macro point of view, foreign trade policy plays a special role in China's economic development strategy. The rapid growth of foreign trade has become an important factor in pushing forward the modernization of the economy. However, the following three points should be heeded in formulating and implementing future trade policy:

1. *Relations Between Export Expansion and the Domestic Supply Condition.* In the last ten years, the fast increase of exports has paralleled the fast growth of domestic demand of consumption. The ratio of foreign trade in China's GNP is now 13 percent, and, as such, it is already very high. A further increase in exports will rely mainly on readjusting the structure of production rather than further cutting domestic consumption.

2. *Relations Between Imports and Domestic Production.* Increasing imports are important for improving technology and the structure of consumption. However, this also undermines the development and growth of infant industries. A selective restrictive policy on the import of consumer goods should be implemented.

3. *Relationship Between Efficiency and the Growth of Trade.* Foreign exchange earnings through export are given top priority. However, improving efficiency (management and technology) through international competition and the division of labor should be given more attention.

ENVIRONMENTAL POLICY

Serious consideration of environmental protection occurred rather late in China. The first national environment conference was not held until 1973, and a ten-year environment program was only formulated in 1975. What is worse, they all failed to be implemented, so that pollution has intensified since then. The ratio of investments for environmental protection in China's GNP was as low as 0.68 percent in the early 1980s. It is estimated that the losses caused by water pollution total 37.7 billion yuan per year, by solid waste 7.9 billion yuan, by pesticide pollution 14.7 billion yuan, and by destruction of national resources 21.2 billion yuan. The total losses caused by environmental pollution was equivalent to 20.7 percent of national income in 1982. However, the Chinese government has taken several measures since 1979. The principle that "pollution must be eliminated by those who create it" was implemented in 1979, and the National Committee on Environmental Protection was established in 1984. The state council required government institutions and enterprises to spend 7 percent of the fund used for capital and technology renovation on pollution control. In the cities, control of the "four calamities"—polluted water and air, drugs, and noise—was placed on the development strategy agenda. Investment in pollution control increased rapidly following the adoption of these measures.

Yet, pollution continues to increase. In 1987 there were 3,617 pollution casualties, the total reparation for pollution was 67.8 million yuan, and the fines imposed on those who polluted was 12.7 million yuan. Because of the deteriorating environment, the public health is now threatened. For example, half the population living in rural areas are jeopardized by various kinds of diseases relating to pollution.

China recognizes that environmental policy can no longer be subordinated to development policy. From October 1987 to October 1989 a survey was carried out on the source of industrial pollution covering more than 168,000 industries in twenty-nine provinces and autonomous regions, with around eight hundred thousand people participating. This survey collected more than 20 million pieces of data. Approximately 1,949 archives and 153 computer data banks on industrial pollution were built up, and this established the base for formulating an environmental protection policy.

The environmental policy now focuses on three objectives:

1. To make national environment protection plans. These plans include developing long-term and midterm plans, as well as annual plans and defining the key polluted areas and industries that need to be controlled;

2. To inspect, investigate, and control pollution. Besides the national committee on environmental protection, various kinds of environmental institutions have been established, such as government administration agencies, research units, and pollution-controlling companies. Environmental protection laws and quite a few regulations have been formulated, including the specification of penalties for those who create pollution; and

3. To increase investments in pollution control. Besides increasing the budget for environmental protection, environmental protection fees have been levied on enterprises. From these fees the special fund for implementing environmental policies can be set up.

China's basic problem in this area lies in the contradiction between economic growth and environmental protection. It is very difficult to determine the optimum tradeoff between the two when a nation is engaged in a drive toward modernization as China is. Nevertheless, the effort must be made.

NOTE

1. GR / (RC + RL), where GR is the growth rate of net output value, and (RC + RL) is the weighted average growth rate of capital input plus labor input.

REFERENCES

Gui Shirong. *On the Macro Economic Management of China*. China Economic Management Publisher, 1987.

Li Maosheng. *Studies on China's Financial Structure*. Shanxi People's Publisher, 1987.

Liu Guogang. *Studies on Models of China's Economic Reform*. China Social Sciences Publisher, 1988.

Li Rongzhang. *Studies on the Capital Efficiency of the Socialist Economy*. China Social Sciences Publisher, 1988.

World Bank. *World Development Report*, 1988.

Yearbook of Chinese Economy, 1987.

Yearbook of Chinese Statistics, 1986, 1987, 1988.

SELECTED BIBLIOGRAPHY

Abdel-Fadil, M. *The Political Economy of Nasserism*. Cambridge: Cambridge University Press, 1980.

Acharya and Associates. *Aspects of the Black Economy in India*. New Delhi: National Institution of Public Finance and Policy, 1986.

Ahluwalia, Isher Judge. *Industrial Growth in India: Stagnation Since the Mid-Sixties*. New Delhi: Oxford University Press, 1985.

Arndt, Sven W. (ed.). *The Political Economy of Austria*. Washington, D.C., and London: American Enterprise Institute for Public Policy Research, 1982.

Baily, Martin N. *Workers, Jobs and Inflation*. Washington, D.C.: Brookings Institution, 1982.

Balassa, B., and Associates. *Development Strategies in Semi-Industrial Economies*. Baltimore: Johns Hopkins University Press, 1982.

Brabant, Jozef M. van. *Adjustment, Structural Change, and Economic Efficiency—Aspects of Monetary Cooperation in Eastern Europe*. New York and Cambridge: Cambridge University Press, 1987.

——. *Economic Integration in Eastern Europe—A Reference Book*. Hemel Hempstead: Harvester Wheatsheaf, 1989.

Brada, J. C., E. T. Hewett, and T. A. Wolf (eds.). *Economic Adjustment and Reform in Eastern Europe and the Soviet Union*. Durham, N. C.: Duke University Press, 1988.

Cargill, Thomas F., and Shoichi Royama. *The Transition of Finance in Japan and the United States*. Stanford, Calif.: Hoover Institution Press, 1988.

Chakravarty, Sukhamoy. *Development Planning: The Indian Experience*. London: Oxford University Press, 1987.

Commander, Simon. *The State and Agricultural Development in Egypt Since 1973*. London and Atlantic Highlands, N.J.: Overseas Development Institute, Ithaca Press, 1987.

Courchene, Th. J., *Economic Management and the Division of Powers*. Toronto: University of Toronto Press, 1986.

England, Catherine, and Thomas Huertas (eds.). *The Financial Services Resolution*. Boston: Kluwer, 1988.

Gui Shirong. *On the Macro Economic Management of China*. China Economic Management Publisher, 1987.

Hadenius, St. *Swedish Politics During the 20th Century*. Stockholm: Swedish Institute, 1988.

Heclo, H., and H. Madsen. *Policy and Politics in Sweden*. Philadelphia: Temple University Press, 1987.

Howitt, P. *Monetary Policy in Transition: A Study of Bank of Canada Policy 1982–85*. Scarborough: Howe Institute, 1983.

Hulten, Charles R., and Isabel V. Sawhill. *The Legacy of Reaganomics*. Washington, D.C.: Urban Institute Press, 1984.

Kozo, Yamamura (ed.). *Policy and Trade Issues of the Japanese Economy: American and Japanese Perspectives*. Seattle: University of Washington Press, 1982.

Krueger, A. O., et al. *Trade and Employment in Developing Countries*. Vol. 1, *Individual Studies*. Chicago: Chicago University Press for NBER, 1981.

Li Maosheng. *Studies on China's Financial Structure*. Shanxi People's Publisher, 1987.

Lipton, D., and J. Sachs. *Creating a Market Economy in Eastern Europe: The Case of Poland*. Brookings Papers on Economic Activity, No. 1, 1990.

Liu Guogang. *Studies on Models of China's Economic Reform*. China Social Sciences Publisher, 1988.

Li Rongzhang. *Studies on the Capital Efficiency of the Socialist Economy*. China Social Sciences Publisher, 1988.

Lucas, R., and G. Papanek (eds.). *The Indian Economy: Recent Development and Future Prospects*. Special Studies on South and Southeast Asia. Boulder, Colo.: Westview, 1988.

McCraw, Thomas K. (ed.). *America Versus Japan*. Cambridge, Mass.: Harvard Business School Press, 1988.

Michaely, M., Choksi, A., and Papageorgiou, D. "The Design of Trade Liberalization." *Finance and Development* (March 1989).

Noguchi, Yukio. "Public Finance." In Kozo Yamamura and Yasuba Yasukichi (eds.), *The Political Economy of Japan*. Stanford, Calif.: Stanford University Press, 1987.

Nwanko, G. O. *The Nigerian Financial System*. London: Macmillan Press, 1980.

Obey, David R., and Paul Sarbanes (eds.). *The Changing American Economy*. New York: Basil Blackwell, 1986.

Palmer, John L., and Isabel V. Sawhill. *The Reagan Experiment*. Washington, D.C.: Urban Institute Press, 1982.

Ranis, G., and T. P. Schultz (eds.). *The State of Development Economics: Progress and Perspectives*. London: Basil Blackwell, 1988.

Reserve Bank of Australia. "The Reserve Bank's Domestic Market Operations." *Bulletin* (June 1985).

———. "Monetary Policy from the Inside." *Bulletin* (November 1985).

———. "Recent Developments in Regulatory and Supervisory Arrangements in Australia." *Bulletin* (September 1989).

Salvatore, Dominick. *The New Protectionist Threat to World Welfare*. New York: North-Holland, 1987.

———. "Import Penetration, Exchange Rates, and Protectionism in the United States." *Journal of Policy Modeling* 9, no. 1 (1987): 125–41.

Sargent, J. *Fiscal and Monetary Policy*. Toronto: University of Toronto Press, 1986.

Sundrum, R. M. *Growth and Income Distribution in India: Policy and Performance Since Independence*. New Delhi: Sage Publications, PVT Ltd., 1987.

Tanzi, Vito. "Forces That Shape Tax Policy." In Herbert Stein (ed.), *Tax Policy in the Twenty First Century*. New York: Wiley 1988, pp. 266–77.

——— (ed.). *Fiscal Policy in Open Developing Economies*. Washington, D.C.: International Monetary Fund, 1990.

Viner, Aron. *Inside Japanese Financial Markets*. Homewood, Ill.: Dow Jones–Irwin, 1988.

Wolf, Thomas A. *Foreign Trade in the Centrally Planned Economy*. Chur, Switzerland: Harwood, 1988.

INDEX

ABOUT THE CONTRIBUTORS

ADEBAYO ADEDEJI is Under Secretary General of the United Nations and Executive Secretary of the Economic Commission for Africa, with headquarters in Adis Ababa, Ethiopia. He is responsible for the Annual Reports on Economic Conditions in Africa.

JOZEF M. VAN BRABANT is Chief of the Centrally Planned Economies Section of the Secretariat of the United Nations, based in New York City. Among his many other publications is *The Planned Economies and International Economic Organizations.*

VITTORIO CORBO is Chief of the Macroeconomic Adjustment and Growth Division of the World Bank in Washington, D.C. Among his many other publications, he has written on public finance, trade, and development in Chile.

ANTONIO COSTA is the Director General of the Economic and Financial Affairs Commission of the European Communities, with headquarters in Brussels, Belgium. He is also the Editor in Chief of the *Journal of Policy Modeling.*

ELIAS C. GRIVOYANNIS is Professor of Economics at Seton Hall University. He wrote his Ph.D. dissertation on the Japanese economy at New York University.

EDUARD HOCHREITER is the Chief of the Foreign Research Division of the Austrian National Bank in Vienna, Austria. He has written extensively on national and international economic and financial matters.

GEORGE IDEN is Principal Analyst in the Congressional Budget Office of the U.S. Congress in Washington, D.C. He has written extensively on economic policies in the United States.

DEENA KHATKHATE is Senior Consultant at the World Bank in Washington, D.C. He was Assistant Director of the International Monetary Fund and Managing Editor of *World Development*.

RAMA RAMACHANDRAN is Associate Director and Visiting Professor of Economics at the Center for Japan–U.S. Business and Economic Studies in the Leonard N. Stern School of Business at New York University in New York City.

LI RONGZHANG is Deputy Director of the Institute of Finance and Trade of the Chinese Academy of Social Sciences in Beijing, China. He has written extensively on economic policies in China.

DARIUSZ K. ROSATI is the Director of the Foreign Trade Research Institute in Warsaw, Poland. He has written the chapter on National Trade Policies in Poland for the handbook of National Trade Policies (forthcoming) in this series.

SUNG-TAE RO is the Director of the Korea Development Institute in Seoul, Korea. Among his other publications is "Monetary Control and the Choice of an Intermediate Target," which appeared in the *Journal of Financial Studies* (vol. 1, no. 1, 1985).

DOMINICK SALVATORE is the Director of the Graduate Program and Professor of Economics at Fordham University in New York City. He is Co-Chairman of the New York Academy of Sciences and is the author of the leading International Economics text. He has written over twenty books, among which are *World Population Trends and Their Impact on Economic Development* (Greenwood Press, 1988) and *National Trade Policies* (forthcoming) a handbook in this series of which he is Editor.

RYUZO SATO is the Director of the Center for Japan–U.S. Business and Economic Studies in the Leonard N. Stern School of Business at New York University, in New York City. He has written extensively on Japanese and international economic policies.

AUREL SCHUBERT is Senior Economist at the Austrian National Bank in Vienna, Austria. His interest and writings have been on economic policies in Austria and other OECD countries.

ZHANG YUNLING is Deputy Director of the Institute of West Europen Studies of the Chinese Academy of Social Sciences in Beijing, China. He contributed the chapter on National Trade Policies in China to the handbook on *National Trade Policies* (forthcoming) in this handbook series.